CAMBRIDGE STUDIES IN
CHINESE HISTORY, LITERATURE AND INSTITUTIONS

General Editors
PATRICK HANAN & DENIS TWITCHETT

China and the Overseas Chinese

China and the Overseas Chinese

A study of Peking's changing policy
1949–1970

by

STEPHEN FITZGERALD

Fellow, Department of Far Eastern History,
Australian National University

CAMBRIDGE
AT THE UNIVERSITY PRESS
1972

Published by the Syndics of the Cambridge University Press
Bentley House, 200 Euston Road, London NW1 2DB
American Branch: 32 East 57th Street, New York, N.Y.10022

© Cambridge University Press 1972

Library of Congress Catalogue Card Number: 77–177938

ISBN: 0 521 08410 5

Printed in Great Britain
at the University Printing House, Cambridge
(Brooke Crutchley, University Printer)

Contents

Abbreviations

ACROCA	All-China Returned Overseas Chinese Association
CCP	Chinese Communist Party
CNS	*China News Service*
CPPCC	Chinese People's Political Consultative Conference
KMT	Kuomintang
MCP	Malayan Communist Party
NPC	National People's Congress
OCAB	Overseas Chinese Affairs Bureau
OCAC	Overseas Chinese Affairs Commission, or Overseas Chinese Affairs Committees in the provinces
OCTS	Overseas Chinese Travel Service
ROCA	Returned Overseas Chinese Association
UFWD	United Front Work Department

*For my parents
and my wife*

Preface

For more than two decades the Chinese Communist government has had to contend with unusual difficulties in its foreign relations, because of its failure to attain a minimum objective of winning universal recognition, and because of the political climate which bred hostile attitudes and antagonistic interpretations of its foreign policies and produced the policy of quarantine and non-recognition. Perhaps it was the fact that the CCP had been in power for longer than the total period of Kuomintang rule that finally persuaded the United States and other like-minded governments of the absurdity of their position on recognition. Whether they are also persuaded that some of the arguments which they used to justify non-recognition may have been equally indefensible, is another question. It may be accepted that Chinese foreign policy cannot be characterised now in such fear-raising simplifications, partly because of the incredibility of early arguments about China's role in the Vietnam War. But the record of China's foreign policy actions before Vietnam is still dominated to some extent by the arguments and viewpoints which sustained the policy of exclusion and containment. This tends to exercise a continuing influence on appreciations of China's past performance. There is, therefore, an historical question, which perhaps may be answered more satisfactorily with the benefit of a twenty-year perspective. But there is also a contemporary question, in that if these arguments of the 1950s and early 1960s are accepted as valid, if the underlying suppositions or beliefs persist, they must also condition present theories – and future policies.

Overseas Chinese policy is in some respects an untypical aspect of China's foreign policy. But it is also fairly representative in terms of popular beliefs about the international behaviour of the Chinese Communist Party. A re-examination of the historical question of the CCP's Overseas Chinese policy, therefore, is relevant both to present interpretations and to wider questions of Chinese foreign policy. There is also a more specific relation to the present state of Overseas Chinese policy. Most of the discussion in the following pages concerns the pre-Cultural Revolution period, but it is also related directly to the post-Cultural Revolution situation. It is not simply that Overseas Chinese policy appears to be moving in the same direction as it was before the Cultural Revolution, but that the fundamental nature of China's Overseas Chinese problem remains the same and does not warrant or, with a rational government in power, even allow significant changes. This is not, therefore, simply an historical account; it also seeks to offer an explanation of the motives underlying present policy.

The two basic questions in the CCP's O verseas Chinese policy, which have determined the focus of this book, are the nature of China's own Overseas Chinese problem, and the extent to which the Overseas Chinese are or may be deployed in the service of the Party's foreign policies. Whatever other factors are involved, the answers will depend ultimately on the perceptions and evaluation of the Chinese government itself and not, even for the second question, on the political behaviour of Overseas Chinese. For this reason, I have concentrated on the China side of the relationship with the Overseas Chinese and the internal evidence furnished by the special nature of Overseas Chinese affairs. Nor has it been my intention to examine in detail the period before 1949 for evidence of CCP policy. It was only after 1949 that the Party was in a position to come to grips with the problem and put its policies into effect, and this is where the import of the subject lies. It is apparent, moreover, that the CCP had given little thought to the Overseas Chinese before 1949; and it was not in fact until the mid-1950s that positive lines of policy began to emerge. Similarly, the policies of the KMT are discussed only where this is necessary to the central subject. It might be interesting to examine, for example, the KMT s truggle to preserve its position among the Chinese in Southeast Asia, but that is a separate subject in itself and not necessarily fruitful in terms of analysis of the CCP's objectives.

The use of the term 'Overseas Chinese' is in many ways unsatisfactory. The implied emphasis on the word 'overseas', particularly as it relates to the word '*ch'iao*' (sojourner) in the Chinese term for Overseas Chinese, '*hua-ch'iao*', may suggest unintended political implications. The CCP itself has had some difficulty with this term. At first it seems to have included all ethnic Chinese outside China. By the mid-1950s it was narrowing to a category comprising mainly Chinese nationals but also including all those who still maintained some attachment to the Chinese homeland. To underline the distinction, the CCP tended to refer to those to whom its policies were directly addressed as 'patriotic Overseas Chinese'. But it also continued to use the term *hua-ch'iao* in reference to Overseas Chinese in general, apparently because the alternatives were equally imprecise or else too unwieldy. In dealing with the policies of the Chinese government it has seemed appropriate to follow its usage, particularly since these policies have been concerned mainly with those who are in fact still 'overseas' Chinese by virtue of some kind of association with China. But in the Southeast Asian context this term seems increasingly inappropriate, and it would seem preferable in English to follow the usage among the Chinese themselves of such terms as *hua-jen* and *hua-tsu*, meaning simply 'Chinese', with a Southeast Asian national identification, and the general term Nanyang, or Southeast Asian, Chinese. For similar reasons, I have avoided using the term 'host countries' because of its judgment about the position of the Chinese in these countries.

The principal sources are the official Chinese media and the Hong Kong and Overseas Chinese press. For national dailies and journals other than the *Jen-min jih-pao* (*People's Daily*), and for the provincial press and the special newspapers and news sheets for Overseas Chinese dependants, I have used the holdings of the Hong Kong Union Research Institute, which amount to some 50,000 items on Overseas Chinese affairs and relations with the Overseas Chinese for the period 1949 to 1968. A separate examination has been made of all items on Overseas Chinese affairs appearing in the *Jen-min jih-pao* from 1949 to 1970, of the *Ch'iao-wu pao* (*Overseas Chinese Affairs Journal*) from the time of its inception in 1956 until it ceased publication in December 1966, and, with some gaps, of *Chung-kuo hsin-wen* (*China News Service*), the Chinese government's newsagency for the Overseas Chinese press. Translations from the Chinese are my own, except where otherwise indicated by footnote references to English or translation series sources. In the case of some Red Guard newspapers for which I have not been able to trace the original Chinese, I have had to make do with English quotations which appear to be accurate literal translations but which sometimes are a little stilted.

Most of the research was conducted during a year in Hong Kong and Southeast Asia. In January and February of 1968 in the course of a visit to China, I endeavoured to check some of my findings, but this was not a particularly suitable time for discussing what had been a controversial subject during the Cultural Revolution. I did, however, have an interview with an official of the Overseas Chinese Affairs Commission in Peking, and a series of discussions with another official who was well-informed about Overseas Chinese affairs. I am particularly grateful to these and other Chinese officials for their efforts to meet my requests and answer my questions.

This book owes much to the encouragement, guidance and support of a number of people to whom I wish to express my deepest gratitude. To my wife, who helped support us both, who shared my involvement with the subject and who gladly endured its problems, and in doing so gave up opportunities of her own. To Gregory Clark, a friend and former colleague both in External Affairs and at the Australian National University and now correspondent for *The Australian* in Tokyo, who helped me from the very beginning, and whose example underscored the necessity for re-examination of long-standing appraisals of China's foreign policy, particularly as they contributed to policies towards China and the enormities of the Vietnam War. To Dan Tretiak of York University, Toronto, for his friendship and unfailing interest and support, and for hours of discussion and detailed and critical comments on the manuscript. To Mrs C. L. P'an, formerly of the University of Hong Kong, who enriched my understanding of politics and society in contemporary China, who painstakingly culled the pages of the *Jen-min jih-pao* without any other reward, and who gave unstinting friendship, as did John and Alice Shih and T'ang Hsiang. And to Jack Harris, philanthropist and friend.

I am indebted also to those who read all or part of the manuscript and offered helpful comments and suggestions: Professor C. P. FitzGerald, Mr J. L. S. Girling, Mrs Ann Kent, Professor J. D. B. Miller, Professor Wang Gungwu, and Mr Ian Wilson, all of the Australian National University, and I am grateful to Mrs Jill Hardy who untangled my impossible manuscript and transformed it into a typescript. And I wish to express my appreciation to the Australian National University, which provided me with a scholarship and with funds to conduct the research in Hong Kong, China and South-east Asia, to the staff of the Universities Service Centre in Hong Kong, and to the Union Research Institute, whose collection of materials was invaluable.

Some of the information and conclusions in this book have already appeared in the following publications: *The China Quarterly*, no. 40, October–December 1969, and ibid. no. 44, October–December 1970; *Far Eastern Economic Review*, vol. LIX, no. 13, 28 March 1968; and *Papers on Far Eastern History* (Department of Far Eastern History, Australian National University), no. 2, September 1970.

STEPHEN FITZGERALD

Canberra
April 1971

1

Introduction

The 'colonies' of ethnic Chinese in Southeast Asia which the Chinese Communist Party inherited when it became the government of China might have been useful to China's new rulers in a number of ways.[1] Yet it is now strikingly apparent that they have not been as significant in China's policies as was generally, and perhaps not unreasonably, expected in 1949; or at least, not significant in the same way. Seldom first in the order of external priorities, the Overseas Chinese have nevertheless been a fairly constant preoccupation for the Chinese Communist Party (CCP), if only because it has been extremely difficult for the Party to work out policies which could both be consistent with its general objectives in Southeast Asia and promise some measure of effective implementation.

The establishment of the communist government posed a number of questions about Overseas Chinese, disturbing to the countries of Southeast Asia. What role did the new Chinese government envisage for them in the conduct of its foreign policy and the pursuit of its avowed revolutionary goals? Would China seek to exploit them as a vehicle for its propaganda and policies, a spearhead for infiltration, and a vanguard of armed insurrection? Was it possible that a communist government in Peking could leave the Overseas Chinese alone or abandon them to work out their own future in the countries of residence?

Perhaps the most common generalisation about China's relations with the Overseas Chinese over the last twenty years has been that they are potentially or in fact a 'Fifth Column'. In the theory developed in the 1950s of China's aggressive and expansionist designs and disruptive international behaviour, there was the proposition that the countries of Southeast Asia were threatened by this Fifth Column, that the CCP's Overseas Chinese policy consisted of a single-minded attempt to mobilise all Overseas Chinese in the political service of China and the pursuit of the Party's revolutionary goals. The 'Overseas Chinese problem' was seldom perceived as a 'problem' for the Chinese government, except in so far as China was believed to have encountered certain obstacles to political and economic exploitation of a relationship which appeared deceptively simple, and which seemed to offer very considerable advantages to the Chinese Communist Party.

This proposition was widely accepted, not only because it suited the purpose of Cold War polemicists. It seemed also to be the obvious position for a communist government in China to adopt, and it was easily credible in Southeast Asia, a fact which some nationalist leaders have sought to exploit for domestic political purposes. For suspicion and fear of the Overseas Chinese relationship with China was a problem which the CCP had inherited from its predecessors. It was bred by the attitudes and behaviour of the Overseas Chinese themselves, and nurtured by the policies of successive Chinese governments, in particular those of the Kuomintang (KMT).

The Fifth Column theory was never seriously tested, but it was an extra-ordinary oversimplification to say the least. Its essential weakness, of course, was that it rested on a combination of untested assumptions about the CCP's intentions, and generalisations about the behaviour and political attitudes of Overseas Chinese themselves. Yet the literature on the subject of the Chinese in Southeast Asia has shown that it is not possible to make generalised conclusions about all or even a majority of Overseas Chinese. To some journalists, Overseas Chinese are almost all merchants or usurers or at least petty capitalists; to the Chinese government, on a theoretical level, over 90 per cent are labouring class. Neither of these assertions is accurate, as sociological studies of Overseas Chinese communities have shown. And the political behaviour of Overseas Chinese, moreover, in itself tells nothing about the objectives of the Chinese government. To the extent that it might do so on closer investigation, there are unusual difficulties in conducting studies in Southeast Asian countries on such a politically charged question as personal attitudes to and relations with China or the Chinese govern-ment.[2]

The only, and one would have thought obvious, alternative is to examine the Overseas Chinese policies of the CCP itself, and that is the purpose of this study. The evidence which emerges from the CCP's policies contests the validity of the Fifth Column theory. It reveals a growing awareness on the part of the CCP that there were complex and intractable problems associated with its overseas population, both in the pursuit of foreign policies in Southeast Asia and in the very nature of the Overseas Chinese relationship with China. The Party's response to these problems is extremely significant, not simply for China's relations with the Overseas Chinese, but also for its whole approach to Southeast Asia.

OVERSEAS CHINESE POPULATION

China's Overseas Chinese policy is concerned almost exclusively with the Chinese in Southeast Asia, since it is in Southeast Asia that they present the greatest obstacles, and the greatest potential for the advancement of China's foreign policy interests, and also because that is where more than 95 per cent of them live.[3] With a few exceptions, the Chinese in other parts of the world have not influenced the policies of the Chinese Communist

Party.[4] The Chinese Nationalists estimated that of a total of 18,301,126 Overseas Chinese in June 1969, 96.02 per cent, which includes the Chinese of Hong Kong and Macao, were in Asia.[5] Estimates of the number of Overseas Chinese have varied according to the definition applied, and even the best attempts suffer from lack of statistical information. Surprisingly, however, authorities working from different criteria tend to arrive at roughly similar conclusions on the total figure. The Chinese Nationalist estimate might be expected to be high, since the concept of *jus sanguinis* to which they adhere means that any person of all or part Chinese parentage is included in their total.[6] But by subtracting the figures for Hong Kong and Macao which only they count as Overseas Chinese, the Nationalist total is close to a widely accepted figure of between 12 and 13 million for Southeast Asia.[7] While the Overseas Chinese taken together constitute only five per cent of the total population of Southeast Asia,[8] they are still a significantly large communal group. A table of estimates of the Chinese population in Southeast Asia is given in Appendix A.

Peking's present estimate of the Overseas Chinese population is not known. In the national census of 1953 the Chinese government produced a figure of 11,743,320, which included Chinese students abroad,[9] and this is the only precise figure it has published. According to the official release, it was calculated by 'indirect investigation', and frequent references to pre-1949 KMT estimates in the official publications of the period suggest that it may have been derived from projections of old KMT estimates.[10] Subsequently, Peking settled on a round sum of 'over 12 million', or 'approximately 13 million'. By 1965, however, when official figures for the population of China still referred to the 1957 estimate, no figure at all was given for Overseas Chinese.[11] This may mean that the government was uncertain how far the dimensions of the problem had altered since 1953, which is suggested also by its failure to increase the number of Overseas Chinese deputies to the National People's Congress (NPC) when the total number was increased in 1964. The reason for the uncertainty probably lies in the fact that since the 1953 census the CCP has made sweeping changes in its policy on Overseas Chinese nationality, which make it more difficult to define what is an Overseas Chinese or to measure how many might come within that definition.

In 1968, I was told by an official of the Overseas Chinese Affairs Commission (OCAC) in Peking that the Chinese government did not know how many Overseas Chinese there were, and that there had been no attempt to compile statistics, even in countries where China had diplomatic representation.[12] While the second half of this statement is open to question, the first is probably true, given the difficulties experienced by other authorities.[13] Moreover, since the Chinese government does not have direct jurisdiction over the Chinese abroad, an approximate total would be sufficient for most purposes. More specific estimates would be necessary only for solving immediate problems like repatriation, or surveying the potential for such things as Overseas Chinese investment.

The status of the Chinese in Hong Kong and Macao is ambiguous. Statistically, they are not included within Peking's category of Overseas Chinese.[14] They are referred to as 'compatriots' (*t'ung-pao*), and where they appear together with Overseas Chinese they are clearly designated as 'Hong Kong and Macao compatriots'. In speeches, documents, and press articles covering twenty-one years of the People's Republic of China, it has not been possible to find one instance in which the Chinese government referred to them as 'Overseas Chinese'. Nevertheless, they are treated as Overseas Chinese for administrative purposes: 'although the compatriots in Hong Kong and Macao cannot be regarded as Overseas Chinese, their position is similar to that of the Overseas Chinese and the various Overseas Chinese policies can generally be applied to them'.[15] In laws and regulations concerning Overseas Chinese they are sometimes included, sometimes not.[16] When they visit China, they use the Overseas Chinese Travel Service, they enjoy some of the privileges accorded to Overseas Chinese dependants, and they are included in programmes arranged for visiting Overseas Chinese. Their relatives in China may be given Overseas Chinese dependant status if they receive regular remittances. Their status, therefore, appears to lie somewhere between Overseas Chinese and ordinary Chinese citizens temporarily under British or Portuguese jurisdiction.

DOMESTIC OVERSEAS CHINESE

The relatives or dependants of Chinese living abroad, returned Overseas Chinese, and Overseas Chinese students are referred to in this study as 'domestic Overseas Chinese'. Although the term is not used in Chinese, policies are invariably stated as applying at least to the first two categories, and in most cases also to the third. While each group has presented distinct problems, the Chinese government has regarded all, including the students, as permanent residents of China, and its general objectives have been the same for all three groups. There are approximately 11 million domestic Overseas Chinese; over 10 million relatives or dependants,[17] between 400,000 and 500,000 returned Overseas Chinese, and between 60,000 and 70,000 students. Over 9 million live in the two provinces of Kwangtung and Fukien, and the remainder are concentrated in Kwangsi, Chekiang, Shantung, and Yunnan, with small numbers scattered throughout the rest of China.[18] The dependants have consisted almost entirely of women, old people, and young children,[19] and despite the financial assistance they received from abroad the CCP claimed that the ratio of social classes among them corresponded in the main with that of the general populace.[20]

Figures published by the Chinese government for the number of domestic

Overseas Chinese do not necessarily represent the actual number currently treated as being in this category. The number of dependants was assessed during land reform on the basis of those who were known to have relatives abroad, and a revised figure has not been published.[21] Official totals for the returned Overseas Chinese represent only the number of arrivals since 1949; many have since merged with the category of Overseas Chinese dependants, some have left China, and some have become submerged in the Chinese masses. Similarly, Overseas Chinese students have tended to become indistinguishable from the Chinese masses once they have graduated.

HISTORICAL BACKGROUND

The Overseas Chinese problem, from whichever point of view, was not one which sprang into existence with the victory of the Chinese Communist Party. Just as indigenous Southeast Asians discovered an Overseas Chinese problem with the stirrings of modern nationalism, so also had Chinese governments for more than half a century been confronted with problems similar to those which faced the CCP. Some of their responses established precedents which the CCP was to follow. Some of their policies compounded the difficulties of the legacy they left to the CCP. Their policy options were all limited, and they have become more limited with the rise of Asian nationalism, the emergence of independent Southeast Asia, and the growth of China's interest and involvement in the region. But since the Ch'ing government first became involved with the Overseas Chinese, no Chinese government has found it possible to ignore them in relations with Southeast Asia. And a relationship between China and the Overseas Chinese carries with it a degree of involvement in the affairs of Southeast Asia and will have some effect, however minimal, on China's relations with the countries concerned.

The question of a policy towards Overseas Chinese did not arise until the end of the Ch'ing dynasty, when the growing wealth of the Chinese abroad and their involvement in domestic Chinese politics forced the Manchu rulers to acknowledge their existence. Because of problems with pirates and rebels, the Ch'ing government expressly forbade emigration and prescribed the death penalty for Chinese subjects who settled abroad. The first changes, like the reluctant abandonment of Manchu isolationism, were the result largely of pressure from the western powers. Written into the Unequal Treaties were clauses in which the Chinese emperor recognised first the fact, and then the right, of Chinese emigration. The motives of the western powers, of course, were to secure rights in China for themselves and freedom to exploit Chinese labour. But with a respect for international legal niceties not reflected in their actions, they drafted the clauses containing their demands so as to incorporate the principle of reciprocity. Hence, many of the treaties accorded the Chinese government the right to protect Chinese subjects abroad, but it was not until the 1880s that the Manchus began to exercise this right, nor was it until 1893 that the law preventing emigration was repealed.[22]

In the last two decades of the dynasty, there was a quickening of interest in the Overseas Chinese, prompted by their support for monarchist, revolutionary or constitutionalist factions in China, and also by a realisation that their wealth was more than just a few 'sands they have scraped together'.[23] This new interest was first demonstrated in the activities of Chinese Consuls in the Straits Settlements,[24] and it ultimately found legal expression in the Nationality Law of 1909. The Law adopted the principle of *jus sanguinis*; any person born of a Chinese father, or of a Chinese mother where the nationality of the father was unknown or indeterminate, was a Chinese citizen, regardless of place of birth.[25]

Many of the considerations which the CCP was to face forty years later in framing an Overseas Chinese policy were either present in the circumstances surrounding the Ch'ing government's acknowledgment of the Overseas Chinese, or were the result of that decision. The possibility of tapping Overseas Chinese wealth has been of concern to successive Chinese governments. The Manchus were motivated by the prospect of financial gain well before they claimed the Overseas Chinese as citizens; the revolution of 1911 was financed partly by Overseas Chinese; remittances and investment were a major preoccupation of the KMT; and to the CCP also, foreign exchange from the Chinese abroad has been of great importance. When the political battles of China in the last years of the Ch'ing dynasty were carried into the Chinese communities abroad, Overseas Chinese were encouraged to identify with Chinese rather than local politics; and this in turn fostered the growth of Overseas Chinese nationalism which has remained to trouble the countries of Southeast Asia and complicate the CCP's policies in the region. It is partly for this reason also that, since 1949, the Chinese Nationalists have been able once more to carry the internal political battle into the Overseas Chinese arena, seeking among the Overseas Chinese moral and financial support in their opposition to the Communist government. The decade before the 1911 Revolution also saw the first efforts by a Chinese government to promote Chinese education among Chinese abroad, an objective which subsequently became a cornerstone of KMT policy, contributing to the growth of Overseas Chinese cultural chauvinism and separateness and inhibiting tendencies to integration. The Communists have taken a somewhat different view of Overseas Chinese education, but it has been a central issue in their policy. The principle of *jus sanguinis* itself created problems of dual nationality which have plagued communist China's relations with Southeast Asia.

Following the 1911 Revolution the KMT maintained the strongest interest in the Overseas Chinese, because it had begun virtually as an Overseas

Chinese party and because it still looked to them for finance. But the string of Peking governments which ruled until 1927 did not ignore the financial and political potential of the compatriots overseas.[26] Between 1912 and 1919, they also attempted to promote and supervise Overseas Chinese education,[27] an attempt was made in 1917 to register all Chinese abroad, and from 1918 until 1922 there was a department for Overseas Chinese affairs within, significantly, the Ministry of Commerce.[28] From 1921, the KMT began to take a greater initiative in Overseas Chinese affairs, attracting more widespread support.[29] It established an Overseas Chinese Affairs Bureau in Canton, which in 1926 became the first Overseas Chinese Affairs Commission. After the establishment of the National Government, it was undecided what to do with the Overseas Chinese Affairs Commission. For brief periods it was placed under the Ministry of Industry and Commerce, and the Foreign Ministry, and for four years it was under the direct control of the Central Executive Committee of the Kuomintang. In 1932, with the independent ministries under the Executive Yüan, it finally assumed the structure which remains in Taiwan today, and which was the model for the Communist's organisation of the same name.[30]

In 1926, the KMT laid down three basic objectives for Overseas Chinese policy: to devise ways in which the Overseas Chinese would have equal treatment in the countries of residence, to facilitate the return to China to study of the children of Overseas Chinese, and to give special guarantees to Overseas Chinese who wished to establish industries in China.[31] The objectives of this first coherent Overseas Chinese policy are remarkably similar to those announced by the CCP when it first came to power, although the motives and interpretation have differed considerably. In February 1929, the new Nationalist government promulgated a Nationality Law, which adopted virtually unchanged from the law of 1909 the principle of *jus sanguinis*, and which is still in force in Taiwan.

It is enlightening to look at the kind of things the KMT said about Overseas Chinese policy in its two decades of rule on the Chinese mainland, even though what it has said about this policy often corresponds more with its ambition and particularly since 1949 with its desperation to win the Chinese abroad, than with its actual performance. The manner in which it approved of chauvinism[32] among Overseas Chinese and sought to discourage any weakening of traditional ties with China, was at least partly responsible for the initial suspicion in Southeast Asia of the Communists' Overseas Chinese policy. If the Nationalists could encourage such ultra-nationalistic tendencies, then the Communists must be even more extreme; and since 1949 the Nationalists themselves have actually fostered this belief in Southeast Asia. One of their reasons for doing so is that they appear to have assumed a far greater identity of motive and purpose between themselves and the Communists, particularly on 'nationalist' issues, than has actually existed.

Yet just as there were other important issues on which they differed, territorial claims for example, so also was it mistaken of the KMT to assume such an identity of views on the Overseas Chinese. Moreover, Communist Chinese nationalism is conditioned to some extent by realpolitik and a measure of internationalism, philosophies which could not be said to have had significant impact on the thinking of the KMT. Whatever the situation, the KMT could have been expected to criticise the CCP's policy. But it is surprising how much of the comment from Taipei reads as though the KMT were simply imputing its own objectives or aspirations to the Chinese Communist Party.

From the very beginning, the KMT regarded Chinese education as the key; without that, the Overseas Chinese might begin to see their future in the countries of residence. From 1927 the Education Ministry, later assisted by the OCAC, instituted a programme for the registration and inspection of Overseas Chinese schools, the establishment of new schools, teacher training for Overseas Chinese, and education for Overseas Chinese youth in China. An instruction issued in 1938 stated that Overseas Chinese children 'should be directed to learn special skills which can be used in serving the homeland'; twenty years later, the CCP was to issue an almost identical instruction, in reference not to the homeland but to the countries of residence. Of 'Six Crises' for Overseas Chinese enunciated by the Central Executive Committee of the KMT in 1940, one was an 'educational crisis', the interference in Chinese schools by foreign governments. It was the duty of Overseas Chinese schools to 'concentrate on raising their nationalist consciousness'.[33] In 1946, emigration was proposed as a means of strengthening Chinese education, one of the rare occasions on which a Chinese government has even suggested official sponsorship of emigration. At the same time 'Overseas Chinese cadres' were to be trained at Chinan University to assist in spreading Chinese culture outwards from the homeland. So important was education in the view of the KMT, that it was written into the 1946 Constitution that encouragement and subsidies were to be given to Overseas Chinese educational enterprises.[34]

If education was the crucial factor in preserving the close association between the Overseas Chinese and China, the purpose of maintaining this link was primarily financial. With every new pronouncement on education, there was either a call to increase the flow of money from Overseas Chinese, or a directive for greater effort to be made in protecting, not simply the persons of Overseas Chinese, but their 'wealth', their 'assets', or their 'material well-being'.

Throughout KMT policy there runs a theme of assertive and possessive nationalism, exemplified in the 'Six Crises' of 1940. There was said to be a 'crisis of national identity' (*min-tsu shang chih wei-chi*), arising from the fact that, since it is difficult for (Chinese) women to enter (the countries of residence) Overseas Chinese are marrying local women, and local births are increasing daily. Their blood is becoming mixed, their language, literature, customs and habits are being transformed by local and foreign influences, making it difficult to avoid losing their national characteristics.[35]

What might perhaps be seen as a desirable trend by Southeast Asian countries, and even by many Overseas Chinese themselves, was regarded as a crisis of national identity by the KMT.

Overseas Chinese would appear to have been responsive to these policies, but this was as much due to the situation and attitudes of Overseas Chinese themselves as to any achievement on the part of the KMT:[36] their historical, and personal, link with the homeland, and the constant renewal of the link by continuing emigration, until the war and Japanese occupation intervened; the fact that in many parts of Southeast Asia the only education available to Overseas Chinese was that which they provided themselves; and the presence of colonial governments which kept a tight rein on local political activity and which tended not to encourage integration of Chinese with the local peoples. Despite the special relationship of some Overseas Chinese with the KMT it is probably the case that most Overseas Chinese who were and are concerned to preserve the link are concerned with China rather than political parties. This made it easier for some to transfer allegiance to the government which came to power in 1949; it also posed problems for that government.

THE INHERITANCE OF THE CHINESE COMMUNIST PARTY

When the CCP came to power in 1949, there were four general problems with which it had to contend, irrespective of policy priorities or specific objectives.

The first was that, in assuming responsibility for the Overseas Chinese[37] the CCP was immediately committed to involvement in Southeast Asia, through a relationship which, if not strictly colonial, in itself carried colonial implications but yet was not easily susceptible to manipulation. Secondly, there was the legacy of the KMT, whose Overseas Chinese policies had done little to engender trust or goodwill from indigenous Southeast Asians and whose position on nationality was to complicate the difficulties facing the CCP.

Thirdly, there was the relationship between Chinese and non-Chinese in Southeast Asia. In varying degrees from one country to another, the Chinese were an ethnically distinct, linguistically and culturally separate, and largely unassimilated minority, an object of resentment to indigenous Southeast Asians. They also belonged to the once dominant power in East Asia and were thought to be, and in many cases were in fact, economically dominant, racially arrogant, unwilling to identify with the interests of the countries of residence, and closely involved with the politics of China and China's supposed ambitions in Southeast Asia. There was, of course, some doubt as to how far these fears of 'the enemy within' were justified. But they were very real in the minds of Southeast Asians, with the result that 'Southeast Asian nationalism early developed an anti-Sinitic tradition which found more open expression as indigenous elites came to power'.[38]

The fourth problem, subsequently admitted in the inaugural issue of the *Ch'iao-wu pao* (*Overseas Chinese Affairs Journal*) in 1956, was that 'the legacy in the Overseas Chinese affairs field amounted to almost nothing, so that in fact, Overseas Chinese work in New China had to grope its way from the very beginning'.[39] Before 1949, the Chinese Communist Party had almost no experience, and appears to have given little thought to an Overseas Chinese policy.

The KMT claimed that there was a threat to its own position from communist influence among the Chinese abroad. There was, of course, a degree of sentiment among Overseas Chinese which favoured the Chinese Communists,[40] and communist groups existed among Chinese in a number of Southeast Asian countries at the end of the Pacific War.[41] But it is doubtful if the CCP was responsible for as much of this influence, or even gave as much attention to the Overseas Chinese, as the KMT thought. The Party had ample opportunities for contact with Overseas Chinese in China, through the first united front with the KMT, through its own contacts with Overseas Chinese families in Kwangtung and Fukien in the early 1930s,[42] and again in the anti-Japanese united front through the KMT and the minority democratic parties which had close connections with Overseas Chinese.[43] Some Overseas Chinese managed to make their way to the liberated areas, and some Overseas Chinese funds reached the CCP. But the Communists were also fairly effectively isolated from the Overseas Chinese after the retreat to North China and the outbreak of the Sino-Japanese War, which certainly restricted their ability to control such communist movements as did exist. They needed, moreover, to concentrate their resources for the struggle against the Japanese and the KMT, and for the administration of the areas under their control. They could not easily afford a costly operation among the Overseas Chinese unless there was some prospect of immediate and substantial material support. In post-1949 writing the CCP has tended to be vague about Overseas Chinese support in the whole Republican period, suggesting that it may have been minimal.

This is not to argue that the CCP totally ignored the Overseas Chinese. It did not. But to the extent that it had formulated a policy for Overseas Chinese, it seems to have been more concerned with soliciting financial assistance and mobilising support for the anti-Japanese struggle in China than with exploiting or communising them for purposes external to China. Official CCP programmes in the border areas included appeals to Overseas

Chinese 'to come to the border area to study, to take part in anti-Japanese work, or to establish enterprises'.[44] The Party seems to have been concerned particularly with assisting Overseas Chinese to return to China,[45] an objective stated in the only reference to Overseas Chinese in Mao's published writings before, or after, 1949.[46] CCP members did turn up in Hong Kong and Southeast Asia in the late 1930s, but many of these had lost contact with the main Communist forces and had been forced to leave China, and were not initially despatched as agents of the CCP.[47]

The KMT's suspicions of the CCP were almost certainly prompted by its own policies, under which, by its own admission, it was training and sending cadres to Southeast Asia with unconcealed political intent. It was probably the case also that their own expectations of the Overseas Chinese led the KMT leaders to believe that support from Overseas Chinese would be equally important to the CCP. But whatever their motives, their accusations represent one of the earliest examples of the misleading practice of describing Overseas Chinese communists as synonymous with the Chinese Communist Party.

The CCP's Overseas Chinese policies immediately after 1949 seem to confirm that the Party had not thought very deeply about the problem in the years before. The fact that there is so little evidence of detailed policy decisions or discussions before 1949 is at least indicative of a low priority accorded to Overseas Chinese work. Even the United Front Work Department, responsible for Overseas Chinese affairs after 1949, does not appear to have been very much concerned with the Overseas Chinese.[48] It is not surprising, therefore, that the Party felt it 'had to grope its way from the very beginning'.

The Kuomintang, like the Ch'ing government until the middle of the nineteenth century, took a very simple view of the Overseas Chinese. The original Ch'ing policy was to ignore them. The KMT claimed them all, believed they could be an instrument of foreign policy, and even listed Overseas Chinese policy as the first objective of foreign policy.[49] The CCP may have been tempted to follow the KMT, or to regard the Overseas Chinese as no more than an additional and sometimes complicating factor in foreign policy. But its own terms of reference, its domestic and foreign policies and its world outlook, were different. Although the interests of foreign policy took first place, the Party found it impossible to take such a simple approach, because the Chinese abroad represented more than an overseas financial and political asset. In the mid-twentieth century, China had its own 'Overseas Chinese problem', and in its attempts to grapple with and solve this problem the CCP's policies have been complex, adaptable, and sophisticated, the objectives have been diverse, and the difficulties encountered formidable.

Part One. The domestic perspective

2

Administration of Overseas Chinese affairs

THE DOMESTIC PERSPECTIVE. A FRAMEWORK FOR
INTERPRETING OVERSEAS CHINESE POLICY

There are certain features of Overseas Chinese affairs which offer quite unique opportunities, not normally available in other areas of foreign policy, for discerning the CCP's often unstated policy motivations and long-term objectives.

At the crudest level of analysis it is sometimes argued that what is important in Chinese foreign policy is not what the Chinese government says but what it does. If this is also intended to imply that what is said can be discounted, it is grossly at fault. But it is true that in most analyses there are often significant gaps which must be tested against China's foreign policy actions and interactions, or else left to be filled by speculation, prior assumptions or informed guesswork. There is always the possibility that the shadow of posture statements may be mistaken for the substance of policy objectives.

The focus of the present study is one-sided. It is based on the Peking perspective on relations with the Overseas Chinese and the evidence in Chinese, as distinct from Overseas Chinese, sources. It might be objected that a better method of evaluating the CCP's intentions is to examine the actual operation of its policies in Southeast Asia. But the unfortunate fact is that there are such obstacles and false trails in the way of this approach that the results of those who have attempted it have been far from satisfactory or conclusive. The general literature on the Chinese in Southeast Asia suggests, moreover, that further attempts are unlikely to yield the kind of information which might enable valid or accurate assessments to be made of the CCP's intentions. The nature and purpose of China's contacts with Overseas Chinese is difficult to investigate; and the scattered, and for the most part unsubstantiated, evidence which does exist provides little basis for drawing general conclusions. The alternative adopted by some writers is to draw inferences from the political behaviour of the Overseas Chinese themselves. As an indicator of the intentions of the government in Peking this is quite unreliable. Where direction and control is not proven, even the activities of Overseas Chinese communists are not necessarily an indication of the wishes of the Chinese Communist Party.

The difficulties of testing one's conclusions on the ground, however, are compensated by other factors. To the Chinese government, and to the Nationalists in Taiwan, the Chinese abroad are only one component, albeit the most important, of a field of activity known as *hua-ch'iao shih-wu* or *ch'iao-wu*, 'Overseas Chinese affairs'. This field embraces both the Chinese abroad and the domestic Overseas Chinese, and a network of organisations in China. It also extends into many major areas of policy; apart from foreign policy, it involves internal affairs, economics and finance, culture, education, women and youth work, and it is spread over a number of provinces outside the two main provinces of Kwangtung and Fukien.[1] This means that there are extra dimensions to Overseas Chinese policy which in foreign policy do not exist, or rather, are more diffuse, less visible, and seldom ever discussed in the public media. While it is difficult, and very often impossible, to discern precisely what influences or determines foreign policy decisions, in Overseas Chinese policy there is a great deal of information about perceptions of external policy problems and domestic influences or determinants in the formulation of external policies. The more one investigates Overseas Chinese policy, the more one becomes aware of the peculiar importance of the domestic perspective, both for its relationship to external policy and for testing the Chinese government's intentions; it enables conclusions to be drawn with greater confidence than is the case with possibly any other area of Chinese foreign policy. To ignore the domestic perspective would conceal much that is important for external policy, and result in a partial, and possibly erroneous view. The following three chapters, particularly the second two, serve to demonstrate this point.

THE FUNCTION OF THE ADMINISTRATION

Given the physical separation between China and the Overseas Chinese, the first question facing any Chinese government seeking to influence them is an organisational one. The Overseas Chinese affairs administration is the framework within which the CCP has tried to work out its relationships with the Chinese abroad, the formal expression of the domestic perspective and its relation to external policy.

The distinction between the special problems of Overseas Chinese policy and the more conventional problems of foreign policy is underlined by the separate and fairly extensive administrative network which the CCP, and the KMT before it, created for Overseas Chinese affairs. But it would be wrong to suggest, as some writers have done, that it is possible to infer something about the CCP's objectives simply from the existence or size of the Overseas Chinese affairs administration.[2] It is not, of course, its existence but its function which is important. Its areas of responsibility can be divided under two general categories. The first is concerned directly with influencing the Chinese abroad; the second, which is also concerned ultimately with policy towards the Chinese abroad and which is necessitated only by the special problems inherent in that policy, is most immediately concerned with domestic affairs.

By far the greater part of the work of the Overseas Chinese affairs administration lies in the second of these two categories. For while external policy is the ultimate justification, the need for the network of organisations which the Communists created stems from a problem which is largely internal. External policy, particularly considerations of Overseas Chinese foreign exchange, dictated that domestic Overseas Chinese should be given a degree of preferential treatment. It is the problems arising from this preferential treatment, problems of mobilisation, supervision, and control, not always visible to the outside world, which explain the necessity for a large Overseas Chinese affairs bureaucracy. So long as the Chinese government continues to solicit Overseas Chinese foreign exchange then at least part of the bureaucracy, if only within the banking system, is likely to continue in existence, regardless of the government's political intentions towards the Chinese abroad.

In other words, the implementation of external policy rests on a network of organisations and a body of administrative programmes which are centred in China. The KMT's Overseas Chinese policy also functioned in this way, but where the CCP's administration has been almost wholly China-based, the KMT sought to complement its administration with a network of extraterritorial organisations in the countries of residence. The CCP's failure to do the same was probably at first a matter of necessity or practical impossibility. Increasingly after the early 1950s, however, it became a matter of preference. Its implementation of external policy has been largely through indirect communication, which is discussed separately in the following chapter.

The administration of Overseas Chinese affairs is not without considerable interest in itself, since it posed unusual problems which had no parallel in China. It has to cover a wide variety of functions and responsibilities not easily divisible under self-contained administrative units. The same could be said of many fields of government activity, but the problems of Overseas Chinese affairs administration are unique. In the first place, it is an area of united front work. It is concerned with people who, by virtue of special characteristics which the CCP found it expedient to recognise and sanction, stand apart from the Chinese masses. This necessitated the establishment of a government institution which caters to these characteristics, and the creation of organisations like the Overseas Chinese Service Departments in the banks, Overseas Chinese schools and settlements, investment corporations, retail purchasing stores, and organisations for relief and resettlement. It meant also the inclusion of non-functional figureheads in Overseas Chinese government bodies, and entailed the creation of a mass organisation with an active role of mobilising domestic Overseas Chinese in politics and labour. In these respects, administration of Overseas Chinese affairs is not unlike the administration of national minorities. But there are significant differences. United front 'status' for domestic Overseas Chinese exists only by virtue of their relationship with the Chinese abroad. They are distinguishable by this classification and the privilege which accompanies it and not by ethnic difference. The degree of special treatment they receive is related directly to policy towards the Chinese abroad. This is distinct from a special policy for, say, Moslem minorities, made in consideration for the effect on Moslem countries, since the effect on the Chinese abroad is the sole purpose of domestic policy. In mobilisation of the domestic Overseas Chinese, therefore, the Chinese government has had to take account of the effect on the Chinese overseas. A further complication which does not arise with minorities is that the domestic Overseas Chinese population has been constantly augmented by arrivals from overseas who have not previously been subjected even to a modified version of the Party's socialist programmes.

A second problem arises from the fact that while situated in China and preoccupied with domestic affairs, Overseas Chinese affairs institutions are at the same time ultimately concerned with external policies. These institutions, therefore, are subject to direction from organisations which are concerned with the wider field of foreign policy; the State Council Staff Office of Foreign Affairs, the Foreign Ministry, and more recently, the Foreign Affairs Political Department of the Central Committee of the CCP.

A third complicating problem, but not unique, is the involvement of Overseas Chinese affairs work in several major areas of domestic government activity, ranging from education to agricultural production. Within these fields of work, however, Overseas Chinese affairs present special difficulties which necessitate regular channels for liaison and consultation between Overseas Chinese affairs bodies and related sectors.

The size of the bureaucracy, of its staffing and budget are not known, and cannot be compared with other institutions. But it should be borne in mind that it is fairly insignificant in relation to the total state bureaucracy or even Party membership before the Cultural Revolution. Domestic Overseas Chinese affairs work, moreover, in the context of national policies is of major significance in only two of China's provinces, and even then it is concerned with only one-fifth of the population of Kwangtung and one-sixth of the population of Fukien.[3]

The following account is applicable only to the situation which prevailed up to the Cultural Revolution. But since the fate of the administration and its leading personnel during and after the Cultural Revolution is an important indication of trends in policy, some knowledge of the administration which went before is indispensable for interpreting these trends. A chart of the Overseas Chinese affairs administration is given in Appendix B.

GOVERNMENTAL INSTITUTIONS

The Overseas Chinese Affairs Commission

The type of structure created in 1949 for the coordination and direction of Overseas Chinese affairs, a Commission,[4] combines in one institution two forms of organisation, an appointed committee and a permanent staff, which together are known as the Overseas Chinese Affairs Commission (OCAC).

The permanent Commission, which in this study is referred to as the Commission bureaucracy or staff to distinguish it from the appointed members (*wei-yüan*),[5] is of the branch agency type; it is the apex of a hierarchy of branches extending to the basic level. At the head of this hierarchy are the members of the Commission, or *wei-yüan*, appointed by the State Council. They comprise first, a small leading group whose main work is in Overseas Chinese affairs; secondly, Party or government personnel from other sectors whose offices entail some aspect of Overseas Chinese work; thirdly, senior cadres of the Commission staff; and finally, a number of prominent returned Overseas Chinese. This structure enables the Commission, in addition to its own direct administrative responsibilities, to act as a central organ for liaison with other central agencies and with lower-level government organs in the provinces.[6] A similar structure exists also in those branches below the Central Commission which are designated 'committees' (*wei-yüan-hui*). Below that level, the organisational unit is often small enough to combine the two functions in one organ, sometimes, but not always, including persons who at higher levels might be appointed members rather than staff.

The Commission is headed by a Chairman (*chu-jen*), equivalent in rank to a minister, and a number of Vice-Chairmen. There have been only two Chairmen since 1949. Ho Hsiang-ning, or Madame Liao Chung-k'ai served from 1949 to 1959. She was to some extent a figurehead, who represented the Revolutionary Committee of the Kuomintang, and provided a link with the 1911 Revolution and Sun Yat-sen, with whom both she and her husband had been closely associated. She appears to have been intended to represent to Overseas Chinese the legitimacy of the Communist succession. Unlike some of her subordinates in the Commission, however, Ho's appointment does not seem to have been purely nominal.[7] She was very active in the public work of the Commission, and delivered major speeches on policy matters.[8] When Ho retired in April 1959 at the age of eighty-two, she was succeeded by her son, Liao Ch'eng-chih, who had been a Vice-Chairman of the Commission since 1949. Liao, although also qualifying as a figurehead and by birth at least an Overseas Chinese, was the key figure in Overseas Chinese affairs, even during the period when his mother served as Chairman. Where Liao was a member of the CCP Central Committee, his mother was not even a member of the Party.[9]

Three Commissions have been appointed since the Communist government was established; in October 1949, March 1957, and September 1959.[10] The timing of the appointment of the Second and Third Commissions is of interest, since in both cases it seems to have been related to significant changes in Overseas Chinese policy. The appointments were made partly to bring the Commission into line with changes in organisation and personnel in related bodies.[11] But in the case of the Second Commission, the new appointments were announced shortly after the CCP had embarked on a policy designed to alter the whole basis of its relations with the Chinese abroad, a policy which certainly required a capacity for different thinking and different approaches within the administration. The Third Commission came at a time when the Party was about to take this policy one step further with the introduction of large-scale repatriation. This programme was to place considerable strain on Overseas Chinese affairs organisations and required strengthening of coordination with related government bodies.[12] The further implications of the way in which administrative changes have been related to policy changes, of which these are two examples, are discussed more fully below.

The significant change in the appointed Commission since 1949 has been a consolidation of its coordinative function and a decline in the importance of figurehead members.[13] Of the seventy members of the Commission in December 1966, forty-three were either permanent Commission staff or representatives of related areas of work. Of the Chairman and Vice-Chairman, four out of eight were Party members in 1966, compared with one out of five in 1949; although representation from the central United Front Work Department fell from three in the First Commission to one in the Third Commission.[14] The composition of the Second and Third Commissions indicates that the Commission's coordinative function had been institutionalised to the extent that the occupants of certain designated offices in the Chinese government were *ex officio* members of the OCAC. Government institutions represented at vice-ministerial level in both the Second and Third Commissions included the ministries of Commerce, Culture, Education, Foreign Trade, Internal Affairs, Labour, and State Farms and Land Reclamation. Also represented in both Commissions were the People's Bank of China, the Consular Affairs Department of the Ministry of Foreign Affairs, branches of the OCAC in the provinces of Fukien and Kwangtung, and OCAC branches or other government agencies in Kwangsi, Kweichow, Yunnan, and Shanghai.[15] A list of members of the Third Commission is given in Appendix C.

The necessity for this coordinative function is apparent when one looks at the range of activities in which the Commission was involved, but the exact role of those members who represented other government agencies is not clear. From the Commission's point of view it was obviously necessary to have some institutional means of consulting with responsible persons from areas on which Overseas Chinese affairs work impinged. Within the confines of Overseas Chinese affairs, therefore, the appointed Commission represented the highest central organ for both consultation and decision-making. But it seems likely that from the point of view of the cooperating agencies the Commission was a subordinate committee for regulating a relatively minor area of work which came within their province. In particular, the level of representation from central agencies suggests that the role of these representatives was to provide direction rather than to act as consultants.

It is not known how regularly the appointed Commission, or sections of it, meets to discuss or direct Overseas Chinese work, and such meetings are rarely reported. The Chairman, the Vice-Chairmen, and the members who are also department directors in the OCAC staff, do constitute a permanent nucleus and may well provide the majority of members attending regular meetings. But since the role of the Commission is intended to be coordinative, it is assumed that it meets more frequently than is reported.[16]

The permanent staff of the OCAC works under the direction of the Chairman and Vice-Chairmen, and the Commission members who are also permanent staff. Its size and composition are unknown.[17] Its functions are divided under a number of departments; numbered departments have been identified up to a Fourth Department and those identified by name are the General Office, the Secretariat, the Culture and Education Propaganda Department, the Production Relief Department, the Liaison Department[18] and a Correspondence Office. Information on the internal functioning of the OCAC is so scant as to make substantial comment impossible, although broad areas of responsibility can be inferred from the titles, and the activities of leading cadres of the Departments. The Culture and Education Propaganda Department appears to handle education in China for Overseas Chinese and external propaganda; the Liaison Department is probably concerned with the Returned Overseas Chinese Associations and political mobilisation for domestic Overseas Chinese; the Production Relief Department handles State Overseas Chinese Farms and resettlement.

Both the appointed Commission and the staff include returned Overseas Chinese whose local knowledge could be of use in matters concerning the Chinese abroad. Twenty-seven, or 42 per cent, of the appointed members of the Third Commission, of whom four were also members of the Commission staff, are known to have been born or to have studied outside China. A report in 1958 stated that of 148 members of the Kwangtung provincial OCAC leaving for work in the countryside, over 60 per cent were from Southeast Asia, most of them having returned since 1949.[19] This percentage may not be representative of the total Commission hierarchy, or even of the full membership of the Kwangtung OCAC, but it does confirm that returned Overseas Chinese are employed extensively in administration of Overseas

Chinese affairs. In 1962, an official report of the death of Wu Sheng-yü, a newspaperman deported from Singapore in 1953, said that from the time of his arrival in China, Wu had been a counsellor (*ts'an-shih*), in the Central OCAC.[20] Although counsellors have not been identified elsewhere in the CCP press, officials who held this position in the OCAC under the Chinese Nationalists were responsible for drafting and examining bills and orders of the Commission and for studying the laws of foreign countries concerning immigration and residence.[21] It seems, therefore, that certain returned Overseas Chinese may have been employed at fairly senior levels in the administration in an advisory and possibly influential capacity. This raises some interesting questions about the influence of Overseas Chinese on policy formulation, which are discussed at the end of this chapter.

The most public activity of the Central OCAC is the convening of conferences at which the state of Overseas Chinese work is reviewed, new policies are announced, and the implementation of policy is discussed. These may be either plenary or enlarged sessions concerned with all aspects of Overseas Chinese affairs, or work conferences which discuss domestic policies. The distinction between plenary and enlarged conferences is not apparent, since both types are attended by delegates from outside the Central Commission and its subordinate branches, and the only obvious distinction is that some delegates do not have voting rights at enlarged conferences.[22] From this, it might seem that more substantial discussions are held at the plenary sessions, but this has not been evident from what is known of their proceedings. It would be unusual, to say the least, for the CCP to permit public debate on policy issues at such conferences, particularly since among the delegates there were many non-Party people, some of them with close personal contacts outside China. The conferences are important, nevertheless, for official statements on Overseas Chinese policies and the problems encountered in their implementation.

One function of enlarged conferences is to elect Overseas Chinese deputies to the NPC. The number of such deputies has been fixed at thirty since the First NPC in 1954, which is roughly one for every 400,000 of a nominal 12 million Overseas Chinese. It was decided that of the thirty Overseas Chinese positions, five should be allotted to Malaya, four each to Indonesia and Thailand, two each to Indo-China and the Americas, and one each to Burma, the Philippines, North Borneo, Mongolia/Korea, Japan, India/Pakistan, Europe, Africa, and Oceania, leaving four unspecified.[23] This distribution is only very approximately related to the distribution of the Overseas Chinese, in that Malaya, Indonesia and Thailand were to have the most deputies. Given the fact that 95 per cent of the Overseas Chinese are in Southeast Asia, the ratio of deputies to Overseas Chinese is quite disproportionate for all countries. As Ho Hsiang-ning pointed out, with only thirty deputies, it would have been difficult to make a more rational distribution, since the remaining five per cent are scattered thinly throughout the rest of the world. The selection of candidates was through 'consultation'. Overseas Chinese were told that election by an enlarged conference of the OCAC was a democratic method, and indeed the only method given the circumstances of the Chinese abroad and the impossibility of conducting direct elections.[24] But any idea that the thirty Overseas Chinese deputies are representative of the Chinese abroad, or even that patriotic pockets of Chinese nationals meet in various parts of the world to elect people to represent them in China, is dispelled by the fact that in the Third NPC, nineteen out of the thirty were appointed members of the Central OCAC, not one of whom resides outside China. The remaining eleven, most of them returned Overseas Chinese, were permanently resident in China. One was known to be a Party member, two were directors of Overseas Chinese schools, and the rest were 'figureheads' who are not known to have held any positions in the Party or the government at any level.[25] As NPC deputies the role of these people is of little consequence in the administration of Overseas Chinese affairs. The CCP has never really attempted to promote them as evidence of genuine democratic representation of the Overseas Chinese in the Chinese government. Their role is to provide a symbol of the Party's professed concern for Overseas Chinese. This is probably one reason why, when the total number of deputies was increased for the Third NPC in 1964, not only was the number of Overseas Chinese deputies unchanged, but the deputies to the Second NPC were simply reelected, with replacements for two who had died since 1958.[26]

A more important function of the OCAC is the convening of work conferences. These are concerned either with current domestic matters generally, or with specific problems like education for returned Overseas Chinese youth, or domestic Overseas Chinese participation in agricultural production.[27] It is at the work conferences that the basic problems of administration are discussed in detail.

One of the recurring problems, and also the most exacting, has been to train cadres, first to understand who should be included in the category of domestic Overseas Chinese and the degree of genuine privilege, as opposed to publicised privilege, to which they are entitled; and secondly, how to balance privilege against participation, freedom against control, and persuasion against force. This was not only a problem for Overseas Chinese affairs cadres; it also created contradictions between Overseas affairs institutions and other cadres who ignored, or refused to accept, the special policy for Overseas Chinese.[28] The problem was never resolved satisfactorily. Basic level cadres appear to have alternated between leaving domestic Overseas Chinese completely alone because they were 'difficult', or treating them in exactly the same way as they treated the Chinese masses. Another problem, not unique to Overseas Chinese affairs, has been the relationship between Party and non-Party cadres. In the period of free criticism in May 1957, leading non-Party functionaries in Overseas Chinese affairs complained that their work was rendered ineffective because subordinate Party cadres refused to take orders from them or report to them.[29] It seems that this problem was particularly acute in Overseas Chinese affairs, where non-Party cadres were often returned Overseas Chinese with suspect bourgeois or capitalist backgrounds. In 1957 the Party Committee in the Kwangtung Province OCAC was attacked for failing to make use of such people, for completely ignoring organisations like the Chih Kung Tang, and for 'building a low wall' between Party and non-Party cadres.[30] Even 'revolutionary' returned Overseas Chinese met with this kind of treatment. In Swatow, Chinese from Malaya and Singapore describing themselves as revolutionaries, complained that they were not trusted and were regarded as politically unsound.[31]

Branches of the Overseas Chinese Affairs Commission

Administration below the centre is performed by a hierarchy of branches in the provincial and local people's governments. These are designated, in descending order, Committees (*wei-yüan-hui*), Offices (*ch'u*), Bureaus (*chü*), and Sections (*k'o* or *ku*), and at the basic level Work Committees (*kung-tso wei-yüan-hui*) or Work Groups (*kung-tso hsiao-tsu*).[32] The type of branch organisation is not decided by the corresponding level of government administration or geographical division, but is based on the importance of Overseas Chinese work in the particular administrative unit. At provincial level, for example, there were Committees only in Fukien, Hopei, Kwangsi, Kwangtung, and Shantung, whereas in Chekiang, Hupei, Kiangsi, and Yunnan there were Offices.

The organisation of Overseas Chinese affairs branches provides for both vertical and dual control, the former through the Central OCAC or its Party Committee, and the latter through the United Front Work Department (UFWD) at the appropriate level. The contradiction between vertical and dual control which Schurmann discusses may not have been so pronounced in Overseas Chinese affairs as it was in some other fields, because of the interrelation between domestic Overseas Chinese affairs and external policies, which are administered at the centre.[33] Central control is reinforced also by the coordinative committee system, in which cadres from lower levels are represented on committees at higher levels. A representative example is Wang Han-chieh, who as Chairman of the Fukien Province OCAC from 1959 was also an appointed member of the Central OCAC and Director of the Fukien Province UFWD, representing in one person the vertical and dual channels of control and a direct coordinative link with the centre.

The branches at the level of provincial government are responsible for the direction of all Overseas Chinese work within the province. They convene work conferences for the whole province, organise cadre training courses, and conduct an almost continuous round of inspections during which meetings are held to discuss the work of the lower branches. On particular problems which require coordinated planning, like resettlement, they occasionally hold inter-provincial conferences; and between the provincial committees in Kwangtung and Fukien at least there appears to have been a formal channel for regular consultation.[34] The provincial level branches have limited direct communication with Chinese abroad, for supplying information and arranging for repatriation, education in China, and investment. It is not known to what extent there is organisational connection between the provincial branches and the provincial Foreign Affairs Offices.

Below the provincial government are the Overseas Chinese Affairs Sections, or in some cities with a large concentration of Overseas Chinese, Bureaus. The Section may be at *hsien* level, but in major Overseas Chinese areas, where there can be up to several hundred thousand domestic Overseas Chinese in one *hsien*, it is usually at district (*ch'ü*) level.[35] The Section is the first level at which there is extensive contact with the domestic Overseas Chinese masses. Where the lower-level Work Committees are charged with the responsibility of mobilising the individual, the Section, although having individual contact on routine administrative matters, attempts to mobilise the domestic Overseas Chinese on a larger scale, through group meetings and Overseas Chinese congresses. The congresses differ from conferences in that they have the widest possible representation from the ordinary domestic Overseas Chinese; conferences are primarily for cadres from the Party, government, and mass organisations. The object of the congresses is to explain the role of Overseas Chinese in national movements and campaigns, or to discuss particular problems in Overseas Chinese policy. In 1958, for example, Overseas Chinese congresses were held throughout the home districts to discuss the general programmes of the Great Leap Forward and the specific tasks for domestic Overseas Chinese in that movement.[36]

At the basic level are the Work Committees, or in *hsiang* with an Overseas Chinese population which is less than 30 per cent of the total, Work Groups.[37] They were not introduced until 1955, but in major Overseas Chinese areas they rapidly became almost universal; in Taishan *hsien* in Kwangtung Province, for example, they had been set up in 240 out of the 250 *hsiang* by late 1955.[38] The composition of the Committees originally resembled the committee system at the centre, comprising personnel from the banks, courts, economic and finance committees, the Public Security Bureau, the United Front Work Department, and the Propaganda Department.[39] The Work Committees are described as the basic administrative organisation for Overseas Chinese affairs; they are under the leadership of the *hsiang* People's Committee, and directed in their work by the Overseas Chinese Affairs Section at district or *hsien* level. Their work is vital to the operation of Overseas Chinese policy, since they have the responsibility of persuading the individual domestic

Overseas Chinese to participate in the Party's general programmes for the Chinese masses, and to communicate with their relatives abroad.

An article in *Ch'iao-wu pao* in May 1957 reveals that there was considerable confusion in the work of the Committees at that time. Their tasks were described as to strengthen liaison with and service for domestic Overseas Chinese, to reflect their ideas, to propagate the policies of the Party and the government, and to persuade domestic Overseas Chinese to write to their relatives abroad to publicise China's policies and solicit remittances and investment. Their tasks so resembled those of the nongovernmental Returned Overseas Chinese Associations (ROCAs), that many cadres mistook them for a mass organisation, and many of the Committees themselves were actually seeking directives from and reporting to the ROCAs. The article called for a rationalisation of the Committees. In some areas they had as many as a hundred members; it was suggested that they should be reduced to between nine and seventeen, and that their operations should not exceed the limits of one natural village. It seems that the coordinative structure was to be abandoned, since it was suggested also that most members should not hold other posts, and that every effort should be made to appoint 'representative' domestic Overseas Chinese.[40]

It is clear from this article also that basic level cadres had failed to control the domestic Overseas Chinese to the extent that the Party wished, and that in some areas the Committees existed in name only. It was at this level that cadres were expected to integrate the public policy which proclaimed special consideration and status for domestic Overseas Chinese, with the Party's aim of making domestic Overseas Chinese participate in all activities with the Chinese masses. Another article in the same issue of *Ch'iao-wu pao* cites an example of how the Work Committees should operate. According to official policy, participation in labour and cooperatives for domestic Overseas Chinese was voluntary, and they should be free at any time to withdraw from cooperatives. In this particular *hsiang*, when the cooperatives were transformed into higher cooperatives, the Work Committee had the task of investigating why some one hundred families had withdrawn from the cooperatives altogether. The Committee reported to the Party and government authorities, and 'solved' the problems of the reluctant families by 'convicing' them that they should join the cooperatives.[41]

Administrative consolidation, 1956

At the Fourth Enlarged Conference of the OCAC in June 1956, Vice-Chairman of the Commission Fang Fang called for a strengthening of the administrative organs for Overseas Chinese affairs.[42] Up to this point, branches of the OCAC had been established in a somewhat piecemeal fashion, coordination with related organs of government varied from district to district, there was unnecessary duplication of duties, and cadres, particularly at the basic level, were failing to grasp the special problem of Overseas Chinese affairs.[43] Fang announced that provincial level OCAC branches were to 'request' the People's Committees to strengthen leadership over them, and were to increase the number and improve the quality of their cadres. Provinces which did not have branch organisations were to establish Offices or Sections; municipalities and special districts under the direct control of provincial People's Committees were to appoint special cadres for Overseas Chinese work. Provinces which already had committees were to increase representation from related sectors. The central OCAC was to establish a training school for cadres already in the service. Work Committees were to be set up in all *hsiang*, *hsiang*-level towns and municipalities in the Overseas Chinese districts.

The rationalisation announced in Fang's speech had, in fact, been under way for some time. It was foreshadowed in Ho Hsiang-ning's address to the NPC in 1954,[44] and had commenced in 1955 with the establishment of Work Committees. Preparations were being made also to reorganise the Returned Overseas Chinese Friendship Associations and establish a national mass organisation; corporations were being formed for Overseas Chinese investment; and special retail facilities were being established to regularise Overseas Chinese purchasing privileges.

The reason for this consolidation may be inferred from what had been happening in Overseas Chinese policy. Since the end of 1954 the Chinese government had been developing a set of policies involving new initiatives in the external sphere and a greater measure of utilisation and control of the domestic Overseas Chinese. Where there had been considerable changes in other areas of government since 1949, there had been no major reorganisation of Overseas Chinese organisations. The strengthening of administration at this stage was designed to achieve more effective coordination in what was a rather untidy area of government work, to ensure that the new policies then being introduced would be understood and implemented correctly, and to bring about a greater degree of control over the domestic Overseas Chinese.

The administrative pattern which resulted from this rationalisation remained basically unchanged until the Cultural Revolution. The only major development occurred in 1960 when the State Council established a special committee for repatriation and resettlement, which was accompanied by a rapid increase in the number of State Overseas Chinese Farms. Since this was closely related to other developments at that time, it is discussed separately in relation to the repatriation policy.

The OCAC and External Overseas Chinese policy

The Chinese government's perception of the place of Overseas Chinese affairs in the context of foreign relations was stated succinctly in a speech by Chuang Hsi-ch'üan, a Vice-Chairman of the OCAC, at the inaugural meeting of the All-China Returned Overseas Chinese Association in 1956: 'Work concerning the Chinese overseas must be subordinate to foreign policy.'[45]

Major external policy decisions, presumably the responsibility of the Political Bureau or its Standing Committee,[46] probably are made in conjunction with the State Council Staff Office of Foreign Affairs, with advice from the Foreign Ministry and the OCAC. It is unlikely that the OCAC has independent responsibility even in minor decisions on external policy, since every measure designed to affect the Overseas Chinese has some bearing on China's relations with the countries concerned. The final arbiter at the government level is the State Council Staff Office of Foreign Affairs,[47] and the only member of the Commission involved in external policy decision-making, Liao Ch'eng-chih, was concurrently a Deputy Director of this Office.[48] The Foreign Ministry also has a leading role in Overseas Chinese affairs to the extent that official government-to-government contact and consular matters concerning Overseas Chinese are handled by the Ministry or its missions abroad. So far as is known, the OCAC itself has not been involved in direct official contact with foreign governments. During the Cultural Revolution, the temporary rulers in the Foreign Ministry attempted unsuccessfully to send an OCAC investigation team to Burma; this would have been the first known occasion on which members or staff of the OCAC had appeared outside China in their official Commission capacity.[49]

The role of the OCAC in relation to the Chinese abroad is one indicator of the intentions of the CCP in Overseas Chinese policy. The work of the Commission is concentrated in the domestic field, but it is nominally the central administrative agency for all Overseas Chinese affairs, and might be expected to be concerned with the implementation of the Party's external policies. To the extent that the Party's intention was to hold the allegiance of the Chinese abroad and manipulate them in the service of China, it would be necessary to establish strong organisational links and firm central direction of Overseas Chinese education, the press, the chambers of commerce and the clan and welfare associations. At the end of 1949, the Chinese government wrote to Overseas Chinese societies, newspapers and schools, asking them to establish direct contact with the Commission.[50] The initial intention, therefore, seems to have been that the OCAC would attempt to control the Chinese abroad, working through their organisations as the KMT had done. In 1949, however, an Overseas Chinese policy had barely evolved, and when a positive policy did emerge after 1954, it did not require the kind of involvement with the Overseas Chinese which apparently was intended in 1949.

According to a Cultural Revolution source, Overseas Chinese affairs cadres were actually instructed that they should interfere with the Chinese abroad as little as possible.[51] The evidence from Chinese sources, even though largely negative, seems to confirm that this was in fact the case; certainly, it would have been consistent with the Party's objectives after the end of 1956. Significantly, the Foreign Ministry has not been represented on the Commission at vice-ministerial level, as other ministries were, and very few members have been drawn from the foreign affairs field. Apart from Liao Ch'eng-chih, only two members of the Third Commission are known to have worked in foreign affairs, and both appear to have been concerned with internal matters.[52] This suggests that the OCAC was not closely involved organisationally with the Chinese abroad, which would have implicated it constantly in matters affecting China's foreign policies and required close supervision from senior levels in the Foreign Ministry.

There was, of course, opportunity for such supervision through the person of Liao Ch'eng-chih. But even Liao's role does not suggest such a function for the OCAC, and if anything tends to illustrate the low priority accorded to the Chinese abroad in the context of national policies. Liao, as a Vice-Chairman and subsequently Chairman of the Commission and a member of the CCP Central Committee, appears to have been the one person in the Commission involved in decision-making on external Overseas Chinese policy. So far as is known, no one person outside the Commission has had specific responsibility for the Chinese abroad. Overseas Chinese affairs, however, was only one of many major areas of work in which Liao was involved in a leading capacity. He was Secretary of the New Democratic Youth League and subsequently a member of the Central Committee of the Communist Youth League, and was active in youth work throughout the 1950s. He has been one of the Party's leading spokesmen in the peace movement, and his visits outside China have been primarily for international peace and solidarity conferences and not for Overseas Chinese affairs. Above all, he appears to have had primary responsibility for China's relations with Japan; party relations, cultural relations, and the important field of Sino-Japanese trade. It is probably for this reason as much as his responsibility for Overseas Chinese affairs that he was a Deputy Director of the State Council Staff Office of Foreign Affairs. In his activities since 1949, Overseas Chinese affairs appear only as one, and possibly the least significant, of a number of important and time-consuming responsibilities.[53]

The role of the OCAC might be more clearly understood by contrasting it briefly with that of the organisations responsible for Overseas Chinese affairs in Taiwan.[54] Peking's Commission operates entirely within China, and it implements external policy by indirect communication with the Overseas Chinese. By its own admission, the Overseas Chinese Affairs Commission of the Chinese Nationalists attempts to maintain the strongest possible control over Overseas Chinese organisations. It has sponsored a whole series of cultural, educational and economic organisations both in Taiwan and overseas, in which Overseas Chinese participate, and through which the Commission seeks to extend its control to the Overseas Chinese masses. Where possible, it still maintains overseas branches of the Kuomintang. Members of the Commission and the Third Department of the Kuomintang[55] make regular tours of the countries of residence to strengthen ties with the Overseas Chinese. The Commission holds special training courses in Taiwan for teachers in Overseas Chinese schools; groups of Overseas Chinese youth are given summer vacation trips to Taiwan during which they receive training with the Taiwan armed forces. The Communists' organisations have maintained links with the Chinese abroad, as the following chapter makes clear, but the extent of direct organisational control appears to have been far less than that of the KMT. The reason is not simply one of greater impediments to the operations of Peking's representatives in Southeast Asia; it is essentially a difference of policy objectives.

'Service' for Overseas Chinese

Where the OCAC is primarily an administrative organisation and does provide some services, there are also three special service (*fu-wu*) organisations for Overseas Chinese; Service Departments in the banks, retail purchasing stores, and the Overseas Chinese Travel Service.

Because of the importance of Overseas Chinese foreign exchange, the banks were a vital component of the administration of Overseas Chinese affairs. In the first years of the Communist government, they appear to have provided the only administration in areas of China where regular Overseas Chinese agencies had yet to be established. Late in 1949 and throughout 1950, Overseas Chinese Service Departments were established in the Bank of China.[56] There were two subdivisions within these departments, one for service (*fu-wu*), and one for business (*yeh-wu*). The former covered special banking facilities, assistance with travel documents and tickets, establishment of guest houses, and handling of commercial and trade enquiries. The latter dealt with the special Overseas Chinese exchange rate, remittances, foreign currency bank deposits, and the provision of low-interest loans.[57] Most of these tasks were purely banking matters, but from the end of 1950 the Service Departments extended their activities to include meeting returned Overseas Chinese and finding accommodation for them, arranging schools for Overseas Chinese students, writing letters for dependants, and tracing relatives. In late 1954, there were thirty-five of these Service Departments, by this time in the People's Bank as well as the Bank of China.

In addition to providing banking and other services, the Service Departments kept a check on the activities of domestic Overseas Chinese, particularly their use of remittances, their correspondence with relatives abroad, and movement in and out of China. They assisted also in the work of registering domestic Overseas Chinese, recording those who received remittances and issuing them with an identification.[58] When the Work Committees and Returned Overseas Chinese Associations were established, the role of the

Service Departments tended to be confined to banking and commercial matters, although they continued to provide travel assistance, much as banks do in other countries. Members of the banks, not necessarily from the Service Departments, continued to hold positions in the branches of the OCAC and to play an important role in Overseas Chinese affairs.[59]

Some of the remaining functions of the Service Departments were taken over by 'Service Agencies', which had existed in some areas as early as 1951, apparently as a section within local branches of the OCAC.[60] Their function was to handle travel arrangements for visiting and returning Overseas Chinese and provide them with guides and interpreters. This meant some duplication of the work of the Service Departments, until 1955, when the Service Agencies began to assume main responsibility for travel, developing into a combination of travel agency and information office. Agencies were established at ports of entry, in the Overseas Chinese home districts, and in tourist centres like Hangchow. They provided the kind of facilities which China International Travel Service does for non-Chinese travellers, and had their own hotels and guest houses for this purpose. In March 1957, they were organised on a national basis as the Overseas Chinese Travel Service (OCTS).[61] The OCTS offered far more extensive itineraries than were available to ordinary foreign tourists, largely because they also handled visits to the Overseas Chinese home districts; and according to the publicity, Overseas Chinese tourists could make application to have relatives who lived in China accompany them on tour. The OCTS does not maintain agencies outside China, and arrangements are handled either by correspondence or through the China Travel Service.[62]

The third form of service, retail purchasing stores, is discussed in Chapter 4. They were established initially by Supply and Marketing Cooperatives, and subsequently in all Overseas Chinese home districts in the form of department stores, retail stores, or simply Overseas Chinese 'counters'. Their purpose was to provide an inducement for domestic Overseas Chinese to solicit remittances. They were used also by visiting Overseas Chinese, and in this respect resemble the special stores for foreigners in China.

PARTY CONTROL

The United Front Work Department of the CCP Central Committee, and its branches at all levels, is the leading Party organ for Overseas Chinese affairs.[63] It would appear from the announcement of the First Commission that it is the Third Office of the UFWD which is responsible for Overseas Chinese work, although this may have changed since 1949.[64] In the Central OCAC and most of the branches, members of the corresponding level of the UFWD have at least one position among the chairman and vice-chairmen or directors and deputy directors, and they apparently control the Party

Committees within the government organisations. The UFWD has representatives also in the Returned Overseas Chinese Associations. It is significant for the CCP's perception of the relative importance of Overseas Chinese that there was no separate Party organ for Overseas Chinese affairs, that they were included within the work of an organ which had other wide-ranging and more important responsibilities.[65]

Lyman Van Slyke, in his study of the united front, has suggested that the fact that Liao Ch'eng-chih ceased to be a Deputy Director of the United Front Work Department in 1956 may have indicated that Overseas Chinese work was no longer a principal concern of the UFWD.[66] If this is so, it is of the greatest importance for Overseas Chinese policy. As far as domestic Overseas Chinese affairs are concerned, the UFWD does appear to have continued to play a leading role after 1956, even though this work may have diminished in importance in the total context of its activities.[67]

It is quite possible, however, since Liao Ch'eng-chih's main work appears to have been in the field of external policy, that the UFWD may no longer have been concerned with the Chinese abroad. Liao's membership of the Department in the early 1950s has two possible explanations.[68] One is that the UFWD has always been concerned solely with domestic policy; that as the only Vice-Chairman from 1949 to 1954 who was also a Party member, Liao was responsible for both external and domestic policy and that in 1954, when Fang Fang was appointed a Vice-Chairman and took over the direction of domestic affairs, it was no longer necessary for Liao to be a member of the UFWD. The other is that the original Overseas Chinese policy of the CCP envisaged direction of external affairs by the UFWD, but that this was no longer applicable in the policy introduced in the mid-1950s. There is some evidence to support this view. In the First Commission, there were, besides Liao, two other members from the central UFWD. In the Second and Third Commissions, however, there was only one central UFWD representative, concerned exclusively with domestic affairs, but representation from provincial branches of the UFWD was increased. In the most detailed Cultural Revolution attack on the Commission it is alleged that the initial policy framed in 1949 was worked out by Liao in collaboration with Li Wei-han, Director of the central UFWD. Most of the attack is directed at policies introduced after 1954, but there is no further mention of the UFWD in this context.[69]

If it is the case that the United Front Work Department ceased to be responsible for external Overseas Chinese affairs, then presumably a separate Party department was involved. One possibility is the International Liaison Department, which is thought to have directed foreign affairs.[70] Another is the Propaganda Department. In official listings of Ministries, Commissions, and other agencies of the central government, it is often possible to identify the CCP department responsible for a given organisation from the way in which the organisations are grouped. In this kind of listing, the OCAC is grouped with agencies which come under the jurisdiction of the Propaganda Department.[71] There is some scattered evidence that the propaganda departments at lower levels also have shared in the direction of Overseas Chinese affairs;[72] their responsibility, presumably, would have been for communication with the Chinese abroad.

The question of which Party department directs external Overseas Chinese affairs is as significant for assessing the intentions of the CCP as the question of the role of the OCAC. One of the aims of united front work is to enlist non-Party people in active support for and participation in the general programmes of the CCP. Direction of external policy by the UFWD would suggest that the Party's objective was to involve all Overseas Chinese in the affairs of China, to bring them under the control of the CCP. Propaganda work, on the other hand, is concerned with communicating Party policies to the masses, particularly in the fields of education and culture. If the Propaganda Department has been responsible for external Overseas Chinese policy, this would suggest that the CCP's aim has been to communicate rather than to control. The evidence for direction by the Propaganda Department, however, is inconclusive.[73]

In 1966 a new Party organ was identified which apparently had responsibility for Overseas Chinese affairs. It was reported in the *Jen-min jih-pao* that a notice had been issued to all Party organisations and cadres in the foreign affairs sector by the 'Foreign Affairs Political Department' of the CCP Central Committee, an organisation previously unknown.[74] None of the components of the foreign affairs sector was mentioned by name, but in July the *Ch'iao-wu pao* published an instruction to the OCAC Party Political Department, also previously unidentified, issued in the name of the Foreign Affairs Political Department. Subsequently, an unofficial Cultural Revolution newspaper identified Wang P'ing, a Deputy Director of the Hopei Province OCAC, as one of the Deputy Directors of the Foreign Affairs Political Department, and alleged that he was directing the work of the Central OCAC Party Committee.[75] Apart from this, nothing is known of the work of this department, although it was probably created at the time that other Party departments were converted into Political Departments in 1964/65. It may mean that the International Liaison Department was no longer responsible for foreign affairs, or possibly that it had never had this responsibility.

NONGOVERNMENTAL ORGANISATIONS

Parallel with the government hierarchy of administrative branches is a nationwide network of associations for domestic Overseas Chinese, with a central body known as the All-China Returned Overseas Chinese Association (ACROCA). Despite its name, the Association and its branches, at least until 1958, were concerned with all domestic Overseas Chinese and not just those returned from overseas. Its function was to provide a 'bridge' between the Party and the domestic Overseas Chinese masses.

Returned Overseas Chinese Friendship Associations were first established in 1950, mostly in Kwangtung and Fukien.[76] When the national body was established in October 1956, it was reported that there were between seventy and eighty Associations at *hsien* and municipal level, with membership ranging from 200–300 to 3,000–4,000.[77] Following the establishment of the ACROCA, when the word 'friendship' was dropped from the title of the associations, new branches were established at provincial level to complete the hierarchical structure. By 1963, it was reported that there were 176 ROCAs in twenty-five provinces and cities throughout China, ranging from Kunming to Urumchi.[78]

Because of their leading and public role in mobilising the domestic Overseas Chinese, far more has been written in the Chinese media about the Associations than about the government agencies. Membership of the national Association is drawn from the lower level ROCAs and 'other Overseas Chinese associations of a similar nature', meaning, presumably, the Chih Kung Tang, some Overseas Chinese commercial enterprises in China, and a few traditional Overseas Chinese societies which had survived from before 1949.[79] The organisation of the ACROCA not only mirrors the OCAC, but most of its leading members are members also of the Commission,[80] and the departments established within the ACROCA were usually headed by leading members of the corresponding departments in the OCAC.[81]

The extent to which the departments of the association have a separate identity, and the precise organisational relationship between the government and the nongovernment bodies are unclear. But dual appointment of leading cadres to similar positions in both organisations appears to have led to some confusion. In the rectification in the Central Commission in late 1957, it was revealed that there had been failure to clarify division of duties between the ACROCA and the Commission's General Office and Third Department.[82] Coordination between the two institutions is extremely close, and at the basic level their duties appear almost identical.

The ACROCA and its branches, like other united front or mass organisations, functions as a means of communicating directives from the centre and taking a leading role in their implementation, and reflecting the views of lower-level organisations and the masses. It also had specific continuing tasks of 'raising the political consciousness' of domestic Overseas Chinese, and organising them to participate in socialist construction; a difficult task since it required a kind of political persuasion which would be effective while maintaining the appearance of special consideration and status necessary for external propaganda. The regulations of the ACROCA list five basic tasks: to lead the ROCAs and Overseas Chinese organisations of a similar nature in uniting and organising domestic Overseas Chinese and strengthening socialist education, to reflect the ideas of the domestic Overseas Chinese and Chinese abroad, to maintain liaison with the Chinese abroad and foster their 'patriotic unity', to urge and assist domestic Overseas Chinese to take part in construction enterprises in China, and to serve domestic Overseas Chinese and assist in the establishment of cultural, welfare, and other public enterprises for them.[83]

Although their work at the basic level seems indistinguishable from that of the Work Committees, the Associations have a special function which is to lead the domestic Overseas Chinese in political campaigns. For example, in the rectification and anti-rightist movement in 1957–8, their role was not simply to mobilise the domestic Overseas Chinese but specifically, to reform their contempt for physical labour and agricultural production, their wasteful practices and taste for city life.[84] By 1957, between the pressures of the Work Committees and the political indoctrination by the Associations, the domestic Overseas Chinese were left with very little of the publicised freedom and privilege which the government proclaimed.

The references to overseas work in the regulations of the Association are not very meaningful, except that by assisting in domestic policy it assisted indirectly in implementing external policy. 'Patriotic unity' is a slogan of Overseas Chinese policy with special connotations which are discussed below; it has been used continuously since 1949, despite the frequently contrary objectives of policy. Where the Associations have had most immediate impact on the Chinese abroad is through newly returned Overseas Chinese, whose first impressions of China in letters to friends and relatives, are formed with the assistance of the Associations. The ROCAs also figured prominently in receptions for visiting Overseas Chinese, and provided an instrument for mobilising 'mass' opinion on foreign events, usually, although not always, involving Overseas Chinese.

A minor nongovernmental organisation in Overseas Chinese affairs is the Chih Kung Tang, originally an Overseas Chinese secret society which dates from the middle of the nineteenth century. In 1925, some of its members formed a political party, which in 1949 participated in the CPPCC as one of the democratic parties of the united front. Many of its members have been associated with the central OCAC or with regional Overseas Chinese affairs organisations.[85] The Chih Kung Tang is described in communist sources as having two tasks: one, to exploit its 'deep historical relationship' with the Hung Men Hui, and, on the basis of China's foreign and Overseas Chinese policies, to assist and cooperate with Overseas Chinese organisations in propaganda and education for Chinese abroad; and two, to unite, educate, and reform domestic Overseas Chinese, to assist them in ideological remoulding, to serve them, to guide them in making contributions to socialist construction and the liberation of Taiwan, 'and through them to influence their friends and relatives abroad'.[86] While these tasks resemble those of the ROCAs and the Work Committees, the Chih Kung Tang has not been significant in Overseas Chinese affairs administration, and from the example cited above (p. 21) it appears that it was often ignored.

INFLUENCE OF OVERSEAS CHINESE ON POLICY-MAKING

Anyone who has delved into the domestic side of Overseas Chinese affairs must be struck by the fact that in China there is an extraordinarily large number of Chinese who have come fresh from an experience, in some cases life-long, of living and working in Southeast Asia. One is constantly intrigued by the question of how far these people have influenced, directly or indirectly, the CCP's opinions about Southeast Asia and, consequently, its policies towards that region. What follows is not so much a conclusion as a theory which has still to be properly explored. But it is advanced only because scrutiny of related Chinese sources over the period from 1949 suggests quite strongly that it may have some validity.

Throughout the first twenty years of its government of China the CCP has been subjected to the encirclement and isolation policies of the United States. Although formal relations have existed with some Southeast Asian governments, it is through the Overseas Chinese that the greatest and most consistent penetration of the isolation barrier has taken place. There have been widespread family and business contacts, Overseas Chinese travellers in China amounting to many thousands each year, a total of half a million Chinese from abroad who have settled permanently in China, and approximately 60,000 students who have passed through educational institutions in all parts of the country and who have remained to live and work in China. The 'bamboo curtain' erected by the United States, therefore, was never effective as far as Southeast Asia was concerned.

The permanent settlers are predominantly in the south, but there are also large numbers in Peking and smaller concentrations in most of the major administrative centres. In other societies it is common for such people, where they have special expertise related to their former countries of residence, to find their way into government service, research institutes, and other positions where their expert knowledge is of use. It would be unusual for the CCP not to have tapped this resource in this way, as it did in other ways more concerned with domestic affairs, and it does seem that the Party consciously used Overseas Chinese to inform itself both about the condition of Overseas Chinese themselves and about the situation generally in each country in Southeast Asia. At one level, about which very little is known, they have probably been used covertly for political intelligence purposes. But the CCP has also been quite overt in its exploitation of this source of information. As discussed above, returned Overseas Chinese have been employed extensively throughout the Overseas Chinese affairs bureaucracy and there appears to have been a system by which prominent Chinese from abroad acted as special consultants to this bureaucracy. Returned Overseas Chinese served as appointed members on the Central Overseas Chinese Affairs Commission and the Overseas Chinese Affairs Committees in the provinces. One of the specific tasks of the ACROCA and its branches was to 'reflect the opinions' of the Chinese abroad. Less formally, lower-level cadres have been instructed to have close contact and discussion with all visiting Overseas Chinese, and for large or important groups of visiting Overseas Chinese there has always been a series of meetings and discussions with Party leaders at all levels.

This much is known. The actual influence which these people had on policy can only be guessed at, but I would suggest that through political intelligence, professional advice, and a wide variety of informal and semi-formal contacts, Overseas Chinese have been an important influence in determining the Chinese government's views about Southeast Asia, not simply about Overseas Chinese. Their own opinions may well have been biased or antagonistic to the peoples of Southeast Asia, but this in itself would have assisted the CCP in a negative way, by alerting it to anti-Chinese hostility within the region. But there was probably a more positive influence, in that Overseas Chinese, for the sake of their own survival, have had to be quite calculating in their response to the political and social currents of the societies in which they live, which meant that they were also capable of furnishing the CCP with detailed assessments and information. The CCP's advantage, of course, was that in the Overseas Chinese it had a vast number of sources from which to draw and check its information, enabling it to round out and evaluate what it received from covert intelligence sources, and to sort out the hard information from the prejudices of the disillusioned and the enthusiasm of the patriots.

Certainly, there was no other single source or channel of information available to the CCP which could have provided it with such detailed knowledge as is reflected in the Party's approach to the Overseas Chinese problem, which in itself demanded a similarly detailed understanding of the wider problems of Southeast Asia with which it is interwoven. To Overseas Chinese must go some of the credit for providing the Chinese government with information about the 'objective situation' of the Chinese in Southeast Asia, the sensitivities and hostilities of Southeast Asians, and the basic weaknesses of China's own position in the region. To the extent that this information has been a contributing factor to China's restrained and con-servative approach to relations with the region, the Overseas Chinese have been not so much a fifth column for China but, in the totality of their influence on the CCP, although unintentionally and possibly to their own dissatisfaction, a lobby for the interests of indigenous Southeast Asians.

3

Communication with the Chinese abroad

THE FUNCTION OF COMMUNICATION

By definition, Overseas Chinese live beyond China's borders and the immediate jurisdiction of the Chinese government. Geographically separated from its overseas population, the CCP is unable to establish overt administrative institutions in the countries of residence without creating problems of extra-territoriality and colonial possession. Implementation of policy, therefore, poses a communication problem which does not occur elsewhere. There are two particular features of this problem which distinguish it clearly from domestic and foreign policies, and which also make it easier to pick one's way between propaganda and posture statements, and to reconstruct the objectives of the CCP.

First, there is no single person or organisation or authority which can speak for all Overseas Chinese or through which the Chinese government can operate, even within each country of residence. The Overseas Chinese are a heterogeneous mass of individuals scattered throughout a number of countries, and as divided in their attitudes and loyalties as the countries in which they live. The fact that they are ethnically Chinese does not mean that they think of themselves as members of one community. Still less does it mean that they think they should be loyal to a Chinese government or that it has authority over them, although some do think in this way.

In practice, therefore, the Chinese government has had to communicate its policies to individuals. It does not have the facility or, more important, the privacy, of foreign policy, which can be implemented by direct communication with foreign governments or political movements which speak and act on behalf of their people. Official contact with foreign governments is not of great significance in Overseas Chinese policy, even if it were possible with all countries. It is confined almost entirely to representations on nationality and protection; and as the Indonesian case has demonstrated such representation does not always have the desired effect on, or for, the individual Overseas Chinese. The advantage in countries where Peking has had representation is not that local governments cooperate in the implementation of China's policies, but that direct contact with Overseas Chinese is facilitated.

In some respects Overseas Chinese policy might not be unlike people's diplomacy, were it not that the Chinese government inherited an existing

2-2

relationship with the Chinese abroad which necessitated acceptance, however unwilling, of special obligations and responsibilities. People's diplomacy can be selective in a way that Overseas Chinese policy cannot. The very fact that there is an Overseas Chinese problem in China's relations with Southeast Asia means that if the CCP wants its policies to be effective, it has to get its message across to the widest possible number of Chinese abroad.

Not only, therefore, does the Party have to communicate with individuals; it also has to communicate to a very large extent in public. Even indirect communication through domestic Overseas Chinese correspondence is public, in that the CCP has no control over the recipients, no guarantee that what it tells the dependants to write will not be given a public airing in the countries of residence. Public communication with the Overseas Chinese, then, is essential for the implementation of policy, and as such is extremely useful for interpreting that policy.

There are, of course, a number of ways in which a Chinese government may attempt privately to enforce its policies on individuals. It may bring pressure to bear on their dependants, or assets, in China. It may use various forms of coercion against individual Overseas Chinese through its official representatives abroad. It may attempt to penetrate and control existing Overseas Chinese societies and associations. In some circumstances, it is possible for the Chinese government to enlist the cooperation of local governments. The only other way in which it can enforce its policies is where individuals or groups of Overseas Chinese submit voluntarily to its jurisdiction. These methods of implementing policy, however, have only limited effectiveness; and even where they may be effective in one situation, the Chinese government cannot ensure that its directives, or pressures, will continue even in that situation to produce the responses it seeks.

Although little is known about the content of private communication, particularly with Overseas Chinese communists, there is reason to believe that the message expressed privately was essentially the same as that proclaimed in public. The object of public communication with individuals with whom the CCP is not in direct contact is to elicit a widespread response necessary to specific Overseas Chinese and foreign policies. It is beyond question that the Party's publicly proclaimed policies after 1954 were intended to be taken seriously by the Overseas Chinese masses. Yet it is clear that they could only be effective if there was a similar response from all Overseas Chinese, that in fact they stemmed in part precisely from a negative assessment of the role of Overseas Chinese communism in Southeast Asia, and that for their successful implementation it was essential that above all both communists and blind patriots should follow the publicly proclaimed advice.

The second distinguishing feature of communication is essential to the first. The Chinese Communist Party may decide and publicise policies for Overseas Chinese, but these will be meaningless without a really effective means of communicating them to the people for whom they are intended. There is, therefore, an important difference between the CCP's communication with Overseas Chinese and with the masses in China. Public communications media in China use a distinct language which requires interpretation, which is decipherable to people who study it every day, particularly to cadres who interpret it to the Chinese masses.[1] Communication of policies which seek specific responses from Overseas Chinese, however, must contain more than the generalisations of external propaganda, but at the same time, since the Chinese abroad cannot be expected to decipher the special jargon of the domestic media, it must also be sufficiently free from this jargon as to be intelligible. Where the Party wishes to make plain its intentions to the Chinese abroad, therefore, it has to communicate *en clair*, and it must anticipate that the majority of those who pay attention to what it has to say will accept its statements as representing the genuine intentions of the Chinese government. Communication with the Overseas Chinese is never entirely free from jargon or propaganda, and to some extent it developed a jargon of its own. But the CCP's real intentions are perhaps more plainly and directly stated in communication with the Overseas Chinese than in most other aspects of Chinese policy.

Given that the Chinese government does not have direct jurisdiction over the Overseas Chinese, that the object of its policies is a disparate mass of individuals, and that the Party's objectives have been less militant than is sometimes supposed, it is difficult to measure the extent to which communication has been successful. The response is for the most part beyond the control of the Chinese government. It cannot assume that a majority of Overseas Chinese will listen to what it says or that those who do will respond favourably. It is possible that this was one factor contributing to the CCP's decision to unburden itself of the Overseas Chinese. The difficulties of accepting responsibility for 13 million people over whom it had virtually no control, must have been particularly frustrating to a government which sought to rule through an apparatus of strong central control capable of producing the right responses and getting results. Evidence of positive results among the majority of Overseas Chinese is possibly almost as elusive to the CCP itself as it is to the outside observer.

METHODS OF COMMUNICATION

A feature of communication which exemplifies the CCP's whole approach to the Overseas Chinese problem is that the statement of fundamental policy objectives does not differ for the Chinese in different countries. The CCP's policy has been a policy for 'the Overseas Chinese', and not a series of separate policies for the Chinese in Burma, for example, or the Chinese in the Philippines. There has been a tendency also for the CCP to ignore differences of class and economic circumstances among the Overseas Chinese to whom its policy is addressed.

There are three general purposes of this communication. The first is to inform the Chinese abroad how the CCP thinks they should behave in relation to the countries of residence. This includes matters like political participation, relations with the local people, economic activity, education, language, and integration. The second objective is to tell them what is expected of them in relation to China. This includes questions of Chinese nationality, support for China's foreign policies, acting as 'envoys' for China, trade, remittances and investment. It also includes what are described as 'internal relations' (*nei-pu kuan-hsi*), which means relations between 'patriotic Overseas Chinese' (*ai-kuo hua-ch'iao*) and those who are anti-Peking, anti-communist, or pro-KMT. The third aspect of communication is from the Overseas Chinese to China, or what is called 'reflecting the opinions' of the Chinese abroad. In this, the CCP seeks to inform itself about the situation of Overseas Chinese, about their attitudes towards China and the Party's Overseas Chinese policy. There is no evidence that the CCP ever attempted to conduct an opinion survey among the Chinese abroad. But as suggested in the preceding chapter, there seems no doubt that Overseas Chinese opinion had an important bearing on the policy decisions of the mid-1950s.

Domestic Overseas Chinese

The role of domestic Overseas Chinese in external policy lies in their personal relationships with Chinese abroad. If every one of them maintained contacts overseas the CCP would have potential channels of communication to almost 11 million of the Overseas Chinese; at the very least, the Party could assume that through the medium of family letters a significant proportion of the Overseas Chinese received and possibly discussed information on developments in China. The personal nature of this communication made it ideal for the Party's purpose. But the problem was to control it; to maintain and if possible increase the number of contacts, and to ensure that the content was favourable to the Chinese government and transmitted correctly its policies for Overseas Chinese.

One of the basic tasks of the Overseas Chinese Affairs Commission and related bodies, therefore, was to provide assistance in letter-writing and tracing relatives. The new government moved quickly to supplant the professional letter-writers who had performed this function for the illiterate and semi-literate before 1949. For while there had been some contribution to education in the home districts by wealthy Overseas Chinese, the illiteracy rate was not significantly lower than the national figure of 90 per cent at the time the communists came to power.[2] In addition to letter-writers, there were also professional couriers, known as *shui-k'e*, (literally, 'water guests'), who travelled between the home districts and the countries of Overseas Chinese residence. These couriers were concerned primarily with collecting remittances, but they also carried letters and messages. The Chinese government did not immediately suppress this practice, but introduced a system of registration to control it.[3] By 1956, however, *shui-k'e* were being condemned as undesirables, and accused, among other things, of currency smuggling.[4]

Assuming that domestic Overseas Chinese were prepared to trust the official letter-writers, it would have been possible to ensure that letters were written regularly, and to exercise some control over their content. But there were frequent complaints in the Chinese press in the early 1950s that domestic Overseas Chinese did not trust government cadres. In the case of bank officials this was blamed, with some justification, on the impression created by the Bank of China in the period before 1949.[5] To overcome this lack of confidence, small inducements were sometimes offered. One was an offer to pay postage in certain cases, and another, intended equally for those who were literate in Chinese, was assistance with writing letters and addressing envelopes in foreign languages.[6] It is probably for this reason also that the task of letter-writing was shared by the Friendship Associations, which were supposed to be representative of the domestic Overseas Chinese themselves.

The task of tracing lost relatives was more limited in scope although its purpose was the same. Scattered figures for the first five years of Communist rule indicate that the number of relatives traced was not great, probably less than 2,000 a year. But it is an indication of the importance attached to domestic Overseas Chinese that the CCP was prepared to make considerable efforts for such relatively small returns. The same applied to a related aspect of this work, for which special cadres were appointed, the delivery of remittances incorrectly or insufficiently addressed. One of the most frequently recurring models of exemplary work-style in Overseas Chinese affairs is that of the cadre who overcomes all obstacles to deliver remittances from abroad.

The attempt to control domestic Overseas Chinese letters went far beyond the provision of the services outlined above.[7] It was one of the foremost concerns of all Overseas Chinese affairs officials, from the Chairman of the Central OCAC to the basic-level cadre. Ho Hsiang-ning, for example, pointed out that one of her tasks as Chairman of the OCAC was to direct the Commission to 'mobilise' Overseas Chinese dependants to write to their relatives abroad;[8] and Liao Ch'eng-chih, in a talk with Overseas Chinese students in 1957, admonished those who had not written to their parents and asked them to write at least once every two weeks.[9] At the basic level, Work Committees were not merely to assist, but to 'organise and direct' the writing of letters.[10] Excessive persuasion was not condoned, but from admissions in the Chinese press and frequent reports in Overseas Chinese newspapers, it is clear that many cadres were guilty of 'commandism' in their supervision of domestic Overseas Chinese.[11]

One of the problems confronting the CCP in this task was the fear of many domestic Overseas Chinese, particularly those who were Party members or government cadres, that contact with bourgeois relatives abroad would taint them politically. This fear was not altogether unjustified, and particularly during campaigns against rightist deviations basic-level cadres tended to see only their bourgeois connections and life-style and to ignore the requirements of Party policy. The Party rationalised the problem of relations between cadres and bourgeois relatives overseas by describing it as a non-antagonistic contradiction. It was pointed out, and emphasised repeatedly, that contact with Overseas Chinese was approved because it was of benefit to the state. The key to this rationalisation was the paramount consideration of foreign exchange, neatly exemplified in Liao Ch'eng-chih's talk with Overseas Chinese students cited above. Some students apparently had refused money from their parents in order to demonstrate their progressiveness. Liao advised them not to do so since it might 'upset their parents'; if they found they could not use the money, they should deposit it in the bank.[12]

The most difficult problem was to control the content of letters. Domestic Overseas Chinese might not object to being asked to write regularly to their relatives abroad, but they might take exception to being told to demand more money, or to inform their relatives how the Chinese government thought they should behave. One method was for the Party to use the various powers of coercion at its disposal to force them to write what it wanted. It is reported in the non-communist press in Hong Kong, that in some cases letters were simply drafted by cadres and given to the dependants to copy out or sign. It seems also that there was some attempt to check on what was being written by opening and reading letters. Even if this was not practised extensively domestic Overseas Chinese had sufficient reason to believe that it might be, and therefore, to be a little circumspect in what they wrote.[13]

The problem remained, however, that it was physically difficult to check on each and every letter;[14] and the use of pressure or intimidation did not necessarily produce the desired results.[15] In the official admissions that mishandling of domestic Overseas Chinese had an adverse effect on the Chinese abroad it is implicit either that the use of pressure was not widespread or, if it was, that it was still impossible to prevent dependants from saying what they wanted. This meant that the success of communication through domestic Overseas Chinese depended on the way they were treated. With special consideration their letters might tend to convey more favourable impressions of the Communist administration, and they might be more amenable to suggestions about the content of their letters. On the crucial question of remittances they were more likely to agree to the Party's wishes if they were permitted the free use of this money and if there was something on which they could spend it. The main task of the administrative machinery described in Chapter 2 was to regulate the necessary special consideration so as to ensure effective communication with the Chinese abroad. This was only a first step since even with the full cooperation of domestic Overseas Chinese the Party could not control the responses of their relatives. But without their cooperation much of what the Chinese government had to say in public media or official contacts would be as *erh-pien-feng*, 'wind passing the ears'.

The success of this method of communication would be more easy to gauge if the Chinese government's objective had been to promote militant chauvinism among Overseas Chinese rather than to encourage existing trends towards identification with the countries of residence. Even the fact that remittances did not regain the pre-war peak cannot be taken as an indicator of failure, because it cannot be known whether the level would have been higher if the CCP had not been in power, and because after 1957 remittances policy was to some extent contradicted by the Party's political aims. Domestic Overseas Chinese communication may have assisted in informing Overseas Chinese about conditions in China and the policies of the Chinese government, but it may not have been as effective as the CCP wished. The Party was unable to prevent domestic Overseas Chinese from communicating views unfavourable to the CCP, which is evident from the reaction of Chinese abroad to social and political upheavals in the home districts.

Public communications media

Complementing the personal communication through domestic Overseas Chinese are the public mass media. Soon after the Communist government was established, the Party set about reaching the Overseas Chinese through their own newspapers and through direct radio broadcasts from Peking. Broadcasts to Overseas Chinese, which commenced in 1949, were from April 1950 handled by an Overseas Chinese Department in Radio Peking, with programmes in standard language or mandarin and four regional dialects.[16] For the Overseas Chinese press, the OCAC provided printed news despatches[17] and Radio Peking broadcast news at dictation speed or what is known as 'dictation news' (*chi-lu hsin-wen*). In October 1952 the main responsibility for news was assumed by a specialised news agency, China News Service (*Chung-kuo hsin-wen she*, hereafter, *CNS*).[18] Radio Peking continued to operate its Overseas Chinese programme, but it had a broader purpose, similar to foreign language broadcasts. Part of its programmes concerned Overseas Chinese policies and news about domestic Overseas Chinese affairs, but by the 1960s at least half of the content was devoted to such things as socialist construction, the life of the Chinese people, state policies, music and opera.[19]

The way in which *CNS* operates is like a combination of the New China News Agency (NCNA) and Radio Peking's international news service. It issues a daily, originally weekly, printed news release, and instead of a wire service operates its own broadcasting station in Peking.[20] This station broadcasts dictation news from the daily *CNS* releases, which until 1970 were distributed from Canton, largely, it seems, through Hong Kong and Macao.[21] There are obvious advantages in this system. The issue of a printed news release is of limited value, partly because of the time lag involved, but mainly because it is subscribed to only by a small number of newspapers. The broadcasts, however, are easily available to editors, and more important, to the Overseas Chinese masses, without necessitating a direct relationship with or prior commitment to the Chinese government.

Unlike the broadcasts of Radio Peking, *CNS* reports, until 1962 at least, have been aimed more directly at the implementation of Overseas Chinese policy. They include major statements on domestic and external policy; reports of conferences and other official activities in Overseas Chinese affairs; regulations on investment, remittances, customs procedures, education, and other matters which might concern the Chinese abroad; news items on domestic Overseas Chinese affairs such as the establishment of villages, farms, and schools, and privileges for domestic Overseas Chinese; reports of visits by Overseas Chinese tourists; and general accounts of construction and production, particularly in Kwangtung and Fukien. The service usually concludes with two or three feature articles designed to show how the home districts are developing under communist rule, how the individual fares, and what his attitudes are towards the programmes of the CCP. The records of *CNS* provide the most comprehensive official chronicle available outside China of the Overseas Chinese affairs of the CCP.

There appears to have been a conscious attempt on the part of the Chinese government to tailor the content of *CNS* reports to the attitudes of non-communist, bourgeois Overseas Chinese. During the Cultural Revolution *CNS* was attacked for this policy. Its reports are said to have been designed to cater to the debased tastes of bourgeois Overseas Chinese, dwelling on the details of celebrations and festivities, pleasure outings, and feasting and drinking by Overseas Chinese capitalists in China. The agency was accused of suppressing political content, of reporting internal political movements only indirectly, and of ignoring proletarian politics.[22] The attack is coloured in places and selective in the examples it cites, but it is not an entirely distorted account of the image which *CNS* projected. The content of *CNS* may have seemed highly political to a non-communist outside listener, but it is obvious that some thought was given to devising reports which would be acceptable and therefore effective among bourgeois Chinese abroad.[23]

The same Cultural Revolution attack has a more puzzling charge, which seems related directly to specific objectives of Overseas Chinese policy. Denouncing Liu Shao-ch'i for directing that the policy of the agency should be to deal only with domestic news, it claims that the original proposal was that it should operate overseas, as the International News Service (*Kuo-chi hsin-wen t'ung-hsün she*). Whether or not Liu Shao-ch'i was personally involved, it is true that *CNS* does not maintain bureaus or correspondents outside China. Moreover, its coverage of news about the Chinese abroad is extremely thin, and limited to statements of Chinese policy, reports on 'persecution' or 'discrimination', protests, and arrangements for repatriation. Very occasionally, there are reports on other activities like Chinese embassy receptions, or statements by groups of Overseas Chinese in support of a Chinese government policy or a local popular movement.

There may be a number of reasons why *CNS* did not operate overseas. It would have meant, for example, unnecessary duplication of the operations of NCNA. But it was also consistent with the objectives of Overseas Chinese policy after 1954. Where the Overseas Chinese institutions of the Chinese government could not operate overtly in the countries of residence, *CNS*, with a legitimate function as a news bureau, would have provided an ideal cover if the CCP had wanted to establish closer organisational contacts among Overseas Chinese. The fact that *CNS* did not establish foreign bureaus is at least negative evidence that this was not the CCP's main concern. The fact that it carried so little news about the Overseas Chinese themselves is an illustration of the China-centred preoccupation of the CCP's Overseas Chinese policy. If 'patriotic unity' for Overseas Chinese had been more than just a slogan, the Chinese government would have been more interested in reporting on the state of patriotic unity among the Chinese abroad. It might also have been more interested in describing exemplary activities of Overseas Chinese to the Overseas Chinese masses. When it did, in the late 1950s, its purpose had little to do with patriotic unity.

Although reporting Overseas Chinese affairs was the foremost function of *CNS*, its despatches included reports on important developments in the domestic and foreign affairs of China. Beginning in 1962 there was a gradual increase in the amount of *CNS* material concerned with national affairs and a corresponding decrease in reporting on Overseas Chinese affairs. This reflected a significant development in Overseas Chinese policy, a trend towards taking less account of the sensibilities of Overseas Chinese than had been the case in the past, ignoring the fact that their thinking was influenced by bourgeois environments and not by a decade and more of socialist indoctrination. The trend in *CNS* despatches was an important visible sign of a downgrading of Overseas Chinese policy to a point where the CCP appeared to be attempting as far as possible to ignore the problem.

The effectiveness of *CNS* as an instrument for communication could only be measured by a complete survey of the Overseas Chinese press, which has not been possible within the compass of this study. The Chinese government chose to present it as a 'popular press association' (*min-chien hsin-wen t'uan-t'i*), ostensibly formed by a group of journalists in China. Apparently it was thought that an 'independent' or nongovernmental news agency would be more effective than, for example, a department of the OCAC.[24] The number of Overseas Chinese newspapers which have used and attributed *CNS* material is quite small, and in Southeast Asia has been confined to newspapers in countries with which China has diplomatic relations.[25] As suggested above, it may have been with this problem in mind, as much as the technical difficulties involved, that the CCP decided to broadcast *CNS* releases rather than establish a subscription wire service. This enabled newspapers in countries like Malaysia to use *CNS* reports without subscribing to the service and without acknowledging the source. This applies both to left-wing papers and to those anti-communist papers which maintain an interest in developments on the Chinese mainland; although the latter seem to prefer to use second-hand reports from Hong Kong and Taiwan and the international news agencies.

CNS is probably as effective an instrument for communication as the Chinese government could hope for, given the political obstacles involved, and the fact that the use of *CNS* despatches, even in the most favourable political climate, is at the discretion of the individual editor. Certainly, through the combined coverage of *CNS* and the dialect and foreign language broadcasts of Radio Peking, the government at least made it possible for almost all Overseas Chinese to receive news about China and Overseas Chinese policies.

The other main vehicle for the communication of policies, although far more limited in scope, was the *Ch'iao-wu pao* (*Overseas Chinese Affairs Journal*), the official organ of the Overseas Chinese Affairs Commission. The *Ch'iao-wu pao* did not begin publication until October 1956, and its introduction at that time appears to have been related to the current strengthening of Overseas Chinese affairs propaganda work.[26] Despite the fact that it was stated to be intended for Chinese abroad, there is some doubt as to how important a consideration this was in the overall objectives of the journal, and how wide a distribution it had overseas. It was available on subscription outside China, but from the content it seems that it was designed primarily for domestic consumption.[27] It would seem that it was the kind of journal which might have been given limited distribution to Overseas Chinese who already had some special connection with China, such as investors, parents of Overseas Chinese students, pro-Peking editors, or 'patriotic' organisations which sought to maintain close relations with the Chinese government.[28] The *Ch'iao-wu pao*, therefore, like *CNS*, also reflects the priorities of the CCP in that it was predominantly China-centred, concerned with domestic affairs more than with the Chinese abroad. It is interesting also that the OCAC itself did not publish a popular journal for the Overseas Chinese masses, or even something like *Peking Review*, which might have been expected if the CCP's intention had been to hold the attachment to China of its overseas compatriots.[29]

Correspondence offices

There are three channels through which the CCP communicates its policies direct to individuals, through official correspondence, visiting Overseas Chinese, and representatives abroad.

Official correspondence with Chinese abroad was sufficiently important to warrant special offices within the OCAC and its province-level branches, with the designation 'Office for Answering Correspondence' (*ta-fu lai-hsin pan-kung-shih* or *fu-hsin-shih*). The Correspondence Offices were quite public in their operations, and their work was openly discussed in the Chinese press. They resembled public relations offices, answering individual queries on all aspects of Chinese policy and not just Overseas Chinese affairs. While it seems likely that the Correspondence Offices were partly responsible for maintaining such formal organisational links as existed between the Chinese government and Overseas Chinese individuals and associations, they seem to have been concerned mainly with replying to letters received.

There were, however, certain advantages in this kind of communication. It was directed at people who had shown enough interest to write direct to the Chinese government and who might be expected to take some note of what was written in reply. Unlike the letters of domestic Overseas Chinese, moreover, the Party had complete control over what was written. Letters from Chinese abroad also provided the government with an opportunity to impress with good public relations, and Correspondence Offices were instructed to answer each letter promptly and in detail.[30] The work of these Offices was important also in that they were the main institutional channel for two-way communication or 'reflecting opinions' of the Chinese abroad. It was actually claimed that letters from Chinese abroad 'were of benefit in formulating and implementing Overseas Chinese policy'.[31] While there was no suggestion that the demands of individual Overseas Chinese could determine or reverse policy decisions, this correspondence provided a good opportunity to sample Overseas Chinese opinion, and as such it probably contributed indirectly to the influence of Overseas Chinese in policy-making discussed in Chapter 2.

Visiting Overseas Chinese

The CCP's treatment of visiting Overseas Chinese provides the most visible manifestation of the Party's concern to propagate its policies for Overseas Chinese as widely as possible, and also of its attempts to enlist Overseas Chinese cooperation in people's diplomacy. Overseas Chinese visitors were not restricted to political sympathisers. They represented most shades of opinion, and at the height of the campaign for peaceful liberation of Taiwan in the mid-1950s, the government even declared that members of the Kuomintang would be welcome to visit China.[32] They have ranged from labourers and shop assistants to businessmen, and from large group tours to individuals visiting relatives in the home districts. The only apparent restrictions, apart from China's exclusion of 'counter-revolutionary elements', were those enforced by the governments of the countries of residence. The majority of visitors appears to have been from countries which recognised Peking, although it was possible for Overseas Chinese to visit China from Hong Kong, and there may have been more from non-recognising countries than appears to have been the case. The Chinese government certainly claimed that this was so, and that they came from as many as forty countries.[33]

The visitors who received most publicity were those who attended May Day and National Day celebrations in Peking. The number of such visitors averaged roughly 1,000 a year, and reached a peak of over 2,000 in 1964.[34] Whether officially sponsored or privately initiated package tours, all were given an official reception during their stay. Many remained in China for several months before or after the celebrations, touring the home districts and other parts of China. Official receptions were arranged wherever they went, and in Peking they attended a series of functions organised by the OCAC, the ACROCA, the CPPCC, and other mass organisations or friendship associations.

The significant point about these tours is that the visitors were always given at least one formal reception in Peking, which the Chinese government obviously regarded as a particularly important opportunity for explaining Overseas Chinese policy. They were usually addressed by Chou En-lai, Ch'en Yi, or other leading members of the CCP, and invariably they were asked explicitly to publicise what they had heard when they returned home. The speeches on these occasions are of great interest, since they represented direct communication by top Party figures to Overseas Chinese, many of whom were highly influential in their own communities. It is unlikely that the speeches reported in the press were simply propaganda and that the visitors were given a different line in private discussions, because most of them were not communists, and had no reason to cooperate in concealing covert intentions of the Chinese government. As with public broadcasts, the CCP had to assume that what was said would be regarded as authoritative, and disseminated as such in the countries of residence. It is significant, therefore, that statements about Overseas Chinese policy made at these receptions have not differed from general broadcast statements to the Overseas Chinese masses.[35]

Individual visitors to the home districts have been far more numerous, but they were accorded similar treatment, on a smaller scale but with the same intent.[36] Not only were they cared for in such a way as to impart a favourable impression of the Chinese government, but they were usually interviewed by Party and Overseas Chinese affairs cadres in their home villages. The purpose of such interviews, as with the large tourist groups, was both to explain the Party's policies and to obtain information about the situation, and the position of Overseas Chinese, in the countries of residence.

To some extent the reception given to Overseas Chinese visitors compares with the practice of most governments in sponsoring visits by prominent people from foreign countries. The difference is that the Chinese government attempted to give individual attention to all visiting Overseas Chinese, and not simply to the prominent or influential. And since it was responsible for the Overseas Chinese and needed to influence them, the CCP has tended to be more direct in its propagandist purpose than most governments might be with foreign guests.[37]

Communication in the countries of residence

Communication in the countries of residence is less easy to document, since it is not usually publicised, and the facts are often obscured by the rumour which surrounds the activities of Chinese government representatives abroad. It is sometimes assumed that every Overseas Chinese who has contact with a Chinese official is being indoctrinated or receiving instructions to carry out subversive activities or subjected to some kind of pressure to act in the service of Peking. This may be the case with many of these contacts, particularly with Overseas Chinese who are also communists. But it is difficult to obtain factual evidence of any kind which might confirm the assumptions or, indeed, provide any definite answer. In the absence of information to the contrary, it would be equally possible to assume that Chinese representatives abroad do not engage in any of the activities suggested above, although this would seem unlikely. This question is discussed further in Chapter 10.

The efforts of the Chinese government to communicate its policies to the widest possible audience by other means certainly suggests that one of the functions of representatives abroad is to implement Overseas Chinese policies. But in Southeast Asia China has been represented only in Burma, Indonesia, Cambodia, North Vietnam, and Laos, and the combined Chinese populations in these countries amount to only 3,800,000, or less than one-third of the total. It has been possible for the Chinese government to operate through semi-official agencies, particularly in Singapore and formerly in Kuala Lumpur, through the Bank of China, but it must be remembered that their activities have been severely circumscribed.[38] In Thailand, the Philippines, South Vietnam, and to a large extent in Singapore and Malaysia it has not been possible for official or even quasi-official Chinese representatives to have widespread personal contacts; and the activities of pro-Peking Overseas Chinese societies, or underground representatives from China if they exist, are inhibited both by the anti-communist policies and measures of the local governments, and by the vigilance of representatives and supporters of the Kuomintang. Even in Indonesia Chinese representatives appear to have been cautious in their relationships with local Chinese because of the attitudes of successive Indonesian governments towards the Chinese minority.

The Chinese government has not concealed the fact that its representatives abroad maintain contact with Overseas Chinese, although from official reports it would be possible to believe that such contact was confined mainly to National Day parties and film receptions. It is not known to what extent there are officials within the diplomatic and consular missions, branches of the Bank of China, and NCNA, whose designated responsibility is Overseas Chinese affairs. Consular officials, certainly, would spend a great amount of time dealing with Overseas Chinese, although much of this contact concerns administrative matters only. Of the senior diplomatic and consular officials presently serving in Southeast Asia none are known to have been a former Overseas Chinese affairs cadre in China. Nor does there appear to have been a general practice of posting back to the former countries of residence Overseas Chinese who have returned to work in China.[39] It might seem that Overseas Chinese with local knowledge and fluency in the local language would make ideal representatives in Southeast Asia. But China, no less than other countries, has been careful to select only trusted cadres for service overseas, and the difficulty of making sufficiently thorough security checks on the early background of returned Overseas Chinese would tend to exclude them from this category.

The Bank of China and the state trading corporations would seem to be an ideal channel for communication, since they deal with businessmen and community leaders and have numerous opportunities for publicising China's policies in the course of their legitimate business. While politics probably does enter into such contacts, and it is a principle of the CCP that trade and politics cannot be separated, it must not be overlooked that there are very considerable commercial advantages in dealing with Overseas Chinese. In practice the Chinese government has not been rigid in its principle of trade and politics; one example of the separation of the two was China's wheat purchases from Australia after the Australian involvement in the Vietnam War.[40] A more striking example is China's relations with Hong Kong, and more recently with Singapore. The question of the use of commercial dealings as an instrument for political pressure is less a matter of verifiable facts and more of 'reports and rumours'.[41] The extent of such pressure would depend on the CCP's expectations of Overseas Chinese in Southeast Asian politics, and if those expectations are as limited as the evidence suggests, then it is unlikely that this practice has been widespread.

The type of Overseas Chinese with whom Chinese officials seek to maintain contact is an intriguing question. If its objectives were revolutionary, the Chinese government might have been expected to concentrate on the 90 per cent which it claimed was labouring class. There is a distinct impression, however, that much of the representatives' attention has been devoted to the non-proletarian element of the Overseas Chinese communities, with the objectives of trade and investment, and the dissemination through community leaders of public policies for Overseas Chinese.

Two important areas of communication have been the press and the schools. China's relations with the Overseas Chinese press have been discussed above, but it should be added that, while China may have provided financial subsidies or sought to influence the proprietors of Overseas Chinese newspapers, it is not known to have established its own publications. This may have made it easier for pro-Peking newspapers to operate, although they have always been vulnerable to censorship and suppression.

The question of China's influence in Overseas Chinese schools is a controversial subject, but the tendency of some political observers to see Chinese government initiatives in these schools simply in terms of political subversion tends to obscure other important factors. The CCP was obviously motivated by some political considerations, but any attempt to use Overseas Chinese schools to administer political indoctrination with subversive intent would have been contrary to the whole direction of Overseas Chinese policy at least since 1954.

But the Chinese education system was an ideal instrument for communication of China's policies and presenting an image of New China, and shortly after it came to power the CCP openly declared its intention to establish direct communication with these schools. Overseas Chinese education subsequently became one of the critical concerns of Overseas Chinese policy and is discussed more fully in chapters 7 and 8. But it might be pointed out here that this is one area in which there has been frequent failure to distinguish between the activities of local 'patriotic' or communist Overseas Chinese and the involvement of the Chinese government. Where there has been obvious pro-Peking communism in Chinese schools, in Burma, Cambodia, Singapore, Malaysia and Indonesia, this influence comes from existing local communist parties. Moreover, much of the alleged communist activity, while possibly inspired by a hard core of communists, stems from patriotism, cultural chauvinism, or sympathy for the Chinese government. This made the school system a potentially receptive vehicle for the CCP's ideas, but the Party also encountered serious obstacles and there is considerable doubt as to how far it was able to extend its influence.

Perhaps the single most important motive in the CCP's attempt to influence Overseas Chinese schools was the desire to dislodge the Kuomintang from Southeast Asia. If there was one respect in which the CCP expected the Overseas Chinese to act in its support, it was in rejecting the leadership of the Kuomintang and combating its influence in Southeast Asia and among Overseas Chinese. If Overseas Chinese were to regard themselves as belonging to China, they could not be permitted to support the Kuomintang. The CCP did not need the Overseas Chinese to legitimise its rule, but it realised that the Kuomintang did, that the KMT used this argument to support its claim to represent China, and that pro-KMT Chinese could influence the attitudes towards China of the governments of the countries of residence. The CCP was aware of the pressures of Asian nationalism to eradicate the separate system of education for Overseas Chinese. Its attempts to influence Overseas Chinese schools were as much a matter of 'internal relations' as an attempt to create communist cells among Overseas Chinese youth. If the aim was subversive, it was subversive of the Kuomintang as much as the local governments.

One of the most interesting ways in which communication has been made in the countries of residence has been through meetings between Overseas Chinese and Chou En-lai. Between 1954 and 1957 Chou met with Overseas Chinese in New Delhi, Djakarta and Bandung, Rangoon, Phnom Penh and Hanoi; and again in 1959 Chou reported that he had spoken with Overseas Chinese during a recent overseas tour.[42] Chou's remarks on these occasions were directed at a wider audience than the few who elected, or were selected to attend the receptions. One part of that audience was the local government, and the speeches appear to have been weighed partly with this in mind. The main audience, however, was the mass of Overseas Chinese; and like the speeches to visiting Overseas Chinese in Peking, these represented the direct authoritative interpretation of the CCP's Overseas Chinese policy, and Chou must have anticipated that they would be taken as such. It would have been impossible for Chinese officials to contact every Overseas Chinese after Chou's departure, and inform them that what Chou had said was intended only for the ears of the local government. Even if it had been possible, it is doubtful if many of them would have responded favourably to such duplicity. It is for this reason that what Chou said on these occasions is of particular significance, and it was in this series of talks that the CCP's conclusions about the future of its relations with the Overseas Chinese were first outlined in detail.[43]

Communication through Hong Kong and Macao

The existence of Hong Kong and Macao facilitates contact with Chinese from countries which do not recognise China. In a sense they are neutral territory, since the British and Portuguese authorities permit communist agencies to operate openly, and it is relatively easy for Overseas Chinese from any country to visit the two enclaves. Macao is probably less significant than Hong Kong, in that it does not have the same facilities for international communication or the commercial and banking establishment which makes Hong Kong so useful. It is important, however, since access appears to be much easier from China to Macao than it is to Hong Kong.

The great advantage of Hong Kong is that it provides a channel for remittances, investment, and trade. It is estimated that over 95 per cent of

Overseas Chinese remittances to China pass through Hong Kong. Without Hong Kong it would still be possible for remittances to reach China, but the amount might be lower from those countries which prohibit or limit Overseas Chinese remittances. The same is true to some extent of Overseas Chinese investment, and possibly also of trade. Overseas Chinese businessmen who deal in Chinese goods through Hong Kong, either directly with state trading corporations or with non-official companies, might find it difficult to deal direct from the countries of residence or in China. The point about Hong Kong is that it is not indispensable to China's financial and commercial contacts with Overseas Chinese, but that it does provide a very great convenience.

In other respects contact with Overseas Chinese in Hong Kong and Macao combines the advantages of communication in China itself and in the countries of residence. To the extent that Chinese intelligence agents operate among the Chinese abroad, their activities are facilitated by the existence of these two enclaves. Hong Kong and Macao also provide an outlet for, and source of, communist and pro-communist propaganda, there are communist film companies and cinemas, communist department stores and exhibitions, and official agencies of the Chinese government.

A final point might be made about administration and communication. The maintenance of a large bureaucracy and the effort expended on communicating with the Chinese abroad might seem to indicate a greater interest on the part of the CCP in maintaining close ties with the Overseas Chinese than has actually been the case. A number of reasons for this have already been suggested. But the main problem for the CCP is simply that the Overseas Chinese exist. Many of them claim the protection of the Chinese government, many Southeast Asian governments hold the Chinese government responsible for their actions, and the CCP itself appears to have felt responsible for solving their problems, or 'the Overseas Chinese problem' as such. The problem exists, and forces its attention on the government. It requires a policy, appropriation of money, an administrative structure, and the creation of special institutions for the people concerned. The problem may always remain unsolved, and so long as it is not solved, the programmes and the structures remain. But the ultimate objective is the elimination of the problem.

4

Domestic Overseas Chinese policy:
1949—1966

Overseas Chinese families are divided into two parts; the main labour force, which is overseas, and the dependants, who are in China. The great majority of the 10 million Overseas Chinese relatives in China are dependants of labouring Chinese abroad; they live in the rural areas, they have a close relationship with the Chinese abroad, and they rely on remittances as their primary or secondary means of subsistence. Careful consideration must be given to this point, otherwise in every comparatively big social reform movement, there will be encroachments on remittances, and some impact will be felt by Overseas Chinese or their families. People in many foreign countries learn about the situation in our country through the Overseas Chinese. The experience of the past few years has shown that the slightest mishandling of the problems of Overseas Chinese families in China has an immediate effect on the attitudes towards China of the Overseas Chinese, and even of the people of the countries of residence.

Jen-min jih-pao editorial, 19 June 1956

In the years since liberation, Overseas Chinese work in Kwangtung Province has veered from left to right, and alternated between severity and leniency.

Huang Chieh, Report to the Fourth Session
of the First Kwangtung People's Congress,
Nan-fang jih-pao, 11 August 1956

The above two statements pinpoint the role of domestic Overseas Chinese in the CCP's approach to the Chinese abroad. The Party recognised that there was a direct relationship between its treatment of the former and the responses of the latter. This did not dictate the objectives of policy. But it did mean that domestic policies were made with this interrelationship in mind. It could be ignored, but only if the Party was prepared to accept the consequences, of which it was fully aware, among the Chinese abroad. So long as it did not deviate too far from the Party's policies for the Chinese masses, domestic Overseas Chinese policy veered from left to right to serve the implementation of external policy.

Domestic Overseas Chinese policies provide a singularly unusual perspective on the CCP's external aims. The Party's objectives are discernible both from instructions about the content and purpose of domestic Overseas Chinese communication with relatives abroad, and from the way in which they were treated. Major changes in external Overseas Chinese policy have always been accompanied by corresponding changes in domestic policy. Where the Party's motives may not be entirely clear from what is said to or about the Chinese abroad, they are often plainly visible in domestic Overseas Chinese policies. At no time was this more apparent than in the redirection of policy in 1957. Moreover, the difficulties encountered in domestic Overseas Chinese affairs have themselves influenced decisions about relations with the Chinese abroad, since domestic Overseas Chinese are an inseparable component of the Party's Overseas Chinese problem. Domestic Overseas Chinese affairs are highly revealing of the problems and policies of the CCP, and there is an abundance of information on this subject in the Chinese media.[1]

THE STATUS OF DOMESTIC OVERSEAS CHINESE

Theoretically, it might be possible for a Chinese government not to have an Overseas Chinese policy, to disclaim all responsibility for the Chinese abroad. Since 1957, the policy of the Chinese Communist Party has tended in this direction, but there have been other considerations which so far have precluded the adoption of such an absolute stand. The fact that it has a positive policy for Overseas Chinese, however, implies that it seeks to influence them, and the most effective means of doing so is through their relatives in China. This provides the justification at least for the existence of a category of domestic Overseas Chinese, even if not the need for a privileged status for that category of people.

The degree of special consideration then depends on the kind of influence which the Chinese government wishes to have on the Chinese abroad. While this has varied over time, the *Jen-min jih-pao* editorial cited above refers to a general and a specific purpose which have remained fairly constant. The general purpose is to create a favourable impression of China, through the Overseas Chinese, among the local people in the countries of residence. This necessitated a certain amount of special consideration for domestic Overseas Chinese, or at least protection from the excesses of social reform movements which might reflect unfavourably on the Chinese government.

It is in the specific purpose, however, that the ultimate justification for privileged status is found. Communication with Overseas Chinese without the advantage of domestic Overseas Chinese is difficult but not impossible, as the Kuomintang has found since 1949. But where the Communist government has treated domestic Overseas Chinese in exactly the same way as the Chinese masses, it has jeopardised the one constant objective in its Overseas Chinese policy since 1949, the attraction of family remittances and investment. The CCP never intended to create a privileged class, but the variety of measures introduced to cater to the special characteristics of domestic Overseas Chinese certainly fostered this impression, both among domestic Overseas Chinese themselves and among the Chinese masses. The problem was to temper these favours with the right amount of pressure on the beneficiaries to participate in socialist construction. This is another reason why policy 'veered from left to right, and alternated between severity and leniency'.

PREFERENTIAL TREATMENT AND
EXEMPTION VERSUS CONFORMITY AND PARTICIPATION:
A NON-ANTAGONISTIC CONTRADICTION

From 1949 to the end of 1954, despite the CCP's constantly reiterated claim that its policy was to protect the Chinese abroad, it made very few gestures at protection, and concentrated instead on the immediate problems of domestic Overseas Chinese. Its first tasks were to identify the Overseas Chinese dependants, and then to regularise their relationships with their relatives abroad. In the process, the Party was drawn into consideration of the place of domestic Overseas Chinese in 'new democratic' China and their role in social and socialist programmes.

In this period there was no question of creating a class apart although the foundations were laid for the emergence of such a class. In the first major statement on Overseas Chinese policy after the founding of the People's Republic of China, Ho Hsiang-ning announced that measures were under consideration for regulating remittances and 'looking after the interests' of Overseas Chinese dependants.[2] It soon became clear that what this meant was looking after the interests of China's foreign exchange earnings, and that any privileges for domestic Overseas Chinese would be tied directly to receipt of money from abroad. Included among the temporary regulations introduced in 1950 for controlling the chaotic currency conditions was a set of 'Temporary provisions for preferential treatment of Overseas Chinese remittances'. These provided for a special Overseas Chinese exchange rate, direct conversion of remittances to People's Currency (JMP), and exemption from remittance fees. More interesting as a sign of what was to come was that they also included a proposal to offer short-term low interest loans to domestic Overseas Chinese.[3] The guiding principle for this policy was the slogan 'Foreign exchange to the state, profit to the individual'; the individual being, not the recipient, but the registered middleman or remittance office.[4] Presumably the intention was that both recipient and middleman would be self-supporting but that neither should be permitted to fatten and profit in the capitalist sense, since the word 'profit' (li-jun) was used interchangeably with 'benefit' (li-yi). In 1950 also, Overseas Chinese dependants were entitled to discount purchasing at retail stores against presentation of remittance deposit slips.[5]

There was nothing particularly privileged about the concessions for domestic Overseas Chinese in 1950. But the fact that they were made available necessitated a decision on who should be entitled to enjoy them. To this end, investigation of domestic Overseas Chinese was begun early in 1950 and continued into and merged with the investigation of class status of the agrarian reform movement,[6] and those classified as Overseas Chinese families were issued with certificates which entitled them to use the limited facilities offered to Overseas Chinese at that time.[7]

There was no suggestion, however, that domestic Overseas Chinese would be permitted to drift apart from the masses or be immune from socialist influence, and this was demonstrated clearly in the agrarian reform movement, the first major test of the opposing requirements of Overseas Chinese policy and socialist reform. In the 'Regulations governing the administration of Overseas Chinese land and property during Land Reform' promulgated in November 1950,[8] some minimal concessions were made to Overseas Chinese landlords, but it is clear from later reports that in practice Overseas Chinese land and property owners were not exempt, and were also subject to various 'excesses' which the Party subsequently tried to rectify. In land distribution, dependants who received regular remittances and who were 'unable or unwilling' to participate in agricultural production, were to be allotted less land than the average or none at all. The intention appears to have been to balance overseas income against land ownership so as to prevent domestic Overseas Chinese from emerging from land distribution in a more favourable position than the average peasant. The reference to those who were 'unwilling' to participate in agricultural production implies a degree of voluntariness but there was little evidence of freedom not to participate at the time and later reports admit as much.

In the agrarian reform movement, therefore, the principle was established that in political and social movements domestic Overseas Chinese were not to be exempt, and in the years which followed immediately on land reform, until the end of 1953, the balance between privilege and conformity was weighted heavily in favour of the latter. Cadres were told that they should concentrate their efforts on mobilising domestic Overseas Chinese to take part in land reform, production and construction, and organising them in the study of politics, culture and current affairs.[9] By 1952 dependants were reported to be joining mutual aid teams, taking part in national campaigns, and attending literacy classes; and many dependant wives were said to be engaged in agricultural labour for the first time in their lives.[10] Nor were returned Overseas Chinese exempt; they were instructed to participate in socialist construction, to practise economy and change their 'wasteful habits'.[11] It was in these years that some of the most lurid stories about domestic Overseas Chinese appeared in the Hong Kong press. They usually concerned 'ransom notes' sent to Chinese abroad, demanding large sums of money in return for the release of imprisoned relatives or the granting of exit permits. Even allowing for the bias of sections of the Hong Kong press, the reports were not without foundation; domestic Overseas Chinese were under considerable pressure at this time, a fact tacitly acknowledged later in official Chinese sources.[12]

The treatment of domestic Overseas Chinese from 1950 to 1953 was related to external policy but in an essentially negative way, since this was a period in which the Party took no external initiatives in Overseas Chinese affairs. Demands on the Chinese abroad were limited; they were asked to remit money, to oppose the Kuomintang, and to support China's position in Korea. Instead of policies the CCP instituted a series of slogans. Many of these could not have seemed very convincing to the compatriots abroad; for example, the claim that the existence of New China meant that Overseas Chinese no longer suffered persecution or discrimination. The Chinese government either assumed that it could count on Overseas Chinese support irrespective of how the dependants were treated, or else was not particularly concerned with the responses of Chinese abroad. When it referred to the situation in the home districts, for example, the CCP stated blandly that Overseas Chinese should welcome and be grateful for the Party's political and social reforms since that was what they had been fighting for since before 1911, and reforms would strengthen China and thus ultimately guarantee the protection of the Chinese abroad.[13]

By 1952 it was apparent that Overseas Chinese remittances not only had failed to reach pre-war peaks, but that they were declining. At first, the CCP does not appear to have considered that measures to halt the trend were either necessary or justified. In early 1953, however, there were signs that the Party was reexamining the decisions of 1950 and investigating closely the actual implementation of policy at the basic level. A fresh look at domestic Overseas Chinese was facilitated at this stage by the fact that the CCP had now complemented its initial reform programmes, and also because it had established some measure of administrative control over domestic Overseas Chinese, within which it was possible to permit a degree of relaxation.[14] But it was obvious also that the reappraisal was prompted directly by the decline in Overseas Chinese foreign exchange.

In mid-1953 the Hong Kong press, always sensitive to developments in Kwangtung Province, began to report indications of a new policy.[15] The reports were confirmed in September, at an Overseas Chinese Dependants Rural Production Conference held in Kwangtung. The purpose of the conference was to discuss the correct implementation of the policy then being introduced, and to assure domestic Overseas Chinese that the Party was sincere in its announced intention to deal a little more leniently with them. With the latter purpose in mind an unusually large number of dependants was invited to attend, representing all classes from hired labourers to rich peasants. Representatives from Fukien and Kwangsi also attended, underlining the importance attached to the meeting.

The discussions revealed new directions in policy which apparently had already been introduced earlier in the year.[16] They were clearly intended to counteract the downward trend in remittances. It was admitted that basic-level cadres had been appropriating remittances or otherwise infringing the right of dependants to receive and use them, and in many cases this had resulted in remittances being discontinued. The first new measure, therefore, was a programme to correct excesses and mistakes which had occurred during land reform. Dependants who had been wrongly classified as landlords or rich peasants were to have their status downgraded, and houses unlawfully confiscated were to be returned. More surprising, a special appropriation of JMP 50 million had been made to help dependants who were experiencing hardships as a result of the land reform movement. In the current campaign to organise the Chinese peasantry into Mutual Aid Teams Overseas Chinese dependants were not to be forced to join, but 'educated and helped' so that they would join of their own accord. The end result may not have been very different, but this measure indicates how far the CCP had gone in acknowledging a need to avoid undue force in mobilising them for production. A new slogan was introduced for remittances: 'Facilitate Overseas Chinese remittances, serve the Overseas Chinese compatriots.' Although domestic Overseas Chinese were still told that remittances should be used to benefit production, the government asserted that it guaranteed their right to keep and use remittances, even for hiring labour and lending money. This was not so much an encouragement to free spending or bourgeois living, as an admission that in the past dependants had not been able to use remittances as freely as they might. Regulations for departure from China were relaxed; all except landlords and 'counter-revolutionaries' would be permitted to leave China if they had sufficient reason. It was announced also that regular investigations would be made of Overseas Chinese work by the branches of the OCAC assisted by special 'roving work teams' (hsün-hui kung-tso tsu), to ensure that policies were carried out correctly.

For the cadre who had to implement the new policy, however, there were difficult contradictions. Dependants were to be permitted to hire labour and lend money, but they were not to exploit the people or behave as capitalists. They were not to rely solely on their income from abroad, and yet they could refuse to take part in productive labour. The right to remittances was protected, but they should be used in such a way as to benefit production. The cadre was left to resolve these contradictions 'according to actual conditions'. This meant that domestic Overseas Chinese receiving remittances were to be 'educated' rather than compelled to participate in agricultural production, and that they should be permitted just sufficient control over their remittances to prevent them writing to ask their relatives to stop sending money. Whatever else, they were not to be permitted to remain outside the system. This point was emphasised by Ho Hsiang-ning a few months after the September conference in a special New Year speech for domestic Overseas Chinese. Several times in the course of this speech, Ho stressed that all Overseas Chinese dependants, returnees and students, must behave as one with the masses in participating in socialist construction.[17]

The contradiction still remained, however, and the CCP seems to have been uncertain what to do about it. The Party's dilemma was illustrated by an instruction issued in October 1953 which directed that no new Returned Overseas Chinese Friendship Associations should be established, and that returned Overseas Chinese should join existing mass organisations for peasants, workers, women, and so on.[18] The purpose was said to be to strengthen cooperation with the masses; obviously, a device to facilitate integration. Yet this was incompatible with the demands of a special policy for a separate category of people, and the idea was abandoned as the Party virtually turned its back on the existence of the contradiction, paid little more than lip-service to the principle of conformity, and moved towards the creation of a privileged class.

1954–1957: 'THE ESSENCE OF OVERSEAS CHINESE WORK IS DOMESTIC OVERSEAS CHINESE AFFAIRS WORK'[19]

In 1954, more far-reaching changes were introduced. The continuing fall in Overseas Chinese foreign exchange was one problem requiring attention, but there were now additional considerations. For the first time the CCP was forced to approach the Overseas Chinese problem in terms of an active foreign policy, the policy of peaceful coexistence. So long as China had 'leant to one side' and its Southeast Asian policy had been fairly inactive, the Overseas Chinese were expected simply to support policies in China, and the CCP could discuss their problems as acts of persecution by imperialism, directed against China. In peaceful coexistence, however, the Party had to give serious thought to the position of Overseas Chinese in its relations with Southeast Asia. The extent to which they might be used to further China's policies would depend on the impressions they formed through their relatives in the homeland. A second consideration was Overseas Chinese investment. Family remittances were for the support of relatives in China, and might continue irrespective of the government which ruled. Investment required confidence in the Chinese government, and the CCP was prepared to admit that such confidence had not been encouraged by foreign publicity and 'fabrications' about its domestic programmes in the preceding five years. Confidence might be restored if potential investors were shown that people in the home districts were secure, free from socialist excesses, and erjoyed a measure of material well-being. One of the conditions of investment was that a large percentage of the returns could not be repatriated; the investor could direct, however, that dividends be paid to relatives in China, which meant that he had to be assured that the relatives would have both the right and the opportunity to use these funds. By the end of 1954, the whole country also was entering a more relaxed phase, which made a relaxed policy for domestic Overseas Chinese more feasible.

Between late 1953 and September 1954, there appears to have been a comprehensive review of all aspects of Overseas Chinese policy,[20] the results of which were first discussed openly at the First Session of the NPC. Chou En-lai spoke about external policy, and Ho Hsiang-ning, in a speech on 26 September, discussed problems of domestic Overseas Chinese affairs.[21]

Ho admitted that there had been very serious shortcomings and mistakes in the past five years. Overseas Chinese problems had been neglected during land reform, and the remittances policy had not been implemented correctly. In some areas policy had not even been transmitted to the basic level. The relationship between the Chinese abroad and their relatives in China was 'a complicated situation', which many cadres had ignored 'to avoid difficulties or save trouble'. Yet it must be realised that 'every measure taken in domestic Overseas Chinese work can have a direct influence on external Overseas Chinese work'. The two 'comparatively important questions' to which attention should be given in domestic Overseas Chinese affairs were remittances and the use of Overseas Chinese capital in rural development, housing construction, and the establishment of schools. Returned Overseas Chinese were to be 'directed and organised to undergo socialist education and reform', but this reform should be carried out with patience and care.[22]

In the statements on domestic Overseas Chinese policy at the NPC and in the months that followed there was a perceptible note of defensiveness, suggesting that the policy may have had to contend, not only with reluctant cadres at the basic level, but possibly also with more serious opposition at the centre. The policy could have been questioned on the ground that it would create a privileged class and engender capitalist and bourgeois thinking, conflicting with fundamental objectives of the Communist Party. It was possibly with such opposition in mind that statements on Overseas Chinese policy tended to emphasise the 'great contributions' of Overseas Chinese to socialist construction, to the Chinese revolution before 1949, and to countering the influence of the Kuomintang in Southeast Asia.

Nevertheless, in the three years from the end of 1954 to the end of 1957 domestic Overseas Chinese enjoyed a greater degree of freedom and privilege than at any other time. The Party's first significant move was to downgrade the status of Overseas Chinese landlords and rich peasants. According to the regulations of 1950 status could be changed only after labour reform of five years for landlords and three years for rich peasants.[23] At the end of 1954, however, it was announced that Overseas Chinese landlords and rich peasants would have their status changed ahead of schedule.[24] It was announced also that this decision applied to landlords who were living overseas or in Hong Kong and Macao, and that not only these, but landlords who had fled China since 1949 were free to return.[25] In addition, all domestic Overseas Chinese were guaranteed that income from remittances or investment would not affect their class status.[26] By 1957, 95 per cent of Overseas Chinese landlord and rich peasant households were reported to have been reclassified as peasant households.[27]

This move was designed partly to dramatise the new policy to the Chinese abroad. It was covered extensively by the communist press in Hong Kong, and progressive totals for the number whose status had been changed were reported enthusiastically in the despatches of *CNS*. It was hoped that the result would be an increase in foreign exchange. An overwhelming proportion of Overseas Chinese households classified as landlord were in Kwangtung Province,[28] and according to an early estimate of the Communist government, 70 per cent of remittances before 1949 had been derived from a small proportion of Kwangtung Overseas Chinese in the Americas.[29] It seems that the Party believed that it had deprived itself of one of the most important sources of Overseas Chinese foreign exchange and that it could rectify the mistake in this way, despite the total restriction on remittances to China imposed by the United States government. Whether it is true that the 'solid bourgeoisie of the South Seas' were not impressed by the classification of themselves or their relatives as peasants[30] is not really relevant to the Chinese government's intentions. By its own criteria, the government was behaving generously, since reclassification also meant restoration of full citizen rights. The government obviously believed this measure would be effective, and many Chinese abroad may have been glad that they were now able to assist their relatives in China.

Soon after the decision to reclassify landlords there was another, more comprehensive measure, a State Council decree on the protection of remittances, issued in February 1955.[31] This decree represented an endorsement by the supreme state body of a policy which was claimed to have been operating since 1950. Despite the claim the Chinese government had never before phrased its policy in such unequivocal terms. Remittances were now the 'lawful income' of the dependants, and the protection of remittances was a 'long-term policy' of the state. Participation in cooperatives, 'patriotic savings', and purchase of state bonds, must accord with the principle of 'complete voluntariness'. Dependants were free to use remittances, and 'no person may interfere with their use of remittances for living purposes, including weddings, funerals and celebrations'. Administrative bodies were directed to facilitate investment, and to guide, help, and 'if necessary commend', Overseas Chinese who made financial contributions to public welfare enterprises. The State Council warned that any encroachment on remittances, in the way of forced loans, withholding payment, appropriation, embezzlement, or stealing, would be punished according to law. The warning itself indicates that such practices were widespread and serious, but despite the directive there were persistent reports in the Chinese press in the following three years that encroachments were continuing.[32]

This directive and the accompanying editorials in the Chinese press provided the most explicit statement ever made by the Chinese government of the justification for the status of domestic Overseas Chinese. Remittances must be protected. The ostensible reason given on this occasion was that it was the desire of the Chinese abroad that their relatives in China should have a 'settled life', but at other times the CCP was quite frank in admitting the value of remittances in foreign exchange earnings. If remittances were to be protected there was no alternative but to treat the recipients in such a way that they would be, by comparison with the Chinese masses, a privileged class.[33] Transmitting the directive to lower levels, leading Overseas Chinese affairs cadres stated that 'the protection of remittances is the central task of Overseas Chinese work'.[34] Meetings were held at *hsien* and *hsiang* level to publicise the policy. Copies of the directive and the editorials of the *Jen-min jih-pao* and the *Nan-fang jih-pao* were distributed by the provincial branches of the OCAC.[35] By the middle of 1955, Ho Hsiang-ning was able to report a slight increase in the flow of remittances.[36]

It was in this context that the Overseas Chinese affairs administration was rationalised and extended in the mid-1950s. It was obvious that domestic policies had not been carried out correctly and for any policy to be effective more efficient administration was essential. It was also imperative that this particular policy should be strictly controlled; privilege should not be permitted to develop unchecked, care should be taken that antagonism did not develop between domestic Overseas Chinese and the masses. The Fourth Enlarged Conference of the OCAC at which the administrative overhaul was announced was followed in the last half of 1956 by lower-level conferences in all Overseas Chinese areas.[37] It is difficult to judge how successful these moves were, but there were signs of administrative rationalisation, and in particular there was a strengthening of local propaganda media. The *Ch'iao-wu pao* began publication in October 1956, and the two Overseas Chinese newspapers in Kwangtung and Fukien, which previously had been news sheets with distribution limited to the Overseas Chinese affairs sector, were reorganised and offered publicly for sale and increased their frequency of publication. Subsequently an Overseas Chinese paper was established in Kwangsi, together with a number of fairly small-scale papers in some of the home districts.

The measure of the CCP's intentions was not only a more lenient attitude. The Party began to provide special facilities so that Overseas Chinese could more easily use their remittances. Extra allotments of grain were introduced to enable them to hold the weddings, funerals, and celebrations referred to in the State Council directive; and where there were temporary difficulties in supply, first priority was supposed to be given to satisfying their needs before those of the ordinary people. There was a general increase in the ration of grain, cloth, oil, meat, and sugar for domestic Overseas Chinese, which put them above the quotas for the masses.[38] This special ration was provided, moreover, not merely to those who received remittances, but to all Chinese who had relatives outside China, including Hong Kong and Macao, and to all who had returned to China since 1949.[39] In 1956 also, Overseas Chinese retail stores were established by supply and marketing cooperatives in the main home districts. In areas where there were only few dependants, retail stores established 'Overseas Chinese counters' or appointed special cadres to deal with Overseas Chinese purchasing. Dependants were able to buy a wide variety of consumer goods, including many that were not available to the ordinary public.[40] By 1957 the stores were supplying luxury consumer goods, jewellery, rare medicines, and expensive foodstuffs like shark's fin, and the government did not fail to publicise this to the Chinese abroad.[41] To enable Overseas Chinese families to build houses, extra supplies of construction materials were made available by the provincial governments in Fukien and Kwangtung. Perhaps most surprising of all was that not only were the dependants encouraged to spend on consumer goods, they were officially permitted to use their remittances on the upkeep of ancestral graves, geomancy, and other 'feudal superstitious practices'.[42]

It appears from the provincial press that throughout this period the principle of 'voluntariness' was observed in practice to the extent that domestic Overseas Chinese who flatly refused were not forcibly drafted into agricultural labour or made to join cooperatives.[43] There was, however, considerable indirect pressure, by which a majority of domestic Overseas Chinese in rural areas was persuaded to conform. Part of this pressure, as perceived by domestic Overseas Chinese now living outside China, was simply social pressure to belong to the group, and the individual's concern not to be an exception in a society where conformity was demanded. The Party also appealed with arguments directed at their capitalist instincts. Participation in labour, while in itself a 'glorious task', would also increase the income of domestic Overseas Chinese, and by helping to change China into an industrialised nation they were helping to bring about improvements in their own living standard.[44] In 1956 and 1957, it was reported that over 90 per cent of returned and dependant Overseas Chinese had joined co-operatives, and without exception every report claimed that those who had joined had increased their income.[45]

It might seem, therefore, that the CCP had managed to achieve an ideal balance between privilege and participation. With the exception of a small number of dependants who lived in the cities and student and returned Overseas Chinese, the domestic Overseas Chinese had been kept within the limits of general domestic programmes, while enjoying a liberal measure of preferential treatment. This was made easier by the fact that the domestic politics of the period were sufficiently relaxed and free from large-scale assaults on rightist or bourgeois tendencies to accommodate the privileged status which financial considerations made necessary for domestic Overseas Chinese.

1958–1965: 'EQUAL TREATMENT'

The point about domestic Overseas Chinese privileges, however, was that they were not the kind normally permissible within China's socialist framework: holidays in Hangchow for model workers, chauffeur-driven cars for busy officials, or higher salaries for experts. They were bourgeois, capitalist, and, by the Party's own definition, even 'feudal'. It was not surprising, therefore, when as early as 1956 there were signs of concern that preferential treatment might have gone too far. Numerous reports, increasing in frequency in 1957, accused domestic Overseas Chinese of taking advantage of the policy to engage in speculation and other illegal activities.[46] The first indication of what was to come was a statement by Vice-Premier Teng Tzu-hui which was actually made at the Fourth Enlarged Conference of the OCAC, a meeting which in other respects seemed to endorse the liberal line. In a talk with a small group of cadres attending the Conference, Teng said that 'returned Overseas Chinese and dependants should not be made privileged'; and in the matter of rations there should be, in principle, 'equal treatment' for domestic Overseas Chinese and ordinary peasants.[47] The phrase 'equal treatment' (yi-shih t'ung-jen) appeared increasingly at the end of 1956 and throughout 1957. In January 1957 the Fu-chien ch'iao-hsiang pao published an editorial calling for a strengthening of socialist education for domestic Overseas Chinese and greater efforts to mobilise them in socialist construction. They were to be instructed to practise frugality in their use of remittances and encouraged to invest their money.[48]

Throughout 1957 reports on Overseas Chinese work revealed a serious problem of peasant resentment of Overseas Chinese.[49] This is hardly surprising given the privileges heaped on them. They did not have to make the sacrifices demanded of the masses, yet they were given first priority in periods of shortage. The relationship between Overseas Chinese and the masses was rapidly becoming an antagonistic contradiction.

There also remained, of course, the unresolved non-antagonistic contradiction between Overseas Chinese policies and policies for the masses. A good example is provided by an experience of the Nanyang Middle School in Shanghai. When an Overseas Chinese student physically attacked another student the school authorities were faced with the dilemma that punishment according to school regulations might violate Overseas Chinese policy, but that failure to punish the culprit might result in a weakening of school discipline and resentment of Overseas Chinese students, and encourage this particular student to further disorderly conduct. Since the incident occurred in 1957, it was decided to apply school discipline, but from the official account it is obvious that such dilemmas had not previously been so easily resolved.[50]

In October 1957, the Editorial Office of the *Ch'iao-wu pao*, summing up the journal's first year of publication, declared that 'our consideration for the special characteristics of returned and dependant Overseas Chinese is a means, and not an end in itself. Special characteristics can be changed and transformed'.[51] The signs appeared to indicate a radical reorientation of domestic Overseas Chinese policy.

In November, the Second Overseas Chinese Affairs Commission held its First Plenary Conference, which criticized excessive consideration and privilege for domestic Overseas Chinese and denounced them for complaining that they were not being treated well enough. The conference foreshadowed measures to curtail privilege, to prevent wastefulness, and to reintegrate domestic Overseas Chinese with the masses. It was announced that all domestic Overseas Chinese should take part in the rectification campaign, participate in production, and undergo socialist education. In future, 'domestic Overseas Chinese work should start from the interests of the 600 million people', and the method of handling this work 'must in no way be one of making privileges'.[52]

The Party's reasons for 'veering to the left' again in domestic Overseas Chinese policy were themselves partly domestic. The current political climate was particularly antagonistic towards privilege, bourgeois manifestations, and tendencies to remain immune from socialisation. Moreover, if there had been opposition to the domestic policy of 1954, the opposition could have found vindication in the problems and abuses which had followed its introduction. The CCP must have taken into account the possible impact on the overseas relatives and friends, but there were two other developments which almost certainly encouraged the Party to ignore them. Despite the generous treatment accorded to domestic Overseas Chinese, remittances had not increased significantly, and in fact had fallen in 1957.[53] Officially the decline was attributed to smuggling and illegal remitting of money.[54] But the Party must have realised by this stage that the level of remittances could not be increased substantially, and that since remittances were made for personal family reasons they might still be maintained without the existence of a privileged class in socialist China.[55] Most important of all in the redirection of domestic policy, however, was the fact that in external policy the CCP was now actively encouraging the Chinese abroad to sever many of the ties which bound them to China, which meant that it was no longer essential that domestic Overseas Chinese be treated with special care.

Immediately after the plenary conference of the OCAC, it was announced in Fukien and Kwangtung that existing arrangements for special rations and purchasing for domestic Overseas Chinese were cancelled. New regulations stipulated that privileges were to be tied strictly to remittances as they had been before 1954; the amount of rations or goods supplied would be calculated strictly on the amount of money received, for which the banks were to issue certificates valid for only one month.[56] In one stroke the Party both imposed control on Overseas Chinese foreign exchange, and drastically reduced the dimensions of the domestic Overseas Chinese problem itself, since the immediate effect would have been to reduce by at least one-third the number of domestic Overseas Chinese.[57] Those who did not receive remittances were to be treated as one with the masses, and they have not since regained domestic Overseas Chinese status. Those who did receive remittances were to be strictly controlled, and their income from overseas was to be channelled into construction and production.

The domestic Overseas Chinese policy which emerged in 1958 remained essentially unchanged until the Cultural Revolution. The contradiction between preferential treatment and participation in socialist construction had been resolved firmly in favour of the latter. Henceforth, the guiding principles in domestic Overseas Chinese affairs were 'equal treatment' rather than 'special treatment'; 'starting from the interests of the 600 million' rather than the 'special circumstances of Overseas Chinese'; and 'all-round consideration' in place of 'special consideration'. Participation in productive labour was no longer voluntary, and socialist education and reform were actually more vigorously pursued to compensate for the laxity of the mid-1950s. To a limited extent special consideration did continue, in the form of purchasing facilities, but tendencies to privilege or bourgeois living were kept in check. Domestic Overseas Chinese were told that they should retain only sufficient of their income from overseas to satisfy daily necessities; the rest should be used in agricultural production.

In February 1958, Fang Fang addressed a large gathering of returned Overseas Chinese and students in Peking, devoting over half of his time to denying that there had been any change in Overseas Chinese policy;[58] to have acknowledged a radical change would have been to admit that the Party had been wrong. Fang pointed out, correctly, that the policy had always been for domestic Overseas Chinese to participate in socialist construction, but he omitted to mention that the Party had been extremely liberal in applying this policy in the preceding three years. All that had happened, according to Fang, was that shortcomings and mistakes in implementation had been corrected, and 'unreasonable' demands for special consideration were now being refused. Domestic Overseas Chinese, Fang reported, were now joining the masses in a high tide of socialist construction. Fang's speech appears to have been made in response to criticism from domestic Overseas Chinese, and possibly also to an adverse reaction from Chinese abroad.

But there was no question of the Party changing its policies because of criticism from Overseas Chinese; nor was there any doubt that the CCP was aware of the effects of this policy on the Chinese abroad. As early as July 1957, Ho Hsiang-ning had criticised the argument that 'reform movements should not be carried out in the home districts, in order to prevent influencing the unity of the Chinese abroad', and dismissed the claim that 'the Chinese abroad are extremely disillusioned with the homeland because of such movements and reforms'.[59] In mid-1958, Fang Fang told an enlarged conference of the OCAC that domestic Overseas Chinese and cadres 'should not always be thinking about special consideration; it should be forgotten'.[60] The existence of special characteristics was still admitted, but where before they had been given special consideration now they were to be 'solved', (*chieh-chüeh*), or in the other words, eliminated.

The programme to integrate domestic Overseas Chinese with the masses was more than simply a temporary measure dictated by the anti-rightist and rectification campaigns of 1957 and the Great Leap Forward. Overseas Chinese affairs, which had been important in Fukien and Kwangtung[61] but which had never occupied a prominent position among national policies, were relegated still further to a position of minor significance even in Fukien and Kwangtung. This was reflected in the domestic Overseas Chinese press, which devoted an increasing amount of space to national policies which had no special relevance to Overseas Chinese affairs, and which pointedly related every measure in Overseas Chinese work to relevant national policies. Where before it had been claimed that 90 per cent of domestic Overseas Chinese had joined cooperatives, indicating that a considerable number, possibly much more than ten per cent, had not, now it was stated that 100 per cent were engaged in productive labour, which suggests that only a small percentage still remained completely immune.[62]

A work conference convened by the OCAC at the end of 1958 confirmed the complete subordination of domestic Overseas Chinese affairs to national affairs and the principle of equal treatment. The conference gave fleeting acknowledgment to the principle of voluntary participation in production, but the directives issued at the conference made it clear that no person would be permitted to remain exempt by virtue of domestic Overseas Chinese status alone. All domestic Overseas Chinese were to undergo systematic socialist education and reform.[63] Overseas Chinese policy was to be 'closely integrated with the central tasks of the Party and government'. Political and ideological work was now the 'first and most important task', and 'even greater attention must be paid to ideological education than is the case with the ordinary people'.[64]

At the end of 1959, official statements reaffirmed publicly what had been apparent for at least a year, that this was not a temporary phase. In a report to the First Conference of the Second Fukien OCAC, Wang Han-chieh announced: 'In future, organising the masses of Overseas Chinese dependants and returned Overseas Chinese to participate in socialist construction will continue to be the central task of domestic Overseas Chinese affairs'.[65] In November, the Editorial Office of the *Ch'iao-wu pao* stated that the current domestic Overseas Chinese policy was to be applied not only during the Great Leap Foward, but in all future movements and campaigns.[66] As for the impact on the Chinese abroad, Fang Fang, in a speech to returned Overseas Chinese and dependants in October 1959, announced that people who were concerned that a 'communist style' among domestic Overseas Chinese would influence the Chinese abroad, were guilty of 'rightist thinking which must be criticised'.[67] Fang's statement marks the final repudiation of the policy of the mid-1950s.

This point must be clearly understood because of its relation to policy towards the Chinese abroad. That is, while more important nationwide policies may have been partly responsible for the way in which the domestic Overseas Chinese policy was introduced in 1957 and the pace at which it proceeded, this policy was geared essentially to the requirements of external Overseas Chinese policy. It was intended to outlast passing campaigns because it resulted from a decision to alter fundamentally the long-term relationship between China and the Chinese abroad.

The only concession which remained was the right to receive and use remittances, interest on investment, and bank deposits. But the Party's suggestions as to their use indicated that only the absolute minimum would be permitted for personal living expenses. In an apparent effort to compensate for the losses incurred through economic mismanagement and natural disasters, the CCP offered in 1959 and again in 1962 an increase in the quota of basic necessities for each JMP 100 of remittances received.[68] Overseas Chinese stores continued to operate as an outlet for special rations, and also to provide scarce foodstuffs for unproductive newly returned Overseas Chinese who began to arrive from Indonesia in large numbers in late 1959. To help relieve the general shortage of food in Kwangtung and Fukien the government also permitted domestic Overseas Chinese to receive food parcels instead of cash remittances, a practice which had been condemned in 1956 and 1957, and which was prohibited once more in January 1963.[69] These measures represented not so much a fundamental change in Overseas Chinese policy as a response to domestic shortages and a sharp decline in foreign exchange earnings in 1961 and 1962.

To the ordinary Chinese in the lean years following the Great Leap, domestic Overseas Chinese must still have appeared as a privileged class.[70] But the concessions they enjoyed were as much a matter of necessity, as of privilege in the sense that it had existed before 1957. And in matters of political education and productive labour, there was, if anything, an intensification of pressure on domestic Overseas Chinese. A succession of Overseas

Chinese conferences from 1959 to 1962 served to confirm, moreover, that the Party had no intention of reverting to the kind of policy which had prevailed from 1954 to 1957. In 1962, when some relaxation might have been expected to occur, a plenary conference of the OCAC reaffirmed in the most positive terms that the policies of the preceding four years had been entirely correct, and would continue to provide the guideline for domestic Overseas Chinese affairs in future.[71] If there was any relaxation, it was only such as the masses also enjoyed.

In one of the last major public statements on domestic policy before the onset of the Cultural Revolution Fang Fang, writing in the *Ch'iao-wu pao*, demonstrated clearly the extent to which the special problems of domestic Overseas Chinese had become submerged in national policies and political movements. The 'key policy' in domestic Overseas Chinese affairs was now class struggle and the struggle between the two lines of socialism and capitalism. Class struggle, Fang said, was particularly acute among domestic Overseas Chinese because of their intimate relationship with relatives in capitalist countries. It was necessary to educate them in 'suppressing capitalism and establishing proletarianism'. There were certain mistaken ideas which obstructed their full participation: the 'concept of privilege', the 'concept of being an exception', the fear of upheavals, and disregard for the principle of 'equal treatment'. All these, of course, had been more than acceptable in the mid-1950s. They were now mistaken ideas and were to be thoroughly repudiated: 'Overseas Chinese affairs work should serve the further development of the socialist education movement, socialist revolution and socialist construction.'

The complete reversal of the Party's policy of the mid-1950s was in some ways exemplified by the curious way in which Fang phrased his remarks about remittances: 'personal remittances should be allowed, since foreign exchange is not harmful, and is even helpful to socialist construction' (*tui wo-kuo she-hui-chu-yi chien-she yeh shih-wu-hai ti, shen-chih shih yu-pang-chu ti*). This off-hand and rather grudging acknowledgment of the benefits the state derived from Overseas Chinese foreign exchange is in marked contrast to previous statements, in which the Party had considered it extremely important. The significance of Fang's remark for policy towards domestic Overseas Chinese was not difficult to discern. He went on to say that while it was permissible for Overseas Chinese families to have a slightly better life and to eat a little better if they received remittances, they must also practise frugality and economy, feudal superstition and waste must be opposed, and surplus remittances should be used for patriotic saving, investment or other enterprises beneficial to state construction.[72]

RETURNED OVERSEAS CHINESE; PROBLEMS OF
RESETTLEMENT AND INTEGRATION

The outstanding obstacle to smooth implementation of domestic policy after
1957 was the problem of Overseas Chinese returning to settle permanently
in China. The Party's aim had always been to apply to returned Overseas
Chinese the same policies as it did to dependants who had never left China.
But so long as it encouraged Overseas Chinese to return it faced a continuing
problem of assimilating the new arrivals into socialist society.

Between 1949 and 1966, almost 500,000 Overseas Chinese returned to
settle in China, including at least 94,000 in 1960.[73] They included deportees
or repatriates, described by the Chinese government as 'refugees', people
returning to spend their declining years in their native villages, and those
particularly encouraged by the CCP, 'higher intellectuals', skilled workers
and agriculturalists, and wealthy Overseas Chinese with money to invest.
Included in this category also were Overseas Chinese students.

Many returned Overseas Chinese had nowhere to live and no means of
support, and some could not speak Chinese. Many also were unaccustomed
to physical labour, and if they were not themselves capitalist, they were, in
the Party's view, influenced by the capitalist environments from which they
had come. A minority large enough to warrant repeated criticism by the
central authorities was obviously dissatisfied with life in China. They
demanded the right to live in the cities, to be given superior accommodation,
to change employment to suit themselves, and to spend money freely on
goods for personal use. If their demands for personal freedom were not met
many of them asked to be allowed to leave China.[74] The Party was prepared
to consider what it termed 'reasonable' requests for exit permits, but it
did not consider personal dissatisfaction a reasonable excuse. Perhaps it felt
that to have done so would have been to admit failure of the system; and
disillusioned Overseas Chinese could be expected to be strong and vocal
critics of the Communist government if they returned to Southeast Asia.

Despite the problems the CCP always welcomed Overseas Chinese to
return to China, with varying degrees of enthusiasm.[75] Its motives were
obviously partly financial, but to some extent also it was influenced by a
desire to maintain prestige, particularly by comparison with the Kuomintang.[76]
From 1959 to 1961, and to a lesser extent since then, resettlement in China
was seen also as part of the ultimate solution to the Overseas Chinese
problem.

The general guideline for returned Overseas Chinese policy was summarised
in a slogan introduced in 1956: 'Resettlement in the district of origin, and
primarily in rural areas; make appropriate use of those with special skills.'[77]
The easiest to handle were those who could return to their native village and
live with relatives or friends, support themselves by work or remittances,

and with the help of the Party and the Returned Overseas Chinese Association, undergo socialist reform. Skilled and professional people also presented few problems in placement, although not necessarily in assimilation.

The difficult cases were those who had no contacts in China and no special skills, and those who wanted to settle down and enjoy life in the cities and towns. A small percentage of the latter who were either wealthy enough to invest in China or regarded by the Party as 'representative' Overseas Chinese,[78] were permitted to settle in towns and cities in special Overseas Chinese apartment buildings or Overseas Chinese villages.[79] The Overseas Chinese villages would not compare unfavourably with modern housing developments in, for example, a country like Australia, on a smaller scale and with fewer amenities, but with equally spacious and possibly more substantial houses. They were largely self-contained, with their own schools, restaurants, and recreation facilities.[80] Residents were offered generous purchasing terms and tax concessions, and could live in the villages on the returns from investment without having to work.

These pockets of bourgeois society were perhaps the best illustration of what the CCP really thought about Overseas Chinese; they were worth looking after if they were financially useful to China. Because they were totally self-supporting, residents of the villages were possibly the only genuinely privileged class of Overseas Chinese, in that they appear to have been exempt from participation, free to enjoy themselves and travel around China. Their treatment resembled that accorded to foreign experts or 'foreign friends'; they were among the Chinese people, they had more freedom of movement and contact than the tourist, but they were still apart from the masses. For the same reasons as the Party permitted the establishment of these Overseas Chinese villages and apartment buildings, they also received possibly more external publicity than any other aspect of domestic Overseas Chinese affairs. Even after 1957 and throughout the 1960s before the Cultural Revolution, the villages continued to operate and expand and the immunity of the residents appears to have continued, although it is not clear what happened during the Cultural Revolution.[81]

There remained the problem of those who had neither relatives, nor money, nor skills, and they appear to have comprised as many as 50 per cent of all returned Overseas Chinese.[82] The government attempted to place them in industry, the bureaucracy, and special Overseas Chinese farms which in 1960 became the principal areas for resettlement and in themselves a basic unit of administration. The first, the Hsing-lung Farm on Hainan Island, was established in 1951 as a matter of urgent necessity, when something had to be done with large numbers of deportees from Malaya. By 1959 there were nine state Overseas Chinese farms, and a year later over thirty.[83] The latest total in Chinese sources, in 1965, was thirty-eight.[84]

These farms, at first either private or joint state–private enterprises and subsequently entirely state-run, presented a number of advantages. First, there was somewhere to put returned Overseas Chinese who had 'difficulties'. They could be resettled immediately, and almost as rapidly mobilised in agricultural production which, hopefully, would become self-supporting. The burden on the state was thus partly relieved.[85] Secondly, the farms provided a partial political quarantine in which the new arrivals could be transformed by socialist education and labour. The Party also found a third advantage by situating the farms in southern China where, it was hoped at least, use could be made of returned Overseas Chinese experienced in the cultivation of tropical and sub-tropical crops. One has the impression that there were not nearly so many of such skilled people as publicity about the farms suggests, and many returned Overseas Chinese were horrified at the thought that they might be expected to produce skills which they never possessed. It seems also that at least some of the farms were established in areas which hitherto had been considered barren and worthless, and it is probably for this reason as well as inexperience that Overseas Chinese had so much trouble in attaining the basic self-sufficiency which the Party demanded of the farms.

From 1954 to the beginning of 1960 there was a gradual levelling off in the number of new arrivals, making the problem of resettlement less acute.[86] But where in 1958 and 1959 the Party had had little trouble in conditioning returned Overseas Chinese to accept the policy of 'equal treatment', in 1960 it had to cope with almost 100,000 Chinese from Indonesia. The Party was forced to acknowledge that there was 'a distance between the life and thinking of the newly returned Overseas Chinese, and that of the people of China', that they did not understand the situation in China, and that it was inevitable that there would be some difficulties in resettling them.[87] For this reason domestic Overseas Chinese policy from 1960 was directed increasingly at the assimilation of recent arrivals. At least nine Work Conferences on Overseas Chinese farms were convened by the Central OCAC or its province level branches between 1961 and 1965. A long report on the National Work Conference of February/March 1962 illustrates the kind of problems the farms were presenting. Quite apart from 'unreasonable' demands, bourgeois influence and 'bad habits', the administration and finances were in a state of chaos, self-sufficiency had not been attained even in the barest necessities, and political work had been badly neglected.[88] It was not until 1965 that the farms appear to have begun to operate with a degree of efficiency, although 'undesirable practices' and 'demands antagonistic to the socialist system' persisted.[89]

The Overseas Chinese farms were essential to the CCP's 'permanent' solution to the Overseas Chinese problem through repatriation, a policy which failed through lack of response from the Chinese abroad. But in 1962 at least, it was still thought that 'the situation in which Chinese overseas will return to China is a long-term one, and the Overseas Chinese farms are necessary not only at the present time, but will continue to be for a long time to come'.[90] The farms were necessary, therefore, so long as there were Overseas Chinese, since there would always be some who would wish or be compelled to return to China to live. If they could be made to operate effectively as the Hsing-lung Farm and several others had done by 1965, they would continue to provide the best means for rapid resettlement and political acclimatisation.

DOMESTIC AFFAIRS AND EXTERNAL POLICY

It should not be imagined that the CCP was entirely successful in its policy for domestic Overseas Chinese. By the time the Party entered its second decade of rule there was no question of them being a class apart merely because they had relatives overseas. The guideline was by then very simple; if they received foreign exchange they were entitled to slightly more food and clothing rations than the masses, but in all other respects they were to participate and to conform. But so long as there were some who were better fed and clad than the Chinese masses, they remained conspicuous. There were also wealthy returned Overseas Chinese in the cities and towns who led a comfortable bourgeois existence, and who were an object of considerable resentment. And while there remained even limited privileges, while there were people who had more than the average peasant and who received money or consumer goods from Hong Kong and overseas, there were opportunities for stretching regulations, for bribery, corruption, and various forms of profiteering. The Party was still faced with the same contradictions it had confronted in 1949.

The fact that domestic Overseas Chinese policy may not have been completely successful, however, does not imply a lack of resolve on the part of the CCP; it would be difficult to name any domestic policy since 1949 which has been wholly successful. The point about the policy, particularly since 1957, is its significance for interpreting the Party's intentions overseas. Post-1957 domestic policy was similar in many respects to policy before 1954. But in relation to external policy it was quite different, and the change in 1957 was of the greatest importance for China's policy towards the Chinese abroad.

Domestic Overseas Chinese policy in the mid-1950s had been a large scale united front operation. The CCP had stated openly and repeatedly that in order to persuade the Chinese abroad to do what it wanted, it was vitally necessary to be more than a little light-handed with their relatives and friends in China. It had claimed that adverse reactions abroad were due only to excesses or mistakes by inefficient or over-zealous cadres. But it was obvious from the policies of the mid-1950s that the Party believed it was necessary not merely to avoid excesses, but to be lenient, even indulgent. 'The essence of Overseas Chinese work', according to Kao Ming-hsüan, was 'domestic Overseas Chinese affairs work'. The fact that the Party was prepared in 1957 to force domestic Overseas Chinese to participate fully in socialist programmes irrespective of the reaction of the Chinese abroad, and in effect, to abandon 'the essence' of Overseas Chinese work, was not only a reversal of the previous policy but a total rejection of the arguments on which it was based. It provided possibly the clearest indication that the CCP was quite serious in its apparent determination to detach the Chinese abroad from China.

Treatment of the domestic Overseas Chinese is not only an indicator of external objectives. The domestic Overseas Chinese problem in itself provided strong arguments against attempting to hold on to the Chinese abroad. The freedom and privilege which had existed from 1954 to 1957 to serve one purpose, was at the same time contrary to fundamental beliefs of the CCP. Unless there was some overwhelming advantage to be gained, and by 1957 the advantage was already more than dubious, the problems of domestic Overseas Chinese, far from being a useful weapon for enlisting the support of the Chinese abroad, had become another argument for disposing of the whole Overseas Chinese problem.

Part Two.
Policies towards the Chinese abroad

5

The 'colonial' legacy; identification of problems. Overseas Chinese policy, 1949–1954

> The government will do anything which is of benefit to the Overseas Chinese but which is not detrimental to the government.
>
> Po Yi-po, Minister of Finance,
> speech to delegation of Chinese
> from Hong Kong, 24 July 1950[1]

The analysis in the following chapters emphasises one way of looking at China's Overseas Chinese policy, the decolonisation model. It is primarily an illustrative model, and no attempt is made to build the analysis around it or to see every aspect of policy in these terms alone. Nor can it be a strict model of China's relations with Southeast Asia; there are too many points of dissimilarity for it to be so. The migration of Chinese to Southeast Asia was never sponsored or directed by Chinese governments, nor has it been followed in modern times by Chinese territorial claims or administrations. The Chinese Communist Party did not inherit anything resembling conventional colonial possessions.

But the model has some value for explaining the predicament of the CCP and its attempts to rationalise the legacy of this unique but troublesome set of associations with Southeast Asia. It also illustrates the evolving nature of the Party's approach to the Overseas Chinese, which is best understood if it is followed through in sequence. It is more appropriate to the policies introduced after 1954 than to those which went before, and for this reason it is more acurately a model of decolonisation than a colonial model. The intention in the following chapters is to use this model as a frame of reference where it seems appropriate to the kind of policy the CCP was pursuing.

In the post-war era of self-determination and national independence, Chinese in Southeast Asia also have been struggling to find a new identity in a new situation, to exercise their own right to self-determination. With the possible exception of Singapore, the quest has not been easy. From one point of view, held by Southeast Asian governments and by many of the Chinese themselves, they must be regarded as individuals or at most as an ethnic minority within the state rather than as a separate entity with a separate collective right to self-determination. It is possible to discern broad categories of identity of attitudes and interests, but in general the Chinese in Southeast Asia do not act in concert for political ends, either regionally or together within the countries in which they reside.[2] From this point of view, therefore, they may determine their political future only in the same way as the indigenous majority, in the political context of the nation states in which they live. To the extent that the countries of Southeast Asia have attained national independence, this is shared by all Chinese who by birth or the acquisition of citizenship are regarded as belonging to those countries.

There is a second point of view which is that the Chinese in Southeast Asia, by virtue of their numbers, their relatively low rate of assimilation and their many ties with China, can be regarded as collective 'colonial' communities, or at least standing in a somewhat similar relation to China as former Asian colonies did in relation to European colonial powers. This view is often suggested in the statements of Southeast Asian governments, it is certainly accepted by some Overseas Chinese, and it represents one of the ways in which Chinese governments have regarded the emigrant communities since the late nineteenth century. It is not so much an opposing view to the first as one which adds a further dimension, although it is often held separately to the first because it is less capable of legal definition and rests more on a political judgment of the relationship between the Overseas Chinese and China irrespective of citizenship.

The ties which in the past have bound the Overseas Chinese to China have been ones of kinship, culture, patriotism, and the 'sojourner mentality' expressed in the Chinese term for Overseas Chinese, hua-ch'iao, and it is on these ties that the close commercial and political links have been founded. In this sense, the 'colonial' situation of Overseas Chinese resembles more those European colonies distinguished by permanent white settlement and political dominance and continuing immigration, rather than those which were occupied, administered, and exploited, but not extensively populated from Europe. But there is some resemblance to the latter in the extent to which Overseas Chinese hold, or more correctly are believed to hold, economic power which is used to exploit the indigenous peoples for the benefit of the Chinese communities themselves and the Chinese homeland. Overseas Chinese 'colonies', therefore, reflect something of the more conventional colonial models, but they lie somewhere between the two and in their totality resemble neither.

The 'colonial' relationship rested on a combination of Overseas Chinese willingness to regard themselves as belonging to China, and Chinese government claims over them and attempts to control them. This complicated the problem of self-determination for Overseas Chinese, and on this level the problem existed also in non-colonial Thailand and predominantly Chinese Singapore. And since Overseas Chinese do not speak with one voice, there could be no simple act of independence. This has been one of the central dilemmas of the Chinese in Southeast Asia. The governments of Southeast Asia, and the Chinese government, may act upon whichever voice they choose to hear as representing the general prevailing attitudes of Overseas Chinese. The individual Chinese may want independence, from China and with the local people. But he may find himself identified with loyalties and aspirations which he does not hold, which determine the policies of the two governments between which he is caught, and which he as an individual has little power to influence.

The nearest approach to a simple colonial position on China's relations with Chinese in Southeast Asia was represented by the policies of the Kuomintang,[3] which regarded jurisdiction over Chinese abroad as a right and responsibility of the Chinese government; in effect, a question of the internal affairs of China. In this view, foreign governments should concede the right of Overseas Chinese not only to give their allegiance to the Chinese government and perform such acts of loyalty as flying the Chinese Nationalist flag or singing the Nationalist anthem, but also to conform, under the direction of diplomatic and consular officials or overseas branches of the Kuomintang, with the regulations and policies for China proper of the Nationalist government. The abduction from Manila in 1970 of two Chinese newspapermen who did not consider themselves nationals of the Republic of China and their subsequent military trial in Taipei on charges of violating in Manila emergency regulations in force in Taiwan, is a recent illustration of Kuomintang policy.[4] It might have outraged the Filipino and international press, but it should not have surprised them since it was entirely consistent with the established position of the KMT. But the KMT itself has found repeatedly that the difficulty in asserting this kind of possession over the Chinese abroad is that it is contingent upon the cooperation of friendly states, which brings it within the ambit of foreign relations and frequently into conflict with foreign governments. It was against the background of the KMT's narrow and limiting view of Overseas Chinese affairs that the CCP had to examine its own position in 1949.

In the first five years of its rule the CCP issued strong public statements, but took almost no initiatives in Overseas Chinese policy. There is little evidence of coherent long-term planning. Decisions on all matters which might define China's relations with the Chinese abroad, such as nationality, were temporarily postponed. Overseas Chinese policies give the strong impression of having been perfunctorily aligned with a stereotyped communist world-view and left to follow precedents established by the Kuomintang. Even the attention devoted to remittances in domestic Overseas Chinese affairs was not supported with comparable efforts in external policy. External propaganda was only marginally tailored to counter the effects among non-communist Overseas Chinese of the CCP's socialist programmes and the anti-communist propaganda of the Kuomintang.

There were a number of reasons for this low-key approach. The Chinese Communist Party was preoccupied with the consolidation of political control and the implementation of reform programmes. Externally its attention and resources were directed towards the war in Korea. Across the Taiwan Straits the United States was reviving the Kuomintang and the CCP could not be sure how far the US was prepared to back the KMT's ambition to recover the mainland. Overseas Chinese, as indicated negatively in the CCP's programmes before 1949 and confirmed in the Common Programme, were low on the list of national priorities; and in the midst of these other preoccupations it was not surprising that they received so little attention. Moreover, the organisations responsible for Overseas Chinese affairs were themselves preoccupied with domestic matters, with controlling the inflow of Overseas Chinese foreign exchange, resettling deportees from Malaya, and placing Overseas Chinese students in suitable educational institutions; and they had some difficulty in coping even with these problems. Above all, initiatives in Overseas Chinese policy were inhibited by the general orientation of foreign policy, which, although it did not 'lean to one side' as much as had been proclaimed, was notably lacking in positive efforts to develop relations with the countries of Southeast Asia. It was not until the emergence of an active, forward-looking foreign policy compelled comparable initiatives in Overseas Chinese policy that the Party began to enunciate long-term policies and objectives.

The Party's view of the relationship even in this period was never formulated explicitly in colonial terms. In its public statements, it stressed that the demands it made of the Overseas Chinese were only consistent with the willing cooperation and unreserved support which it received from them, rather than a right exercised by the Chinese government. Even if it was privately admitted that there were colonial overtones in the relationship in the early 1950s, all that could be done was to make the best of the situation until an acceptable solution could be worked out. For the problem was that the colonial situation was inherited, and the CCP appears to have been unprepared in the first years of its rule to deal with it in a creative or positive way.

Until 1954, the Party was very much feeling its way, and it claimed that there had been virtually nothing in the experience of 'old China' on which it could have drawn in framing a policy.[5] But in many respects the CCP tended to follow the familiar lines of the KMT's Overseas Chinese policies, and although more important preoccupations precluded positive action, it is here that the colonial approach is discernible. In the Common Programme, protection of Overseas-Chinese was listed as an objective of foreign policy, just as it had been, even if far more prominently, in the Nationalists' constitution of 1946. The CCP also attempted to establish direct organisational links with the Overseas Chinese, as the KMT had done; and while it may not have been very active in the pursuit of its policies and it lacked the long-established contacts and influence among Overseas Chinese which the KMT had, its policy slogans tended to echo those of the KMT; protection, remittances, education, culture, and patriotism, overlaid with the language of socialism.

The CCP stated repeatedly that its policies represented a complete break with those of the Kuomintang but in these early years the resemblance was unmistakable. This may have been conscious, an effort on the part of the CCP to establish itself in the eyes of the Chinese abroad; what the KMT had done or professed to have done for their interests and welfare the CCP would continue to do, but more efficiently, successfully and selflessly.[6] It may even have been that the Party believed initially that there were no alternatives to the policies of the KMT. Without defining its terms too closely, the Party tended throughout this period to approach the Overseas Chinese in much the same way as did the KMT, as an extension of the Chinese population. Statements addressed to the Chinese abroad implied that they accepted obligations and responsibilities demanded by their intimate relationship with the Chinese homeland. And so long as the CCP regarded even a proportion of Overseas Chinese as nationals of the People's Republic of China it was under some obligation to express its concern for its subjects abroad, in terms unavoidably similar to those of the KMT.

Despite the inactivity in this period and the failure to define long-term goals, a number of themes emerged and a number of precedents were established. From the experience of its first five years as the government of China, the Party acquired some understanding of the complexities of the Overseas Chinese problem, and came to realise that there were alternatives to the KMT policy.

NATIONALITY

The best illustration of the CCP's approach to Overseas Chinese in this period was its attitude to nationality. Because of indecision, or a deliberate postponement of decision, or possibly because of reluctance to make known a decision already taken, the Chinese government failed to make any precise definition of the national status of the Chinese abroad, to say what it meant when it used the term Overseas Chinese. According to one opinion the Nationality Law promulgated by the KMT in 1929 remained in force after the CCP came to power.[7] This implies that the CCP accepted the KMT's definition of nationality and the legal procedures for acquiring and renouncing it, and rejected the concept of dual nationality. Not only is this improbable, but in fact, all laws and statutes and the entire judicial system of the Nationalist government were formally abolished in the Common Programme,[8] and the CCP has never framed a nationality law of its own.

At no time, however, did the CCP actually state that it rejected the concept of *jus sanguinis* on which the KMT nationality law was based; and the evidence suggests that for public purposes at least the Party accepted a very broad interpretation of nationals of the People's Republic of China. The criteria on which this interpretation was based were never stated and the outer limits of China's overseas population never defined. For the purpose of land reform Overseas Chinese land had been defined as that which belonged to people who had lived and worked abroad for one year or more.[9] But this definition was for a specific domestic purpose and did not necessarily imply that all Chinese who had lived and worked overseas for more than one year were Chinese nationals. Two years later the Hong Kong *Chou-mo pao* offered the following definition: 'According to the stipulation of the People's Government, an Overseas Chinese is one who has resided overseas for more than three years. He does not necessarily have to understand a foreign language.'[10] In the narrowest sense this definition only clarified the position of those born in China whose status was not affected by marriage, residence, or different interpretation by the governments of the countries of residence.

In the Common Programme, the 'Chinese resident abroad' were stated to be one of the components of the people's democratic united front with the right to representation in the CPPCC.[11] The Common Programme does not make any further definition except, perhaps, by implication, that Overseas Chinese represented in the CPPCC should be 'patriotic', which would have excluded a very large number. The census of 1953 listed some 11.5 million Overseas Chinese as part of the Chinese population.[12] Although the Party did not explain what means of 'indirect investigation' were employed to arrive at this figure, its proximity to contemporary KMT figures suggests that the CCP's criteria for determining the status of Overseas Chinese may have been similar to those of the KMT. The thirty Overseas Chinese deputies elected to the NPC in the following year were supposed to represent all of these Overseas Chinese. This is not specified in the electoral law or the constitution, but according to an article by Hu Wei-fu in the *Jen-min jih-pao* these deputies represented an approximate total of 12 million Chinese resident abroad, or roughly one to every 400,000.[13] The term 'Chinese resident abroad' (*kuo-wai hua-ch'iao*), which occurs in the Common Programme, the 1954 Constitution, and the official census figures, seems intended to mean Chinese nationals. But there is an ambiguity in that this term, and others like it, are also frequently used without any intended legal meaning of nationality.[14] Despite the vagueness and the ambiguities of the CCP's approach to the nationality question, however, it seems that in this period the Party was prepared to claim the broad undifferentiated mass of Overseas

Chinese as nationals of the People's Republic of China, irrespective of their own attitudes or the attitudes of the governments of the countries of residence, and irrespective of the Party's own ultimate intentions.

Although it was not until after 1954 that the CCP clarified its position on nationality, it was not unaware of the problems of dual nationality.[15] When Chou En-lai gave notice of the introduction of a new Overseas Chinese policy at the First NPC he singled out dual nationality as the problem most requiring attention, and subsequent statements in 1954 indicate that the question had already been discussed at some length. But even though the Party had been aware of the problem it had made no attempt to resolve it, since nationality was the fundamental issue in Overseas Chinese policy, involving the whole question of China's relations with the Chinese abroad.

There is a further possible reason why the Party was reluctant to take any action on this question; the problem of the rival claims of the Kuomintang. If the CCP relinquished its claim to part of the Overseas Chinese population without formal arrangements with the countries in which they lived, this might have been construed as *de facto* acceptance of a situation in which Overseas Chinese could be nationals of the People's Republic of China or of the Republic of China. It was possibly partly for this reason that the CCP's first attempts to solve the problem after 1954 were through formal treaty arrangements. In the meantime the simplest solution was to claim all Overseas Chinese as Chinese nationals and, without specific legal commitment, to create the impression that the CCP followed the KMT and the principle of *jus sanguinis*. For purposes of protection and repatriation, the Party was prepared to accept as Chinese anyone who considered himself or was considered by the local authorities to be Chinese.

PROTECTION

To the extent that the CCP assessed it as being of positive value to China, the relationship with the Overseas Chinese was worth preserving, and this raised questions about the necessity, and the Chinese government's capacity, for protection. If all Overseas Chinese were potentially valuable, was it necessary to act in every case involving an individual Overseas Chinese? Or should protection only be extended to pure Chinese nationals? Or patriotic sympathisers and communists? Should the Chinese government act more strongly in cases of political oppression or economic persecution? Where state relations were friendly or where they were hostile? Was there a point at which the obligation to protect should override the possible effects on foreign relations? In the decade from 1949 to 1959 the CCP moved through a number of positions on protection, reflecting its changing evaluation of the benefits to be derived from the Chinese abroad.

Despite its failure to make any precise definition of nationality, the CCP did recognise in this period the right of Overseas Chinese to Chinese government protection. In the Common Programme it was promised that 'The Central Government of the People's Republic of China shall make every effort (*chin-li*) to protect the proper rights and interests of Chinese resident abroad',[16] but it soon became apparent that the CCP's words were not supported by concrete actions, and that by protection it did not mean exactly what seemed to be implied in the Common Programme. In the first two years, when the CCP's expectations of the Overseas Chinese appear to have been relatively high, the Party asserted a willingness to protect them far beyond its capacity to do so. It claimed that where the KMT had abandoned them to their fate as 'overseas orphans', they need no longer feel isolated or without succour; in their many trials the Overseas Chinese would find that the homeland was their mainstay (*k'ao-shan*, literally, 'reliable mountain'). In her first New Year broadcast Ho Hsiang-ning spoke passionately of the 'bright dawn' of New China, which allegedly heralded an immediate improvement in the status of Overseas Chinese in the eyes of the world.[17] This statement and others like it were made with a flourish which evoked an image of the governments of Southeast Asia retreating in the face of Chinese gunboats and ultimatums.[18] But the Chinese government had no gunboats, and its ultimatums, which usually went unheeded, were carefully worded so as not to commit the government to positive specific action.

It was not long, therefore, before continuing pressures on the Chinese in Southeast Asia created a serious credibility gap between China and those of its citizens abroad who looked to it for protection. There had been no appreciable improvement in the status of Overseas Chinese after 1949; restrictions and discrimintory measures continued in Thailand, the Philippines, and Indonesia; Chinese newspapers were censored or closed in a number of countries; and Chinese were being expelled from Malaya for supporting a cause in which they might have expected the full backing of the Chinese government. Small wonder that 'some people thought it strange that since China was now liberated the imperialists were more vicious towards Overseas Chinese rather than more benign'.[19] Chinese officials had some difficulty in explaining the credibility gap; the fact that the imperialists were incensed at the victory of communism in China and were venting their hatred by intensified persecution of China's citizens abroad was cold comfort to the unfortunate Overseas Chinese who expected a show of strength from the new Chinese government.[20]

The first change was forced, therefore, by an awareness of political realities in Southeast Asia and the CCP's own inability either to afford the kind of protection it promised, or to afford any really effective protection without influencing foreign relations. By January 1951, a short fifteen months after the CCP had claimed that the problems of Overseas Chinese were over and promised 'to make every effort' to protect them, Ho Hsiang-ning announced that the situation of the Overseas Chinese 'is certain to become increasingly difficult', and that Overseas Chinese should depend for their survival 'on the strength of their own efforts'.[21] Although protection of Overseas Chinese was still proclaimed as a basic principle of Overseas Chinese policy and a 'glorious task of the Chinese people',[22] from the beginning of 1951 self-reliance became the keynote of the policy for protection.[23] The government continued to register official protests, but for lack of diplomatic contact, these protests usually had to be lodged in the *Jen-min jih-pao* rather than with the governments concerned. Sometimes they might be supported by a telegram to the suffering compatriots.[24] Quite often they were not even issued by the Foreign Ministry or the OCAC, but came from returned Overseas Chinese, trade unions, the democratic parties, the Red Cross, or mass organisations.

In March 1951 the Chinese government made one gesture in support of its words, with an attempt to send an investigation team to Malaya.[25] It is debatable whether the CCP seriously believed that the British would comply with its request. It may have been simply an attempt to dramatise China's professed concern for the Overseas Chinese in a way which provided publicity without risk. The almost certain refusal would mean that the government would avoid having to conduct an investigation which could have had little effect on the Chinese in Malaya or influence on British policies. As an added precaution the telegram to Attlee was sent by an unofficial *ad hoc* committee. The Chinese government would thus have been able to take the credit for any achievement, but to avoid a situation which might have been construed as a diplomatic defeat or otherwise harmful to the image of the CCP.

The call to Overseas Chinese to protect themselves was, in fact, a matter of practical necessity. It is difficult to imagine what the Chinese government could have done at that stage to enforce its will on the ruling governments in Southeast Asia. Moreover, with the war in Korea, the potential threat from Taiwan, the active hostility of the United States and its policy of military encirclement, the CCP was sufficiently preoccupied with its own defence to want to avoid provoking serious disputes in Southeast Asia. Even so, the Party's verbal responses were still relatively muted for a nationalist-minded government which declared itself an unwavering member of the socialist camp, and whose nationals abroad were being ruthlessly persecuted by imperialism or its stooges.

The real point was not simply China's incapacity to protect the Chinese abroad; it was that expressed in the remark by Po Yi-po cited at the beginning of this chapter: 'the government will do anything which is of benefit to the Overseas Chinese but which is not detrimental to the government'.[26] This statement is not merely an indication of the CCP's attitude towards protection; it is an expression of the theme underlying all Overseas Chinese policies since 1949. The Party's failure to be more positive about protection was a reflection of the priority accorded to Overseas Chinese in the context of foreign policy. The Kuomintang, particularly since 1949, has considered Overseas Chinese so important that it has often been prepared to place their interests above those of foreign policy.[27] The CCP on the other hand, even at this early stage was not prepared to allow Overseas Chinese problems to dominate any aspect of state policy, nor was it prepared to commit itself too readily on issues of protection which were of no potential benefit to China.

One indication of the CCP's record on protection is that the official media could find very little to say about positive achievements in this field. The 'proper rights and interests' of the Overseas Chinese could be variously interpreted. The Party tended, therefore, to claim domestic Overseas Chinese policies as examples of the kind of protection allegedly envisaged in the Common Programme, and gave rather less attention to 'continual and powerful protests' in defence of the Chinese abroad.[28] Significantly, in later accounts of its record in protecting Overseas Chinese the CCP tended to ignore the first five years altogether. By the end of the decade the usual practice was for the Party to cite as the first of its achievements an incident involving the Chinese in Vietnam at the end of 1954.[29]

The attitudes which the Party formed in the first five years towards questions of nationality and protection were of vital importance in shaping the policies introduced after 1954. The Party had discovered that to claim the Overseas Chinese as nationals of the People's Republic of China involved an obligation which it was unable, and not necessarily willing, to fulfil. It had either to make promises to the Overseas Chinese and threats to the local authorities which it could not support; or, if it were capable, to take actions which could embroil it in some form of hostile confrontation with neighbouring countries. The most it had been able to achieve was to accept for resettlement political deportees. This in itself was a clear demonstration of failure, since the CCP had protested against deportations, and at first had even demanded that deportees from Malaya be permitted to return.[30] The obligation of protection, therefore, was one of the first and most burdensome liabilities involved in accepting responsibility for Overseas Chinese.

As a commentary on the experience of the first five years and a prelude to the policy that was to follow, the Party made a revealing alteration to the clause on protection of Overseas Chinese in the Common Programme when it was transferred to the 1954 Constitution. The wording of the new clause was identical with the original with the exception that the words 'shall make every effort' (*chin-li*) were omitted.[31] The Chinese government had not made every effort to protect the Overseas Chinese in the preceding five years, nor was it prepared to commit itself to do so in the future.

GREAT PATRIOTIC UNITY

The Communist government had accepted the Overseas Chinese as nationals of the People's Republic of China, apparently without distinction or exception. What did it expect of its overseas nationals in return? In the earliest statements on Overseas Chinese policy, the CCP introduced a phrase, 'great patriotic unity' (*ai-kuo ta t'uan-chieh*), which subsequently became a standard term in the vocabulary of Overseas Chinese affairs, embodied in slogans like 'Overseas Chinese should join together in great patriotic unity around China'. This phrase, strongly reminiscent of the Overseas Chinese policies of the Kuomintang, was derived from the concept of the united front, of which Overseas Chinese were a component, and the original meaning appears to have been quite literal; all Chinese abroad were an integral part of the united front in China, they were expected to unite together with Overseas Chinese from all classes, organisations, and walks of life, without regard to past political affiliations.[32] The Chinese government continued to use the term in this sense until 1954, and to a limited extent beyond then as a slogan.[33] In practical terms it was supposed to mean that all Overseas Chinese should give their allegiance to the new government and not to the Kuomintang, and support and publicise its domestic and foreign policies.

It is worth examining the evolution of this term because it persisted when the CCP was pursuing obviously contrary objectives, and it provides the clearest example of the distinction between policy and posture statements. The use of 'patriotic unity' in its literal meaning reached a high point in 1951. When the Party was most remote from the Overseas Chinese, as it was in the early years, it was most vociferous in calling on them to engage in 'patriotic' activity.[34] As its contacts increased and it became more aware of the problems associated with its overseas population its calls became less insistent and less specific. The most militant expression of the original conception of patriotic unity in Overseas Chinese affairs was a statement by Liao Ch'eng-chih in June 1951. Liao outlined the current tasks as follows:

To unite all patriotic Overseas Chinese compatriots, to educate them in patriotism, and (enlist their) support for the People's Republic of China; to expose the crimes of the Chiang Kai-shek bandits in betraying the country and harming the Overseas Chinese, and to smash all their rumours and slanders; to protect the proper rights and interests of the Overseas Chinese and to oppose all crimes of persecution against them; to expand Overseas Chinese educational and cultural work and develop their tradition of establishing schools and newspapers; to disseminate widely the great achievements of the homeland in political, economic, and cultural construction, and to propagate the thought of Mao Tse-tung, New Democracy, the Common Programme, and all policies and laws of the People's Government; to promote friendly relations between the Overseas Chinese and the people of the countries of residence, and further their cultural exchange, their unity and mutual assistance, for the mutual preservation of world peace.[35]

The tone of this report suggests that the Overseas Chinese policy of the CCP was just as imbued with militant Chinese nationalism as that of the KMT had been. Together with its communist overtones, and current beliefs in the non-communist world about China's relations with the Soviet Union, the monolithic communist bloc and China's 'expansionist' designs, it must have appeared to justify the worst apprehensions of ruling authorities in Southeast Asia. If the Overseas Chinese were to support the new Chinese government it meant supporting a communist regime; to publicise its policies and the thought of Mao Tse-tung was to publicise communism, revolution, guerilla warfare, and the overthrow of imperialist and colonialist rulers and their stooges; to support its foreign policy was to support the Soviet bloc against the 'free world' in which most of the Overseas Chinese lived.

Like contemporary pronouncements on foreign policy, however, this statement was militant in tone but not supported with positive action. To have pursued this policy with the militancy and vigour which Liao's report seemed to demand would have been to commit the Chinese government to policies in Southeast Asia which it was unwilling to support; Overseas Chinese policies would have dictated foreign policy. It seems, moreover, that already there was an element of conscious rhetoric in such statements, for it was at this time that the CCP was actually withdrawing its guarded support for the communists in Malaya. And according to a Cultural Revolution source, it was at this time also that Liao himself was actually attempting to curb chauvinist and communist activity among Overseas Chinese. The less offensive aspects of this policy, such as opposition to the Kuomintang and the promotion of Chinese education and culture, were pursued within the limits of the CCP's capacity to do so although these limits were fairly narrow. It was difficult to promote Chinese education when, for example, the government in Thailand was attempting to eradicate completely the separate education system for Chinese; or to support the Overseas Chinese press when communist newspapers were being suppressed in all but two countries in Southeast Asia.

Although there were signs, even in 1951, that the Party was having doubts about the usefulness of the Overseas Chinese, it is conceivable that there could have been a serious attempt to translate this policy into action if the objectives of foreign policy had demanded it. But by the time the CCP had disposed of its more urgent problems and turned its attention to Southeast Asia, its thinking on both Overseas Chinese and foreign policy had changed to an extent that it was unlikely that such an Overseas Chinese policy would have been considered appropriate even in the context of a militant and aggressive foreign policy. Patriotic unity in the sense described above ceased to be the dominant theme in Overseas Chinese affairs, although to satisfy its own nationalist instincts, for the benefit of chauvinists among the Overseas

Chinese and particularly for the benefit of the Kuomintang, the Party continued to use it as a slogan even when it was obviously in conflict with current policies.

At the same time as it was used in the political and united front context, patriotic unity was invested with a number of other meanings which had little to do with the policies outlined above. Increasingly, the term was identified with one or other of these meanings and not used in its original sense.

The first derived meaning concerned protection. The CCP's argument about self-protection was advanced one stage further with the proposal that Overseas Chinese would have more chance of defending themselves against discrimination and persecution if they were united, instead of fighting among themselves. Thus Ho Hsiang-ning in her second New Year broadcast announced: 'Our overseas compatriots must further strengthen their unity... (to) oppose the imperialists' crimes of persecution, and their only recourse is to depend for their survival on the strength of their own efforts.'[36] The suggestion that this was their 'only recourse' is an eloquent commentary on how much protection they could expect from the CCP, but in the following years Ho's statements on this question became even more explicit: 'Only through this kind of unity will (the Overseas Chinese) have the strength to protect their own rights, and only through their own strength will they be able to survive in the difficult and complicated situations in which they find themselves';[37] 'to preserve their right to exist and their proper rights and interests, they must unite even more closely';[38] 'If the Overseas Chinese wish to protect their own proper rights and interests, they must rely on their own unity and mutual assistance'.[39] By 1954 this message was included in the list of official May Day slogans; Overseas Chinese were called on 'to unite together, to foster a spirit of mutual assistance, to protect their own proper rights and interests, and to love China'.[40] Just before the Party began to redirect its Overseas Chinese policy in 1954 Lien Kuan, a member of the OCAC and the UFWD, wrote in the *Jen-min jih-pao* that 'the patriotic unity of Overseas Chinese is of great practical significance to the Overseas Chinese themselves';[41] patriotic unity had become a euphemism for self-protection, a slogan to indicate to the Overseas Chinese how they should look after themselves rather than how they should demonstrate political allegiance to the Communist government in the homeland.

A second meaning imparted to patriotic unity, closely related to self-protection, was opposition to the Kuomintang. To some extent protection was merely an obligation which for reasons of national prestige and propaganda the CCP felt obliged to appear to fulfil. Opposition to the Kuomintang was a question of national importance. As suggested above, the survival of the Kuomintang may have been partly responsible for the CCP's original reticence about nationality, and throughout this period it was virtually the only respect apart from remittances in which the Party actively sought to mobilise Overseas Chinese for its own ends. The existence of the Kuomintang is the key to some of the more militant aspects of the CCP's Overseas Chinese policy and some of its apparent contradictions.

It is essential, however, to distinguish the Party's motives in combating the influence of the KMT among the Chinese communities abroad. Its primary concern has been with the KMT's continuing existence in the island of Taiwan with the support of the United States, and not with Overseas Chinese pro-KMT sympathy in itself. There is in fact little evidence that the CCP 'considers it psychologically and politically important to obtain positive support from the Chinese abroad', or that 'the Communists appear to feel that Overseas Chinese support is symbolically necessary for the ratification of their succession to power in China'.[42] It is true that in the early 1950s the CCP sought to establish its legitimacy in the eyes of Overseas Chinese, but this was because it wanted to eliminate one of the props to the KMT's claim to legitimacy and also because it wanted to use the Overseas Chinese for purposes unrelated to the Kuomintang. If the KMT had been an ineffectual Third Force among expatriate Chinese intellectuals in Hong Kong or the United States, opposition to KMT influence among Overseas Chinese would not have been important. But the KMT has occupied a portion of Chinese territory, it has claimed to be the legitimate ruler of China, and it claims the allegiance of Overseas Chinese as evidence of its legitimacy. So long as the KMT has considered it 'psychologically and politically important' to obtain the support of the Overseas Chinese the CCP itself has felt compelled to take corresponding measures to combat the influence of the KMT. The CCP asserts not so much a claim to represent Overseas Chinese as the right to represent China.

In the post-1954 period, this situation posed a dilemma for the Chinese Communist Party. As with nationality, so with political and cultural attachments to China, the Party was prepared to encourage desinification so long as the Overseas Chinese transferred their attachments to the countries in which they lived and not to the Kuomintang. It was partly for this reason that, while urging Overseas Chinese to identify with the countries of residence, the Party continued the seemingly contradictory policy of urging those who were unwilling to do so to 'join together in patriotic unity'. In effect, what the Party was saying was that if they must continue to regard themselves as Chinese, they should look to Peking and not to the Chinese Nationalists in Taiwan.

In its earliest pronouncements on Overseas Chinese policy, the Party urged the 'patriotic'[43] or pro-Peking Chinese abroad to make every attempt to unite with KMT supporters who were prepared to see the error of their ways, while at the same time isolating and exposing 'die-hard' KMT elements. In her first New Year broadcast Ho Hsiang-ning called on the Overseas Chinese to welcome former KMT supporters to the 'patriotic democratic camp', and to wage resolute struggle against hard-core elements of the KMT.[44] One of the basic policies adopted at the First Enlarged Conference of the OCAC was 'to keep up the struggle against the traitorous Chiang Kai-shek bandits and their crimes against the Overseas Chinese'.[45] It does not appear that the CCP expected the Overseas Chinese to launch physical attacks on KMT supporters, since physical assaults might have been counterproductive in terms of undermining KMT support and dangerous in terms of China's relations with the region at that time.[46]

In practical terms the Party attempted to destroy KMT links with Overseas Chinese societies and organisations and establish its own direct links or rival societies. It attempted to counter the effects of the non-communist and pro-KMT press through pro-Peking newspapers. In Overseas Chinese schools, although the CCP's opportunities for direct control were severely limited, the Party attempted to undermine the opposition by following the KMT's own example of providing teaching materials.[47] While the CCP may have been lukewarm in its efforts to protect the Overseas Chinese against persecution, it was incensed when it considered that foreign governments were favouring the KMT and its supporters, and frequently expressed its wrath in public protests.[48] In Burma and Indonesia, it sought to persuade the local governments to prohibit KMT activity among Overseas Chinese, to outlaw the KMT itself, and to deport KMT agents. In its propaganda, the Party sought to discredit the KMT with accounts of its inefficiency, corruption, and extortion, and personal stories of Overseas Chinese in China and abroad who had lost their remittances, their homes, their livelihood, and their lives at the hands of ruthless KMT officials.[49] The Overseas Chinese policy of the KMT was compared in the most unfavourable light with that of the CCP, although here the Party was on shaky ground; despite its claim it had done no more, for example, than the KMT had done to protect the Overseas Chinese. In presenting its own policies the Party tended even in this period to emphasise nationalism rather than communism, to base its appeals on patriotism and cultural chauvinism. The CCP's victory was portrayed not so much as a victory for international communism as for China, and it was inconceivable that any truly patriotic Overseas Chinese could support the KMT, the stooge of imperialism which had failed the Overseas Chinese and the Chinese nation, when the CCP had brought freedom and independence and self-respect to the whole Chinese people.[50] Patriotic unity in this sense was not a question of being pro-communist or anti-communist, but of being for the Peking government, or at the very least against the KMT.

A third policy to which the term patriotic unity was applied was the call to Overseas Chinese to contribute to socialist construction in China through investment, purchase of government bonds, and contributions to public works in the home districts. In this respect also the Party had some difficulty in distinguishing its own policy from that of its predecessor; like the KMT, the CCP also was stretching out its hand for Overseas Chinese money. It is possibly partly for this reason that it did not solicit capital investment in this period as actively as it did in later years, concentrating instead on attempting to restore family remittances by publicising the security and stability of life in the home districts. When it did appeal for direct investment and donations, the Party argued that for fifty years it had been the ambition of Overseas Chinese that China should be strong, united, and prosperous. That ambition had almost been realised, but its full realisation would require contributions on their part. Hence, patriotic unity became a call 'to unite more closely around the Central People's Government and Chairman Mao, and strive for the greater prosperity of the homeland'.[51]

Perhaps the sloganeering involved in the use of this term underlines more than anything else the value of the domestic perspective. From the message seemingly communicated in statements of this kind, it might be possible to construct an interpretation of Overseas Chinese policy quite different from that presented in this study, but it would also be seriously at fault. For the domestic perspective, and also the formal statements themselves, indicate that when CCP spokesman called for patriotic unity among Overseas Chinese this could not be taken at face value.

OVERSEAS CHINESE POLICY AND FOREIGN POLICY

The CCP's expectations of Overseas Chinese within the context of patriotic unity were essentially internal, either to Overseas Chinese themselves or to the relationship between them and China. There remained a question of where they fitted into foreign policy. The nature of foreign policy before 1954 was such that Overseas Chinese were not an important consideration. But despite the lack of forward initiatives in both foreign and Overseas Chinese policy, the CCP did give some indications of its view of the proper relationship between the two and the appropriate behaviour for the Overseas Chinese themselves in relation to foreign policies of the Chinese government.

The Party's approach was essentially China-centred, in that Overseas Chinese were asked to be concerned with and support policies which usually had no direct bearing on China's relations with the countries in which they lived. For example the two major issues on which the CCP regularly called for support were Korea and Taiwan. The Chinese abroad were asked to explain and propagate China's policy on these two questions, and through the domestic Overseas Chinese the Party sought both moral and financial support for the Chinese armies in Korea, precedents for which can be found more than a decade earlier in the war against Japan.[52] Another example was the Japanese peace treaty. This was the occasion for the first full-scale mobilisation of domestic Overseas Chinese 'opinion' in the form of mass rallies, protests, and telegrams. At the same time the Party mounted an intensive campaign to persuade the Chinese abroad to oppose the peace treaty.[53]

Where ideological matters were concerned the Party was less demanding, and there is little in its public declarations to substantiate the argument that this was the only respect in which it demanded obedience and action from the Overseas Chinese. Patriotic unity did not mean that Overseas Chinese should be communists or 'act as the vanguard of international communism'.[54] The point about the united front was that it represented an alliance between communists and non-communists, and so long as Overseas Chinese were not pro-KMT or actively anti-communist the CCP did not appear to mind whether they were communists or not.

Although its primary appeal was to Chinese nationalism, the Party did address the Overseas Chinese in the language of communism and inter-nationalism, which inevitably raised questions about their role in China's foreign relations. They were urged to struggle against imperialism and colonialism, on the assumption that they would be sympathetic to the cause by virtue of their class background. The CCP asserted that all Overseas Chinese were originally poor peasants or handicraft workers who had fled from the exploitation of feudal and imperialist forces to scratch a living in Southeast Asia, and that their class composition had not altered significantly over the years. It was unthinkable, therefore, that they could support colonial or reactionary regimes unless their minds had been poisoned by the deceptions of the reactionary press and the rumours of the Kuomintang.[55] The Party did not state what kind of struggle it expected the Overseas Chinese to wage, whether it should include armed struggle, or whether the ruling governments in independent Burma and Indonesia should be regarded as tools of imperialism like the governments in Thailand and the Philippines, and, therefore, to be struggled against. If armed struggle was intended, the CCP was in no position to support it; and as the discussion below of the Party's response to the Malayan emergency suggests, armed struggle seems to have been precluded. In most cases, moreover, the call to struggle against imperialism and colonialism, like the call to patriotic unity, was accompanied by important qualifications. Either the Overseas Chinese struggle was to be 'in support of the struggle of the Chinese government', which meant support for its position on the issues of Korea, Taiwan, and the United States; or it was to be a struggle 'in defence of the proper rights and interests of the Overseas Chinese themselves'.[56] The 'proper rights and interests' were defined sometimes as the 'right to freedom of residence and occupation, and security of life and property',[57] and even as 'the right to express support for the People's Republic of China'.[58] But at no time did the CCP declare that the rights of Overseas Chinese included the right to wage revolutionary armed struggle, to overthrow imperialist or reactionary governments and establish communist or Overseas Chinese rule.

Underlying the CCP's approach to all these matters was an uncompromising principle, established at least as early as 1949 and probably earlier, that Overseas Chinese policy should be subordinate to foreign policy. This has remained the guiding principle in Overseas Chinese policy ever since, with only one possible exception, the period when elements of the so-called 'extreme left' usurped power in the Foreign Ministry in 1967. At no other time from 1949 to 1970 have Overseas Chinese policies been permitted to develop independently to a point where they might have forced developments in foreign policy. This did not mean necessarily that Overseas Chinese policy always had to serve foreign policy; it could also pursue its own objectives so long as these did not conflict with or obstruct the pursuit of foreign policy objectives.

This principle had a number of far-reaching effects in terms of the kind of relationship which evolved between the CCP and the Chinese abroad after 1954. These are discussed separately at the end of this chapter, but first it is proposed to examine in some detail one outstanding example of the order of priorities dictated by this principle, which occurred soon after the Party came to power. The new Chinese government claimed to be extremely indignant that the British government, while seeking to establish diplomatic relations with Peking, was 'ruthlessly persecuting' the Chinese in Malaya.[59] But this did not deter China from establishing relations with Britain; nor did China sever relations when the 'persecution' continued or when, for example, the British government refused to accept the Chinese investigation team in 1951. The Malayan communist insurgency contained many object lessons about the political role of Chinese in Southeast Asia and was certainly most influential in terms of subsequent CCP policy towards Overseas Chinese. China's policy towards the insurgency not only illustrates the primacy of foreign policy in practice; it also contained some of the earliest signs of the decolonisation policy which emerged in the mid-1950s.

THE COMMUNIST INSURGENCY IN MALAYA

The first five years of communist rule in China coincided with the most concerted effort to have occurred so far by Overseas Chinese communists in Southeast Asia to win power through armed struggle. The objectives of the Malayan Communist Party (MCP) seemed to echo the national policies proclaimed in Peking; its methods were similar to those which the Chinese Communist Party had used in its own successful struggle for power. But what was the attitude of the CCP towards a communist insurrection in a neighbouring country by a party composed almost entirely of Overseas Chinese who were regarded, presumably, as nationals of the People's

Republic of China? It was at first equivocal, and subsequently increasingly unenthusiastic, not about the objectives of the MCP, but about the particular circumstances in which those objectives were being pursued.

Since the Malayan insurgency was both communist and Overseas Chinese, many observers concluded that the movement was created and controlled by the Chinese Communist Party. There was a widespread belief that the Party was determined to carry the revolution into Southeast Asia through the medium of Overseas Chinese, a belief which gained popular currency through the indiscriminate application of the terms 'Chinese Communist' and 'Communist Chinese' to both the Chinese Communist Party and Overseas Chinese communists, suggesting a complete identity between the two.[60] The Malayan insurgency appeared to be a clear manifestation of the 'export' of the Chinese revolution, a conclusion apparently so obvious that it often went unquestioned and did not seem to require evidence to support it. This interpretation was, however, open to question on at least three counts.

In the first place, it was not apparent then, nor has it been established since, that the CCP provided anything more than moral and propaganda support for the Malayan communists or that the MCP was controlled and directed by Peking. Although the MCP had its beginnings in the late 1920s, its development to a point where it was capable of mounting a full-scale armed insurrection was the direct product of the Japanese occupation, a time when the Chinese Communist Party was battling for its own survival against the Japanese invasion forces and the armies of the Kuomintang. The Party was quite unable to provide material assistance, and such external support as the Malayan guerillas did receive came from the British.

In the first two decades of its existence the MCP had acted mainly under instructions from the Comintern, although it did maintain links with the Chinese Communist Party.[61] The international communist movement, however, was Moscow's preserve; and the CCP has not attempted, either then or after 1949, to establish its own International with the kind of organisational authority and control which Moscow had sought to exercise over fraternal parties.[62] After the Japanese occupation of Malaya, the MCP leadership, like revolutionary nationalists in other parts of Asia, was able to see in the anti-Japanese struggle an opportunity for winning power and independence. It did not need the CCP to tell it so, even though it may have accepted the CCP's advice on other matters and followed its example in the use of guerilla warfare and the united front.

When the MCP began its armed struggle against the British in June 1948, therefore, it had as much claim to independence from the CCP as the CCP itself did from Moscow. In twenty years it had accumulated its own experience in political and industrial agitation, sabotage, and guerilla warfare, although its leadership was weak and it depended on Moscow for ideological inspiration. The claim that the Malayan insurgency and similar movements throughout Asia in 1948 were launched on instructions issued at the Calcutta Youth Conference in February 1948 has been shown to be open to question; but even if it were true, the Conference was not sponsored by the CCP and the line presented by the sponsors was evidently non-Maoist.[63] Although in 1949 Liu Shao-ch'i was to proclaim the Chinese revolution as a model for the rest of Asia, neither then nor in mid-1948 was the CCP itself in a position to 'export' its revolution; and even if it had been, the Chinese leaders had learnt from their own experience with Moscow that external direction of revolution was potentially disastrous.[64]

By the time the CCP had established itself in control of China the Malayan emergency was already well under way, and the Party had to decide whether it should support a communist revolution by Overseas Chinese. There is no doubt that the Party approved of the objectives of the MCP, and although it was unable to provide material support it was prepared to help with literature and propaganda. But that is as far as it was prepared to go. The question of Chinese Communist Party cadres being sent to Malaya appears to be more supposition than fact; curiously there do not appear to have been any such cadres apprehended in Malaya. While it appears that the MCP took advice and inspiration from the Chinese Communist Party,[65] such contact as did exist between the two parties has never been established as a relationship between a superior CCP controlling a subordinate MCP.[66] According to Victor Purcell, the CCP 'confined itself to verbal encouragement',[67] and this is certainly borne out by the Party's position on the Chinese in Malaya.

The second count on which the theory about China and the MCP was open to question was that it never took account of what the CCP itself had to say, and this makes interesting reading. Whatever else may have prevented the CCP from giving greater support to the MCP, it was obviously inhibited by Overseas Chinese domination of the Malayan Party and its increasing isolation from the other races in Malaya. There had been several attempts by the MCP to widen its membership to include Malays and Indians, but these had never been successful and the party which took to the jungles in 1948 was virtually an Overseas Chinese party. The Chinese government made it clear that it did not consider this an ideal situation. It did not then admit, nor has it admitted since, that the MCP was an Overseas Chinese party; and such public support as it did give to the communists' struggle was always addressed to the 'Malayan peoples'. This posed a contradiction, which would have been more acute had China been pursuing an active, forward foreign policy in the area. Ideologically, it was committed to supporting a just struggle of all the Malayan peoples, in which it would have been logical to encourage Overseas Chinese to join. But to do so could only increase the preponderance of Overseas Chinese in the MCP and contribute to its growing isolation.

The CCP's first response left the contradiction unresolved. If it did, in fact, adopt the line dictated by ideology and the strategy of 'lean to one side', it was expressed in a most indirect manner. The Party did not call directly on all Chinese in Malaya to take up arms with the guerillas in the jungles, but it did proclaim a policy which might have been construed as such.[68] For example, in one statement in 1950 Ho Hsiang-ning said: 'I call on the Overseas Chinese in Malaya to unite together and continue the struggle for their proper rights and interests.'[69] The call 'to continue' the struggle appears to refer to the only real struggle then in progress, that of the MCP.

But the CCP never committed itself beyond this point, with the result that its statements were always ambiguous. As similar calls addressed to Chinese in other countries illustrate, there were other forms of struggle which were neither armed nor communist, and the CCP's statements on Malaya could be interpreted in this way. On this particular occasion Ho actually went on to define the rights for which the struggle should be continued in terms which had nothing to do with the communist insurrection; these were 'the right of our compatriots to express support for the People's Republic of China and the state policy promulgated by the Central People's Government of support for world peace and democracy; and the right to oppose US imperialist aggression in Taiwan and Korea'. To the Chinese in Malaya, therefore, it was never clear whether the Chinese government intended them to join the communist struggle, or even whether the Chinese government itself would come to the support of the MCP.[70]

The CCP may have been ambiguous about its own position on the Malayan struggle, but it still asserted that the Chinese in Malaya were quite within their rights to take political action. It pointed out that Chinese formed some 45 per cent, or 'almost half' of the population, and that they had lived in Malaya for generations.[71] The economy of Malaya, it was argued, had been built on the 'blood and sweat' of the Overseas Chinese, and the country's prosperity was based on Overseas Chinese development of rubber and tin. In the war against Japan they had proved themselves by fighting the Japanese after the British had fled.[72] The implication was that the Chinese in Malaya had as much right as any ethnic group to be politically involved; and the further unstated implication was that if conditions were ripe for revolution, the Malayan Chinese, together with the 'Malayan peoples', were within their rights to take revolutionary action if they so wished. In one editorial comment the *Jen-min jih-pao*, demanding that deportees be permitted to return, urged the Chinese in Malaya to struggle for what it termed their 'legal' rights,[73] and at a Peking rally in December 1950 it was asserted that 'the Overseas Chinese have the same inviolable rights to live in Malaya as do the local people'.[74] If the Chinese in Malaya had the same inviolable 'legal' rights as the 'local people', they could not be nationals of the People's Republic of China. To some extent, this may have been an attempt by the CCP to dissociate itself from the Malayan communists. But it is interesting also for what it reveals about the Party's underlying view of Chinese nationality, and perhaps explains why the Communist government refused at this stage to commit itself to more precise definitions.

The involved and defensive arguments about an anti-imperialist struggle which should not have required defensive justification suggest a measure of uncertainty and uneasiness about the whole situation. The trouble was that while Overseas Chinese revolution was certainly not a proclaimed policy of the Chinese government, in Malaya the existing revolutionary situation cast a different interpretation on Peking's propagation of general formulae to the Overseas Chinese masses. Nowhere else did the CCP face Overseas Chinese leading an armed communist insurrection, and nowhere else could its calls on Overseas Chinese to struggle in their own defence be construed as an incitement to revolution.

From the beginning of 1951 the CCP became steadily less equivocal in its attitude toward the Chinese in the Malayan insurgency. It was in January 1951 that Ho Hsiang-ning officially endorsed the policy that Overseas Chinese should protect themselves. Although she did not refer specifically to Malaya in this context, Malaya was the one country in the region where Overseas Chinese were clearly, in the CCP's terms, subject to imperialist persecution, and the Party's continuing emphasis on self-protection would appear to have been aimed above all specifically at the Chinese in Malaya. Ho's statement served as a warning, particularly to those who may have been waiting to see how far China would back the MCP, that the homeland was not going to come to the rescue of Overseas Chinese communists in Malaya, or elsewhere. In the last months of 1950 and in early 1951, Chinese statements also betrayed increasing concern for those it termed 'innocent' Overseas Chinese.[75] The innocent were often simply the alleged communists or sympathisers deported by the British. But increasingly, as British efforts to quarantine the guerillas became more effective, genuinely innocent people began to suffer, either from communist terrorism, or simply through disruption to their lives, loss of property, resettlement, or internment. The MCP was losing, rather than gaining, support among the Malayan Chinese.

China's attempt to send an investigation team to Malaya served to underline the emerging direction of policy. In a telegram to the British Prime Minister, a 'Committee for the Relief of Refugee Overseas Chinese in Malaya' announced its intention to send a seventeen-member investigation team to Malaya and asked that members be given the right to carry out 'relief and welfare work'.[76] The indirect and unofficial manner in which this move was made was in itself indicative of a certain reserve on the part of the Chinese government. In April 1951, after the British refusal had been announced in the House of Commons and the Committee's telegram still remained unanswered, the Chairman of the Committee, Hsiung Chin-ting, gave an interview to an NCNA reporter. Hsiung reviewed the situation in Malaya without once referring to the insurgency or the Malayan Communist Party, and outlined the measures taken by the Chinese government to resettle the 'refugees'. He concluded by saying that the Chinese government's action had drawn widespread publicity and approval from the Overseas Chinese.[77] This was almost certainly all it was intended to do, and having made this gesture, the Chinese government began to retreat from its original position. It spoke less and less of the struggle of the Chinese in Malaya and Chinese government protection of their rights and interests, and more about the government's 'care and consideration' for deportees when they arrived in China.[78] Its protests to the British government became less insistent, and it no longer demanded, for example, that deportees be allowed to return to Malaya.

According to the 'revolutionary' critics of the OCAC in 1967, at about this time Liao Ch'eng-chih ordered Chinese in one unidentified country to withdraw from the local revolutionary movement and return to China. If the allegation is true it probably refers to Malaya, since large numbers of Chinese left Malaya at this time and the Chinese government established special committees and made other provisions to receive and resettle them. The charge that Liao actually ordered them to withdraw may be open to question, but as the revolutionary rebels' argument suggested, if the CCP had intended to mobilise the Overseas Chinese to 'stick to their posts' and carry out revolutionary struggle, it would not have so compliantly accepted the revolutionary activists deported by the British or encouraged large numbers of Chinese to return voluntarily to live in China.

The CCP had never openly supported the MCP or urged the Chinese in Malaya to join the insurgency. By 1951 it was already apparent that the Party was no longer prepared even to suggest by implication and ambiguity that it approved of Overseas Chinese taking up arms against the British.[79] The first signs of change in the CCP's attitude, moreover, preceded by almost a year the MCP's directive of October 1951, calling for an end to violent tactics against the masses and the establishment of a broad united front.[80] Even allowing for problems in communication this suggests that, while the MCP may have been influenced by the CCP, the Chinese party was not exercising direct control of the Malayan movement. The fact that the MCP had used indiscriminate and self-defeating terrorism in the first place was in direct conflict with the CCP's own principles for waging guerilla warfare. And the MCP's periodic attempts both then and throughout the 1950s to win support by appeals to the Chineseness or cultural chauvinism of the Chinese population ran counter to the Overseas Chinese policies of Peking, and were hardly the tactics of a CCP-controlled organisation.

The CCP's approach to the MCP insurgency was dictated by a number of considerations, not the least of which was the vulnerability of the new government and a desire not to provoke open confrontation with the rulers in Southeast Asia. The Party already had one war on its hands in Korea. It may be also that the CCP was sensitive to the fact that the British who controlled Malaya also controlled Hong Kong, strategically close and economically useful to China.

There were, however, more specific reasons for the verbal withdrawal in 1951. In the first place, the policy of support for Overseas Chinese struggle against imperialism and colonialism does not appear to have been intended to involve the Chinese government in support for revolutions led and dominated by Overseas Chinese. In its initial response to the situation in Malaya the CCP had allowed itself to imply greater support than it apparently intended, to the extent that in the view of many observers Peking was clearly the mastermind behind the MCP. The retreat from this position was probably influenced by the fact that China was accused of engineering the insurgency, which had earned considerable hostility for the CCP and could have led to the kind of tension between China and Southeast Asia which the Party was anxious to avoid. There was also, of course, the fact that the MCP was losing, although the Party's doubts were already evident well before it was apparent that the MCP had little chance of success.

The third aspect of the emergency which makes nonsense of the Fifth Column argument is not so much the MCP's failure as the reasons for its failure. Not only had the MCP failed to win support from the non-Chinese population; the insurgency was contributing to a communal polarisation dangerous both for the Malayan Chinese and for the ultimate cause of revolution in Malaya. If this were not enough, not even a majority of the Chinese in Malaya supported the communists, a situation harmful to basic CCP policies of attracting foreign exchange and opposing the Kuomintang.[81] The communists were becoming increasingly alienated from the rest of the community, and were succeeding only in creating racial antagonism and bloodshed.

If the Malayan emergency demonstrated anything about China's 'subversive Fifth Column', it should have served to refute rather than reinforce the argument that Overseas Chinese were an ideal instrument for China-based communist revolution. Many observers failed to see the very obvious fact that the outcome in Malaya was not only a victory for the British but a defeat for the MCP and a clear illustration of the limitations of the 'Overseas Chinese Fifth Column'. The Chinese government, however, did not fail to understand this lesson. The deep-rooted suspicion and resentment in Southeast Asia of the Overseas Chinese and their relationship with China was in itself a barrier to the success of Overseas Chinese revolutionary movements. The prospects for success were perhaps better in Malaya than in any other country in the region, but the revolution could succeed only with popular

4

support from all racial groups and genuine representation of all groups in the party leadership. Prospects for achieving such a unified movement had been damaged, possibly irreparably, by the efforts of the MCP. If this was the case in Malaya, then in other countries where they were a much smaller minority, Overseas Chinese acting as a communal revolutionary group could cause considerable political upheaval, but there was the almost inevitable prospect that, as in Malaya, their efforts would only engender or exacerbate hostility towards the revolution, towards Overseas Chinese in general, and by association, towards China itself. If the CCP had wanted to use the Overseas Chinese as a revolutionary force, the best it could have hoped for would have been for them to participate as individuals in broadly based local movements; but the same dangers were inherent even in this kind of situation. In Indonesia and the Philippines, for example, 'there were inevitable frictions, with the seeming result that in (the) two parties...Chinese elements were actively curbed by the indigenes'.[82] Since 1965, the Indonesian case has demonstrated even more convincingly the problems of real or alleged Overseas Chinese participation in indigenous communist movements.

Where the Chinese government had found protection to be a major liability in the possession of an overseas population, the Malayan insurgency had shown one of the potential assets, political exploitation in the service of communism, to be of doubtful value. If a locally generated Overseas Chinese communist movement could be a liability to the development of China's relations with Southeast Asia and to the cause of revolution, there was no reason to suppose that a Peking-directed movement would fare any better.

THE FOUNDATIONS OF POST-1954 POLICY:
ONE POLICY OR MANY?

In the period before 1954 Overseas Chinese policy had been largely negative, and in its positive aspects almost entirely China-centred. But perhaps the most far-reaching development in this period concerned the relationship between Overseas Chinese and foreign policy.

The principle that Overseas Chinese policy should serve foreign policy raises a question of whether it is possible to speak of 'an Overseas Chinese policy', or whether, as some writers have claimed, there was a series of Overseas Chinese policies which varied according to the requirements of foreign policy towards each country in the Southeast Asian region.[83] How much room was there for flexibility where the Party had different foreign policies towards each country in Southeast Asia? The CCP's conclusion, in some ways its most significant, was that the possibilities for varying Overseas Chinese policy between one country and another were extremely limited.

An argument which has been advanced for three quarters of a century by non-Chinese Southeast Asians and interested Europeans and North Americans is that the Overseas Chinese can be used easily by the Chinese government to serve the interests of its policies towards any country at any time. What is meant by this argument in reference to post-1949 China is that its policies for Overseas Chinese differ significantly between, for example, fraternal communist North Vietnam and anti-Communist Thailand. What it also tends to mean is that change in Overseas Chinese political behaviour depends very much on the policies of the Chinese government, that throughout Southeast Asia the Overseas Chinese have attitudes and characteristics in common which enable the Chinese government to manipulate and exploit them at will.

Leaving aside the erroneous proposition that it is the Chinese government which is mainly responsible for change in Overseas Chinese political behaviour, the implication of this argument is that the problems of Overseas Chinese are regional or universal, essentially the same in each country. This is seen in the tendency to indiscriminate generalisation about the character and behaviour of 'the Overseas Chinese', on anything from their supposed capacity for making money to their alleged potential as fifth columnists for China. This kind of thinking underlies the attitudes of those Southeast Asians who see the experiences with Overseas Chinese of their neighbours as capable of exact reproduction in their own countries. But it is also a fundamental assumption in the policies of the Kuomintang. The formal adoption of the principle of *jus sanguinis* was in itself an assertion of a universal approach which assumed an unbreakable common bond between all Chinese at home and abroad.

What has not been fully appreciated is that the CCP also came to adopt a similar position, which required that it should have one set of policies for Overseas Chinese in all countries. Already in the period before 1954 it was apparent that Overseas Chinese policy did not differentiate between the Chinese in different countries,[84] a tendency which was to become more pronounced after 1954. The CCP arrived at this view by a line of reasoning quite different from that of the KMT, and the resulting policies were also very different. Where the KMT had taken a colonial position on the Overseas Chinese and attempted to maintain it even where it might jeopardise harmonious foreign relations, the CCP set out to make Overseas Chinese policy serve foreign policy, but found it either inexpedient or extraordinarily difficult to make the necessary adjustments simply to serve the often passing interests of foreign policy.

There appear to have been a number of problems which persuaded the CCP to this view. First, there was the 'objective situation' of the Chinese in Southeast Asia, the position they had come to occupy after almost a century of large-scale migration, and the ingrained attitudes towards them of the local peoples. Problems of dual nationality and protection were common to all countries in the region, and on both counts Overseas Chinese were a potential liability. Anti-Chinese feeling has been most obvious where ethnic, religious, and cultural differences have been sharpest. But the history of the last twenty years is littered with the legislative or coercive measures of Thai, Vietnamese, and even Burmese authorities, which have sought through pressures on Chinese commerce, education, and society generally to break up the Chinese communities and curb their economic and political influence. The CCP ran up against this problem everywhere in Southeast Asia, and while it did not mean that flexible policies could not be attempted, it undoubtedly limited the extent to which Overseas Chinese could be used successfully and suggested that overall they might be a negative factor in foreign policy.

To this problem was added a further one of the changing attitudes of the Overseas Chinese themselves. Any attempt to manipulate Overseas Chinese in one country for purposes of Chinese foreign policy depended for its success on a combination of control from China and willingness to serve on the part of Overseas Chinese. While it is true that there have been many who would respond readily to direction from Peking, in general the Overseas Chinese have been an increasingly non-compliant constituency in the period since 1949. This tendency has also been universal, including in those countries which have had close and friendly relations with China.

If these two problems seemed to suggest that Overseas Chinese should be treated as a general problem, so also did the Party's own experience of Overseas Chinese as a factor in foreign policy and its observation of their effectiveness as a political force in Southeast Asia. In commercial terms, the Overseas Chinese were an undoubted asset, but in political relations with Southeast Asia they were on most counts a liability. As a communist party, the CCP could not have failed to have been interested in the potential of the Overseas Chinese for promoting revolution; as a realistic government it could not have failed to draw lessons from the debacle of the Malayan insurgency. Moreover, from the various incidents about which the CCP had protested in the preceding five years, it must have been aware that there were in many countries underlying hostilities towards the Chinese which had nothing to do with communism, and that the Overseas Chinese could easily become a contentious issue in foreign relations without any initiative on the part of the Chinese government or of the Overseas Chinese themselves. It is not surprising, therefore, that Liao Ch'eng-chih, according to a Cultural Revolution source, instructed that 'Overseas Chinese shall not make revolution. They will not succeed even if they make revolution.'

If the potential of Overseas Chinese was so severely circumscribed there was little that could be done to make Overseas Chinese serve a variety of foreign policies. By the end of 1956 it was clearly apparent that the CCP was attempting to implement an Overseas Chinese policy which, while subordinate to foreign policy, was intended to have universal application.[85]

This in itself is an indication of the Party's attitude towards the Overseas Chinese. If it had believed that they could be exploited successfully as an instrument of Chinese policy it would have been essential to distinguish between, for example, policy towards the Chinese in Burma and policy towards the Chinese in the Philippines. But a universal policy for Overseas Chinese could not contradict the principle of serving foreign policy only so long as it did not conflict with China's foreign policy towards any one country, or exceed the lowest point on the scale of the CCP's revolutionary actions or ambitions. This is indicative of a far more negative attitude towards the Overseas Chinese than has sometimes been claimed.

6

Self-determination, nationality, and peaceful coexistence: 1954–1956

China has approximately 12 million nationals resident abroad. They have lived together in friendship for many years with the people of the countries of residence, and they have made positive contributions to the development and prosperity of the local economies. For the most part they do not participate in political activities in the countries of residence. For the last few years, the position of the Overseas Chinese in those countries which are unfriendly to China has been extremely difficult. We hope that these countries will be able to refrain from discriminating against our nationals and respect their proper rights and interests. For our part, we are willing to urge the Overseas Chinese to respect the laws of the local governments and local social customs. It is worth pointing out that in the past, reactionary Chinese governments never made any attempt to solve the problem of Overseas Chinese nationality. This not only placed the Overseas Chinese in a difficult position, but was often the cause of discord between China and the countries of residence. In order to improve this situation, we are prepared to solve this problem, beginning with those Southeast Asian countries with which we have diplomatic relations.

> Chou En-lai, Report to the First Session
> of the First National People's Congress,
> 23 September 1954.[1]

Work concerning the Overseas Chinese must be
subordinate to foreign policy.

> Chuang Hsi-ch'üan, Vice-Chairman of the
> OCAC, Report to the inaugural meeting
> of the All-China Returned Overseas Chinese
> Association.[2]

One effect of the CCP's decision to subordinate Overseas Chinese affairs to foreign policy was that it led the Party to look at Overseas Chinese strictly in terms of their usefulness to China, and to give scant attention to considerations of traditional or nationalist sentimentality, so important in the thinking of the KMT. This was necessary for the Party's purpose, but it was also of critical importance in that it opened up new options in Overseas Chinese policy, which to the KMT would have been unthinkable.

In particular, the Party was forced to reflect seriously on the colonial aspect of China's relationship with the Chinese abroad. The adoption of flexible foreign policies in Southeast Asia meant that in certain situations the CCP had to modify China's traditional role in relation to Overseas Chinese. This necessarily raised a question of what was essential to this role if the relationship was to be preserved; and the essence had unmistakable colonial overtones. First, it meant an assertion of possession over and a claim to the allegiance of communities of people, not territory; communities in which the number of local-born and long-term residents was increasingly preponderant, in countries whose right to independence the CCP recognised and championed. Secondly, it required that the CCP attempt to maintain an active presence among the Overseas Chinese, to foster Chinese education and cultural traditions, and to prevent what the KMT had called the crisis of national identity or the transformation of Overseas Chinese by local and foreign influences (*t'u-hua, yang-hua*). The CCP itself at no time publicly admitted that its own policies had such colonial implications, but it was aware that such charges were made, and in the colonial model it found an answer to the Overseas Chinese problem and a possible means of opting out of its inheritance: a programme which corresponded roughly to a long-term plan for self-determination and decolonisation.

The CCP's decision on this matter was probably taken very early, but the available evidence only suggests a decision taken as late as between September 1953 and April 1955. Nor it is clear that the Party even at this stage had in mind the kind of full-scale decolonisation attempted from 1957 onwards. The first measures were more in the nature of a concession to the principle of self-determination.

The official turning point was signalled by Chou En-lai's statement at the First National People's Congress in September 1954. This was also the first formal acknowledgment of the existence of an 'Overseas Chinese problem'. The foundation of this new policy had been laid in the five years since 1949, but it was also a direct product of the policy of peaceful coexistence. As the Ch'ing government had discovered, Overseas Chinese were not really a problem to China until relations began to develop with the countries in which they lived, and when the Chinese Communist Party set out to play a more dynamic role in international affairs it was forced to consider this problem in its relations with Southeast Asia. How could they be used to advantage, and to what extent did they present an obstacle to the development of relations with the countries of residence? For the first time, the Party attempted to assess the dimensions of the Overseas Chinese problem, to weigh the advantages and disadvantages in terms of its own self-interest and its foreign and domestic policies, and to translate its conclusions into policy action.[3]

In the CCP's perception of the problem in this period there was a discernible conflict between two considerations; its evaluation of the usefulness of the Overseas Chinese, and the requirements of peaceful coexistence.

PEACEFUL COEXISTENCE AND DUAL NATIONALITY

In 1954, the Party may have had misgivings about the value of the Chinese abroad, but there were still potential assets which might be exploited to advantage. From the point of view of foreign policy, however, there was the fact that Overseas Chinese in many parts of Southeast Asia were resented, either for economic and social reasons, or, in the eyes of Asian nationalists, because they appeared as an alien minority which considered itself culturally superior, which did not regard the countries of residence as a permanent home, and which owed allegiance to China and was potentially subversive.[4] To those who feared China, the Overseas Chinese were the visible manifestation of Chinese 'colonialism'. To those who feared communism, they were the vanguard of communist infiltration, subversion, and revolution. To those who feared or resented the Overseas Chinese, the 'Jews of the East' as the Thai king, Rama VI, is alleged to have called them, China, Nationalist or Communist, was an object of suspicion and hostility. A combination of China, communism, and the Overseas Chinese seemed to present a formidable threat to the stability and security of Southeast Asia.

This problem had been raised with the Chinese government by a number of Asian leaders, notably by Nehru in talks with Chou En-lai in New Delhi in June 1954.[5] The content of Nehru's argument was not reported at the time, but in September he summarised his views in a speech to the Lok Sabha:

One of the reasons why...the countries of South-East Asia fear this great country China, has been the large Chinese populations in these countries...This fact rather frightens them. In the old days and until now the Government of China did not recognise the right of any person to divest himself of Chinese nationality. A very peculiar situation was created as a result. On occasions there was some kind of dual nationality. That was also a factor in making the position of the Chinese communities in all these South-East Asian countries very embarrassing to those countries.

Nehru also pointed out that the international aspect of communist parties could mean that 'other countries might well utilise such a party for their own advantage. That is the fear that Burma and Thailand and other South-East Asian countries have.' Referring to Chou's NPC speech, he said that he hoped that this would help to remove some of the difficulties and apprehensions in Southeast Asia.[6] When Nehru visited Peking in October 1954, he raised the question of the Overseas Chinese once more, this time at the behest of the Indonesian Prime Minister.[7]

If the Chinese government was genuinely interested in improving relations with Southeast Asia, it was necessary to try to dispel the belief that it was exploiting the Overseas Chinese for political purposes antagonistic to the countries of residence, to neutralise hostility towards Overseas Chinese by encouraging them to be sensitive to the causes of such hostility, and if possible, to turn them to positive advantage. For the next two years, therefore, the CCP's efforts were directed towards this end, in a way which inevitably involved a degree of recognition of the Overseas Chinese right to self-determination. But the Party was not prepared to go further because it still believed there were positive advantages in the relationship.

The Party's first solution to its Overseas Chinese problem was to attempt to eliminate dual nationality; to make a clear division between those who were Chinese nationals and those who were not, to direct the former to behave as the Chinese government instructed them to, and to relinquish responsibility for the protection, and the behaviour, of the latter. This policy, which Chou En-lai is said to have outlined to Nehru in the discussions in 1954[8] and which he announced at the NPC in September, formed the basis of the CCP's approach to the Overseas Chinese for the next two years.[9] Ideally, the Chinese government would conclude formal agreements with all countries of Overseas Chinese residence, as a result of which only those who felt bound by allegiance to China or who for other reasons wanted Chinese nationality, and those whose status was not in dispute, would remain nationals of the People's Republic of China.

Potentially, there were considerable advantages to Peking in such an arrangement. In terms of peaceful coexistence, it could help to remove sources of friction in bilateral relations. It might contribute also to a general improvement in China's image in Southeast Asia, in that China was apparently quite prepared for Overseas Chinese to become nationals of the countries of residence and, therefore, subject to local and not Chinese jurisdiction. A further advantage in terms of foreign policy was that the proposal was an inducement to those governments which were suspicious of China's relations with the Overseas Chinese to establish direct relations with Peking.[10] Moreover, if formal treaties could be arranged there was no question of surrendering to the KMT the claim to represent the Overseas Chinese. And since former Chinese nationals would be entitled in theory to the same rights in their adopted countries as the local people, the CCP would be able to claim that it had done all that was necessary to satisfy national prestige.

The other aspect of the policy, the promise to ensure that Chinese nationals would not interfere in local politics, served a twofold purpose. First, it served to notify the Chinese abroad that what was involved was not a simple legality. Those who renounced Chinese nationality were on their own; those who retained it would be subject to the jurisdiction of Peking. Secondly, it was intended to reassure the countries of residence that China was not exploiting Overseas Chinese for political purposes. Even before negotiations commenced with Indonesia on the problem of dual nationality, the Chinese government launched a propaganda campaign to remove the stigma of 'subversive' from the Chinese abroad, claiming that they had always respected local laws and customs, that they had made invaluable contributions to the local economies, that they had never interfered in local political quarrels or the internal affairs of the countries of residence, and even that they were unwilling to do so.[11] In October 1954 the *Jen-min jih-pao* published a new official version of Liao Ch'eng-chih's report to the First Enlarged Conference of the OCAC in June 1951, omitting all reference to Liao's call for propagation of state laws and policies, dissemination of the thought of Mao Tse-tung, and 'education in patriotism' for the Chinese abroad.[12] The Party began also to attempt to turn the Overseas Chinese to positive advantage as propagandists for peaceful coexistence. Where before they had been asked simply to publicise policies usually unrelated to Southeast Asia, they were now to be instruments of foreign policy, to play a direct role in the promotion of relations between China and the countries in which they lived.[13]

The most important aspect of this move was that the CCP was prepared formally to abandon the principle of *jus sanguinis*, which had guided the policies of its predecessors since 1909, and the Party was clearly aware that it carried implications beyond the solution of the immediate problem of dual nationality or the improvement of relations with Southeast Asia. The decision was not only a concession to Southeast Asian governments. It also constituted recognition of a trend to weakening of the Overseas Chinese attachment to China and to identification with the countries of residence, a trend which Ho Hsiang-ning had acknowledged as early as January 1950.[14] Many Overseas Chinese already regarded themselves as nationals of the countries of residence, and not all those who elected to take local nationality did so because they felt this would offer them an opportunity to obtain protection and local citizenship rights while still maintaining allegiance to China. The Chinese government had been faced with the problem of deciding whether the benefits of the relationship were worth attempting to resist the trend by encouraging or bringing pressure to bear on dual nationals to opt for Chinese nationality. To support such a policy, it would have been necessary to take corresponding measures to foster political and cultural attachments to China. Such a course of action, however, would have highlighted the colonial aspect of the relationship and risked undermining the government's objective of improving relations with Southeast Asia. But in choosing not to resist the trend, it accepted that there would be a gradual dwindling in its overseas population.

The CCP did not at this stage indicate how many of the Overseas Chinese it considered to have dual nationality. Six years later it was stated officially that only 40 per cent of all Overseas Chinese, a little over five million, were 'pure' Chinese nationals; the remainder were either dual nationals or had acquired local nationality.[15] It is impossible to estimate from this figure what the Party's assessment might have been in 1954. There had been no significant increase in the number of 'pure' Chinese nationals in the intervening years, but there had been developments in Southeast Asia which would have increased the number of dual nationals.[16] It is possible that in 1954 the Chinese government had no clear idea of how many Overseas Chinese were dual nationals, but it must have expected that anything up to 50 per cent would be affected by its proposals to eliminate dual nationality.

THE SINO-INDONESIAN TREATY ON DUAL NATIONALITY

The Chinese government moved quickly to demonstrate the seriousness of its intentions, in discussions with the only two non-communist Southeast Asian governments with which it had diplomatic relations, Indonesia and Burma. Substantive negotiations were commenced with Indonesia in November 1954,[17] and when the Burmese Premier, U Nu, visited China in December, it was agreed that the two governments would hold consultations on nationality at the earliest possible opportunity.[18] On his return from China, however, U Nu stated that a decision on nationality would have to await the negotiations taking place between China and Indonesia.[19] The outcome of the Sino-Indonesian negotiations left much to be desired, which may explain why China was unable to conlude a similar treaty with Burma. Perhaps it was for this reason that Chou En-lai chose a visit to Burma at the end of 1956 as the occasion to announce details of a new policy, in which nationality treaties were of secondary importance.

The Sino-Indonesian negotiations culminated in the signing of the Dual Nationality Treaty in April 1955,[20] the only formal agreement China was able to conclude. The instruments of ratification were not exchanged until January 1960, after an acrimonious dispute between the two governments arising out of the Indonesian ban on alien retail traders; and implementation did not commence until a supplementary agreement had been signed in December 1960, when almost a year of the two-year period of option had already passed. From China's point of view, the treaty had failed to provide a quick solution to the problem of dual nationality, it had tended to disrupt rather than improve relations with the Indonesian government, and in Indonesia, there was continued discrimination against all Chinese, whether nationals, dual nationals or Indonesians of Chinese descent.

Quite apart from the problems of implementation, the treaty itself was not exactly as the Chinese government might have wished. There was no question of China forcing its terms on Indonesia, and the Indonesian views prevailed on a number of important points.[21] According to Donald Willmott, sources close to the negotiations reported that the Chinese side wanted to renounce its claim to all those who had become Indonesian citizens under previous legislation, but the Indonesian side insisted that they should be treated as dual nationals and required to opt once more.[22] Similarly, the Chinese were prepared to relinquish the claim to all dual nationals who did not make a positive declaration to accept Chinese nationality; this was known as the 'passive' system for acquiring Indonesian citizenship. The treaty, however, incorporates the 'active' system, under which there should be positive acts of acceptance of Indonesian citizenship and renunciation of Chinese nationality; and under the terms of article five, all who failed to do so would become Chinese nationals irrespective of whether or not they had exercised the option.[23]

It has been pointed out that the provision by which Chinese who chose Indonesian citizenship could regain Chinese citizenship by establishing residence outside Indonesia, 'makes it possible for Chinese to adopt Indonesian citizenship purely as a matter of expediency, without a genuine transfer of loyalty, secure in the knowledge that they are not cutting their ties with China irrevocably'.[24] This may have been the attitude of many Chinese in Indonesia, but it may not have been the Chinese government's intent, and subsequent developments in Overseas Chinese policy appear to indicate that it was not. It may even have been that the Chinese side anticipated that it might face situations such as that which arose in 1959–60 or the problems which followed the 1965 coup.[25] The provision was not unreasonable for a nationality treaty, and since it stipulated also that any person who regained Chinese citizenship had to establish residence outside Indonesia, presumably in China, and would automatically lose Indonesian citizenship, there was no real problem, since they would have great difficulty in returning to Indonesia.

Publicly, the Chinese government expressed nothing but enthusiasm for the treaty, although the *Jen-min jih-pao* commented that it could be expected that there would be 'a few problems' in future relations between Chinese nationals and Indonesians of Chinese descent.[26] Imperfect though the treaty may have been, it represented a major propaganda achievement for the policy of peaceful coexistence. The CCP had been anxious to reach an agreement as soon as possible, and the Bandung Conference presented an ideal opportunity to demonstrate to the assembled Afro-Asian leaders the sincerity of China's proclaimed intentions.[27] Chinese statements emphasised particularly that the treaty was a precedent for the settlement of problems of a similar nature with all other countries, not simply those with which China had diplomatic relations.[28] At the Bandung Conference, Chou En-lai had seized the opportunity to capitalise on the successful negotiations with Indonesia with an offer to solve the problem of Overseas Chinese nationality with other countries concerned.[29] Hopefully, if other governments could be induced to negotiate on this question, they might be persuaded to enter into more permanent relations.[30]

If nothing else, the treaty had served its purpose as propaganda for China's foreign policy. To what extent had it clarified Chinese policy on Overseas Chinese nationality? The Party's position, set forth in a series of statements accompanying the treaty, was that it was now prepared to solve the problem on two conditions; one, that there should be formal agreements between

China and the countries concerned, and two, that dual nationals should have the right to choose freely between the two nationalities. This meant that the CCP was prepared to renounce its claim to all Overseas Chinese dual nationals if they chose to opt for local nationality.

Although the Chinese government had pressed for an agreement in which Indonesia would accept the greatest possible number of dual nationals as Indonesian citizens, in its public statements it made no attempt to suggest which way it would prefer the Chinese in Indonesia to opt. It simply expressed respect for the wishes of those who chose Indonesian nationality and declared that China would protect and show solicitude for those who chose Chinese nationality.[31] Although the Chinese government's intentions seemed plain, it was not prepared to renounce its claim by a simple declaration, since that would have been to relinquish its bargaining counter in manoeuvres for diplomatic recognition, and to appear to surrender to the Kuomintang its claim to the sole right to jurisdiction over, and disposal of, the Overseas Chinese. The *Jen-min jih-pao* editorial on the treaty, for example, pointed out that 'the solution of the problem of Overseas Chinese dual nationality cannot be decided unilaterally. Only through consultation between China and the countries of residence of the Overseas Chinese on the principle of equality and mutual benefit can a just and reasonable solution be attained.'[32]

In addition to clarifying its public position on nationality, the CCP appears to have derived from the negotiations with Indonesia and the exchanges with other Afro-Asian leaders at Bandung a greater understanding of the Overseas Chinese problem as seen by the outside non-communist, non-Overseas Chinese world. While the Party's statements at the end of 1954 had revealed an awareness of the concern felt in Southeast Asia, the Bandung Conference was possibly the first occasion on which leading members of the Chinese government were confronted directly with the suspicion of China's relations with the Overseas Chinese which existed in the minds of many Asian leaders. Henceforth, the CCP was to be more sensitive to the anti-China hostility which the presence alone of the Overseas Chinese could generate in Southeast Asia.[33] One point which had obviously made an impression on the Chinese at the conference was the suspicion that China was exploiting the Overseas Chinese for subversion. Writing in the *Jen-min jih-pao*, Chang Hsi-jo referred to the 'nonsensical talk' about an Overseas Chinese Fifth Column which had arisen at the Bandung Conference. He asserted that it was a well-known fact that 'revolution cannot be exported', and that although the Overseas Chinese were patriotic it was 'absolutely unthinkable' that the Chinese government would use them to interfere in the internal affairs of other countries.[34] Another impression which the CCP appears to have gained from the conference was that Overseas Chinese were resented for looking down on the local people. In a talk with Overseas Chinese in Bandung Chou En-lai called on all Overseas Chinese to resist the temptation to arrogance because of the strength of New China; 'the higher the international position of China, the more modest should Chinese people be'.[35]

The Dual Nationality Treaty was attacked by the Kuomintang as a 'sell-out', 'a plot to barter the nationality of the Overseas Chinese compatriots'.[36] According to the KMT, there was no such thing as a dual nationality problem in Indonesia, and the Overseas Chinese were told to ignore the requirements to register with communist officials.[37] The CCP had taken care to avoid the appearance of abandoning to the KMT its right to jurisdiction over the Overseas Chinese, but it was sensitive to the KMT's charge and attempted to counter it in propaganda about the treaty, emphasising that it represented a positive measure for protection of Overseas Chinese. As suggested above, however, the CCP's real concern was not so much with the KMT's propaganda, as with its existence in Taiwan. When Ho Hsiang-ning issued a call for vigilance against KMT attempts to undermine the treaty, and suggested that it might be good if the Indonesian government acted on the suggestion of Indonesian parliamentarians and public opinion to suppress KMT organisations and newspapers,[38] her concern was with the rival claims of the KMT as much as with Sino-Indonesian relations or the welfare of Overseas Chinese. The CCP renewed its call to Overseas Chinese to 'win over and unite with' supporters of the KMT, since, as Ho Hsiang-ning had said earlier in the year, 'to win over one more compatriot who has been tricked by the Chiang gang is to make a powerful contribution in support of the liberation of Taiwan'.[39] In fact, the KMT was to some extent forced to follow the line taken by the CCP at the end of 1954, although it has never been as explicit in public statements, and there have been conflicting statements by KMT officials.[40] The Nationality Law of 1929 has not been revised or amended, and to the extent that the KMT considers itself bound by any of its laws or regulations still remains in force in Taiwan.

SELF-DETERMINATION

For more than a year after the signing of the treaty, the CCP continued to base its policy on the offer to negotiate similar treaties with all other countries, even those hostile to Peking.[41] The elimination of dual nationality, however, although intended as a gesture of cooperation and goodwill in the spirit of peaceful coexistence, was only a legal technicality. It need not have had any relation to China's political objectives towards the Overseas Chinese, and it could do little towards removing the underlying suspicion of China's relations with its overseas population. It was as a necessary complement to the treaty offer, therefore, that the Party mounted its campaign to persuade the governments of Southeast Asia that they had nothing to fear from the Overseas Chinese and, equally difficult, to persuade Chinese nationals abroad that they should be law-abiding and not interfere in local politics.

There was, of course, considerable doubt as to how far the CCP could guarantee the behaviour of its nationals abroad. But it did demonstrate the sincerity of its purpose, if not its ability to control them, by appealing to them constantly in public statements and private discussions to be law-abiding and stay out of local politics.

By mid-1956 the CCP's reasons for wanting a solution to the problem were no less compelling, yet its one initiative had been an almost complete failure. There had still been no other response to the offer of negotiations, and the Indonesian government was talking of renegotiating its treaty. The offer had not induced any country to recognise Peking, it had not made any perceptible impact on suspicion of the Overseas Chinese or contribution to friendship and coexistence in Southeast Asia. At the same time, the arguments in favour of retaining the allegiance of the Overseas Chinese were increasingly less persuasive. In the home districts there was a growing contradiction between the life of domestic Overseas Chinese and the ordinary Chinese masses, as well as abuse of privileged status and a general laxity towards domestic Overseas Chinese which permitted a degree of privilege beyond that which the Party had contemplated. The benefits which the Party had hoped to obtain by preferential treatment had failed to materialise.

The failure of the CCP's initiative, therefore, was not only a diplomatic defeat for the policy of peaceful coexistence; it represented a signal failure to reach a satisfactory or conclusive resolution to problems in Overseas Chinese affairs. Unless the CCP was prepared to retreat to its former position of ignoring the Overseas Chinese problem, it had to find some alternative course of action. The alternative had already been suggested by the implications of the Sino-Indonesian Treaty.

The problem with the treaty proposal as it stood was that it was confined to dual nationals only. Yet the CCP had given considerable publicity to the fact that the principle on which the treaty was based was the 'complete freedom of the individual to make a personal choice according to his own wishes'.[42] If the Party was prepared to renounce its claim to dual nationals by allowing them complete freedom of choice, then to the governments of the countries of residence, to the dual nationals themselves, and also to pure Chinese nationals, there was no obvious reason why Overseas Chinese should not exercise that choice without the benefit of formal treaties.

At the end of 1956, partly in recognition of this argument, the CCP widened the scope of its proposals. Formal treaties were no longer the basis for solving the problem, although the offer to sign such treaties was still dangled hopefully before the non-recognising countries of Southeast Asia. The new proposals also extended, by implication, to pure Chinese nationals. The first hint of a revised attitude was contained in a statement by Li Wei-han, Director of the United Front Work Department, at the Eighth Congress of the CCP in September 1956. Li announced, without referring to dual nationality or nationality treaties, that it was China's policy 'to permit Overseas Chinese to choose their nationality on the principle of their own free choice'.[43] Shortly after this announcement, Chou En-lai confirmed that the Party had dropped the idea of formal treaties as a precondition to the solution of dual nationality, in a talk with the former Chief Minister of Singapore, David Marshall. Chou told Marshall that 'the Chinese government is willing to see the Chinese in Singapore obtain the Singapore citizenship which they seek of their own free will, and be completely loyal to the country in which they live'. He went on to say that 'any Chinese resident in Singapore who voluntarily obtains Singapore citizenship will no longer be a Chinese citizen'. He said that the Chinese government would be happy to sign an agreement embodying these principles after Singapore became independent, but he did not say that such an agreement was a precondition for the renunciation of China's claim to Chinese who elected to take Singapore citizenship.[44] Chou's remarks were made also on the understanding that Chinese eligible for Singapore citizenship were not only those born locally, but also some 230,000 who had been born in China and who had established residence qualifications entitling them to apply for citizenship.[45] In other words, pure Chinese nationals were no longer excluded from the category of people who could renounce Chinese citizenship.

In December, in a talk with Overseas Chinese in Rangoon, Chou gave a detailed exposition of the Chinese government's new position on Overseas Chinese policy.[46] On the question of nationality Chou said that Overseas Chinese 'who acquire the nationality of the countries of residence by voluntary decision and according to local laws, are no longer Chinese people (*jen-min*)'. The use of the term *jen-min* is significant, in that it implies much more than the formal renunciation of nationality. It was obviously intended, since it was to occur again in other statements on this question. Chou went on to say that those who did take local nationality should be loyal to the countries in which they lived, that a very clear division should be made between them and those who still retained Chinese nationality, and that they should break all ties with Overseas Chinese societies and organisations. Chou also said that it was not possible that 'all people will make this choice, and there will always be some who remain Overseas Chinese'. To the latter he renewed in the strongest and most specific terms the injunction he had first made in September 1954. They should on no account take part in any political activities, 'for example, in political parties, elections, or any Burmese political organisation'. Chou asserted that 'we do not promote the organisation of communist or other democratic parties among Overseas Chinese...(if they want) to participate in political parties, they should return to China. But it is impermissible to do so locally; this would invite misunderstanding in the countries of residence.' The remark about not seeking to promote communist parties may seem to be pure propaganda, intended for the ears of the governments of Southeast Asia. But in the context of the policies which followed at the end of 1957 it would seem to be a reasonably honest statement of the CCP's position. The wider implications of Chou's Rangoon speech are discussed in the following chapter, but in terms of nationality it confirmed that the CCP's new position was that all Chinese abroad could make a unilateral renunciation of Chinese nationality, described as 'a freedom and a right' of Overseas Chinese.[47] The Rangoon speech subsequently became an authoritative text for Overseas Chinese policy.

The introduction of this policy provides a clear illustration of the CCP's determination to apply the same basic policies to all Overseas Chinese regardless of the countries in which they lived. The treaty offer itself had been intended ultimately to have universal application but it appeared to discriminate in favour of Chinese in those countries which already recognised Peking. It may have been partly for this reason that the precondition of direct bilateral negotiations was abandoned, since the only immediate prospects for solution were in Burma, Indonesia, North Vietnam and possibly Cambodia. Chou had spoken on similar lines with Chinese in Cambodia in November 1956.[48] In the course of his talk in Rangoon he indicated that he had done the same in Hanoi.[49] But he was also to repeat the substance of this talk to Overseas Chinese from all Asian and most other countries, either in the course of his tours abroad or in Peking.[50] The new policy was presented in the same terms to Chinese in Hanoi as it was in Djakarta and in South Vietnam. Even in the case of Singapore, which was to become virtually an Overseas Chinese state, and which did not face the same communal problems as Overseas Chinese in other countries, the Chinese government made no distinction.

As Chou's talk with Marshall indicates, the Chinese government had not completely abandoned the hope that it would be able to conclude nationality treaties. The offer appears to have been continued not only in the belief that it might be exploited as a means of establishing diplomatic contact, but in the expectation that in itself it might be accepted as an earnest of the CCP's desire to improve relations with Southeast Asia, and its stated intention of restraining Overseas Chinese from interfering in Southeast Asian politics. Since the CCP had now announced that Overseas Chinese could renounce Chinese nationality without treaty guarantees, it was important also to continue to assert that the government of the People's Republic of China, and not the Kuomintang, had the right to jurisdiction over Overseas Chinese. If the problems of the Kuomintang had influenced earlier decisions, however, it seems that by the end of 1956 the Party was prepared to disregard them. It was not that it believed that it had won the support of a majority of Overseas Chinese, but that it now regarded the KMT supporters among Overseas Chinese with contempt or condescension rather than concern.[51] Moreover, if the trend was towards weakening of the Overseas Chinese attachment to China, this would affect support for the KMT even more than for the CCP. The KMT might claim to be the legitimate government of China, but it was obviously not sitting in Peking, or Nanking, and it did not control the Overseas Chinese home districts. Except for hard-core KMT supporters, identification with China meant that part of China ruled by the communists. If the attachment to China was weakening, there was no reason to look to the discredited KMT remnants in Taiwan. To some extent also, the CCP may have been encouraged to ignore the KMT by the fact that its own policies on nationality had prompted a gesture in a similar direction from the KMT, and would have been difficult for the KMT to attack.

The CCP's new approach to Overseas Chinese nationality was exemplified, perhaps unexpectedly, in its reaction to the forced naturalisation of Chinese in South Vietnam. A retrospective decree promulgated on 21 August 1956 stipulated that all people born in Vietnam of Chinese parents were required to become Vietnamese citizens. Accompanying the decree were a series of measures designed to eliminate Chinese education and to exclude Chinese from eleven specified retail trades.[52] This development was reported briefly in the back pages of the *Jen-min jih-pao* in September; there was no editorial comment by the *Jen-min jih-pao* nor any statement by a spokesman of the Chinese government.[53] In March 1957, the South Vietnamese government began a general registration of Chinese, and on 17 April it announced that identity cards of all locally born Chinese would become invalid on 9 May. It was not until this time, after nine months' silence during which the KMT had kept up a constant stream of protests and statements, that the CCP chose to make a public comment. On 20 May, Ho Hsiang-ning issued a brief statement pointing out that:

the People's Republic of China has many times expressed its willingness to solve the problem of Overseas Chinese nationality together with the countries concerned, in a spirit of friendly consultation and on the basis of the principles of international law. It is quite obvious that a reasonable settlement of the problem of Overseas Chinese nationality in South Vietnam also can be reached only on the basis of respect for the will of the Overseas Chinese themselves and through consultation between the countries concerned.

She asserted that the Vietnamese government's decree was 'in violation of international law' and 'unreasonable and unilateral', and called for its repeal.[54] The following day a *Jen-min jih-pao* editorial enlarged slightly on Ho's statement, and outlined the basis for Peking's argument that the decree was in violation of international law and basic human rights.[55] A week later, the ACROCA issued a short statement,[56] and in early June the Chinese government cabled 30,000 yüan (US $10,000) for the relief of those deprived of their livelihood by the ban on Chinese participation in the eleven retail trades.[57]

The Chinese government made no further statement on the situation.

At no time did it claim that Chinese in South Vietnam should not take South Vietnamese nationality, nor did it make any reference to the representations of the KMT. Its complaint rested solely on the grounds that the principle of free choice had been ignored, that the decree violated accepted principles of international law, and that the Saigon government had not respected the right of the People's Republic of China to a voice in decisions concerning Overseas Chinese.[58] The significance of the Chinese response was that not only was the Saigon government hostile to China, not only did it have close relations with Taiwan and sympathise with the Nationalists' aim of returning to the mainland, but it was also in control of one half of a partitioned country, of which the other half was ruled by a communist government, a fraternal ally of Peking, which sought ultimately to control the whole of Vietnam.

Clearly, the CCP had already moved beyond the limited objective of eliminating impediments to its policy of peaceful coexistence. It was now concerned with finding a workable and lasting solution to the Overseas Chinese problem itself. Its own approach to nationality was to progress even further, from a 'passive' to an 'active' position, which became one of the platforms of the decolonisation policy which emerged in 1957 and which is discussed in Chapter 8.

7

Policy reassessment, 1956. Foreign exchange and education

Between 1954 and 1956 the CCP had attempted to remove the impediments which Overseas Chinese presented to the advancement of its foreign policy interests in Southeast Asia. If Overseas Chinese policy is viewed only in these terms, however, it could be mistaken as no more than a propaganda cover for subversion or a measure for placating the governments of Southeast Asia while peaceful coexistence remained a tactical necessity. According to such a view, the Party would have regarded the Overseas Chinese as an invaluable instrument which, if not immediately exploitable, was not to be discarded. If the Party appeared not to exploit the Overseas Chinese, it was simply because it had done so covertly or because circumstances had not yet required such action and alternative tactics were temporarily more fruitful. Any measure which might be construed as disengagement from the Overseas Chinese was simply a tactical retreat, to serve the immediate interests of foreign policy or to provide indirect protection until Overseas Chinese could be protected effectively by the threat or use of force, and if required, mobilised in the cause of communist revolution.

But since foreign policy is subject to change, a radical redirection of foreign policy should result in an equally radical change in Overseas Chinese policy. This seemed to be the case for a brief period during the Cultural Revolution, but the point about Overseas Chinese policy in the Cultural Revolution is how quickly it reverted to the previous norm once control was reestablished in the foreign affairs sector in Peking. While foreign policy may change according to the situation in China, in the countries in which China is interested, or in the world at large, the situation of the Overseas Chinese, their special relationship with China and their position in Southeast Asia, cannot be altered by a change in Chinese foreign policy. Any fundamental change in the CCP's approach to Overseas Chinese which does not take account of this fact, and which aims at active political exploitation of Overseas Chinese, is likely to result in a policy with a high probability of failure.

The CCP was well aware of this fact. It was also aware that its Overseas Chinese problem was more than simply a question of whether and in what circumstances Overseas Chinese might be exploited in the service of foreign policy. The Party's attempts to solve the problem of Overseas Chinese nationality and to persuade its nationals abroad that they should behave in such a way as to benefit China's policy of peaceful coexistence, were only the most visible sign of the dilemmas with which the Party was confronted.

It is not exactly certain when the CCP came to a firm decision about the future of its relations with the Chinese abroad, since its domestic and external policies up to 1956 still seemed to indicate that the Party believed the assets of Overseas Chinese outweighed the liabilities. A decision appears to have been made some time in 1956, by which time the Party was in a position to make some assessment of the progress and achievements of the 1954 policy. In June 1956, the Overseas Chinese Affairs Commission convened its Fourth Enlarged Conference, the first such conference since July 1954. The main report at the conference was given by Fang Fang, and was devoted exclusively to domestic affairs.[1] There were no obvious indications of a radical change in policy towards the Chinese abroad, and it seemed that the domestic Overseas Chinese would continue to receive preferential treatment. But in retrospect, it seems that important policy changes were discussed at this conference, that they were probably approved in principle at the Eighth Party Congress in September and passed to the Overseas Chinese sector for detailed implementation. Implementation then proceeded in stages over the next fifteen months, and it may have been hastened by the widespread assaults on Chinese language, education, and commerce, which in 1956 and 1957 occurred in most parts of Southeast Asia. Throughout 1957, the pattern of change was apparent in all aspects of Overseas Chinese affairs, until all policies were either changed or modified in conformity with a single overriding objective of detaching the Overseas Chinese from the Chinese homeland. In March 1957 the State Council appointed a new Commission which, at its First Plenary Conference in November 1957, confirmed that the trends which had emerged since the end of 1956 amounted to a dissolution of the Overseas Chinese 'empire'. What reasons did the CCP have for arriving at this decision?

Assets, real and potential

The OCAC Conference of June 1956 appears to have instituted the administrative measures which paved the way for the reimposition of strict controls on the domestic Overseas Chinese. But the conference itself actually reaffirmed very strongly the principle that domestic Overseas Chinese should be treated carefully in order to prevent an adverse response from their relatives abroad, and to enlist their support in projecting a favourable image of China in the countries of Southeast Asia. The *Jen-min jih-pao* editorial on the conference had singled out foreign exchange and publicity for China as two respects in which they could be useful to the Chinese government.[2] These were also the two ways of exploiting the Overseas Chinese which might be least objectionable to Southeast Asian governments. But there were other ways in which the CCP might still hope to use the Chinese abroad to advantage.

The policy of peaceful coexistence seemed to preclude open exploitation of the Overseas Chinese masses for subversion or communist revolution. There were prospects for exercising indirect influence on Southeast Asian affairs through the medium of patriotic Overseas Chinese, although such influence would need to be exercised with discretion and restraint if it were not to conflict with the objectives of foreign policy. Overseas Chinese were also an ideal cover for political intelligence in Southeast Asia. But the number of active intelligence agents would only be minimal in proportion to the total Overseas Chinese population and there is no reason why intelligence operations would necessitate the retention of the political allegiance to China of all Overseas Chinese.

Another way in which the Overseas Chinese might be used to advantage was as a channel for trade, and consequently, political influence. Although the Chinese government did refer to trade in the context of Overseas Chinese policy, it has never been one of its major platforms. The emphasis was more on investment in China and contributions to socialist construction in the homeland. To some extent, the CCP appears to have been suspicious of the politics, and the business practices, of Overseas Chinese businessmen,[3] although this did not prevent it from taking every opportunity to trade through the Overseas Chinese business world. Moreover, by the mid-1950s, the Party was beginning to accept that trade with foreign countries need not be determined by correct political thinking or attitudes towards China. It appears to have accepted also that allegiance to or cultural ties with the homeland were not necessarily a concomitant of the Overseas Chinese businessman's desire to trade with China.[4] If the Party's intention was to use trade as a means of exerting political pressure, it could achieve similar results even if the objects of this pressure were not Chinese. It should not be overlooked, moreover, that the CCP does not necessarily always regard trade as a 'political weapon', and that it may be content with the very real commercial advantages of trading through the Overseas Chinese. China's trade with Southeast Asia has not been a case of seeking out and trading exclusively with Overseas Chinese. Since Overseas Chinese dominate the Southeast Asian commercial world, there is little alternative but to trade through them; and since they also have the most efficient network of communications and outlets throughout the region, they present by far the most ideal channel for the export of Chinese goods. The same opportunities exist whether the Overseas Chinese identify with China or with the countries of residence; and they exist for any other country which trades with Southeast Asia. There does not seem to be any reason why trade, in itself or as a political weapon, should have persuaded the CCP that traditional, non-commercial ties with the Overseas Chinese should be maintained.[5]

The prospects for exploiting the Overseas Chinese in a variety of ways were attractive, but they did not necessarily require the active allegiance of all Overseas Chinese, nor were they sufficient to compel the CCP to preserve traditional political and cultural links with the Chinese abroad if this were to conflict with wider interests of state policy. If necessary, the Overseas Chinese were expendable.

Liabilities

Problems of the colonial relationship. The CCP's approach to nationality and the political behaviour of Overseas Chinese indicated that it was sensitive to the colonial overtones of the relationship. But its response to this problem, the enunciation of the principle of self-determination, had drawn the Party into further consideration of the rights and wishes of the Overseas Chinese. Why should the right to self-determination depend on intergovernmental treaties, in which the Overseas Chinese themselves had little or no part? And if increasing numbers of Chinese abroad were acquiring local citizenship by birth or naturalisation without the benefit of treaties with the Chinese government, did this not indicate a trend away from the traditional relationship of the Overseas Chinese with China, and a tendency on their part to regard themselves not as Chinese but as Southeast Asians?

The attitudes of Overseas Chinese ranged all the way from 'patriotism' to disinterest, but no Chinese government could disregard the trend to identification with the countries in which they lived. Unlike a colonial people, the Overseas Chinese in most places could ignore any claim which the Chinese government might make to their allegiance. The CCP could not compel them to retain allegiance to China, a fact which it had already recognised. In the short term, this trend need not have influenced the CCP's policy. But in its calculations it could not overlook the fact that the trend was likely to continue, and that any long-term plans for exploiting the Overseas Chinese would be marked by diminishing returns.

But more important, was it consistent with the CCP's political beliefs to cling to a 'subject' people outside China's boundaries who seemed to be demanding independence? Although not all Overseas Chinese held this view, any attempt to arrest the trend might be seen as colonially oppressive, and would have been in conflict with the existing forces of change.

Problems of foreign policy. The CCP's external Overseas Chinese policies had been largely unsuccessful. The nationality question remained unsolved, and the Sino-Indonesian Treaty was almost an embarrassment. If the Chinese government's injunction to Overseas Chinese to be law-abiding was intended to be taken seriously, it had obviously been ignored in a number of countries, for example, by Chinese youths in Singapore in 1956, and China was often credited with the responsibility. The Party's hopes of exploiting the Chinese abroad as instruments of foreign policy had not been realised, and they remained a liability in most of its relationships or 'non-relationships' with Southeast Asia. They were by no means the potential political force for China which they might have seemed in 1949.

If the Party's purpose was antagonistic to or subversive of the local governments, there were considerable disadvantages in relying on Overseas Chinese to achieve this purpose. Even if the CCP had not believed that revolution cannot be imported, the Malayan insurgency had demonstrated that Overseas Chinese were possibly the least effective instrument to promote and lead the revolution, and that their participation might even be disastrous for the revolutionary cause. The Party's insistent injunction to the Chinese abroad to be law-abiding and respect the policies of local governments is one indication that this point had been well taken. Where the CCP's object was to establish diplomatic relations, the Overseas Chinese were a deterrent rather than an inducement to recognition of Peking, a fact which hostile governments did not fail to exploit. In 1958, for example, US Secretary of State Dulles warned the governments of Southeast Asia that recognition of Peking would probably result in their subversion and overthrow by Overseas Chinese backed by Peking. The Chinese government's angry denunciation of Dulles' warning indicated a high degree of sensitivity to the belief in Southeast Asia and the west that the Overseas Chinese were a subversive political arm of the CCP.[6] Where friendly relations did exist, as with Indonesia, the Overseas Chinese were a potential source of discord. That the CCP was actually aware of these problems was implicit in the policy introduced in 1954, in the subsequent attempts to find new solutions to the dual nationality problem, and in the constant accompanying propaganda effort to dispel the belief that the Overseas Chinese were a threat to the security of the countries of Southeast Asia.

Problems of domestic Overseas Chinese. The most immediate problem, although not necessarily the most important, was the domestic Overseas Chinese. After two years' experiment with privilege and preferential treatment, the Party was able to assess the value in returns to China; and if there was still some question at the end of 1956 that the potential of Overseas Chinese might be realised through the domestic Overseas Chinese, that question was answered at the end of 1957 with a resounding negative. In other words, the Party now considered that preferential treatment of domestic Overseas Chinese was no longer essential. And since the purpose of preferential treatment had been to exploit ties between China and the Overseas Chinese, the implication was that these ties themselves were no longer important. Subsequently, as political pressures on domestic Overseas Chinese were increased and renewed demands were made on them to extract money from their relatives abroad, it appeared not only that the Party had given up the attempt to create a favourable impression on the Overseas Chinese, but that it was not even concerned if its policies resulted in alienation of sympathisers.

FOREIGN EXCHANGE AND EDUCATION

In the context of the policy reassessment at this time, foreign exchange and education have a special significance. It is not necessarily that these two aspects of Overseas Chinese affairs were the most decisive factors in the CCP's redirection of policy in 1956, although that claim might be made with respect to foreign exchange. Rather, they lie at the very foundation of the relationship between the Chinese government and Overseas Chinese, and their significance to the CCP at any time is of special interest; foreign exchange, because it was the one respect in which Overseas Chinese were of direct material benefit to China, and education, because it was the most important means of preserving their Chineseness, and hence their attachment to the homeland and potential value to the Chinese government.

Neither belongs entirely to domestic or foreign affairs and in this they epitomise the peculiarities of Overseas Chinese affairs. They also illustrate the strictly utilitarian approach which followed from the CCP's subordination of Overseas Chinese affairs to foreign policy. But above all, they were in some ways the essence of the colonial relationship and were therefore extremely important in the decolonisation policy which followed.

Foreign exchange and technical assistance

The importance of foreign exchange was evident from the CCP's policies for domestic Overseas Chinese, particularly from 1954 to 1957. But there is also evidence that in the positive aspects of policy, the Party was ultimately more interested in exploiting Overseas Chinese for domestic economic purposes than for external political ones. If this was the case, then the level of foreign exchange will have been a critical determinant in the Party's approach to the whole Overseas Chinese question. The problem, however, has been to determine how much foreign exchange the Chinese government has received. The annual estimates of western sources have differed by as much as US $100 million, which makes it extremely difficult to assess their material value to the CCP. Other aspects of the Party's Overseas Chinese policy suggest, however, that by 1957, the returns were not considered sufficient to warrant continued cultivation of the Overseas Chinese, and that the fall in remittances and their diminished importance in relation to total foreign exchange earnings was a most significant factor in the Party's decision to sever the traditional relationship.

When the CCP came to power it may have envisaged many possibilities for exploiting the Overseas Chinese. But the only respect in which they presented a tangible, measurable advantage, was financial. Overseas Chinese remittances in the years 1929 to 1941 had averaged between US $80 and $100 million annually, and even in the post-war period had ranged from US $66 to $130 million.[7] In some years before the war, remittances had been sufficient to offset huge balance of payments deficits, and in 1938 the level had reached US $200 million.[8] The new Chinese government's prospects for obtaining substantial foreign aid were limited to what could be extracted from the Soviet Union which, under the agreement of February 1950, undertook to provide China with credits of US $300 million in five annual instalments.[9] If the CCP could restore Overseas Chinese remittances to pre-war levels, this would constitute an annual net gain in foreign exchange well in excess of that available from the only major source of foreign aid. The Party was well aware of this fact, and appears to have expected that Overseas Chinese would provide the main source of foreign exchange in the first years of its rule.[10] The CCP sought to draw on the resources of the Overseas Chinese in three ways: through family remittances, direct capital investment, and the recruitment of Overseas Chinese with technical or professional qualifications.[11]

By far the most important were family remittances, and the measures taken to maintain or increase the flow of remittances, discussed above, constituted the main objective of the Overseas Chinese affairs bureaucracy. Provided that these remittances reached China through official channels they had the effect of a direct grant of foreign exchange which, unlike the aid from the Soviet Union, did not have to be repaid. There was, however, a constant problem of currency smuggling and illegal traffic in consumer goods from Hong Kong and Macao; and according to CCP sources the extent of these unlawful remittances was still of very considerable proportions even in the late 1950s.[12] Of similar although more direct benefit to the Chinese government were donations to construction or public welfare enterprises in the home districts; the building of houses, roads, bridges, and schools.

Overseas Chinese capital investment was not all derived directly from overseas. Some, possibly the great majority, came from domestic Overseas Chinese, and this was one of the objects of pressure on domestic Overseas Chinese to use remittances to benefit socialist construction.[13] Since 1955, the main channels of investment both from domestic Overseas Chinese and from the Chinese abroad, have been the Overseas Chinese Investment Corporations.[14] The advantage of the corporations was that they enabled the CCP to exploit private capital without the necessity for private enterprises in socialist China. They also facilitated the pooling of small sums of money contributed by domestic Overseas Chinese for financing industrial and other large-scale enterprises. It seems, moreover, that the CCP saw in the corporations an effective means of regularising 'voluntary' investment by domestic Overseas Chinese. In the early 1950s, when the Party had been particularly insistent that domestic Overseas Chinese should use their remittances for the benefit of the state, there had been corruption and coercion among basic-level cadres which had produced unfavourable reactions from the relatives abroad. The corporations offered a means of circumventing the corrupt or over-zealous cadre, and at the same time, by the guaranteed annual dividend, provided an inducement for domestic Overseas Chinese to invest remittances and to request more from their relatives abroad.

The third method of utilising the resources of Overseas Chinese was, in effect, a form of technical assistance. In the early years this was dictated partly by the need to place returned Overseas Chinese in productive employment, initially in the cultivation of tropical industrial crops, particularly rubber.[15] It was not, however, solely a question of finding useful employment for those who had already returned. In broadcasts to the Chinese abroad, particularly in the mid-1950s, the CCP invited anyone with special skills to return to work in China. In 1956, this developed into a campaign, directed also at those described as overseas students,[16] to persuade 'higher intellectuals' (*kao-chi chih-shih fen-tzu*) to return to serve the homeland in socialist construction. This appeal was directed mainly at scientists and engineers, but the government also stated that it would welcome translators, teachers, education administrators, and production technicians.[17] Higher intellectuals were offered special terms and conditions, including a salary equivalent to the one they were currently receiving overseas. There does not appear to have been a massive response to this appeal, and the campaign subsided at the end of 1957 and was not subsequently revived.

In effect, therefore, the Overseas Chinese provided a vast source of 'foreign aid' to the Chinese government. The extent to which the CCP has been able to exploit it, however, has been the subject of widely differing interpretations. The Chinese government has never issued figures for the amount of Overseas Chinese foreign exchange received through official channels, and even if it had there is still the question of illegal remittances.[18] The difficulty of arriving at precise estimates is reflected in the following statement by Alexander Eckstein: 'remittances may have ranged between US $10 million and $100 million annually. The flow was probably nearer the upper limit in the early 1950's and 1960's, and it probably reached its low point in 1959. Between 1952 and 1958, it may have averaged $50–60 million.'[19] A systematic examination of Overseas Chinese remittances has been attempted by Chun-hsi Wu,[20] but despite the thoroughness of his investigations Wu himself has had to rely upon estimates and guesswork. His conclusions differ from most others and no two authorities are agreed on the annual figures for the period since 1949; although most seem to agree that the lowest point was reached in 1959. As an indication of estimated trends, and also as an illustration of the wide discrepancy between individual estimates, Wu's figures may be compared with those of the United States Central Intelligence Agency.[21] A further fifteen selected estimates for varying periods between 1950 and 1965 are given in Wu's study.[22]

Wu estimates that remittances accounted for between 26.1 per cent and 42.1 per cent of the currencies obtained by China from non-communist countries between 1950 and 1963.[23] The Central Intelligence Agency estimates that remittances accounted for 4.8 per cent of total international receipts for the period 1950–64.[24] The CIA estimate of the volume of remittances is probably the highest to have been made, but Wu's is by no means the lowest.[25]

Since it is so difficult to put a figure on the extent to which economic gain has influenced the CCP's political decisions concerning the Chinese abroad, the only alternative is to try to form some impression of the Party's perception of its value from official statements. At times, particularly in the period 1954 to 1957, Chinese officials came very close to admitting that foreign exchange was the single overriding objective of Overseas Chinese policy. The treatment of domestic Overseas Chinese certainly suggests that this may have been the case, and it is possible that the Party was restrained from admitting it more openly only by the fact that it was constantly accusing the KMT of extorting money from the compatriots abroad.

In the seventeen years from 1949 to the end of 1965, the one concern which remained constant in Overseas Chinese policy was the necessity to attract foreign exchange. The first article on Overseas Chinese affairs published in the *Jen-min jih-pao* after October 1949, and before a coherent Overseas Chinese policy had emerged, was a long discussion of the importance of increasing the amount of Overseas Chinese remittances.[26] In 1965, when external Overseas Chinese policy had almost ceased to exist and domestic Overseas Chinese affairs were being submerged in the affairs of the Chinese masses, the Party continued to assert that remittances were of benefit to the state and should be encouraged.[27] Even after the beginning of the Cultural Revolution, the Bank of China in Hong Kong advertised for Overseas Chinese investment, and the Chinese government appears to have continued to pay dividends on investment in the Overseas Chinese Investment Corporations, at least until early 1968.[28] The great majority of formal decrees, instructions, and regulations issued by the government in the field of Overseas Chinese affairs have been concerned directly or indirectly with foreign exchange, and protection of remittances was one of the two policies ever stated to be 'a long term policy of the state'.[29]

There were also more explicit statements. When the new Overseas Chinese policy was introduced in 1954 Ho Hsiang-ning stated that there were three important questions in Overseas Chinese affairs; the first was nationality, and the other two were remittances and investment.[30] According to Ssu-t'u Mei-t'ang in December 1954, the foremost problem in Overseas Chinese affairs was implementation of the remittances policy.[31] In April 1955, Kao Ming-hsüan described the protection of remittances as 'the central task of Overseas Chinese work',[32] and at the Second Session of the NPC in July a similar statement was made by Ho Hsiang-ning: 'Overseas Chinese sectors at all levels should make (remittances policy) their central task.'[33]

According to an article in the *Kuang-ming jih-pao* in December 1956, 'the relationship between China and the Overseas Chinese is a question of mobilising the manpower and material resources of the Overseas Chinese to support and engage in socialist construction of the homeland.'[34]

These statements all seem to indicate that foreign exchange was a first priority, and the last, particularly, suggests that the whole relationship was perceived solely in these terms. But it should be noted that they were all made between 1954 and 1957.

According to Doak Barnett, any decrease in Overseas Chinese remittances affects 'the entire economy of the two provinces (of Kwangtung and Fukien)'.[35] Occasional references in the Chinese press appear to confirm that this was the case. In 1956, for example, Overseas Chinese investment was reported to have accounted for 10 per cent of the total local industrial investment in the two provinces; and in the same report it was stated that 23 per cent of all middle-school students in Fukien were enrolled in schools established with Overseas Chinese capital.[36] In 1957, the Kwangtung ROCA, in an open letter to all Overseas Chinese affairs organisations in the province, stated that illegal remittances had reached such a scale that losses were being suffered in state economic construction.[37] The equivalent value of smuggled goods seized by the authorities in 1956 was said to have been sufficient to import 4,400 tons of fertiliser, and currency smuggled into China in the period 1950 to 1956 is alleged to have amounted to Hong Kong $1,600 million.[38]

Although the actual volume of Overseas Chinese foreign exchange cannot be determined with any certainty, therefore, it does appear to have been a very significant factor in the Party's decisions on Overseas Chinese policy. Most significant in terms of policy changes in 1957 was the general downward trend, which had persisted in the mid-1950s despite strenuous efforts by the CCP to reverse it. The trend reflected in western estimates is confirmed by Chinese government statements, several of which appeared in the middle of 1957.[39] There was also the fact that the Party had been unable to prevent illegal remittances, and a considerable amount of foreign exchange was being lost in this way. It seems, moreover, that the value of Overseas Chinese remittances was diminishing in proportion to China's total foreign exchange earnings.[40] In 1949, the Party anticipated that this would be the case, and it is probably true that by 1957 China was 'in a better position... than during its first few years to forgo the financial and other material help from the Chinese abroad'.[41]

The Party must have realised also, after three years' experiment with preferential treatment for domestic Overseas Chinese, that the decrease was attributable to factors other than 'socialist excesses' in the home districts. One, which may not have reduced the flow of remittances but which limited the amount by which the flow could be increased, was the imposition of currency export restrictions in the countries of residence.[42] More important was that the actual number of Overseas Chinese remitting money for family support was decreasing year by year.[43] There had been no substantial migration from China to Southeast Asia since the establishment of the CCP's authority in South China,[44] which meant that as Overseas Chinese and their relatives died and contact between distant relatives became more remote, there were fewer and fewer Overseas Chinese with direct dependants in China or distant relatives whom they might feel obliged to support.[45] There was, moreover, a disproportion between the number of Overseas Chinese with whom the CCP was primarily concerned for political reasons, the 95 per cent in Southeast Asia, and the remittances derived from them. According to one Chinese report, only 30 per cent of remittances had been derived from Southeast Asia in the period before 1949;[46] Chun-hsi Wu estimates that the percentage was 50.20 for the period 1950 to 1964.[47] A considerable proportion originated in Hong Kong and Macao, which would not have influenced the Party's political decisions concerning the Overseas Chinese.[48] Another factor, which is impossible to estimate but which must have offset the value of remittances to some extent, was the cost of maintaining the Overseas Chinese affairs bureaucracy and the provision of special ration facilities for domestic Overseas Chinese.

In financial terms, therefore, while there is no doubt that Overseas Chinese were extremely valuable, they were a declining asset. But the CCP was by no means prepared to relinquish this asset, which necessitated the introduction of special safeguards when the Party's political objectives were moving in a contrary direction in 1957. The intention of these measures, moreover, was very similar to that underlying the policies of ex-colonial governments which seek to maintain a special economic relationship with former colonies after they have become independent.

Education of Overseas Chinese youth

The established patterns of Overseas Chinese education seemed to offer the Chinese Communist Party an excellent means of influencing both the Overseas Chinese communities themselves and the internal affairs of Southeast Asian countries. In Southeast Asia there was an extensive Chinese education system, heavily oriented towards China, even if still influenced fairly widely by the KMT in 1949. In China there was the practice, which might easily be exploited to advantage, of renewing and reinforcing the Overseas Chinese attachment to the homeland through education at the source, as it were, of Chinese culture, a practice which had existed since the early years of this century. Many of the China-educated Overseas Chinese returned to positions of influence in the schools, in the professions, in business, in the internal power structures of the Overseas Chinese communities, and in the politics of the countries of residence. Overseas Chinese education might seem to have been ready-made vehicle for the export of the Chinese revolution.

But while the CCP did not neglect education in the countries of residence, its programme for the education of Overseas Chinese youth has been centred in China. The reason seems to have been a combination of practical difficulties and, particularly after 1954, political doubts.

There were, in fact, considerable obstacles to Chinese government manipulation of Overseas Chinese schools. There had already been attempts by some Southeast Asian governments to eradicate the separate system of Chinese education,[49] and evidence or suspicion of control from China, Nationalist or Communist, could only add further incentive to these efforts. The anti-communist sympathies of most of the governments in power in Southeast Asia reinforced their hostility to Chinese schools after the communist victory in China, and most of them needed no pretext for placing schools under surveillance, ordering their closure or imposing restrictions on Chinese education in general. The CCP's earliest statements on the subject of Overseas Chinese education suggested either that the Party was unaware of the sensitivities and possible reactions of local Southeast Asians or that it had no intention of translating its policy into action. As it became more involved with the Overseas Chinese it was forced to consider how far it was prepared to go in the face of the resentment and pressures of indigenous Southeast Asians, particularly in view of its express desire to establish good relations with the region.

There were other obstacles, such as the problem of attempting to direct Overseas Chinese education by proxy, and the difficulty of exporting trained and trusted teachers when all countries in the region imposed strict barriers against immigration.[50] But the greatest problem, as the CCP discovered by the mid-1950s, was the question of control. If the CCP had specific political purposes in seeking to exercise direction over the affairs of Overseas Chinese schools, it was essential not only that these schools should be free from outside interference, which was impossible, but that the activists should be disciplined and should control the schools in such a way as not to conflict with Peking's Overseas Chinese policy or its foreign policies towards the countries concerned. Any activity which aroused official suspicion, for example, or which created problems for the Overseas Chinese community in general, was likely to create problems also for whatever policy the CCP was pursuing among the Overseas Chinese and for China's relations with the country concerned.[51]

Despite the fact that by 1956 the Chinese government appears to have believed that it had extensive influence, if not control, over a large number of 'patriotic' Overseas Chinese schools, this does not seem to have been the case.[52] There was an initial intent to establish a strong presence in Overseas Chinese schools, which seems to fit together very neatly with the obvious manifestations of communism and pro-Peking patriotism in Chinese schools in Southeast Asia. But the problem was not so simple. The policy change in

1954 tended to preclude political mobilisation of the compatriots abroad, and the Party's attempts to neutralise hostility towards the Overseas Chinese and allay the suspicion that they were a fifth column for China meant particularly that Overseas Chinese schools should not be seen as centres for subversion and the dissemination of pro-China revolutionary propaganda. Not only do the Party's injunctions seem to have had little or no effect in Overseas Chinese schools which were not communist or pro-China, they also went unheeded by communist-infiltrated schools. The militant activities of Overseas Chinese students in Singapore and Malaya and their blatant appeals to Chinese chauvinism ran directly counter to the whole direction of China's Overseas Chinese policy.

The CCP's interest in the Chinese education system in Southeast Asia was dictated as much by a desire to destroy the KMT as to enlist Overseas Chinese youth in the service of China. But by 1956 the Party had discovered that even the initial step of establishing a presence in Overseas Chinese schools was no easy matter; even in countries like Indonesia the CCP had still not succeeded in uprooting the influence of the KMT. The CCP had also discovered that it was simply not within its power to control the activities of Overseas Chinese schools if they chose to ignore its injunctions. The problem of Overseas Chinese schools, however, was only one symptom of the real problem in China's relations with the Overseas Chinese, their growing reluctance to give their allegiance to China.

In any event, the main focus of the Chinese government's policy for Overseas Chinese education was in its domestic programmes. In the years immediately following the communist victory in China, there was an un-precedentedly large influx of young Chinese from the Nanyang, the great majority of them seeking an education. From 1949 until 1957, the CCP pursued an extremely liberal policy towards these students. It provided them with state subsidies and the privileges accorded to domestic Overseas Chinese, it waived minimum educational qualifications, and does not appear to have refused anyone who could claim to be a student, regardless of age, ability, or political background.

Given the enormous problems facing the new Chinese government and the CCP's more urgent priorities in socialist construction, the treatment of Overseas Chinese students may seem a little surprising, the more so since the numbers involved were not a handful of cadres being trained for Southeast Asia. From the official figures, it seems that the average number of arrivals each year for the first seven years was almost 6,000.[53] According to the most recent aggregate figure, some 60,000 Overseas Chinese students had arrived in China by April 1960, and it is not even certain whether this figure includes the children of Overseas Chinese returning to settle in China, who were entitled to the same consideration, as were also the children of domestic Overseas Chinese.[54]

This would seem to indicate a very strong motivation on the part of the CCP, but the Party appears to have acted from a mixture of motives, and to some extent also from necessity. In the first place the Chinese government was confronted with many thousands of young Overseas Chinese arriving on its doorstep, some of them deported from their countries of residence, but most of them voluntarily and filled with enthusiasm for the new order in China. For reasons of national pride and prestige it would not have been easy to refuse them, partly because they were at that stage apparently regarded as Chinese nationals, and partly because they were a symbol of the support and approval for the new Chinese government which the Party claimed from the Chinese people and hoped for from the rest of the world.

The CCP was also concerned to establish itself in the eyes of the Overseas Chinese for both political and economic reasons and in order to undermine support for the KMT. Overseas Chinese had been studying in China since the 1911 Revolution. What they had expected from the KMT as the government of China, the CCP would continue and surpass; it would not close its doors against any student and would treat them all with greater care and consideration than they had ever received in the past.[55]

There were other practical advantages. The CCP did not encourage emigration, and Chinese immigration was no longer acceptable to the countries of Southeast Asia. The number of 'active' links could be maintained, or at least prevented from disappearing, by a continuing movement of Overseas Chinese back to China. In the case of students, the most immediate benefit to the Chinese government came in the form of foreign exchange. According to one official report, the 'overwhelming majority' of Overseas Chinese students was supported by family remittances from abroad.[56] The students were instructed, therefore, to communicate regularly with their parents, since this was an important means of enabling parents, 'to assist the school in the education of their children';[57] they were also told not to refuse, out of concern for political purity, to accept the money which their parents sent them.[58] It was for the purpose of further exploiting this source of foreign exchange that the students were permitted the use of the special retail stores, and it was probably also for this purpose that in some Overseas Chinese schools the fees for the Overseas Chinese students were as much as three times the amount required from ordinary students.[59]

There was one other advantage, which also points to the most important but least publicised aspect of the CCP's policy for Overseas Chinese students in China. Many of the students already had basic or secondary educational qualifications, which meant that the Overseas Chinese school systems could be drawn on, at no cost to the Chinese government, to supplement the underdeveloped education system of China as a source of qualified students for higher education or partly educated youth who could be assigned to work in positions where literacy was required.

5

The startling fact underlying this programme for the education of Overseas Chinese youth was that the CCP intended that all Overseas Chinese students should serve China, not in the countries of residence, but in China. The Party did not readily admit to such an intention in the first years of its rule. But from the end of 1954, when the number of Overseas Chinese students was becoming unmanageable, the Party's statements left no doubt as to what it meant. Students were told that they were being educated so that they could 'go to posts in various areas of construction in the homeland', there 'to struggle for the realisation of socialism with the people of the whole country'.[60] The Party actively discouraged them from leaving China and made it very difficult for them to do so, even if they failed to pass school entrance examinations. They were told that

(your) aim in returning to China is to study and to take part in socialist construction... therefore, if you fail your exams, you should submit to the overall arrangements of the state and be content to continue your studies or take employment. Unless there is some compelling reason, you should not consider lightly making application to leave China.[61]

The Party's constant injunctions on this subject are an indication of the degree of dissatisfaction of the Overseas Chinese students, but as with returned Overseas Chinese personal dissatisfaction was not considered a 'sufficiently compelling' reason for obtaining an exit permit.

Some of the Overseas Chinese students have returned to Southeast Asia, but more frequently they have not been able to go beyond Hong Kong or Macao. Despite KMT claims to the contrary, the great majority of those who have left China have been disillusioned rather than successfully indoctrinated, as the case histories published in the KMT's own media so eloquently prove. The CCP was prepared to educate Overseas Chinese, but it was not prepared to give them valuable places in educational institutions without any return, and it was determined to utilise their qualifications by making them stay, permanently, in China. This was one of the first signs that the CCP was prepared to break with traditional practice in its approach to Overseas Chinese education.

The advantages to the Party notwithstanding, Overseas Chinese students also presented special problems, partly because of their bourgeois backgrounds and partly because of the strain they placed on the education system. In 1955, for example, Lo Li-shih addressed a message to Overseas Chinese parents, pointing out that educational facilities in China could not keep pace with demands, and that even the children of workers and peasants had to be denied opportunities for education. Parents should not be disappointed, therefore, if their children failed their exams and were sent to work in agriculture or industry, since China needed young people with a 'cultural level' above the basic level.[62] The students had to be housed and processed on arrival in Canton, which necessitated the formation each year of an *ad hoc* committee, which handled the difficult problem of sorting out students from various educational and political backgrounds and assigning them to appropriate institutions.[63] The assignments were not always, it might be added, to the students' own satisfaction; but given the numbers involved, this is probably not surprising.[64] To facilitate the process of orientation, the Party created a system of 'supplementary schools' (*pu-hsi hsüeh-hsiao*).[65] The function of these schools was stated to be a bridge to regular schools. In addition to coaching for exams, they also prepared students whose previous education did not fit them for regular education in China, and offered courses in written Chinese and standard spoken language.

Originally these schools seem to have been only for those students who were below standard or who arrived too late to sit for the combined entrance examinations.[66] But it seems likely that from the very beginning they were also used for political education, since this gradually emerged as their most important function, and it is probable that by the late 1950s, all Overseas Chinese students were required to spend some time in one of these schools or classes. By 1960, it was stated that their purpose was 'to coach newly returned Overseas Chinese students in culture and politics, and to inculcate the habit of labour'.[67] In other words, they provided a means of political orientation and reeducation for the students, and an opportunity for the Party to screen the new arrivals and prevent them from spreading incorrect thinking and discontent among their fellow students in regular institutions.[68]

Since the CCP's purpose was to prepare the students for work in China, they were not isolated from other students once they had left supplementary schools. They tended, however, to be concentrated in schools designated as 'Overseas Chinese', those which were partly or wholly supported by private Overseas Chinese capital. This applied mainly to primary and middle schools since, while Amoy University and Chungshan University in Canton took a large proportion of Overseas Chinese students, they could not handle all of the tertiary level students, either in terms of numbers or courses offered.[69] In 1958, Chinan University, which had been the first Overseas Chinese educational institution in China, and which had been closed after the CCP came to power, was revived and relocated in Canton, with a 50 per cent enrolment of Overseas Chinese students.[70] Two years later, the Overseas Chinese University was established in Ch'üan-chou in Fukien Province, and this university was supposed to cater exclusively for Overseas Chinese students.[71] One other tertiary institution, the Peking Foreign Languages Institute, established in 1964, was intended to provide training for Overseas Chinese translators and middle-school teachers.[72]

There were both political and economic advantages in concentrating the students in Overseas Chinese schools. The number of Overseas Chinese students usually averaged no more than 50 per cent of the total enrolment in Overseas Chinese schools. This meant that they were integrated with ordinary students and exposed to their politics and subjected to their leadership through the Communist Youth League, while at the same time being concentrated in a way which facilitated supervision and control of their special problems.

It was also a device for persuading the Chinese abroad to subsidise education for non-Overseas Chinese students. The CCP recognised very early the value of Overseas Chinese contributions to education in the home districts, and while there were, of course, continuing voluntary donations after the Party came to power, it lost no opportunity to increase the amount by cajolery, pressure, or appeals to patriotism. The CCP gave its blessing to existing Overseas Chinese schools and revived some which had become defunct,[73] it created new ones and in some cases simply conferred the title 'Overseas Chinese' on existing schools, and it persuaded groups of dependants to 'request' the establishment of such schools in their own districts. The Party then appealed for donations from Chinese abroad and suggested to their dependants in China that they might donate some of their savings or 'surplus' remittances. By placing a reasonable proportion of Overseas Chinese in these schools, the CCP could hope to obtain greater financial support for the education of the Overseas Chinese students themselves, while at the same time earning foreign exchange and obtaining a subsidy for educational facilities for at least one ordinary student for every Overseas Chinese student enrolled. Until 1957, the CCP tended to underemphasise its dependence on Overseas Chinese subsidies, but subsequently official statements openly admitted that the shortage of state-run schools meant that Overseas Chinese schools were vitally necessary to meet educational requirements in Kwangtung and Fukien.[74]

There is some doubt about official Chinese claims that the number of Overseas Chinese returning independently as students actually increased in the mid-1950s.[75] If there was an increase in the number enrolled as Overseas Chinese students this probably came from the children of permanently returning Overseas Chinese.[76] Reports from the countries of residence suggest that the number of young Chinese leaving to study in China was in fact declining markedly,[77] and the reasons are not difficult to find. For students who contemplated going to China there was the prospect of being compelled to remain and work in China, possibly at physical labour. For those who had studied in China and managed to leave, it was not easy to return to the countries of residence, and their qualifications were not always recognised. For Overseas Chinese parents, education in China did not provide a traditional Chinese education, it was not necessarily cheap, and they might have little hope of seeing their children again unless they themselves returned to China. By 1956 also, there were greater educational opportunities elsewhere, particularly in higher education.

There were, however, still very substantial numbers attending schools and universities in China, and the CCP found itself increasingly unwilling to cope with them. As early as April 1955, an official spokesman of the OCAC suggested that students who were in bad health, of average ability, unqualified or with an insufficient educational basis, should not 'recklessly' set off for China but should give careful consideration to the problems involved.[78] By the second half of 1956 the Party had moved from cautionary warnings to the imposition of restrictions on the type of students accepted and the degree to which an exception was made for their special characteristics. They were no longer permitted, for example, to repeat courses, but were instructed to accept employment if they failed their exams. Parents were told that primary school students would no longer be accepted unless they were returning with their parents to live.[79]

The problem was compounded by the obvious dissatisfaction of the students with the education they received, with life in China, and with the prospect of being assigned to work in China after completing their studies. If the reports in the *Ch'iao-wu pao* and the provincial and Overseas Chinese press in Kwangtung and Fukien in 1956 and 1957 represent an official, edited version of the activities of Overseas Chinese students, then the government would appear to have faced major problems of delinquency, as well as open rebellion against its authority. The students were accused of 'creating disturbances and assaulting people'[80] and attacked for 'running every day to the Public Security Bureau or the embassy to arrange exit procedures'.[81] It was reported that their ideological level and political consciousness were not good, that they had wasted their remittances and then demanded assistance from the state, and that there had been wrangling and fighting over 'regionalism'.[82] This last refers to organised crime and gang fighting between students from different countries, describing themselves as the 'Singapore gang' or the 'Indonesian gang'.[83] Throughout 1957 there was a barrage of complaints against what was described as the 'small minority', for indiscipline, bourgeois habits, waste, drunkenness, gambling, gang warfare, indecent assaults on women, and even murder, and for attempting to claim immunity from all forms of discipline, punishment, and physical labour, on the basis of their Overseas Chinese status.[84] The problem was described as a contradiction between China's planned education and the unplanned arrival and unruly behaviour of Overseas Chinese students.[85]

Where Overseas Chinese foreign exchange was at least still an asset, even if diminishing, Overseas Chinese education was becoming a serious liability.

In almost every aspect of Overseas Chinese affairs, therefore, there were good reasons for the CCP to want to rethink its policies. And if the prospects for exploiting the Overseas Chinese relationship with China seemed little more than attractive, the arguments for severing the relationship were increasingly compelling. It was evident that a more effective solution to the problems had to be found, but the Party's options were limited. It could revert to a policy similar to that which it had adopted in the first two years of its rule, in which case the existing problems in foreign relations would be exacerbated. It could continue the policy of 1954, in the hope that the outlook would improve; but the prospects for improvement were negligible, and the immediate problems would still remain unsolved. Or it could attempt to devise some means of dissociating the Overseas Chinese from China in the minds of Southeast Asian governments, and therefore in fact. It is the last of these alternatives which the Party chose, not just as the most effective means of improving relations with Southeast Asia, but as the most practical means of unburdening itself of its own Overseas Chinese problem.

8

An experiment in decolonisation

Overseas Chinese policy since 1957 is described as an experiment because, when the CCP moved from a position of simply accepting the Overseas Chinese right to self-determination to one approximating active decolonisation, there was no question, nor could there be, of a simple transfer of power. Overseas Chinese had to be encouraged individually, not merely to go through the formal procedure of shedding Chinese nationality, but to accept that their future lay with the countries in which they resided. On the other hand, the CCP was anxious to avoid giving the impression that it was abrogating its responsibilities and simply dumping the problem on the countries of Southeast Asia; foreign policy remained the predominant concern. The Party also wanted to be sure, as far as was possible, that in releasing the Overseas Chinese it did not simply drive them into the waiting arms of the KMT. And finally, there were certain elements in the relationship which the Party wanted to maintain, which was much more difficult with an individual than with a political or economic entity. This policy was an experiment also in that it was not entirely successful, or at least, in terms of the CCP's initiatives, not measurably so.

The Party sought to attain its objective by a twofold process of disengagement and the advocacy of specific courses of action for Overseas Chinese which amounted to a formula for integration. The process began in late 1956, but it did not emerge fully until early 1958, and in one important respect, resettlement, until late 1959. It should be pointed out that the CCP itself at no stage specified its objectives as bluntly as they are set out below. It was left to the individual Overseas Chinese to work this out, although many of them failed, or were unwilling, to see what the Party was about.

DISENGAGEMENT
Overseas Chinese and the united front

The most obvious manifestation of disengagement from the Chinese abroad was in the new hard line for domestic Overseas Chinese, discussed in Chapter 4. That the effects on their relationship with relatives overseas were clearly calculated is evident from changes in the role of the UFWD and in the concept of the position of Overseas Chinese in relation to the Chinese people. If the Overseas Chinese were to be detached from China they could no longer be part of the Chinese people's united front.

The changes in the UFWD itself at this time have already been discussed. While their precise nature remains unclear, they do appear to indicate a downgrading of external Overseas Chinese affairs in the work of the Department. This was not, of course, stated explicitly. But it was stated explicitly in reference to the united front or mass organisation for Overseas Chinese, the ACROCA. Where the tasks of the ACROCA had included liaison with the Chinese abroad, reflecting their opinions, and strengthening their patriotic unity,[1] in 1958 it was announced that the work of the ACROCA would be reoriented to cater primarily for newly returned Overseas Chinese.[2]

In September 1956, it was still maintained that the Chinese abroad were an integral part of the united front,[3] but in a long statement at the Eighth Party Congress that month Li Wei-han almost ignored Overseas Chinese affairs.[4] Three months later, an article in the *Kuang-ming jih-pao* commented that the role of the united front in Overseas Chinese affairs was centred in domestic affairs, while externally the Overseas Chinese were simply 'envoys of peace'.[5] By mid-1957 it was obvious that the united front argument about domestic Overseas Chinese was no longer accepted. In her speech to the NPC in July, Ho Hsiang-ning declared:

Some people say that because of the special characteristics of Overseas Chinese, reform movements should not be carried out in the home districts, in order to prevent influencing the unity of the Chinese abroad. There are even some who say: 'the Chinese abroad are extremely disillusioned with the motherland because of such movements and reforms'. This kind of talk does not fit the facts, nor does it fit the aspirations of the Overseas Chinese.[6]

But it was not simply a question of abandoning united front tactics with regard to the relations between domestic Overseas Chinese and Chinese abroad. The Party also applied a new analysis to the situation of Chinese abroad. They had been included originally in the united front because they were said to be an integral part of the Chinese people; by 1960, the Party was claiming that the Overseas Chinese had 'forged flesh and blood relationships with the local people, and are, in fact, an integral part of the local people'.[7]

Foreign exchange

If there is insufficient evidence to conclude that foreign exchange was the single most important concern of Overseas Chinese policy and that when it dropped below a certain level the CCP decided to 'abandon' the Overseas Chinese, it does appear that by 1957, it was not considered important enough to dictate the political objectives of policy. But there was no suggestion that the CCP would deliberately cut off existing sources of foreign exchange, or fail to make the most of opportunities which offered for attracting more.

If the Party's intention was to sever political and cultural ties while maintaining the financial relationship, it would have been necessary to take precautionary measures to ensure that the financial relationship did in fact continue. The protection of remittances had already been guaranteed in the State Council directive of August 1955 as a long-term policy of the state. In late 1957, a number of new measures were introduced which represent an attempt to separate the financial relationship from political objectives, or to protect the former from the effects of the latter.

One of these measures was the limiting of special facilities to those domestic Overseas Chinese receiving remittances. Remittances from abroad, as the CCP discovered, were not made for the benefit of the Chinese government; and it would be quite wrong to accept that they can be 'seen as a barometer of China's standing among...her nationals abroad'.[8] Remittances are made for family support, and, like trade, do not depend on political affiliation or even on the degree of identification with the countries of residence.[9] There may be some who are prepared to deny their dependants because they do not like the communists; there may be many more who have been alienated by the CCP's pressures and demands for money. But the majority might be expected to continue to send money if this would benefit their dependants. From the end of 1957, therefore, the Party was prepared to guarantee a minimum benefit in the form of a slightly better standard of living. The intention was that the tie between domestic Overseas Chinese and the Chinese abroad would be reduced to a purely material, and personal one, that remittances, and the family relationship on which they depended, would continue so long as there were dependants in China.

A second measure introduced in 1957 concerned investment. In August 1957, the State Council issued two directives, on the Overseas Chinese Investment Corporations, and the establishment of schools.[10] In the first of these directives, the government guaranteed an annual dividend of 8 per cent on investment in the Corporations, of which 50 per cent could be repatriated in foreign exchange. It was guaranteed also that share capital invested by Overseas Chinese would remain their lawful property after China had completed 'socialist construction'. This directive was in large part an inducement for remittances, not only because domestic Overseas Chinese could invest in the Corporations, but because there was also a provision whereby investors should be given priority in employment in enterprises managed by the Corporations. It was intended also to attract direct Overseas Chinese investment without the need for family ties, patriotism, or political commitment. The Party appears to have believed that the measures promulgated in the directive would make investment in China attractive as a purely business proposition. Commenting on the directive a spokesman of the OCAC pointed out that in certain countries Chinese businessmen, particularly those engaged in retail trades, were facing economic difficulties, and that, while the government advised them to transfer their capital to local industry, many might find that they were unable to do so and that investment in China would be a profitable venture.[11]

The directive on the establishment of schools, which guaranteed the donor a voice in decisions concerning the name of the school, its location, and the appointment and dismissal of staff, and which instructed local people's councils to 'commend and reward' the donors, appears to have been an attempt to capitalise on what was described as an 'excellent tradition' before it disappeared. Donations from Overseas Chinese had provided a useful subsidy for education in Kwangtung and Fukien long before the CCP came to power. But the CCP appears to have calculated that there was a dwindling number of wealthy, older-generation, China-born 'sojourners' who might be impelled, by patriotism or a sense of identity with the people and the villages they had left behind, to make donations to public works in the home districts. The Overseas Chinese policy on which the Party was then embarked, moreover, was certainly not calculated to foster similar feelings in the new generation of Overseas Chinese.

The question of Overseas Chinese foreign exchange may have contributed to the Party's decision about relations with the Chinese abroad for a number of reasons. The value of this source of foreign exchange was decreasing, both in volume and in relation to total foreign exchange earnings; it was beyond the Party's power to halt this trend; but there was reason to believe that the level of foreign exchange might not be affected by domestic Overseas Chinese policies or the objective of disengaging from the Chinese abroad, provided the Party was prepared to make certain provisions and guarantees. The interesting point about these measures, of course, is that in their intent they resembled the kind of relationship which colonial powers have sought with former colonies; an acceptance of their political independence, but a reluctance to forgo completely the economic benefits of the colonial situation.

Education

Changes in education policy in 1957 were differently motivated but equally significant. To some extent also, they may be seen as a response to an unacceptable domestic problem. But the problem was no longer acceptable only because of external policy, and the import of the changes in education policy was strongly underlined by the Party's recommendations about the future course of Chinese education in the countries of residence.

The contradiction which had arisen in the education of Overseas Chinese could not be allowed to develop. As the pressures on domestic Overseas Chinese increased throughout 1957, the CCP virtually abandoned its policy of education for Overseas Chinese youth in China. This was first suggested in a report on a special conference of the OCAC in January, at which Overseas Chinese parents were urged to provide primary and secondary education for their children in the countries of residence.[12] In May, it was announced that in future, China would accept only above-average, high school graduates.[13] Students who were average in ability, over-age, under-qualified, or sick, were specifically excluded, and any other students who wished to study in China were told that they must be totally supported by their parents. Moreover, all students were warned that they must expect to conform to the requirements of the state, that they should be ideologically prepared for life in China, and that they should give serious thought to the fact that 'they may meet or discover many new problems which they had not expected... they should not imagine that study in China is all smooth sailing'.[14] From this time forth, Overseas Chinese students were made to conform with the principle of education serving proletarian politics and productive labour.[15]

In effect, the Overseas Chinese were informed that students were no longer welcome to study in China. This was denied in public statements, but the regulations were applied administratively, and any Overseas Chinese who took the trouble to read beyond the opening sentences of Chinese statements was warned that, while he might be accepted as a returned Overseas Chinese and placed in employment, he might not be accepted as a student; if he was, he would not be treated as an exception and he could not expect to leave China.

In August 1957, a spokesman of the OCAC pointed out that 'the number of Overseas Chinese children is very great, and there are difficulties in studying in China'. Consequently 'the state actively urges the Overseas Chinese to pool their resources and establish schools, in order to solve the problem of their children's education on the spot'.[16] This did not mean a sudden closure of Overseas Chinese schools or an end to education for those students who were already in China, nor did it mean that the Chinese government flatly refused all applicants from 1957 onwards. But the CCP has not reverted to the policy which prevailed before 1957, nor has it again encouraged Overseas Chinese to think that their children will be willingly accepted for education in China. Had it not been for the massive repatriation of Chinese from Indonesia in 1960, it seems likely that there would have been very few Overseas Chinese studying in Chinese schools in the 1960s; by the time of the Cultural Revolution, the great majority of Overseas Chinese students appears to have been drawn from the repatriates from Indonesia and India.[17] Even these, however, did not have the same opportunities as had existed until 1957, and many of them appear to have been assigned to work in rural areas either immediately, or after a short period in supplementary schools.[18] In the last years of the decade and in the early 1960s, the Party claimed spectacular increases in the number of Overseas Chinese endowed schools,[19] but most of these appear to have resulted from renewed pressures on the dependants.

The change in education policy in 1957 is significant in a number of ways.

The Kuomintang had argued that Overseas Chinese attachment to China should be maintained at all costs, and that this could only be done through the preservation among the Overseas Chinese of Chinese language and cultural traditions. The promotion of Chinese education, in China and abroad, had been and to a large extent is still the fundamental concern of KMT Overseas Chinese policy. At the very least, the CCP's policy after 1957 marked the end of any pretence of maintaining links with the Overseas Chinese by reinforcing Chinese culture through education in the homeland. Moreover, if the Party had ever entertained the idea of 'flooding' Southeast Asia with communist-indoctrinated Overseas Chinese youth, which is doubtful, this also would appear to have been abandoned.

The events of 1957 are significant also as an indication of the gulf which separated many Overseas Chinese from Communist China. Not only had the number of Overseas Chinese willing to submit themselves to the rigours of life in China declined, but the students who did go to China found it difficult to adjust to the communist system, even though most had gone for 'patriotic' reasons or because they considered themselves revolutionaries. Chinese government statements indicate that it was very much aware of this problem, and it is likely that its experience with Overseas Chinese students caused it to reconsider the nature of seemingly 'patriotic' activities by Chinese youth in Southeast Asia and influenced its assessment of the Overseas Chinese as a whole.

The full significance of the restrictions on education in China, however, is that they were accompanied by and specifically linked with a policy for desinification of Overseas Chinese schools in the countries of residence. The CCP had told the Overseas Chinese that they could not expect an education to be provided for them in China, and that it was 'more important (for) Overseas Chinese to establish schools abroad, to enable Overseas Chinese students to receive a suitable education in the countries of residence'.[20] At the same time it proposed that Chinese schools in the countries of residence should transform themselves into schools orientated primarily towards the local environment and acceptable to the local peoples.[21] It proposed that Overseas Chinese schools should concentrate on teaching the local language, history, geography and culture, and skills suitable for local employment.[22] The Party even suggested that the local language should be used as the medium of instruction since it was 'necessary' that the great majority of Overseas Chinese should know the local language, although some time might be reserved for the study of Chinese.[23] The existence itself of Chinese education among the Overseas Chinese was actually described as a 'problem', and official statements left no doubt that the CCP's aim was to eliminate this problem:

There still exists among Overseas Chinese and local people of Chinese descent the problem of preservation of the traditional language of the Chinese people and Chinese education. For this reason, Overseas Chinese schools must educate Overseas Chinese children so that they will become thoroughly familiar with the local language, history and geography, and respect the culture of the countries of residence.[24]

The CCP made every effort to ensure that its message was clear and unequivocal: 'Chinese education (*hua-wen chiao-yü*) must serve this policy and move in this direction.'[25] On the one hand, Overseas Chinese students were no longer welcome in China, while on the other, they were told that in the countries of residence Chinese education as a separate system based on Chinese language and culture should be abandoned.

If this policy was partly a response to pressures on Chinese education in Southeast Asia, the CCP was also mindful of the almost inevitable consequences. Just as the attempts of Southeast Asian governments to suppress Chinese schools went beyond the elimination of a separate education system, so also was the CCP's education policy one step, and probably the most crucial, in its attempt to detach the Overseas Chinese from China and persuade them to identify with the countries in which they lived. If it could be assumed that the majority of Overseas Chinese concerned would accept the Chinese government's advice, then the education policy would assist the governments of Southeast Asia in undermining the very foundation of the Overseas Chinese relationship with China. In 1967, the revolutionary rebels in the OCAC accused Liao Ch'eng-chih of assisting in 'strangling and ruining the culture and education of Overseas Chinese', one point on which the KMT might agree. In effect, the CCP was acting on the precept which guided the Overseas Chinese policy of the Kuomintang: 'without Chinese education there can be no Overseas Chinese'.

The 'three-good' policy: nationality, non-interference and resettlement

The external aspects of education policy belong more to the formula for integration than to the process of disengagement. Where it was intended to have a direct impact on the Chinese abroad, disengagement centred on what was known, from early 1958, as the 'three-good' Overseas Chinese policy. In addition to being an essential step towards decolonisation, this policy was also clearly directed towards removing the Overseas Chinese problem in relations with Southeast Asia.

Nationality. Until the end of 1957, the CCP had always stopped short of suggesting which way it would prefer the Overseas Chinese to choose on the question of nationality. The Party's statements, particularly since the end of 1956, could have been interpreted as implying that it would prefer them to choose local nationality, but it had never stated so publicly. In November 1957, this last restraint was finally removed. In her report to the First Plenary Conference of the Second OCAC, Ho Hsiang-ning announced that the Chinese government 'advocated' that Overseas Chinese should choose local nationality,[26] and in January 1958 she broadcast this message to the Chinese abroad.[27] A joint statement at the Fifth Session of the First NPC in February 1957 by sixteen leading Overseas Chinese affairs officials, including Liao Ch'eng-chih, was even more direct:

The broad masses of Overseas Chinese resident abroad must now put aside any reservations, and, on the principle of free choice, choose local nationality. They must live and work in peace in the countries of residence, actively cooperate and coexist with the local people, and strive for the peace, happiness, and prosperity, of the countries in which they live. This will be of assistance in promoting friendly relations between China and the countries of residence.[28]

Both in 1957 and subsequently, Chinese statements on nationality emphasised not only that it would prefer Overseas Chinese to choose local nationality, but also, and more important, that 'those who choose local nationality are no longer Chinese nationals; they must be loyal to the country of their choice'.[29]

The CCP's attitude to nationality provides one of the clearest examples of the way in which its whole approach to the question of relations with the Chinese abroad has been either misrepresented or misunderstood. There has been no significant modification of this position, and so far as is known it has not even been changed by the Cultural Revolution.[30] Yet it is not uncommon to find assertions about the CCP's Overseas Chinese policy, written after 1957, which begin with the claim that the Party regards all Overseas Chinese as nationals of the People's Republic of China and refuses to recognise the right, or even the fact, of acquisition by Overseas Chinese of foreign nationality.[31]

Non-interference. Since the Chinese government was not in a position to haul down the flag and sail away, there remained a problem of how to deal with those who objected, the 'patriotic' Overseas Chinese. Even if it had been legally possible for all Overseas Chinese to acquire citizenship of the countries of residence, as Chou En-lai said in his Rangoon talk: 'there will always be some who remain Overseas Chinese, and if they are still Overseas Chinese that means they are still Chinese nationals'.[32] The Chinese government was still responsible for its overseas nationals and it could not avoid responsibility for a wider group who, through their own behaviour or through local discrimination or persecution, were likely to be a continuing problem in Southeast Asia. The second and third 'goods' were intended to cope with this problem.

The second 'good' was in fact a continuation of the policy of urging Chinese nationals not to interfere in local politics, but it was urged more strongly and in more specific terms, for which Chou En-lai's Rangoon speech was the best example and the model for subsequent policy statements. But Chinese nationals were not only told to respect local laws and customs and religious beliefs. They were actually instructed to respect the 'policies' of the governments of the countries of residence.[33] Given the domestic and foreign policies of the governments to which the CCP was referring this particular injunction may seem somewhat surprising, but it is highly revealing of the Party's thinking on the Overseas Chinese problem.

One of the most difficult problems was the attitudes and behaviour of the 'patriotic' Overseas Chinese, those who, while not necessarily communist supported the communist government, whose chauvinist attitudes were largely responsible for the belief that all Overseas Chinese were willing servants of Peking, and who refused to think of themselves as anything but Chinese or accept that the Chinese government could be serious in what it appeared to be saying. The CCP had long been sensitive to this problem, and had instructed the patriotic Overseas Chinese to suppress tendencies to arrogance and chauvinism. Their persistence was regarded as an obstacle to the success of the 'three-good' policy, to the extent that in January 1958 the existence of chauvinism was said to be the main problem confronting those responsible for communication with the Chinese abroad.[34]

It was in an attempt to overcome this problem that the CCP began to suggest certain limitations to the 'patriotic' activities of Chinese nationals overseas. Patriotic activities were to be confined to 'internal' relations, in matters of assistance, welfare, and relief. Patriotic newspapers were to concern themselves mainly with promoting cultural and trade relations between China and the countries of residence and developing friendly relations between the local people and the Chinese people. Patriotic schools were to limit their activities to cultural work, teaching the language of the countries of residence as well as Chinese, and teaching students to love the countries of residence as well as China.[35]

Resettlement. The third 'good' was such a dramatic development in terms of China's relations with the Overseas Chinese that it is quite extraordinary that it did not receive more attention at the time, and it can only be surmised that this was due to the refusal of Southeast Asian and western politicians and observers to believe that the CCP was capable of anything less than aggressive foreign policy action, including manipulation of Overseas Chinese for the advancement of its interests in Southeast Asia.

While the CCP had still hoped that it might be able to conclude nationality treaties and establish diplomatic relations with all Southeast Asian countries, protection of Overseas Chinese had ceased to be a major issue. Since 1954, Chinese protests had been fewer and more restrained. The South Vietnam case particularly had demonstrated that the Chinese government was unwilling to take a strong stand on protection.

In the context of its policy objectives after 1956, however, the CCP renewed its attention to the problem of protection, this time with additional complications presented by the policy of decolonisation, since part of the reason for this policy was precisely a desire not to become embroiled in disputes over Overseas Chinese with Southeast Asian governments. There was a more difficult question, since nationality problems had not been settled, of how far or up to what point, the Chinese government was obligated to extend protection to the individual when it was encouraging a process of 'self-decolonisation'. The CCP still did not have the means to protect Overseas Chinese; it could not persuade Chinese nationals and 'patriots' to behave as it wished them to; nor could it ensure that Overseas Chinese became loyal citizens of the countries of residence or prevent the recurrence of incidents involving the Chinese abroad which were damaging to its relations with Southeast Asia.

The Party turned, therefore, to the only possible alternative. For a complete solution to the Overseas Chinese problem it would have to be prepared to accept, and possibly itself repatriate, substantial numbers of Overseas Chinese for permanent settlement in China.

During the Fifth Session of the First NPC Overseas Chinese affairs spokesmen raised the question of large-scale resettlement of Overseas Chinese who might be 'compelled' to return to China.[36] It was anticipated that this would involve not only Chinese nationals, but dual nationals and possibly even some who had already renounced Chinese nationality.[37] Attacking the 'conservative thinking' that China's population was already too large, the joint statement by sixteen Overseas Chinese deputies pointed out that in the normal course of events the numbers would not be very great,

but the problem is not so simple. We must on no account base our calculations on a one-sided approach. What if there are some Overseas Chinese who are compelled, for various reasons, to return? What would we do then? For this reason, it would be best to make preparations in advance.[38]

This explains why China has apparently been prepared to ignore the legal status of the Overseas Chinese it has been willing to resettle, a point on which the CCP has been accused of duplicity. The argument runs that the CCP's assertion that it renounced claims to certain of the Overseas Chinese was negated by the fact that it declared that any person of Chinese descent was welcome to return to China. But resettlement, of course, was founded on policy objectives quite the reverse of those assumed by people who made this charge, and the Indonesian government's unilateral abrogation of the Treaty in 1969 showed that the CCP's position was both justifiable and necessary.

There was no sudden increase in the number of Overseas Chinese returning to China; nor did the government go out of its way to 'recruit' returnees. The advance preparations to which the joint statement referred were announced by the Editorial Office of the *Ch'iao-wu pao* in April, which pointed out also that the principle underlying Overseas Chinese policy was 'to serve the advancement of our relations with the national independent states of Southeast Asia'.[39] It was at this time also that the Returned Overseas Chinese Associations were reorganised to cater for the expected influx.[40]

Although the advance preparations were announced in 1958 the scale of resettlement contemplated by the Party did not become apparent until the end of 1959, in the wake of the problems which had arisen from the ban on alien retail traders in Indonesia.[41] It was estimated that at least 300,000 Chinese in rural Indonesia would be affected by the ban,[42] which not only prevented Chinese from engaging in retail trade, but was accompanied by a series of regulations issued by regional military commanders compelling Chinese to move into the cities and towns.[43] Chinese newspapers were restricted, Chinese schools were closed, and there was a general increase in discrimination against all people of Chinese descent.[44]

The kind of situation which had arisen in Indonesia was such as had been anticipated in the joint statement by Overseas Chinese deputies at the NPC in February 1958, and the CCP was apparently now in a better position to be more positive in its presentation of this policy. On 12 December, the *Jen-min jih-pao* declared that China was ready at all times to resettle any Overseas Chinese from any part of the world who 'met with difficulties or who wished to return for other reasons'.[45] At a conference of the ACROCA in the same month, Fang Fang declared:

The government is resolved and prepared to receive compatriots returning from abroad. Regardless of whether there are 500,000, 1 million, or several million, they will all be welcome. We have the capacity, and have made preparations for the work of receiving them.[46]

Fang pointed out that China had already successfully resettled 300,000 Overseas Chinese and 50,000 students since 1949, and said that the Party expected a minimum of 600,000 returnees in 1960 alone. He also outlined in some detail the specific measures already taken, or planned, to cope with a massive influx of people into South China.

The proposed '500,000, 1 million, or several million' was repeated by other spokesmen, and it soon emerged that the CCP believed that 'all' (*ch'üan-pu, yi-ch'ieh*) Overseas Chinese who were unable or unwilling to remain in the countries of residence should return to China,[47] and that where necessary China would even take the initiative to 'withdraw' (*chieh-hui-lai*) or 'repatriate' (*chieh-yün*) them.[48] It was made clear that the proposal was to embrace the Chinese in all countries, and to underline this point specific reference was made to countries like the Philippines, where the position of the Chinese and the state of relations with China differed significantly from the Indonesian case. According to the Cultural Revolution document discussed in Chapter 9, there was a plan to withdraw from three to five million Overseas Chinese from various parts of the world over a period of seven or eight years. This corresponds roughly with the 40 per cent estimated by the Chinese government in 1960 to be pure Chinese nationals.[49] The rate of withdrawal also corresponds with official estimates published at the time of the 600,000 expected in 1960.

This extraordinary proposal was more than simply an impressive gesture forced on the Chinese government by the problem of refugees in Indonesia. It was embodied in a special decision of the CCP, which subsequently appeared in the form of a State Council directive in February 1960.[50] Such directives are not made for propaganda purposes, but are designed to set forth specific policies for implementation by the units concerned. Moreover, the proposal was not an isolated response arising for the first time in the context of the Indonesian problem. For two years resettlement had been proclaimed as a basic component of the Party's solution to the Overseas Chinese problem; the statements of 1958 had not mentioned the figure of several million, but the Party had considered the possibility, and there was contingency planning for such an eventuality. When, therefore, it was confronted with the Indonesian crisis, there was already an established policy which provided the basis for the decisions announced in December 1959. If the 'conservative-thinking' to which the joint statement at the NPC in February 1958 had referred had continued to provide some opposition during the intervening years, it is conceivable that the Indonesian situation furnished the decisive argument in favour of active promotion of this policy. In any event, when the Indonesian government declared that it was unable to carry out the repatriation, the Chinese government sent its own ships to transport almost 100,000 refugees back to China; it did the same in India in 1963, and again in Indonesia in 1966–7.

It was clear also from the accompanying developments in China that this was neither a propaganda stunt nor an isolated response to the events in Indonesia. There was an extensive administrative reorganisation involving the establishment of a Committee for Reception and Resettlement.[51] There had been similar committees in the past, established on an *ad hoc* basis to deal with large numbers of Overseas Chinese returning, for example, from Malaya in the early 1950s. The 1960 Committee, however, was established by State Council directive, and it had a coordinative function and a hierarchy of branches not unlike the OCAC itself.[52] Branches were established at provincial level in Kwangtung, Fukien, Kwangsi, and Yunnan, with special offices in Canton, Swatow, Chan-chiang, and Haikow. Below province level, committees were established at least down to *hsien* level.[53] The national Committee was headed by Liao Ch'eng-chih, and included representatives from the Central OCAC, the Customs Office of the Ministry of Foreign Trade, the Ministries of Commerce, Labour, Internal Affairs, and Education, and the four provincial governments concerned. The administrative headquarters for the whole organisation was established in Canton, with a large staff under the direction of Chung Ch'ing-fa, a member of the Central OCAC and a former counsellor and chargé d'affaires in the Chinese Embassy in Djakarta.[54] Most surprising, the 'major part' of the workers in the Central OCAC was transferred to the Canton office.[55] The provincial governments in Fukien, Kwangsi, and Yunnan also appointed to this office Overseas Chinese affairs officials, and cadres from their departments of communications, agriculture and land reclamation, commerce and health.[56]

Following a joint directive of the OCAC and the Ministry of Commerce ordering that organs be established in all relevant areas for distribution of specially allocated rations and supplies,[57] a Central Administrative Office for Distribution was created, with branches at province level and below.[58] The government also made a special budgetary appropriation for the returnees;[59] it planned to increase the number of Overseas Chinese farms to sixty-four, and to establish a number of supplementary, technical, and agricultural schools for Overseas Chinese;[60] and it offered inducements for those who might be reluctant to return to China.[61] The whole direction of domestic Overseas Chinese policy was reoriented to the task of reception and re-settlement.[62]

The Chinese government asserted that its willingness to repatriate Overseas Chinese was proof that

the Chinese people have never sought, nor will they in the future seek, to exploit the Overseas Chinese to harm any country, or to utilise the so-called 'surplus' population as a means of 'expansion'. This also serves to smash thoroughly the slanders spread by imperialism and foreign reactionaries that the Overseas Chinese are China's 'fifth column' for subversion, and that an increase in the Chinese population will become a 'threat' to China's neighbours in Asia.[63]

Not surprisingly, no foreign government appears to have taken notice of this statement, and yet it was an accurate representation of China's Overseas Chinese policy, and it poses a very interesting question about repatriation and the 'Fifth Column'. To the revolutionary rebels in the Cultural Revolution, the Chinese in Indonesia should not have been repatriated, but urged 'to wage mass self-defence struggle'; repatriation was 'out-and-out escapism and capitulationism'.[64] The section of the Overseas Chinese which China apparently proposed to withdraw from Southeast Asia were the pure Chinese nationals and those who were unwilling or unable to integrate in the countries of residence or who were likely to be a source of dispute between China and the countries concerned. These were the Overseas Chinese who were most vulnerable to discrimination and possible deprivation of livelihood, the ones most alienated from the societies in which they lived, and the ones who would tend most to look to China for protection and guidance and, possibly, to serve in the promotion of its political objectives. Potentially, they were the most susceptible to Chinese influence, the core of any Chinese Fifth Column. That the CCP was prepared to withdraw them is a clear indication not only that it was not interested in using them as a subversive Fifth Column, but also of how intent it was on dissolving the Overseas Chinese 'colonies'.

The resettlement programme, therefore, is one of the most important indicators of the motives behind all of the CCP's Overseas Chinese policies from the end of 1956. The Indonesian crisis merely served to demonstrate this fact. If the government had been prepared, as the revolutionary rebels say it should have been, to disregard the reasons for its failure to solve the Overseas Chinese problem, to ignore the predicament of the Overseas Chinese themselves, to cling to a colonial relationship, to abandon its policy of friendship and coexistence with Indonesia, and to overlook the lesson of Malaya, it might have backed the Overseas Chinese in a campaign of resistance. Since it was not prepared to do so, and the Indonesian government was not prepared to protect the 'proper rights and interests' of these particular Overseas Chinese, repatriation was the only practical alternative.

It was not, however, an outstanding success, simply because such large numbers of Overseas Chinese could be expected to want to return to China only where their situation was desperate and the prospect of life in China seemed to offer some hope for improvement. Once again, the CCP's plans were frustrated by its inability to dictate the responses of the compatriots abroad. The immediate problem of the Chinese in Indonesia was relieved by the repatriation of 94,000 people in 1960; and the exchange of instruments of ratification of the 1955 Treaty in January 1960[65] and the signing of a supplementary agreement in December[66] gave hope for improvement. In February 1961, a *Jen-min jih-pao* editorial declared that China would continue to send ships to bring back those who have 'encountered difficulties and who wish to return'[67] but by the end of October 1961 only another 10,000 had accepted the offer.[68] In China itself, there were also problems in resettlement. In a letter to Subandrio in December 1959, Foreign Minister Ch'en Yi had asked that Indonesia repatriate the Chinese, and do so in small groups to enable China to absorb them.[69] But the repatriation of 94,000 in one year had created problems, both in assimilation, and in cost to the Chinese government.[70] There was also the danger, arising from the special consideration given to the returnees on their arrival in China and their subsequent reluctance to forgo the 'small freedoms' they were permitted at first, that continued repatriation on such a scale would produce the kind of situation in domestic Overseas Chinese affairs which the Party had been attempting to eradicate since 1957.[71]

The resettlement policy was not abandoned. The Party accepted that 'the situation in which Overseas Chinese will return to China is a long-term one',[72] and it continued to develop the Overseas Chinese farms in order to resettle them. But the ambitious scheme of repatriating several million Overseas Chinese in seven or eight years was adjusted to the realities of domestic Overseas Chinese problems and the attitudes of the Overseas Chinese themselves.

INTEGRATION

According to Foreign Minister Ch'en Yi, the 'three-good' Overseas Chinese policy was intended as 'a complete (*ch'üan-mien*) solution to the Overseas Chinese problem'.[73] It may have been a complete solution, at least in terms of foreign relations, if the Overseas Chinese had heeded the CCP's advice. But it was only a partial solution to the problem of decolonisation. The policies outlined above were all limited in the extent to which they could have a positive effect on the Overseas Chinese problem. At most, if they had been heeded by the majority of Overseas Chinese and accepted as genuine by indigenous Southeast Asians, they might have helped to create favourable conditions for the achievement of the Party's purpose. The success of the Party's policy, however, depended ultimately on the willingness of the Overseas Chinese to identify and integrate with the local people and on how far local conditions permitted such identification and integration. The CCP could do little about the latter of these two problems, but it could attempt to influence the attitudes of the Overseas Chinese themselves. In conjunction with the above policies, therefore, the Party began to urge the Overseas Chinese to take specific courses of action which, if followed, would have had the effect of creating or accelerating existing tendencies towards identification with the countries of residence and breaking down some of the barriers to integration. This policy was directed at the causes of the Overseas Chinese problem in Southeast Asia, at the real and alleged characteristics of Overseas Chinese which emphasised their relationship with China or which set them apart from the people of the countries in which they lived.

There were two features of the way in which the Party transmitted this advice to the Chinese abroad which require explanation. The first concerns propaganda and slogans. To a large extent, these continued unchanged, as they had done also after the change in policy in 1954; patriotic unity, 'smashing the Chiang gang', and support for socialist construction in China remained standard slogans in speeches or statements on Overseas Chinese affairs. In 1957 and 1958 there was a peculiar intensity to this sloganeering, accompanied by exaggerated claims to achievement frequently at variance with the Party's own detailed reports. This was due in part to the political movements which followed the Hundred Flowers, and in 1958 and 1959, to the general euphoria about achievements which pervaded the Chinese media.

But there were other reasons arising specifically from Overseas Chinese affairs. After eight years in power, those responsible for Overseas Chinese affairs had failed to solve existing problems or to make any positive achievements. In their unsuccessful attempts they had condoned a permissiveness in domestic affairs of a kind now under attack in all sectors. The policy required, therefore, defence and justification. The CCP did not admit that Overseas Chinese policy had been incorrect; it claimed achievements for that policy and continued to use its slogans. There appears also to have been some opposition to the new policy, sufficiently persistent to warrant statements in its defence from time to time. In the context of the political movements which dominated the domestic scene in the late 1950s, therefore, the language of Overseas Chinese slogans tended to become quite extreme; the Overseas Chinese were united as never before in patriotic unity, they were devoting all their strength and resources to construction in China, the numbers returning to help build socialism were increasing year by year, and students continued to return in droves. Abroad, they had made great contributions to China's policy of peace and coexistence, they had strengthened relations with the local people, and thoroughly isolated and exposed the agents of the Kuomintang.

It is essential, therefore, to realise that the redirection of Overseas Chinese policy was made within this verbal framework, to distinguish policy from propaganda.[74] The same is necessary, of course, for any aspect of Communist Chinese affairs. But the circumstances of the change in Overseas Chinese policy and the constant use of patriotic slogans which accompanied it, suggests a need for particular caution.

The second, and more important feature of its propagation of this policy, was that the CCP used a device more typical of its promotion of policies in the domestic communications media; the combination of an approved, and in this case slightly idealised, model experience with an exhortation to the less advanced or backward to emulate the model. The Party's intentions can be discerned, therefore, both from the model and from the exhortations, and there should have been no doubt in the minds of Overseas Chinese just what those intentions were. The use of this device rested on a somewhat oversimplified distinction, first enunciated in Chou En-lai's talk in Rangoon, between those who were said to have 'merged with' or 'become one with' (*jung-ch'ia yi-ch'i, ta-ch'eng yi-p'ien*) the local people, and a category generally referred to as Chinese nationals, but which was more loosely defined since it appeared to include all those whose attitudes and responses denoted some kind of involvement with or attachment to China.[75] This distinction approximated to the kind of division the CCP had wanted to achieve by nationality treaties, and it was on this basis also that the 'three-good' Overseas Chinese policy was developed.

The elements of the model to which Chou referred in his Rangoon talk were the acquisition of local citizenship, and intermarriage.[76] The second one is interesting because it suggests that the CCP was thinking in terms of complete assimilation. At no time did the Chinese government use the term assimilation (*t'ung-hua*), and on this occasion Chou omitted reference to Malaya and Indonesia, possibly in recognition of the greater impediments to assimilation in those two countries. But frequent reference in Chinese statements to intermarriage and the use of the terms 'to merge with' and 'to become one with' suggests that the CCP believed that this was a desirable end, even if not practical or possible in all situations.[77]

In his injunctions to those who still identified with China, Chou concentrated on language, culture and education, chauvinism, and economic exploitation. He said that the language of the countries of residence should be studied by all Overseas Chinese, not just the young; it should be taught in the schools, but it should also be used in Overseas Chinese newspapers.[78] The fact that Overseas Chinese refused to learn local languages was a sign of 'conservatism', 'laziness', and 'chauvinism'. He explained chauvinism as meaning 'conceited, looking down on everyone, self-opinionated, and superior', and he 'entreated' the Overseas Chinese to suppress such attitudes. He urged Overseas Chinese businessmen to be honest and law-abiding in all their dealings, to be 'model settlers', and to transfer their capital from commerce to industrial development, arguing that, while the returns from industrial investment were slow, Overseas Chinese businessmen should make long-term calculations if they planned to live permanently in the countries of residence. The object of these last remarks was obviously the widespread belief in Southeast Asia that the Overseas Chinese were economic parasites who could be used by the Chinese government to gain an economic stranglehold on the region.[79] If Overseas Chinese businessmen had accepted this advice, it might have encouraged them to feel that they had a permanent interest in the countries of residence and resulted in greater acceptability by the local people.[80]

The themes outlined in Chou's talk were repeated and expanded over the next four years, always with the emphasis on the crucial area of language, education, and culture, discussed above.[81] Businessmen were urged to invest in joint ventures with local governments or individuals for development of the local economy.[82] They were even told to improve the lot of their employees and to undertake social welfare work for the community at large.[83]

The Party's model became progressively more explicit. In its most idealised form, it presented Overseas Chinese born in the country of residence, married to indigenous Southeast Asians, completely assimilated, and wanting nothing but 'to become local people' (*ch'eng-wei tang-ti jen-min*).[84] Two successive statements by Ho Hsiang-ning in January and February of 1958 provide a clear illustration of the model, alleged to be represented by the 'greater part' of the Overseas Chinese, and of the steps which the remainder were expected to take in following this example:

We are aware that the greater part of the Overseas Chinese compatriots have merged with the local people economically, culturally, and in their way of life, that they wish to remain permanently in the local countries and hope to become local citizens. Our government completely understands and sympathises with this aspiration, and is willing to discuss the solution of the dual nationality problem with the countries concerned. We advocate that Overseas Chinese should choose the nationality of the countries of residence, according to their own free will. This is good for the Overseas Chinese themselves, for the countries of residence, and for friendly relations between China and the countries of residence. Naturally, those who choose local nationality are no longer Chinese nationals; they must be loyal to the country of their choice and take an active part in its construction.[85]

We ask those who retain Chinese nationality to continue to respect the policies and laws of the countries of residence and the customs and habits of the local people. We urge Overseas Chinese commerce to transfer to local industry, or in joint management with local national capital to participate in economic construction which will benefit the national independence of the countries of residence. Overseas Chinese children should learn the local language, geography, history, and skills, so that they may be educated and make a living in the local countries.[86]

It was in February also that the Overseas Chinese were told 'to put aside any reservations' and choose local nationality;[87] subsequently, the government urged 'as many as possible' of the Overseas Chinese to act on this advice.[88]

To the ardent patriots, the CCP added a new dimension to the concept of patriotism. In his talk with visiting Overseas Chinese in October 1960, broadcast to the Chinese abroad, Fang Fang said that it was 'a manifestation of patriotism' to take local nationality, to study the local language and culture, to love the countries of residence and to unite with the local people.[89]

The decolonisation policy as it had emerged in 1958 was exemplified in the Party's reaction to the Indonesian situation in 1959–60. This was not because the policy was applied only to countries which recognised Peking, but because a major problem arose in Indonesia and the existence of diplomatic relations made it possible for the CCP to take some practical measures to implement its policy. The CCP ignored the Indonesian government's moves against Chinese education in 1957; it even attempted to ignore the ban on alien retail traders when it was first announced in May 1959. When Subandrio visited Peking in October, he declared that the rights and interests of Overseas Chinese in Indonesia would be respected, and that Indonesia would proceed to ratification and implementation of the Sino-Indonesian Treaty. China gave an understanding and public recognition of the fact that Chinese in Indonesia must accept that they would be affected, perhaps adversely, by measures to promote Indonesia's economic development.[90]

At the end of 1959, when the displacement of Chinese in Indonesia had begun to reach massive proportions, and there was no sign that the Indonesian government intended to abide by the undertaking to ratify the treaty, the CCP decided to act. In a letter to Subandrio written on 9 December, Ch'en Yi demanded that the Indonesian government ratify the treaty as soon as possible, protect Chinese nationals, and arrange for repatriation to China of Chinese who had lost their homes and their means of livelihood or who were unwilling to continue to live in Indonesia.[91] The Chinese media then mounted a full campaign over the Chinese in Indonesia, more intensive than the response to any other Overseas Chinese incident or situation between 1949 and the Cultural Revolution.

China's response to the Indonesian crisis demonstrates a number of points. First, it showed the decolonisation policy, particularly as it was reflected in repatriation, to be the principal objective of post-1957 Overseas Chinese policy. Secondly, it provided a dramatic illustration of the over-riding interests of foreign relations. The Chinese government made it clear that it was 'willing to make every effort to prevent the undermining of friendly relations' by the 'Overseas Chinese problem which exists between our two countries'.[92] And when the supplementary agreement was signed in December 1960, the *Jen-min jih-pao* echoed a sentiment which had been expressed by the Chinese government several times throughout the crisis: 'Even though there have been some unhappy incidents between our two countries in the past year over the problem of the Overseas Chinese, this is, after all, only a temporary problem, a minor difficulty.'[93]

Thirdly, the Indonesian incident provides the best example of the selective basis on which China has chosen to respond to incidents involving the Chinese abroad. It would have been difficult for the government to have ignored the predicament of the Chinese in Indonesia in 1959, as it had done when the Indonesian government began to eliminate Chinese education in 1957. In this case, there was widespread physical hardship and suffering; and according to one report, the Indonesian Army General Staff wanted to expel one million Chinese from the country.[94] Moreover, the discriminatory measures to which the Chinese government chose to respond in this way were precisely of the kind which created communal antagonism and worked against the CCP's policy for integration. The Chinese government responded with restraint and only after considerable delay to the Saigon government's attempt to force South Vietnamese citizenship on its Chinese population; it issued a single protest over a series of arrests in Thailand in late 1958; it seldom even commented on the problems of Chinese businessmen in the Philippines. Yet it did, under considerable provocation, protest strongly and publicly about the Chinese in Indonesia in 1959. Clearly, the Chinese government was selective in its protests. The cases of Vietnam in 1956–7 and India in 1962–3 provide a further clue to the basis for its selectivity. In both cases there was discrimination against Overseas Chinese as a race, involving hardship and deprivation of livelihood for considerable numbers of people. In neither case did the government base its protest on the argument that they were Chinese nationals; it alleged that the actions were in violation of international law and an infringement of human rights. In the case of

Indonesia in 1958–60, which according to some interpretations should have been ignored, the magnitude and the nature of the discrimination made it almost impossible for the Chinese government to ignore. It had nothing to do with the Indonesian government's pressures against retail traders as such; similar incidents, both in Indonesia and elsewhere, had been ignored in the past, and were to be ignored again in the future. The CCP's most vigorous protests have never been against incidents involving political activities of Overseas Chinese; the arrest and detention of Overseas Chinese leftists or communists has usually been ignored, or, where the local government action is sufficiently widespread to be construed as having a racial bias, as in Thailand in 1958, treated with a perfunctory protest.

The CCP responded, therefore, according to the nature of the incidents rather than the state of relations with the governments concerned; where obvious acts of racial discrimination or persecution on a wide scale would have been difficult to ignore. The Party itself may not have been moved by humanitarian motives, although it seems likely that it was, and it was certainly most vocal in cases where its action could be construed as arising from humanitarian considerations, or where lack of response might be taken as cynical disregard for the plight of Overseas Chinese. Moreover, the incidents to which the Party chose to respond most loudly were those which in any country, be it Thailand or Indonesia, tended to exacerbate racial animosities and inhibit integration of Overseas Chinese. The repatriation policy illustrates this point.

It is interesting that the Chinese government made particular efforts to counter charges of Overseas Chinese subversion at this time, a time when most western observers regard the period of peaceful coexistence as having already passed. An article in the *Ch'iao-wu pao* in July and August 1959, for example, accused the United States of manufacturing and propagating these charges in an effort to create racial divisions within the countries of residence, to engender hostility towards and fear of the Overseas Chinese, and to undermine or prevent development of relations between China and the countries of Southeast Asia.[95] If, as appears to have been the case, the Party had concluded that the Overseas Chinese were an unlikely instrument for successful subversion in Southeast Asia, and if it was genuine in its attempts to solve the Overseas Chinese problem and improve relations with Southeast Asia, it must have been particularly galled by propaganda which sought to foster an image of the Overseas Chinese as a menacing communist Fifth Column spread throughout the whole of Asia. It was this particular article which stated explicitly that Overseas Chinese policies were intended equally for friendly countries, hostile countries, and even for areas under the control of imperialism. Subsequent Chinese statements were careful to emphasise this point, not that it seems to have had much effect on hostile foreign governments.

The principles which had guided Overseas Chinese policy since 1957 were reaffirmed in the State Council directive of February 1960, in terms which indicated that, at that stage at least, the Party regarded its decision as final: 'the above policies are the consistent policy of our government, and will remain so in the future (*chiang-lai yeh pu-hui kai-pien*)'. It was not only a consistent long-term policy, but as Ch'en-yi said, it was intended as a 'complete solution' to the Overseas Chinese problem.

This policy remained basically unchanged at least until the Cultural Revolution. It is the key to understanding the Party's intentions towards the Chinese abroad, and it is in relation to this policy that the other aspects of post-1956 policy may be seen in perspective. The CCP had been faced with a circle of dilemmas. Its attempts to grapple with the problem and realise on the potential of the Overseas Chinese had failed; yet it was still burdened with responsibility for the Overseas Chinese, a problem which it could not ignore, but over it had virtually no control. Foreign governments were uncooperative and could not be forced to accept the CCP's offers or assurances; the Overseas Chinese could not be removed or mobilised by mass campaigns or forced indoctrination to do the Party's bidding. The unique advantage of the 'Fifth Column' in Southeast Asia rested on the special relationship of the Overseas Chinese with China. It could not be exploited successfully while there was widespread and deep-rooted suspicion and hostility towards the Overseas Chinese in the countries of residence; its preservation was a barrier to the development of normal relations with Southeast Asia. To overcome this, it was necessary for the Overseas Chinese to abandon the attitudes and the culture which set them apart from the local people, and to dispel the belief that their first loyalty was to China. But this meant destroying the foundation of the ties which bound them to China, and therefore, the special advantages which they seemed to present as a non-integrated Fifth Column.

This did not mean that the Party immediately abandoned the Overseas Chinese, or that it gave up all thought of attempting to utilise them within the limits of its policy and their potential. It did mean, however, that the Party was prepared, not simply to accept, but positively to encourage and assist the transformation of the group of people known by their relationship with China as *hua-ch'iao* or 'overseas' Chinese, not into 'foreign nationals' but into *hua-yi*, 'people of Chinese descent', or Southeast Asians.

AFTER COLONIALISM: 1961–1966

'If you have no work to do, that means you have made achievement.'[96]

Overseas Chinese policy in the 1960s bears some of the hallmarks of a post-colonial policy, if only because the CCP was increasingly less concerned with the problems of the Chinese abroad. In conventional colonial situations, the end result of decolonisation is the dismantling of administrative structures, the disappearance of the Colonial Office. The directive attributed to Liao Ch'eng-chih quoted above suggests that the CCP had such an end in mind; the final achievement would be for the Overseas Chinese bureaucracy to work itself out of existence. Liao went on to say:

You must not fear that people say you have not worked hard to protect the Overseas Chinese. Overseas Chinese can protect themselves. You must not interfere with them and show your opinion. The more opinions you put forth, the more troubles will the Overseas Chinese have.

During the Cultural Revolution, the Overseas Chinese Affairs Commission appears to have been abolished, although it is doubtful whether the CCP could really claim that its 'colonies' had all become independent.

In other respects also the CCP's policy fits the post-colonial model. The separation was not complete, nor was it intended to be. The Party was particularly concerned to maintain commercial links and the opportunity to tap the financial resources of Overseas Chinese by exploiting a kind of 'special relationship' similar to that which Britain, France or the United States have claimed with their former colonies. And like these powers, it might also attempt to influence or even interfere with the politics of the former subjects; but the rules of the game are different and the powers have to act under some restraints. In the case of China and the Overseas Chinese such restraints were far greater than in conventional models because of the reasons which prompted the CCP to decolonise in the first place. There is a parallel also in the behaviour of the decolonised; some demand independence, some go along with it, and some regard it as a disaster. The Chinese government had to contend with a group representing this last point of view. In a number of limited ways they were useful to China, but they could also be embarrassing, and they tended to impede the progress of the decolonisation policy and to undermine the effects which that policy was intended to have among indigenous Southeast Asians. For this reason, they were not encouraged. Finally, in a far more general and less closely parallel sense, China suffered in a similar way to former colonial powers from the tendency to blame them for the ills of former colonies, to see their black hand behind everything which is opposed or antagonistic to what is perceived as the interests of the independent 'states'.

By comparison with the fanfare which had surrounded the policy changes in 1954, the reorientation of the CCP's approach to the Overseas Chinese in 1956 and 1957 had been singularly undramatic. The grand gesture, the 'instant solution', and the showmanship of the Sino-Indonesian Treaty were replaced by a more subdued approach. Where before external policies had depended in large part upon appeals to foreign governments, they were now directed primarily at the Overseas Chinese themselves. The Party also appears to have decided that it would have to think in the long term if it wished, not even to solve the problem, but to secure the slightest benefit in the form of improved relations with Southeast Asia. In October 1956, for example, T'ao Chu announced that the problems of Overseas Chinese could not be solved overnight; 'if they cannot be solved in one year, then they will be solved gradually year by year, and it should be possible to solve most of them in ten years'.[97] It was simply not possible to provide an instant solution. Even if the Party's policy worked, it would take at least a generation, possibly two, and there was no way of avoiding situations such as had arisen in Indonesia, through no fault of the Overseas Chinese or of the Chinese government. At the beginning of the 1960s, therefore, Overseas Chinese policy was to a large extent still at an impasse.

From the end of 1961, there was a shift in emphasis in the Party's approach to Overseas Chinese affairs. This was characterised by an increasing preoccupation with domestic matters, and a corresponding lack of attention to the problems of the Chinese abroad. The presentation of external policy, moreover, was quite unlike anything which had gone before. Where the Party had always been sensitive to the fact that Overseas Chinese did not respond in the same way as was expected of the Chinese masses, it now began to provide them with unadulterated communist jargon. The content of *CNS* despatches devoted to special interest items for Overseas Chinese tended to give greater attention to the participation of domestic Overseas Chinese in production, construction, and political campaigns. In special broadcasts and in talks with visiting Overseas Chinese, Chinese officials spoke less of Overseas Chinese matters and more of general domestic and foreign policies, as they might for ordinary international consumption or any non-political visiting delegation. When the Party did refer to its relationship with the Chinese abroad, it was often in terms which bore no relation to the observable facts, and which can be explained only in terms of the policies and slogans of domestic affairs.[98] The only respect in which policy remained relatively unchanged was in the continuing interest in foreign exchange. The Overseas Chinese Investment Corporations continued to operate and to pay annual dividends, minimum privileges were maintained for domestic Overseas Chinese receiving remittances, and the government continued its general exhortations to the Chinese abroad to contribute to socialist construction in China.

Since 1954, the CCP's Overseas Chinese policy had been marked by constant attempts to seek new answers, new approaches to the Overseas Chinese problem itself. From 1961, this was no longer apparent. There was, however, one new element, which was not so much a policy as a theoretical rationalisation. It was first suggested in the statement in 1960 that the Overseas Chinese were 'an integral part of the local people'. In its communications with the Overseas Chinese, the Party began to identify them with the people of the countries of residence rather than as a separate group requiring separate policies and special attention. This identification appeared to include even those who may still have been pure Chinese nationals, since policy statements tended to lump together 'Overseas Chinese' with 'people of Chinese race with local citizenship'.[99] They were told that they 'should grasp their fate in their own hands', but that their fate was 'intimately bound up with that of the local people'.[100] They should 'do everything which was of benefit to the local people, but avoid doing anything which was not'.[101]

It appears, therefore, both from specific references to the Chinese abroad and from the way in which general propaganda tended to ignore their special characteristics, that the Party was attempting to impose a theoretical integration which did not exist, to behave as though decolonisation were an accomplished fact. This approach would seem to be a logical development of the Party's attempts to detach the Overseas Chinese from China. Or at least, it would have provided a justification for ignoring them. If they were to be regarded as one with the local people, then by implication, it would appear that the Party had discarded the principle of Overseas Chinese non-involvement in local politics. It might appear also, that for the first time Overseas Chinese policy could be construed as applying differently in different countries. When the Party used the slogans of anti-imperialism in statements to the Overseas Chinese, as it did increasingly throughout this period, this could be understood as a general attempt to mobilise all Overseas Chinese in the cause of revolution.

The evidence, however, does not really support such a view. In the first place, this was not Overseas Chinese policy as such. If anything, it confirms that the Party had relinquished all idea of working through the Overseas Chinese to achieve its political aims in Southeast Asia. The Party urged no more on Overseas Chinese than it did on the peoples of the countries of residence, and in most cases a great deal less. It was simply that they were no longer treated as having a special role by virtue of their relationship with China, for whatever purpose. At no stage did the Chinese government urge the Overseas Chinese to instigate revolutionary struggles or take independent action apart from the local people. The slogans of anti-imperialism were part of the standard vocabulary of the Party's domestic and international propaganda, and the Overseas Chinese were simply included in the category of people struggling against imperialism, modern revisionism, and the reactionaries of all countries.

The point is illustrated by the Party's attitude to the role of Overseas Chinese in two situations in which the CCP was publicly committed to support of armed struggle, the Indonesian Confrontation against Malaysia, and the national war of liberation in South Vietnam. In both cases the Chinese government appealed to Overseas Chinese to support the struggles. In neither case was the appeal directed specifically at Overseas Chinese, but to the 'local people', including the Chinese. The appeals were not issued in special messages or directives; they were not even phrased as explicitly as the Party's injunctions to Overseas Chinese to stay out of local politics. They occurred in isolated statements, introduced in the context of general remarks about the international situation. In the case of Malaysia, the Party was not unaware of the communal problems involved, and 'scrupulously avoided open identification with the communal interests of the Overseas Chinese there, while at the same time taking up the slogans of Indonesian nationalism'.[102] The Chinese government simply expressed the 'hope' that 'all races', including the Chinese, would oppose the 'neo-colonialist' plot of Malaysia.[103] The Chinese were asked to react in unison with the prevailing forces, which in this case included the forces of Indonesia. Moreover, if confrontation had succeeded, as the Chinese government apparently believed it could, a Chinese population which had supported the Malaysian government or sat on the sidelines would have been rather vulnerable, and would probably have become a source of contention between China and a new regime in Malaysia.

In Vietnam, the point is not that the Chinese government did issue an appeal but that it did not do so before 1965, in this case for specifically Overseas Chinese reasons. By early 1965, when not only CCP but also the United States judged that the Saigon government was no longer viable and that victory was within the grasp of the communist forces, the CCP appealed to the Chinese to join with 'all other peoples' in supporting the Liberation Front and the struggle against Saigon.[104] The point is that it appealed to the Overseas Chinese only to join in what it perceived to be the last stages of a local popular revolutionary struggle, when it was both expedient and desirable for them to do so.

In the two cases of Malaysia and Vietnam, therefore, it is clear that the CCP was urging Overseas Chinese, not to struggle by themselves or even to engage in protracted struggle with an indigenous movement, but to support what the Party assessed to be the prevailing political forces, the will of the majority of local people, and the imminent victors. The Party had not urged such a course of action on the Chinese in these two areas before, nor has it done so in Thailand, for example, or the Philippines. And its attitude towards the Overseas Chinese in this respect is exemplified, perhaps, by the extraordinary silence about the Chinese abroad which descended early in 1968.

While in general propaganda statements Chinese were included as an integral part of the local people, to the extent that the Party still addressed itself specifically to the Overseas Chinese problem it continued to make the distinction between those who identified with China and those who did not. It still recognised that the objective situation had not changed, that the problems of Overseas Chinese had not been solved. Separate policy towards the Overseas Chinese, therefore, continued on the basis of the objectives set forth in 1957 and 1958. This was implicit in the CCP's attitude towards Overseas Chinese participation in militant struggle in Southeast Asia. The implication of the Party's policy was that Overseas Chinese should be opportunist, sensitive to the possible effect on their lives of a changing political situation, and adaptable to the local political climate, not to the policies of China. This is borne out by the Party's attitudes towards the Chinese in Thailand or the Philippines, and also, according to the revolutionary rebels of the OCAC in 1967, in post-coup Indonesia, where Liao Ch'eng-chih is alleged to have said that Overseas Chinese should not 'struggle in self-defence', since it was 'better to be right than left at present'.[105]

Despite the CCP's attempt to ignore the Overseas Chinese, the principles of the 'three-good' policy and the formula for integration were still stated explicitly, although as the Party gave less and less attention to the Overseas Chinese problem, such statements tended to be little more than condensed versions of the model for integration.[106] These were not, however, meaningless slogans, like patriotic unity, and when the occasion demanded, the advice to identify and integrate with the local people was urged in more specific terms. In October 1962, for example, Fang Fang told a group of visiting Overseas Chinese that Overseas Chinese commerce should be redirected not only to local industry but also now to agriculture, and that Overseas Chinese education and culture should be directed towards the local countries (*mien-hsiang tang-ti*) and, by implication, away from China.[107] In October 1964, he told another group of visitors that the Chinese abroad should develop their 'outstanding tradition of loving the local people, respecting their customs and habits, working with them and enduring the same hardships, and merging with them. You should never, in thoughts or actions, look down on or be disrespectful to the local people, or set yourselves apart from them by great nation chauvinism.'[108] That the third 'good' of Overseas Chinese policy, repatriation and resettlement, also continued as part of the CCP's solution to the problem, was demonstrated in the repatriation of Chinese from India in 1963 and from Indonesia in 1966–7.

The two strands of policy, therefore, operated side by side. In general propaganda, the Overseas Chinese were an integral part of the local people; in practical terms of the position of the Chinese in Southeast Asia and their relationship with China, the same problems still existed and the Party still advanced the same formula for their solution. Overseas Chinese could be a revolutionary force, but only as part of a wider entity and not as an extension of the Chinese Communist Party. So long as they remained, or appeared to remain, as separate 'colonies' of China in Southeast Asia, they were a liability to the successful pursuit of any political objectives in the region, from peaceful coexistence to revolution.

Given the complexities of the Overseas Chinese problem and the fact that the CCP could not control the responses of the Chinese abroad, it is not surprising that the Party was unsuccessful in its attempts to provide a complete solution to the problem, which remains a difficult and complicating element in China's relations with Southeast Asia. What is surprising, perhaps, is that the assumption that the CCP regards 'the Overseas Chinese' as an invaluable fifth column not to be discarded has not lost popular currency and is still held by some writers on Southeast Asian affairs to be unquestionable.[109]

9

The Cultural Revolution.
Overseas Chinese policy under attack[1]

The Cultural Revolution infected every aspect of Overseas Chinese affairs, from the institutions in China to policy towards the Chinese abroad. The struggles in the OCAC brought to a standstill all regular activity within the Overseas Chinese affairs bureaucracy. This in turn influenced both domestic and external policy, although in each case in combination with other developments which were ultimately more disruptive. The domestic Overseas Chinese were affected equally by the general assault on alleged bourgeois and capitalist manifestations throughout China; external policy was turned upside down as a result of extremist activity within the 'foreign affairs circle' and the general orientation of foreign relations.

The most interesting aspects of the period since 1966 are the criticisms of pre-Cultural Revolution Overseas Chinese policy, and the direction of policy in the post-Cultural Revolution period. These are discussed in the second and third sections of this chapter. But first, it is proposed to outline the impact of the Cultural Revolution on Overseas Chinese affairs from 1966 until early 1968, when the Overseas Chinese Affairs Commission disappeared from view, since the fortunes of the administration provide one of the main clues to the likely trend of policy after the Cultural Revolution.

THE IMPACT OF THE CULTURAL REVOLUTION
Overseas Chinese Affairs institutions

From the official Chinese news media, the first indication that the established authorities in the Overseas Chinese Affairs Commission may not have survived was the disappearance of the Chairman, Liao Ch'eng-chih. He appeared at Peking airport on the morning of 3 July 1967 to receive the ashes of a Chinese aid expert killed in clashes between Overseas Chinese and Burmese authorities in Rangoon.[2] That afternoon, he failed to attend a rally to denounce the Burmese government's 'persecution' of Overseas Chinese, and from that day he has not been cited in the official media.[3] The Commission itself was seldom mentioned after Liao's disappearance, and has not been cited at all since February 1968, when an unidentified Commission spokesman issued a statement on the situation in Burma.[4] In the same period, only four people known to have been members of the Commission in recent years have been reported active by the Chinese press; and not one has been identified by association with Overseas Chinese affairs.[5] The only institution which continued to function throughout the Cultural Revolution was the *China News Service*.

The events which preceded the virtual suspension of operations in the Overseas Chinese affairs circle may be reconstructed from the official and unofficial press. The first known move, following the pattern of more momentous developments in the Cultural Revolution, was in Shanghai. In September 1966, returned Overseas Chinese Red Guards went from Peking to Shanghai to take part in an attack on the Shanghai branches of the OCAC, the Returned Overseas Chinese Association, *CNS*, and the United Front Work Department. They published an article setting forth their complaints and giving some details of the struggle;[6] an article which also confirms, incidentally, the supposition that up until the time of the Cultural Revolution Fang Fang had had the pre-eminent role in the direction of domestic Overseas Chinese affairs. The article accuses the leading Shanghai cadres of carrying out the 'Liu–Teng line' at the direction of the Shanghai United Front Work Department and Fang Fang's 'Black party committee' in the Central Commission in Peking, and denounces them for attempting to suppress the revolutionary zeal of the masses of returned Overseas Chinese. There is no indication of how the struggle in Shanghai was resolved, but from isolated reports it appears that the revolutionary rebel returned Overseas Chinese involved in this attack continued south to carry the Cultural Revolution into Fukien and Kwangtung, possibly assisting in power seizures and the creation of alliances and factions within the Overseas Chinese organisations at provincial and lower levels. Their presence was reported in South China throughout the first half of 1967.[7]

In the Central Commission, the struggle appears to have been held in check until January 1967.[8] According to the revolutionary rebels, the supporters of Liu Shao-ch'i and Teng Hsiao-p'ing in the Commission were a group comprising Foreign Minister Ch'en Yi, Commission Chairman Liao Ch'eng-chih, and Fang Fang, Su Hui, Wu Chi-sheng, Wang P'ing, and Chang Fan.[9] The evidence for their political leanings was apparently the fact that Liu Shao-ch'i's *Hsiu-yang* (*Self Cultivation*) was required reading in the Commission. Through Fang Fang and his wife Su Hui, they controlled the OCAC Party Committee, which had become a 'joint dictatorship' and an 'instrument for suppression'. In mid-1966, Ch'en Yi, Liao and Fang appointed work teams from the CCP's Foreign Affairs Political Department to carry out the bourgeois reactionary line in the Commission.[10] They were able to thwart the attacks by the revolutionary rebels by sponsoring a 'conservative' organisation known as the United Power Seizure Committee.

Until January 1967, the 'power-holders' appear to have held off the attack successfully, since the rebels report that cadres still did not dare to oppose the Party Committee. On 20 January there was an attempted power seizure by two groups, the OCAC Revolutionary Rebel General Command Headquarters, and the Returned Overseas Chinese Tung Fang Hung Commune in the Capital.[11] The attempt failed, however, because of direct intervention by Ch'en Yi and Liao Ch'eng-chih, who ignored a warning by Mao and the Central Committee that the rebel movement should not be suppressed. They continued to support their own conservative organisation, the United Power Seizure Committee, and in a special meeting called by Chou En-lai they attempted to promote this organisation as the sole representative of the Commission. In mid-February, bending to pressure from above and below, the power-holders tried to unite the opposing factions in an acceptable Cultural Revolution formation, the Three-Way Alliance. This only served further to infuriate their attackers, because they insisted that before the Alliance was formed both sides should first carry out rectification. The rebels saw this as a stratagem by Ch'en and Liao to maintain themselves in power, since at the same time they continued to manoeuvre behind the scenes with conservative elements in the Foreign Ministry, and to protect their protégés and supporters in the OCAC.

By March, the power seizure movement in Peking was gathering force, and the attacks in the foreign affairs circle intensifying. An indication of the mounting pressure on the OCAC establishment is that at one point eighteen revolutionary rebel and Red Guard organisations both from the Commission and other organisations in Peking were taking part in the attacks on leading OCAC cadres. Ch'en Yi and Liao Ch'eng-chih, both vulnerable on fronts other than Overseas Chinese affairs, began to make placatory gestures towards the rebels, although their conservative approach was revealed in the fact that they tried to suggest that there should be an end to provocative or inflammatory broadcasts and writings. By early April, however, the rebels seem to have been in a commanding position. Lin Hsiu-te, a Vice-Chairman of the Commission, was 'dragged back' to Fukien,[12] a special group was established to struggle against Fang Fang, Ch'en Man-yün was arrested as a 'spy',[13] and on 4 April, a mass rally was held to criticise Ch'en Yi and Liao Ch'eng-chih. In June, it appears that the rebels had ousted the main power-holders, and had collected the material they needed to incriminate the 'top capitalist-roader' in the Commission, Liao Ch'eng-chih. It was in mid-June that a 'preparatory Group for Criticism of Liao and Fang' published a review of Overseas Chinese policy in the *P'i Liao chan-pao* (*Criticise Liao Combat Bulletin*). Fang and the other Party Vice-Chairmen of the Commission had been out of sight for many months, and Liao lasted two weeks from the time of publication of this attack.

Little is known of how the struggle developed after June 1967. I was told by a member of the OCAC in February 1968 that a revolutionary alliance had been established in the Commission, but that decisions had not been made on any of the cadres, including Liao, and a revolutionary committee had yet to be established.[14] Liao was reported under criticism for other misdemeanours, including the alleged promotion of the autobiography of the last Manchu emperor, Henry P'u Yi, as an 'education in patriotism' for Overseas Chinese.[15] In February 1968, a Hong Kong newspaper quoting an unnamed unofficial Peking newspaper, listed twenty-two members of the Commission alleged to have been 'purged', and claimed that Liao had committed, among others, the crime of offending Chiang Ch'ing.[16] The Peking Foreign Language Institute, whose students were in the forefront of the power seizure in the OCAC, established a revolutionary committee on 8 February 1968, the last of the three Overseas Chinese educational institutions in Peking to do so.[17] Some of the students of the Institute have been discredited for association with the 'May 16' group, and the 'left extremism' of Wang Li,[18] and the Director, Chang T'ieh-t'ao, was reported in an unofficial newspaper to have been arrested as an international spy.[19] The only other organisation which appeared at one point to have resolved its problems was the Fukien Province branch of the OCAC, which as early as February 1967 was reported officially as having a provisional revolutionary committee, an organ which has not been referred to since.[20]

The creeping paralysis which overtook Overseas Chinese affairs in 1967 was discernible also from official news media. Throughout the first half of 1967, revolutionary rebel Overseas Chinese replaced the established institutions in the performance of official duties. They were at rallies to protest against alleged persecution of Chinese abroad; they were on hand in Shanghai, Kwangtung, and Fukien, to greet refugees from Indonesia, and had apparently seized power from the special reception committee established for this purpose in Chan-chiang.[21] In May, they held a meeting with Yao Teng-shan, the 'red' chargé d'affaires from Djakarta who was soon to wreak havoc in the Foreign Ministry.[22] In the official reports, the revolutionary rebels were either returned Overseas Chinese or cadres of the OCAC; and although the unofficial newspapers indicate that rebels from other organisations were involved in the Overseas Chinese affairs struggle, there is no indication that these included Overseas Chinese dependants.

In the post-1965 repatriation programme for Indonesian Chinese, there was a marked difference between the reception for the first group, which arrived in October 1966, and the last group which reached China in May 1967. The first was met by Liao Ch'eng-chih, Lin Yi-hsin, a Vice-Chairman of the OCAC, and a relatively senior delegation of provincial and local Overseas Chinese affairs officials. In November, the second group received a telegram from Liao Ch'eng-chih transmitting the solicitude of Mao, Lin Piao, and Chou En-lai. By May 1967, when the fourth and last group arrived in China, there was no message of sympathy, nor was the group met by anyone identified as belonging to an Overseas Chinese organisation, faction, or committee.[23]

A similar process was observed in the All-China Returned Overseas Chinese Association, and the Returned Overseas Chinese Associations throughout China. One of the functions of these associations in the past was to organise and lead rallies or meetings on issues involving the Chinese abroad. From April to August 1967, there was a new eruption of anti-Chinese activity in Indonesia, there were riots in Hong Kong, Overseas Chinese were expelled from Mongolia, and Chinese in Rangoon clashed with the Burmese government. It was a period in which rallies and demonstrations were held every few days, yet on no occasion did the ACROCA or its branches appear, and it has not been mentioned in the official press since. The same phenomenon appeared in every other area of domestic Overseas Chinese affairs. The traditional broadcasts to Overseas Chinese at New Year, Spring Festival, May Day, and National Day have not been made since January 1966;[24] the *Ch'iao-wu pao*, like most other periodicals, suspended publication in 1966; and visiting Overseas Chinese were not reported at national celebrations in China from October 1966 until October 1969.[25] At the height of the Cultural Revolution Overseas Chinese businessmen at Canton Trade Fairs were not accorded the special treatment they were always given in the past.[26] Many, if not all, the Overseas Chinese apartment buildings and restaurants had the words 'Overseas Chinese' removed from their names. The Overseas Chinese villages have not been referred to since mid-1967.

Public references to the struggle in Overseas Chinese affairs appeared in brief reports in *CNS*, mainly in connection with former Overseas Chinese students. In July 1968, students from the Peking Returned Overseas Chinese Supplementary Middle School setting out to work in the countryside, criticised the 'counter-revolutionary distortions' of 'achieving fame and family', 'individual struggle', and 'special characteristics of returned Overseas Chinese', 'promoted by China's Khrushchev and his agents in educational and Overseas Chinese affairs circles'.[27] The longest news item in *CNS* on domestic Overseas Chinese for almost two years appeared in September 1968. Overseas Chinese students in the border areas of North China (*pei-ta-huang*) alleged that Liu Shao-ch'i's agents in Overseas Chinese affairs had opposed Mao study, worshipped book-learning and opposed labour for Overseas Chinese students. They alleged that in the fifteen years prior to the Cultural Revolution, only 1.2 per cent of students in the Peking Overseas Chinese School had gone to the countryside for labour. The article indicates also that problems of Overseas Chinese students had persisted despite the Cultural Revolution; many, for example, wanted to drive tractors rather than do manual labour.[28]

By early 1968 the organisational network for Overseas Chinese affairs appeared either to have been destroyed or else to have come to a complete standstill.

Domestic Overseas Chinese

The position of domestic Overseas Chinese in the Cultural Revolution was rather unclear. The last substantial statement on this question before the movement began in earnest was a *Jen-min jih-pao* report on an Overseas Chinese Political Work Conference held in Peking in April 1966.[29] The Conference report did not refer to the specific problems of Overseas Chinese in the Cultural Revolution, except to say that reform of bourgeois Overseas Chinese should be recognised as a long and complicated process. The conference decided that the Cultural Revolution should be carried out by and among Overseas Chinese affairs cadres, and dependant and returned Overseas Chinese. It did not mention the Chinese abroad.

There is much evidence of Overseas Chinese student involvement in the Cultural Revolution; but what of the dependants and relatives, and the older returned Overseas Chinese? The apparent inertia in the organisations responsible for them, together with the targets of the Cultural Revolution, suggest that individual domestic Overseas Chinese as a group should have been subjected to intensive criticism, denunciation, and attack, but this has not been reflected in the official or unofficial news media.

In the last half of 1966 there were reports in the Hong Kong non-Communist press that domestic Overseas Chinese and visiting Overseas Chinese were being insulted, humiliated, and physically assaulted by Red Guards. The Hong Kong communist press admitted that such incidents had occurred, but claimed that these had now been stopped, and that notices issued by Red Guards guaranteed special consideration for domestic Overseas Chinese.[30] There were, however, other pressures. From September 1966, special purchasing coupons for Overseas Chinese receiving remittances were no longer issued, on the ground that they had been introduced during the 'three lean years' and were no longer necessary now that temporary shortages had been overcome.[31] There were also reports of Red Guards writing to Overseas Chinese informing them that their houses and property in China should be donated to the state.[32] In August 1967, the Canton customs was known to be inserting into parcels arriving from Hong Kong and Macao a notification that the broad revolutionary masses disapproved of people going to Hong Kong and Macao, or writing to their relatives to ask for parcels.[33] Reports of detention and interrogation of visiting Overseas Chinese, and the confiscation of letters and parcels, continued into 1968.

Attacks directed specifically at domestic Overseas Chinese as a group since 1966, however, have been rare. Where many of the major directives which charted the course of the Cultural Revolution filtered through to the outside world, no directive concerning domestic Overseas Chinese has so far been detected. It is difficult to believe that domestic Overseas Chinese could have been protected, even in the unlikely event that the central authorities had wanted to do so. Nor would it have been possible physically to isolate them. Fierce faction fighting occurred in the home districts, and to the more extreme rebels, no person or group, least of all bourgeois elements, was immune from attack.

The explanation may be that by the time of the Cultural Revolution domestic Overseas Chinese were neither so numerous nor so conspicuous as they had been in the 1950s, as a result of the CCP's attempts to eliminate the characteristics which set them apart from the masses. In the five years immediately preceding the Cultural Revolution, moreover, there were some indications that many returning Overseas Chinese were already politically attuned to the policies of Communist China rather than conspicuously bourgeois or capitalist;[34] and students had been warned from the late 1950s that they must conform to the socialist system. For those who remained in the category of domestic Overseas Chinese, special consideration was seldom sufficient to enable capitalist high-living, and many relied entirely for their subsistence on small family remittances. It seems possible, therefore, that by the time of the Cultural Revolution the number of domestic Overseas Chinese who might still have been vulnerable would have been considerably less than the ten million families claimed by the Chinese government in 1956.

This does not explain, however, why so little evidence appeared of attacks on Overseas Chinese in the cities. It was in the cities and towns that the Cultural Revolution was most violent; and it is in cities and towns that the Overseas Chinese presence was most noticeable, in shops, apartment buildings, guest houses and restaurants, and Overseas Chinese villages. It is quite likely, of course, that reports of attacks simply have not reached the outside world, but there is a further possible explanation. With the exception of specifically Overseas Chinese institutions, domestic Overseas Chinese have tended not to participate in Party or government organisations,[35] at least not in significantly large numbers. Those who have done so have participated as ordinary members rather than as Overseas Chinese representatives. This means that as a distinguishable group they have not been in the mainstream of internal Chinese politics, and would have remained outside the organised attacks and struggles within Party and government bodies. Certainly, few have been in leading Party positions where they might conceivably have been working for 'capitalist restoration', or 'hoodwinking the masses'. The one group clearly identifiable as Overseas Chinese and involved in an area of intense struggle were the Overseas Chinese students, and according to Hong Kong reports they have been subjected to struggle and forced to make self-examinations because of their bourgeois backgrounds.[36] It is not certain, however, whether they were attacked because they were Overseas Chinese, or whether they were caught up in the general onslaught on the student population.

It seems likely, therefore, that the domestic Overseas Chinese did not present the kind of target which would be exposed to Cultural Revolution attack, either in numbers, or in manifestations of bourgeois living. It is significant, perhaps, that the reports of physical assaults in Kwangtung involved not so much domestic Overseas Chinese, but visitors, and those who maintain close and frequent contact with Hong Kong and Macao. There is still no explanation, however, for the lack of information on struggles within the provincial and local Overseas Chinese affairs bureaucracy. It can only be surmised that struggle occurred but did not attract the attention of unofficial newspapers which reached Hong Kong, or that problems were resolved without undue faction fighting, as appears to have been the case in the Fukien OCAC.

External Overseas Chinese policy

The aspect of Overseas Chinese affairs which attracted most attention was external policy, which in 1967 had the appearance of an offensive to mobilise all Chinese abroad in the cause of revolution. The appearance now seems to have been deceptive. And although it would be quite false to argue that there was no connection between the Cultural Revolution and the incidents involving Chinese in Macao and Hong Kong, in Mongolia, Burma, Cambodia, and Indonesia, it would be more difficult to demonstrate that these incidents represented a new general policy for Chinese in Southeast Asia. There is, in fact, little sign that the Chinese government has made decisions of any sort in Overseas Chinese affairs since 1966, and the official press and radio have devoted less attention to the Chinese abroad than at any other time since the establishment of the People's Republic of China. The internal responses in the period to the end of 1967 show no sign whatever of a policy consciously formulated and related to what went before and what was to come. To the extent that there was a policy in this period, it was little more than a series of reflexes based on literal application of Mao's thought to Overseas Chinese problems.

The incidents of 1967 had one element in common; they occurred in places where Peking has, or had, diplomatic or other representation. There would seem to be a relation between the two, although there is no evidence of directives from the ruling authorities in China. It seems likely that the incidents occurred where they did because Peking representation indicates a degree of tolerance of a Peking presence by the local authorities; the Chinese government, and local individuals and institutions, have had freedom to publicise Peking's policies. In those areas, therefore, where the local authorities had permitted pro-Peking activity among Overseas Chinese, and where the backwash of the Cultural Revolution arrived with greater speed and immediacy, it should not have been surprising that certain Overseas Chinese reacted by attempting to emulate the struggle which had seized the

Chinese government and its representatives abroad. In some cases, there was direct provocation by Chinese officials, but this appears to have been the product of internal struggles among the officials themselves or possibly the result of unauthorised activity in Peking.

The fact that incidents of this nature did not occur in other countries also suggests that they were locally generated and not directed by Peking. Moreover, the incidents themselves and Peking's response tended to blur into one image; whereas it is evident that in each case the incidents preceded Peking's assertions about the rights of Overseas Chinese. Following the expulsion of Yao Teng-shan and his supporters from the Foreign Ministry, and the subsequent fall of his patrons in the Central Cultural Revolution Group, incidents of this kind have not occurred. Yet there were a number of situations involving Overseas Chinese which a new militant Overseas Chinese policy would certainly have sought to exploit, and these passed unnoticed or with perfunctory comment. Throughout 1967 the Chinese government issued 103 protests in one form or another, all but seven between January and the end of September. By December, less than six months after the Rangoon riots, the Penang devaluation riots were completely ignored.

In the course of the incidents themselves there is little to suggest that they were the result of a planned Peking initiative. The riots in Macao and Hong Kong in some ways typify the events which happened elsewhere, even though these are not strictly Overseas Chinese areas. In societies almost totally Chinese, on territory claimed as Chinese but ruled by western governments and in close physical contact with the Cultural Revolution, local communists took to the streets in militant opposition to colonialism and in passionate defence of what they understood to be the thought of Mao Tse-tung. Peking then reacted in support of the compatriots in the two enclaves. The domestic situation in China, particularly at the time of the Hong Kong riots, called for protests couched in the most militant and offensive terms. The Portuguese capitulated, but it was a hollow victory for the Macao communists; Peking did not follow through with sterner demands, moderates regained influence among the local communists, and by 1968 Macao, outwardly at least, had regained much of its former stability. The British, on the other hand, resisted, and in so doing brought reprisals on British diplomats and nationals in China, but not on Hong Kong itself. There was little support from Peking for the Hong Kong communists, apart from a barrage of statements. By October 1967, it was apparent that the Hong Kong rebels could not expect any direct support from Peking. In China, responsibility for Hong Kong was passed to an *ad hoc* committee in Kwangtung Province,[37] an arrangement which permitted expressions of disapproval without requiring formal protests or stronger action in Peking except in cases of 'serious provocation'. The authorities in Hong Kong maintained all along that the riots were spontaneous and not planned in Peking.

The Burmese incident followed a similar pattern, with the exception that the first clash at the end of June was preceded by agitation among Overseas Chinese by Red Guards who had arrived from Peking.[38] Considering the circumstances in the foreign affairs circle in Peking at the time, there is strong reason to doubt that the despatch of these Red Guards or their activities in Burma had the approval of the leading organs in Peking.[39] The OCAC appears to have had almost nothing to do with the Burmese incident, and the Foreign Ministry did not insist when the Burmese government refused to allow the Commission to send an investigation team to Burma. In contrast with China's open and continuing support for the Burmese Communist Party, the responses to subsequent measures by the Burmese government against Overseas Chinese were restrained and shortlived, and in November 1967 Peking reverted to the pre-Cultural Revolution position that Chinese in Burma had always respected local laws and customs.

The Cambodian incident is even less convincing as an example of Peking-directed Overseas Chinese insurrection. Red Guard-type activity by Overseas Chinese in Cambodia provoked Prince Sihanouk into denouncing the 'export' of the Cultural Revolution.[40] This was after the fall of the extremists in the Foreign Ministry, and there was no protest from Peking. In October 1967, Chou En-lai is reported to have sent two messages to the Prince undertaking that China would in no way interfere in Cambodia's internal affairs.[41] Since the stated reason for Sihanouk's concern was the behaviour of Chinese in Cambodia it seems that these assurances referred in part specifically to the Overseas Chinese. Subsequently, the Chinese Embassy in Phnom Penh, which presumably had engaged in the same kind of unauthorised activity as had occurred in Rangoon, attempted to associate Overseas Chinese with activities which might win the approval of the Cambodian government; for example, Overseas Chinese were invited to the opening of the Siem Reap airport built with Chinese aid.[42] In the case of Mongolia, a minor confrontation with the Mongolian authorities resulting in the expulsion of a handful of Overseas Chinese, was already an event of the past long before the protests began in Peking.

Indonesia is in most respects an exception. Indiscriminate and widespread persecution of Overseas Chinese had been occurring since the 1965 coup. The Chinese government had made some ineffective gestures of protection, but protests went unheeded and repatriation was finally abandoned. Even before the suspension of relations in October 1967, the Chinese government was in no position to arouse the Indonesian Chinese, even if it had wanted to. Chinese officials in Indonesia were subject to restrictions and surveillance, their diplomatic and other offices were sacked on a number of occasions, and the prevailing anti-Chinese mood deterred all but the most committed or the most desperate from having contact with Chinese officials or taking up the revolutionary cause; those who did so met with violent reprisals. The great majority of incidents appear to have been provoked, not by the Overseas Chinese but by local elements, frequently with the support or acquiescence of government and military officials.[43]

The content of Peking's protests and commentaries centred on one theme, the assertion by China of the 'sacred and inalienable right' of Overseas Chinese to love Chairman Mao, to study and propagate his thoughts. Suppression, oppression, or persecution of Overseas Chinese, although 'doomed to failure', was nevertheless a violation of this right, an insult to China, the Chinese people, and most of all to Mao himself. The 700 million Chinese people stood pledged to support patriotic Overseas Chinese in their struggles against fascist persecution or oppression and in defence of Chairman Mao and the prestige of the Chinese homeland. In this struggle, Overseas Chinese should unite with the local people to defeat the common enemy. These slogans, of course, were not exclusively for Overseas Chinese; Peking was even more vocal about the right of the 'world's people' to love Mao and propagate his thoughts. Overseas Chinese were simply joining the vast legions of the world's people waging heroic struggle against imperialism, colonialism, revisionism, and all reactionaries.[44] Attempts to suppress Overseas Chinese constituted a more direct manifestation of a sinister plot against China and Mao engineered by a joint conspiracy of the United States and the Soviet Union in collusion with local reactionaries and 'criminals' like Chiang Kai-shek. The Chinese statements of 1967 bore very little relation to reality, and at times they bordered on fantasy; they represented a view of the world situation in the terms and language of the domestic Chinese situation. In the references to common struggle, there was a clear indication that what was meant was revolutionary armed struggle.[45] This was no longer present by the end of 1967, which also seems to confirm that the responses of mid-1967 did not represent a general revolutionary policy for Overseas Chinese, but were the result of reflexes and pressures which had little to do with external incidents which prompted them.

OVERSEAS CHINESE POLICY, 1949–1966:
A CULTURAL REVOLUTION VIEW

To some writers, the CCP has never regarded the Overseas Chinese as anything but a vanguard of Chinese communism in Southeast Asia. To the revolutionary rebels in the Cultural Revolution, it should have done, but consistently failed to do so. Apart from the few asides in news stories about former Overseas Chinese students, the official media have not carried detailed criticisms of Overseas Chinese policy before the Cultural Revolution. But a number of attacks appeared in the so-called 'Red Guard newspapers' produced in the OCAC and related bodies.[46] One such article, in the *P'i Liao chan-pao* (*Criticise Liao Combat Bulletin*), published by the 'Preparatory Group for Liaison Post of Criticism and Repudiation of Liao Ch'eng-chih and Fang Fang', offers a retrospective critique of external Overseas Chinese policy from 1949 until the Cultural Revolution.[47]

The *P'i Liao chan-pao* is the only direct internal information about the CCP's Overseas Chinese policy to have come to light, which alone makes it an interesting document. Its particular significance is that it substantiates the interpretation of Overseas Chinese policy presented in this study. It has not been cited as extensively as it might have been in the foregoing chapters, partly because of its bias in seeking to discredit Liao Ch'eng-chih, but primarily because of the argument that the CCP's intentions are discernible from the already available evidence, which stands very well on its own merits. The article may be taken as a corroboration rather than a starting point or an indispensable piece of evidence.[48] But it does appear, both from internal evidence in the article itself and from what is known of the Cultural Revolution in Overseas Chinese affairs from other unofficial newspapers and the official press,[49] that it is a genuine document which represents accurately the general line of the CCP's policy towards the Chinese abroad. Most of its allegations can be verified from other sources or deduced from publicly stated policy. There is distortion, not in the recording of factual events, but in the ideological significance attributed to these events in the retrospective judgment of the Cultural Revolution.

Overseas Chinese and foreign policy

The *P'i Liao chan-pao* alleges that Liao Ch'eng-chih, 'the top party person in authority taking the capitalist road in the Central Commission for Overseas Chinese Affairs', for eighteen years was a 'black fighter' posted in the Commission by Liu Shao-ch'i, faithfully implementing Liu's policy of 'three capitulations and one annihilation',[50] and 'betraying the interests of the patriotic overseas Chinese'.

The first section of the article charges that Liao's general guiding line for external Overseas Chinese affairs was Liu Shao-ch'i's 'philosophy of survival', that he advocated that Overseas Chinese should do whatever seemed necessary to live in peace and harmony in the local environments: '(Liao Ch'eng-chih) abolished the class struggle and enforced capitulationism in overseas Chinese affairs abroad. As a result, overseas Chinese affairs abroad deteriorated to a very big extent, and the consequences were very serious.' In support of this charge, the following accusations are made. Shortly after 1949 progressive Chinese abroad organised, spontaneously, mass movements to carry out propaganda for China and to mobilise the Overseas Chinese in support of China's position in Korea and in opposition to the Kuomintang. Liao is said to have ordered the suppression of these movements, on the pretext of 'rectifying the prominence of the "left"', but in reality because he believed such movements would 'irritate' the local governments and prejudice the chances of the Overseas Chinese for 'permanent survival'. Similarly, Liao is alleged to have ordered dissolution of organisations set up to 'educate and organise' Overseas Chinese and engage in 'patriotic activities', because he feared that the existence of such organisations might arouse the suspicion of local governments. The authors claim that this prevented the Overseas Chinese masses from launching counter-attacks when they were persecuted by imperialism and reactionaries. Liao also dissolved groups established by Overseas Chinese 'on their own initiative' for studying the works of Chairman Mao, and he 'repeatedly' refused to permit political studies in Overseas Chinese organisations and schools, not only because he feared local governments might be irritated, but also because he believed that this might 'make them think that we were going to carry out revolutions and "subversive activities" locally, and "impair diplomatic relations"'. Overseas Chinese were instructed to 'mind their own business', 'to stick to their own posts', 'not to criticise the internal affairs of the local governments', 'to obey the local laws and respect the local customs and habits', and to 'carry out all their work publicly and lawfully'. The class struggle was abandoned for the sake of 'survival' and 'subsistence'.

The ideological deviations and crimes which the policy is said to have represented are, like many accusations in other fields, a distorted interpretation in Cultural Revolution terms of events which predate the Cultural Revolution. The article claims that Liao's policy was opposed to an instruction by Mao Tse-tung that 'class struggle must also be carried out in overseas Chinese affairs'. In his published writings, Mao has made only one reference to Overseas Chinese and that was before 1949. But the practice during the Cultural Revolution of directing events by 'Chairman Mao's latest instructions', suggests that this may be a product of the Cultural Revolution. Even if it is not, the term Overseas Chinese affairs probably signifies domestic Overseas Chinese and institutions only. It is true that many of Mao's instructions have been conveniently vague, but there are a number of terms he could have used to designate 'Chinese overseas', if that is what was intended.[51]

The article claims to demonstrate that Liao was a 'counter-revolutionary revisionist'. But there is no reason to suppose that his policy was not the product of consensus or majority decisions, with the concurrence or approval of many who, in the Cultural Revolution, claimed or were claimed to be loyal 'Maoists', possibly even including Mao himself. One Chinese leader, for example, who was identified openly and unequivocally with the external Overseas Chinese policy under attack, was the 'Maoist' Chou En-lai. Mao himself occasionally met with visiting Overseas Chinese, and there was no suggestion, either from Chinese sources or from the visitors themselves on their return from China, that Mao may have urged on them a policy different from that enunciated by Chinese leaders directly responsible for Overseas Chinese affairs.

The details of the charges, however, do bear a close resemblance to the externally observed facts. This being the case, it is not surprising that militant Red Guards and revolutionary rebels should have found the policy objectionable and contrary to what they believed a true Maoist policy should be. In saying that Liao was guided by the 'philosophy of survival', the article implies that the Party's primary concern was with the interests of the Chinese abroad, whereas in fact this was only one side of the question. For while Chinese policy did amount to something which might be called a philosophy of survival, it was concerned to solve the CCP's own problems as much as those of the Overseas Chinese themselves. The authors are more accurate where they claim Liao feared patriotic activities by Overseas Chinese would irritate the local governments, impair diplomatic relations, and arouse suspicion that China was manipulating Overseas Chinese to carry out subversion. The specific instructions cited for Overseas Chinese to obey local laws, respect local customs and refrain from participation in local politics, could have been taken verbatim from almost any major speech for the Chinese abroad from 1954 to 1966.

Certain allegations in this section of the article are not verifiable. There is no documented instance where the CCP specifically ordered the dissolution of Overseas Chinese political organisations, although Chou's remarks in Rangoon and elsewhere and the whole burden of Overseas Chinese policy after 1954 suggest that this was what was intended. It seems more likely that the Party simply discouraged such organisations and accepted without comment or with formal protest their suppression by local authorities. To have acted otherwise would have been contrary to the orientation of Overseas Chinese policy: if Overseas Chinese were to be law-abiding, then in every country in Southeast Asia with the possible exception of North Vietnam they could not be waging class struggle; if they were to stay out of local politics, then they could not be nurtured on Maoist political ideas or engage in revolution.[52] It is significant for assessing the credibility of this account of Overseas Chinese policy that when, in 1968, the first tentative moves were made towards restoring a semblance of normal foreign relations with African and Asian countries, the CCP reverted to the line that Overseas Chinese had followed consistently the instruction of the Chinese government to abide by local laws.[53] Had this been an empty propaganda slogan seized on by Red Guards for want of other evidence, it is unlikely that the Party would have bothered to restore it, since the essentially practical moves in foreign relations did not at that stage include a softening in the militancy of accompanying propaganda.

Overseas Chinese and revolution

The interest of the second section of the *P'i Liao chan-pao* is that it presents what is alleged to be the Chinese Communist Party's analysis of the role of Overseas Chinese in relation to local revolution. It is alleged that in 1951 Liao, in collaboration with Chang Wen-tien, Wang Chia-hsiang, and Li Wei-han,

under the pretext that Overseas Chinese affairs must be conducted in a way different from that before the liberation since the founding of New China had caused a change in the status of overseas Chinese, put forth the fallacy that 'Overseas Chinese are Overseas Chinese and cannot be regarded as a minority nationality of a place' and drew up the wrong policy that 'Overseas Chinese affairs must be strictly distinguished from the local revolution' and 'overseas Chinese should not interfere with the local internal affairs and should under no circumstances take part in the local civil struggle' ...*Liao Ch'eng-chih even said straightforwardly: 'Overseas Chinese shall not make revolution. They will not succeed even if they make revolution'.* (Italics added.)

The specific examples in this section concern two countries which are not identified by name; and since the conditions described could apply to a number of countries, it is difficult to check the charges against external evidence. In one instance, Liao is said to have 'forcibly dragged out all overseas Chinese from the local revolutionary organisations and sent them back home'. In the other when the 'black programme' of preventing the Overseas Chinese from making revolution was transmitted to the country concerned, there was great confusion, and

Some people of the overseas Chinese revolutionary organisation in that area found from this black program a so-called 'theoretical basis' disproving the participation of Overseas Chinese in the struggle against X, and took this opportunity to carry out splittist activities and sabotage the local people's revolutionary struggle... To implement his so-called directive that 'overseas Chinese should not interfere with local internal affairs', he also forcibly dissolved all local Overseas Chinese progressive organisations and suspended the running of the only progressive newspaper in that area.

The article gives 1951 as the year in which this policy was introduced, and it was in that year that the Chinese government began to indicate that it did not approve of the struggle of the Overseas Chinese communists in Malaya. It was at that time also that large numbers of Chinese returned to settle in China from Malaya and Indonesia.

The distinction which Liao is said to have drawn between Overseas Chinese and local minority nationalities is highly significant. It indicates that the CCP was thinking consciously of the colonial implications of its relationship with the Overseas Chinese, who were not an indigenous minority but a minority connected with an external power. It is significant also in that it would appear to apply to Malaya as much as to any other country in the region. The ultimate concern, of course, was the possible effect on

China, and according to the article the purpose of Liao's instruction not to take part in revolution was 'for fear that this would place China's "foreign affairs in a passive position" and that imperialism would say mischievously that China carried out subversive activities through overseas Chinese'.

Abandonment of the Overseas Chinese

The third section of this article concerns protection, the response to discrimination against or persecution of Overseas Chinese. It argues that the correct response should have been to direct the Overseas Chinese to wage a 'tit-for-tat struggle', whereas Liao 'capitulated and did nothing else'. In this section, a number of specific charges are made, most of which are verifiable from external evidence. The first concerns the forced naturalisation in South Vietnam in 1956–7. The article asserts that Liao not only 'dared not mobilise the overseas Chinese to rise in struggle', but that 'he even withheld for almost one year the public announcement of a protest'. The second of these assertions is certainly true, and the first is implicit in the general Overseas Chinese policy of the time. In the specific response to the South Vietnam incident, there was no suggestion that Overseas Chinese should rise in struggle.

The article next alleges that Liao acquiesced in the Indonesian programme for restrictions on Overseas Chinese schools in 1957. Liao 'thought that Indonesia wanted to enforce "nationalisation" and to "develop its national culture", and that this was "a matter of sovereignty", of Indonesia'. Liao was 'the executioner assisting the Indonesian reactionaries in strangling and ruining the culture and education of Overseas Chinese'. There is no record of a Chinese protest on this matter, nor, in fact, was there any mention in the CCP's response to the South Vietnamese decree of 1956 that Diem had also ordered the immediate closure of all Chinese schools. To have objected in either case would have been contrary to the current policy on education for Chinese abroad. It was at the end of 1956 that the Chinese government began to urge all Overseas Chinese to study the local language and steep themselves in the local culture, and to instruct Chinese schools to adopt the local language as the medium of instruction. Continuing on the subject of Indonesia, the article claims that following the ban on alien retail traders in 1959,

Liao Ch'eng-chih did not mobilise and organise the Overseas Chinese to wage mass self-defence struggle. On the contrary, he suggested the plan of withdrawing 600 thousand overseas Chinese from Indonesia in one year. At the same time, he even suggested 'withdrawal of three million to five million overseas Chinese from various parts of the world in seven or eight years to come'.

If Overseas Chinese were not to take part in revolution or interfere in local politics, if the Chinese government was not prepared to protect their interests in Southeast Asia but planned to withdraw them to China, what then were its long-term objectives? The answer provided in this article is given in the words of a directive to the units concerned, attributed to Liao Ch'eng-chih:

It is better for you to keep further away from the overseas Chinese. If you have no work to do, that means you have made achievement. You must not fear that people say you have not worked hard to protect the overseas Chinese. Overseas Chinese can protect themselves. You must not interfere with them and show your opinion. The more opinions you put forth, the more troubles will the overseas Chinese have... They want to live in the countries of their domicile permanently. You must try to understand them.

By the authors' account,

the overseas Chinese were deprived of their revolutionary rights, the revolutionary traditions of overseas Chinese were strangled, the revolutionary forces of overseas Chinese were betrayed, the overseas Chinese were bereft of their proper rights, and the revolutionary friendship of the overseas Chinese with the local people was destroyed.

According to the authors of the article, Liao had said that the Overseas Chinese 'should be allowed to join in demonstrations against communism and China'. This may be a piece of invention, but if the CCP's policy was to sever the connection and encourage Overseas Chinese to identify with the local people, then it must have conceived that such situations could occur.

Unfortunately, no defence of these charges or justification of the policy has become available outside China. It would have been difficult in Cultural Revolution terms to defend, since the facts on which the charges are based could not be dismissed as fabrications. The authors' purpose was to discredit Liao Ch'eng-chih, but there was no need to resort to invention since from a revolutionary rebel point of view almost every aspect of post-1954 Overseas Chinese policy was proof that the policy had been far from revolutionary. It is interesting that the attack is directed only at Liao Ch'eng-chih within the Commission. This tends to confirm that Liao was concerned primarily with external policy and that he was also the only one of the Commission members so concerned, since other Party members in the Commission have been under attack, but not so far as is known for external policy.

There are two ways in which this article is of value. In the first place, it suggests that the official public policy was in fact the policy of the Chinese Communist Party and not simply external propaganda. It has been pointed out that policy for Overseas Chinese has to be stated more clearly because of the problems of communication, and this article would suggest that Overseas Chinese would have been quite correct in accepting at face value the CCP's injunctions to sever their ties with China and identify with the countries of residence.

The second point is that the article presents a little more information than has been available in the official media. The Party's motives and intentions may be discerned from what it says and does, but it is valuable to have further confirmation, particularly of what was actually said privately. In this respect, the directive attributed to Liao Ch'eng-chih in the final section is possibly the most interesting part of the article. In theory, if the CCP's Overseas Chinese policy could be made to work, the Overseas Chinese affairs bureacracy in China would no longer be necessary, and this is the implication of Liao's directive. If this was the ultimate objective, the directive on participation in revolution sums up the underlying motive; Overseas Chinese 'will not succeed even if they make revolution'.

The *P'i Liao chan-pao* shorn of its polemical trimmings would make an effective summary of the conclusions of this study. It has not been essential to the argument, but it is a highly interesting piece of corroborative evidence. As the only piece of direct internal evidence it does not dispute or disprove the main contentions argued above; it also provides additional information to support them.

OVERSEAS CHINESE POLICY BEYOND THE CULTURAL REVOLUTION

What is the import of developments in the Cultural Revolution for future policy towards the Chinese abroad? The eruptions of 1967 were followed by a period of roughly one year in which it was very difficult to determine what was happening, and it seems likely that the problems of Overseas Chinese were put to one side while the Chinese leadership wrestled with far more important problems. From late 1968, signs of renewed activity in Overseas Chinese affairs began to emerge, and while the Chinese government has not produced anything which might be taken as a definitive statement of Overseas Chinese policy, these signs bear all the hallmarks of a resumption of the policy which operated before the Cultural Revolution.

Domestic affairs

Given the prolonged silence on policy towards the Chinese abroad, one is forced to turn to the domestic scene to try to make some sense out of what has happened; and the sources are not as forthcoming as they have been in the past, which in itself may be significant.

The most interesting development is that the Overseas Chinese Affairs Commission may have been abolished. It is more than three years since the Commission was mentioned in the official media. Party members of the Commission have not resurfaced in any capacity, and the few known members who have appeared have not done so in this capacity. They did not even attend, for example, the first separate reception for Overseas Chinese and

Hong Kong and Macao delegates since 1966, given by Huang Yung-sheng in October 1970.[54]

According to a report from Taiwan, Mao is alleged to have issued an instruction in 1967 that 'all foreign affairs units should be merged with the Ministry of Foreign Affairs'.[55] The Commission was still in existence in February 1968. If it has been disbanded, this may have occurred towards the end of that year or early in 1969.[56] This seems to be suggested by the obituary notices for two prominent members of the Commission, Hsieh Nan-kuang and Ch'en Ch'i-yu. In such notices it is customary to list all present and, often in the case of 'united front' people, past offices and affiliations. The omission of all reference to Overseas Chinese affairs and the absence of Overseas Chinese at the funerals for those who died before 1969 may have been due to confusion or uncertainty. That this was still the case with Hsieh in July 1969 and particularly with Ch'en in December 1970 seems to indicate that the Commission may no longer exist.

The merging of economic ministries may be rationalised on grounds of efficiency, and there is continued, even increased, activity in the areas which they administered. The disappearance of the OCAC, however, in the context of other developments in the field, would have a more directly policy-oriented explanation. It would seem to represent the end-point of the line alleged to have been laid down by Liao Ch'eng-chih, that achievement could be measured by a continuing decrease in the amount of work done in the Overseas Chinese affairs sector; in effect, the winding-up of the 'Colonial Office'. It should be emphasised, however, that there has been no official statement on the status of the Commission, and that in unofficial remarks in 1971, Chinese government personnel stated that it was still in existence.

The same does not apply to other areas of the administration, but the emphasis seems to be following the pre-Cultural Revolution trend. Attention is concentrated almost exclusively on the Overseas Chinese farms, the organisational foundation for the 'complete solution' to the Overseas Chinese problem. Roughly one-third of the farms have been discussed in the despatches of CNS, and one new one has been established, apparently partly for Overseas Chinese who returned from Burma after the clashes in 1967.[57]

Reporting on the farms brings out two points about Overseas Chinese policy. First, there is a clear implication of repudiation of the argument of the rebels in the OCAC that the repatriation programme was wrong and contrary to Maoist policy. The line of reasoning is that Overseas Chinese owe everything to Mao because he has enabled and assisted them to return to settle in China; and this seems to be the only specific way in which the protection of China is extended to the Chinese abroad.[58] Secondly, the obvious purpose of discussion of the farms is to demonstrate that domestic Overseas Chinese are in no respect different from the broad masses of the people. What seems to have happened is that domestic policy is running on the lines set down in the late 1950s and that the focus of the administration is centred on the farms. Given the context in which this policy was first enunciated, there is the implication that external policy also is moving in the same direction.

The fate of the Overseas Chinese schools is a little less certain. Revolutionary Committees were established in the three Overseas Chinese educational institutions in Peking by early 1968, and this was described by *CNS* as a victory in the Overseas Chinese affairs circle. The Peking Supplementary School, which in 1967 was used as a base for attacking the OCAC and which for almost a year was referred to as the 'Peking Returned Overseas Chinese School for Destroying Bourgeois Ideology and Fostering Proletarian Ideology', subsequently reverted to its former title.[59] Some of these schools may have continued to function,[60] although most reports on Overseas Chinese students have concerned former students now at work in the countryside and in remote border areas.[61] But while other schools and universities have been undergoing a long and difficult process of rectification and reorganisation as a preliminary to resuming normal functioning, the ultimate fate of the Overseas Chinese schools may be rather different. Reports in late 1969 and 1970 suggested that all Overseas Chinese schools were to be closed, or more probably, converted to ordinary schools.[62] The number of students returning to China appears to have fallen to insignificant proportions, and the problem of Overseas Chinese education is officially completely ignored. Overseas Chinese have been reported in new enrolments, but not necessarily in 'Overseas Chinese' institutions. It seems, therefore, that the Cultural Revolution may have brought to a logical conclusion the policy for Overseas Chinese education which had been developing for the preceding decade.

The models for domestic Overseas Chinese behaviour are the forty-one 'heroic' Overseas Chinese youths who returned from Indonesia after the coup. Identified completely with domestic policies, they have become activists in Mao study and the practical application of national directives. Settled on the Ch'uan-shang Overseas Chinese farm, many of them have joined the Party and the Communist Youth League, and one, Yü Ya-chou, became a member of the Fukien Provincial Revolutionary Committee. They merited the first report on domestic Overseas Chinese affairs in the *Jen-min jih-pao* since the collapse of the repatriation scheme in mid-1967.[63] Their example indicates that while some distinction may be made administratively in the farms and possibly even the schools, while an Overseas Chinese policy may operate in the form of resettlement, there must be a conscious effort to erase completely the distinction between domestic Overseas Chinese and the masses.

Whatever else may have happened to domestic Overseas Chinese, therefore, it is likely that the process of assimilation has been accelerated since the movement passed its peak. Reports from Hong Kong claim that dividends are being paid on investment, and that 1969 saw a significant increase in remittances. But in late 1970 a movement was introduced, known as the 'three overseas' movement, which aimed at discouraging dependence on overseas remittances and supplies, [64] which means that there is little likelihood of a return to the liberal policies of the 1950s. The only point on which the media have referred explicitly to past policies concerns this question, with the firm assertion that 'special characteristics' must be opposed.

External policy

The trend of external policy since 1968 is consistent with domestic developments, even though there are some elements which are superficially contradictory.

The Chinese government has asserted that it is 'determined to protect the proper rights and interests of the Overseas Chinese'. [65] Lin Piao, in his report to the Ninth Party Congress included patriotic Overseas Chinese in the revolutionary unity of the Chinese people. [66] *CNS* reports have asserted that China's enemies will never 'disrupt the relations between Overseas Chinese and the homeland', and that Overseas Chinese will 'devote themselves to opposing the aggressive designs of US imperialism and social revisionism, and to the liberation of China's territory, Taiwan'. [67] The Draft Constitution of the Chinese government is reported to have allowed for Overseas Chinese representation in the National People's Congress. [68] At a reception in Peking in October 1970, Huang Yung-sheng 'urged patriotic Overseas Chinese to support the struggle of the revolutionary peoples of all countries against US imperialism and all its running dogs'. [69]

It would be wrong, however, to conclude too hastily that the Chinese government now regards the Overseas Chinese in a significantly different light, despite Moscow's claim that they are being used as 'detonators' in Southeast Asia and a channel through which the CCP is attempting to force Southeast Asian governments 'to accept China's Great Power chauvinism and to allow it to establish a sphere of influence there'. [70] In the first place, it is clear that the Chinese leadership is in a dilemma about the Overseas Chinese, similar to that which it faced in the early 1960s. It appears to be trying to approach them in the same way as it does the non-Chinese peoples of Southeast Asia, as though decolonisation were a *fait accompli*. But it realises also that it is still stuck with the problem; hence the care taken in its statements to establish that it is referring to the 'patriotic' Overseas Chinese, and also, presumably, the emphasis on the Overseas Chinese farms. Secondly, there are some indications that what is really meant is 'great patriotic unity' in any one of its derived meanings. This is so particularly with Huang Yung-sheng's address cited above. The Overseas Chinese struggle is struggle with their non-Chinese compatriots in the countries of residence, without redeemable promises on the part of the CCP; their patriotism is manifest in contributions to socialist construction, opposition to the KMT, and the liberation of Taiwan.

The most significant feature of public statements and reports however, is that they appear almost calculated in avoiding reference to the Overseas Chinese in the area where the problem really matters, Southeast Asia. The public statements have been extremely general, and by far the majority of reports on Overseas Chinese protests, statements in support of China, and attendance at celebrations and receptions, concern the Chinese in North America, Japan, Europe, Africa, and such unlikely places as Ceylon and Pakistan.

That this is not accidental is illustrated by the CCP's approach to events concerning the Chinese in Southeast Asia since 1968, and towards four incidents in particular; the Indonesian abrogation of the Dual Nationality Treaty, the May 13th riots in Malaysia, the misfortunes of some Overseas Chinese in the aftermath of the US invasion of Cambodia, and the deportation of the Yu Yitung brothers from the Philippines.

The tone was first set by the CCP's failure to take any notice of the Penang riots at the end of 1967. It was accompanied by the reintroduction of two of the central refrains of pre-Cultural Revolution policy, the injunction to be law-abiding and the claim that Overseas Chinese have contributed to the economic and cultural life of the countries of residence.[71] In its most recent protests before the silence descended, the CCP was responding only to what it described as racial, rather than political, discrimination or persecution.[72]

CNS ran a short item on Indonesian proposals to abrogate the Treaty in November 1968, arguing that this was in violation of the Treaty conditions, particularly as they concerned the right of Chinese to opt for Indonesian nationality at the age of eighteen,[73] a point on which the CCP's ultimate intentions had first emerged in 1955. When the Treaty was actually abrogated in April 1969, however, the CCP forbore to comment.[74]

The May 13th riots took the Party completely by surprise. It did not respond with anything more authoritative than an NCNA report,[75] which indicated in passing that the CCP was quite aware that the principal victims were Chinese. But there was no attempt to single this out for special protest. Moreover, it referred to the victims as *hua-jen*, with a clarification which suggested it accepted that most were Malaysian citizens, another of the platforms of decolonisation.

The Chinese in Cambodia escaped lightly by comparison with the Vietnamese, but there were several anti-Chinese incidents which might have been expected to provoke some comment from Peking. Once again neither government spokesmen, nor Foreign Ministry officials, nor press editorials responded to the incidents. CNS reported them, with the comment that they were an attempt to create a gulf between the Chinese and Cambodian peoples, and with the use of a term unusual in Chinese sources, *Chung-kuo ch'iao-min*, Chinese emigrants.[76] As with the use of *hua-jen*, and later *hua-tsu*,[77] in reference to Malaysia, the CCP appears to have been studiously avoiding giving the impression that its comments implied some kind of legal claim.

The extraordinary episode of the abduction of the Yu Yitung brothers from Manila to Taiwan aroused such an international outcry that even the Nationalist Chinese felt compelled to make some public gestures of conciliation and to give some pretence of a fair trial. The incident was covered by a straight news report in the Chinese media.[78]

The point about these incidents is that together they cover every major problem with which the CCP was likely to be concerned: they occurred in countries hostile to China, they involved racial discrimination, political persecution, the direct presence of US troops, the rival claims of the KMT, dual nationality, Chinese culture and the Chinese press, problems of integration, problems concerning relations with China.

Every indication seems to point, therefore, to a continuation of pre-Cultural Revolution policy, and for reasons which remain essentially the same. It is not so much that foreign policy has entered a new phase marked by realistic analysis of foreign political situations and a new offensive to break through the US-imposed isolation barrier, but that the objective situation of the Overseas Chinese has not changed and their potential as a political arm of China remains as negative as ever. It is likely, therefore, that the CCP will continue to be guided by the considerations which in the past have restrained it from seeking to exploit the Overseas Chinese for purposes of revolution, and that it will continue to see decolonisation as the only solution to its Overseas Chinese problem.

10

Overseas Chinese policy, Overseas Chinese communism, and foreign policy

The fact that the most widely held view about China's intentions towards the Chinese abroad bears so little resemblance to the CCP's own perception of the problem or the policies it attempted to implement is perhaps not so surprising, when set against the kind of judgments about Chinese foreign policy which produced the Fifth Column theory. And although Overseas Chinese policy may not in itself be one of the foremost concerns of the CCP, it is still highly relevant to the wider spectrum of China's foreign policy: first, because it is closely bound up with fundamental questions concerning China's relations with Southeast Asia; and secondly, because it is from assumptions about a whole range of similarly limited aspects of China's international behaviour that supporting evidence for general theories about China's foreign policy is drawn.

OVERSEAS CHINESE POLICY

The intriguing question is whether the CCP would have turned to decolonisation if it had believed that the Overseas Chinese could be of positive value; that is, would its political belief in the justice of the self-determination and independence of the peoples of Asia in itself have been sufficient to persuade it to this course? Since there were obvious liabilities in the relationship, and since the Overseas Chinese were such a special problem which by its very nature placed severe limitations on the policy options available to the CCP, the Party never had to face such a clear-cut alternative.

The evidence in the Party's own sources does not really furnish an answer to the question. Because of their position in relation to both China and the countries of Southeast Asia, the problem of the Overseas Chinese was one which demanded attention. There was no point in accepting the liabilities of a large overseas population without attempting to make use of whatever advantages it offered. The CCP could not avoid a decision on whether the relationship was worth preserving. Leaving aside remittances, which the CCP itself finally attempted to separate from political considerations, there were two questions remaining: could the Overseas Chinese be politically useful to China, and if so, what was involved in maintaining the relationship in such a way that their potential might be exploited.

If there were particular advantages in pursuing political objectives through Overseas Chinese, the costs of maintaining the relationship were high. Domestically, it required policies fundamentally incompatible with the CCP's socialist principles, as well as a large administrative and financial investment. Externally, it involved shoring up those props to the relationship that were most colonial in appearance, which reinforced the characteristics of Overseas Chinese that set them apart from the local people, and which inevitably involved problems in foreign relations. It also meant the assumption of impossible responsibilities for protection. And it meant attempting to dictate the behaviour and responses of a population over which the CCP could exercise almost no control.

But if the costs of maintaining the relationship were high, the benefits to be derived from it were low, and were likely to decrease over time and also in proportion to direct Chinese government involvement. For it was precisely because of their special relationship with China and their position in the countries of residence that the Overseas Chinese were both a liability in establishing or developing friendly relations with Southeast Asia, and an unsuitable instrument for the pursuit of more covert objectives. Cultural separateness, economic domination, racial arrogance, and political attachment to China made the Overseas Chinese a suspect minority in Southeast Asia and an unlikely channel for effective influence for the CCP. Ironically, the Overseas Chinese who were best placed to serve China were those who had already achieved, or who were moving towards, integration or identification with the countries of residence, the least likely to respond to appeals or instructions from Peking. If the CCP wished to make the Overseas Chinese an effective political instrument it would have been necessary to attempt two courses of action that were mutually incompatible and counter-productive. On the one hand, it meant maintaining the special relationship, with all its colonial implications; and on the other, it meant dispelling the belief that the Overseas Chinese represented a threat to Southeast Asia, which could only be achieved by destroying the foundation of the ties which bound them to China and, therefore, any special advantage which they might present as a non-integrated 'Fifth Column'. Faced with this seemingly irreconcilable contradiction, it is not surprising that the CCP came to accept that it was impractical to base its relationship with the Overseas Chinese on a single premise of mobilisation in the advancement of the Party's political interests in Southeast Asia, that it was difficult to frame a policy in disregard for the wider implications of the Overseas Chinese problem, and that the solution to the problem was ultimately beyond its control

It is clear then that the Party saw decolonisation as a way out at a time when it had also decided that from many important points of view the Overseas

Chinese were either a liability, an unrewarding responsibility, or at most a dubious asset. It made no pretence about many of the problems associated with Overseas Chinese, such as education, the difficulties of the domestic Overseas Chinese, and in the internal media, the falling graph of Overseas Chinese remittances. It was less forthcoming about its negative assessment of the political potential of Overseas Chinese in the service of China. But in the late 1950s it fulminated against charges that the Overseas Chinese were a fifth column, in a manner which conveyed something of the Party's frustration in its own attempts to use the Chinese abroad in any capacity at all. It does seem unlikely that the CCP would have attempted such a 'complete solution' if it had believed that its political objectives in Southeast Asia could be furthered significantly and successfully through the agency of Overseas Chinese.

But the fact that the Party had other reasons for wishing to unburden itself of the Overseas Chinese does not mean that it was not moved by the argument for self-determination and decolonisation on its own merits. At minimum, the tendency of Overseas Chinese to exercise their own independence from China had a significant influence on the Party's thinking. The political value of Overseas Chinese to China rested on their special relationship with the homeland, the fact that they gave their allegiance to China and were prepared, in theory, to serve the interests of the Chinese government. As the relationship weakened, China's prospects for influencing them would diminish, and this the CCP had found out. But the independence of Overseas Chinese also confronted the Party directly with the fact that to attempt to continue a traditional relationship would run counter to the forces of change. Decolonisation for the CCP, therefore, was perhaps not unlike that of the European powers, a response to a demand.

The response may have been more ready, however, in view of the Party's political commitment; and it may be wrong, in terms of China's attitude towards both Overseas Chinese and the non-Chinese peoples of Southeast Asia, to dismiss decolonisation as a cynical act dictated entirely by selfish political considerations. The European colonial powers not only imposed their rule on reluctant and virtually defenceless peoples, but in many cases they clung to their colonial possessions in the face of popular demands for independence. Similarly, the Kuomintang has not yet been prepared to regard decolonisation as an acceptable policy towards Overseas Chinese.

The CCP acted in recognition of a new situation among the Chinese in Southeast Asia, which is significantly different from that of the pre-war generation of Overseas Chinese. This is partly due to the steadily decreasing ratio of the China-born to the locally born. But it is also due to the attitudes of independent Southeast Asian governments and their uneasy relations with China, and the nature of the present Chinese government. As a result of these factors there are serious personal and political implications for the individual who owes his allegiance to China. This in turn has confronted the Overseas Chinese with the more fundamental question of what is involved in being a kind of outpost of the Chinese homeland, politically, culturally, emotionally, and even psychologically.

The signs of change were already evident in some countries at the beginning of the twentieth century, but it has accelerated since the end of the Pacific War, the emergence of Communist China itself, and the withdrawal of the old colonial powers from Southeast Asia. While there are still considerable differences between individual Overseas Chinese and between the situation of the Chinese in each country of Southeast Asia, the present generation of Overseas Chinese is far more inclined to regard itself as belonging to the countries of residence than to China. It may not be prepared to abandon its language and cultural traditions, but that does not mean that it regards itself as bound to China by nationality or political affiliation, or that it is prepared to serve the Chinese government. It may not be prepared to integrate, but that does not mean that it is not willing to identify completely with the countries of residence.

It would be surprising if the CCP were not influenced by the direction in which the Overseas Chinese themselves were moving. Their demands for independence would have made it difficult, both practically and ideologically, for the Party to try to preserve the colonial relationship. And while it can not be known whether this was the decisive factor in the Party's assessment, it was almost certainly one important factor, which provided political justification and in itself a fairly compelling argument for decolonisation.

Decolonisation did not resolve the CCP's Overseas Chinese problem where it concerned the attitudes of non-Chinese Southeast Asians. It is even impossible to determine whether the Party's policy resulted in significant changes in the attitudes and behaviour of Overseas Chinese, or whether it simply facilitated or hastened existing tendencies. But the principal reason for the failure of this policy as the ultimate solution is that the CCP could not control the Overseas Chinese or dictate their responses, from which non-Chinese Southeast Asians might draw some comfort.

OVERSEAS CHINESE COMMUNISM

There is little doubt that the decolonisation policy was intended to be taken seriously by the mass of Overseas Chinese. It cannot be dismissed as a simple propaganda exercise to deceive the governments of Southeast Asia, if only because it was urged in such detailed and specific terms and was supported by positive measures which should have had the effect of minimising the traditional links which formed the association between China and the Overseas Chinese. Nor can it be regarded as a temporary expedient to serve the passing interests of peaceful coexistence. If this had been the case, it would have been essential to preserve and cultivate the relationship and to attempt to ensure that the special characteristics of Overseas Chinese society did not become submerged in the local societies. The CCP can hardly have failed to have been aware of the objectives underlying Southeast Asian pressures on Overseas Chinese, and that its own instructions to them were contributing directly to the attainment of those objectives. If at some future date the Party wished to reactivate the Overseas Chinese it might appeal to them in other ways, but it might find that it had lost the one really effective way of appealing to them, as Chinese, speaking the Chinese language, identified with China, with Chinese culture and with Chinese traditions. That this was not simply a tactical manoeuvre is best exemplified by the resettlement policy.

The critical question, therefore, is whether the policy was applied also to Overseas Chinese communists, communist sympathisers, and the ardent patriots who were willing to serve the CCP in any cause. As suggested earlier, the policy addressed to the undifferentiated mass of Overseas Chinese appears to rest on an analysis of the potential of Overseas Chinese as a political force in Southeast Asia, and as such provides the best indication of the CCP's perceptions and expectations of Overseas Chinese communism.

The minimum objective of Chinese foreign policy in Southeast Asia might be described as a situation in which China can coexist with all countries in the region. At one end of the scale this means a series of communist governments subservient, or at least sympathetic to Peking and Peking's view of the world. At the other, it means diplomatic recognition from and trade with governments which might be non-communist, but which are prepared to coexist with China. Opposition to the United States is not the primary objective; but the kind of situation which the CCP wishes to achieve necessitates the exclusion of United States, and latterly also Soviet, influence, where that is hostile to the People's Republic of China. The Chinese government has been willing to accept the latter of the above two extremes; it has not scorned the practical advantages of peaceful coexistence or the accepted norms of trade, diplomacy, and other international intercourse. It is also prepared to encourage developments in the direction of the former. It is in the extent to which the CCP provides such encouragement, assistance, or direction, that the crucial question of China's foreign policy lies.

To what extent, then, might Overseas Chinese communists be of service to the Chinese government? They might be used to form the nucleus of communist parties, with the express purpose of overthrowing established governments by revolutionary action, or to create civil disorder so that other indigenous revolutionary forces might seize power with assistance from, and ultimately control by, Overseas Chinese. They might be encouraged to participate directly in indigenous revolutionary or communist movements, or instructed to provide such movements with money, supplies, intelligence, refuge, and facilities for distributing propaganda. They might be called upon to disseminate communist propaganda and to mobilise popular opinion against established governments, or to influence governments to support China's policies or to oppose what was considered detrimental to China's interests in the countries of residence.

But the very obvious fact is that the problems which persuaded the CCP that the Overseas Chinese masses could not be an effective political force for China would seem to apply even more to Overseas Chinese communists. In fact, it is probably the case that the effectiveness of the Overseas Chinese as a political arm of China is potentially greatest in the context of non-communist, non-subversive policies, and that it may diminish in proportion to the extent to which the Overseas Chinese are used for communist purposes or with subversive intent. Overseas Chinese communists face a choice between operating among Overseas Chinese or among the non-Chinese population. If they choose the former, they run the risk of consolidating the movement on a racial basis, which as the MCP discovered creates barriers to further development and is potentially disastrous for the revolutionary cause. If they choose the latter, they confront the same basic difficulties of communal antipathy or nationalist resentment and suspicion of the Overseas Chinese relationship with China which inhibit any effective political action by Overseas Chinese in the service of China. If the Chinese Communist Party was as keenly aware of the problems confronting the non-communist Overseas Chinese masses as its policies indicate, then it must also have been aware of the problems confronting Overseas Chinese communists.

But it is almost certainly the case that the development of the CCP's thinking on the problem was in the reverse order; from problems of communism to problems of the masses. That is, as a communist party advocating and supporting revolutionary change in Southeast Asia, the CCP's first concern in Overseas Chinese policy was with the problems and potential of Overseas Chinese communism; and its conclusions about this question determined and were mirrored in its publicly stated policy for the non-communist masses. If the CCP had believed that Overseas Chinese communists could be an effective instrument for China, then all Overseas Chinese would have been potentially valuable. The fact that it was prepared to detach and desinify the Overseas Chinese masses, therefore, suggests very strongly that it had first decided that the Overseas Chinese could not be used as a fifth column, and also that its publicly stated policies were intended to be applied equally to Overseas Chinese communists.

It can be demonstrated, of course, that Overseas Chinese communists identify closely with the CCP,[1] it must be assumed that there is close liaison with Peking where that is possible, and it is to be expected that the CCP will attempt, within the limits imposed by its own policies, to influence

Overseas Chinese communists to work together in the pursuit of common goals. What is more interesting in relation to the objectives of Overseas Chinese policy is that it has not been possible to establish that Overseas Chinese communists, particularly the militant activists, are controlled and directed by the CCP. In the case of the MCP, for example, there is both negative and positive evidence to suggest that it has acted independently of whatever advice the CCP may have offered.

It is both the logic of the CCP's position, and the failure to discover any evidence of organisational control of Overseas Chinese communism from Peking, which leaves the assertions of many writers on the subject open to serious question. Most of the discussion on the subject has been a matter of stringing together unrelated information in an artificially coherent pattern, or drawing inferences from communist activity among Overseas Chinese.[2] But the critical question of control has never been answered. It is not sufficient to claim that the CCP maintains an underground organisation among the Overseas Chinese,[3] when these claims are neither documented nor substantiated by other evidence. Nor is it possible, given the loose usage of the terms Chinese Communist and Communist Chinese referred to earlier, to assume that the frequent occurrence of these terms indicates the guiding presence of the CCP. There is one notable example in which members of an alleged 'Chinese Communist Politburo' arrested in the Philippines in 1952 turned out to be supported by the local branch of the KMT and the Nationalist Chinese Embassy.[4] Even the claims of Overseas Chinese communists themselves can be suspect, since they seem to have seen some political advantage in claiming the 'powerful backing' of China, even when this was not forthcoming and was contrary to the wishes of the CCP.

Communism in Southeast Asia, of course, is not unique to Overseas Chinese. Nor is it the case that most Overseas Chinese are communists or communist sympathisers; 'the majority of the overseas Chinese...do not present a serious problem to their countries of residence or actively serve the cause of Communist China'.[5] There may be special reasons why communism should appeal to a section of the Overseas Chinese; for example, exclusion from or lack of opportunity in nationalistic Asian societies.[6] But while communism or pro-communist sympathy among Overseas Chinese may be encouraged by the politics of the Chinese homeland, it is not dependent on proselytisation by the CCP.

The *P'i Liao chan-pao* makes the point that communist activities among Overseas Chinese were organised 'spontaneously' and 'on their own initiative', and asserts that the CCP sought to restrain such activities because Overseas Chinese revolution could not succeed. The Party's Overseas Chinese policy would seem to have been based in part upon this premise. So long as the CCP is inhibited by considerations which prevent it from giving more direct material support to Southeast Asian communists, the same considerations will apply also to Overseas Chinese communists. But so long as the 'Overseas Chinese problem' remains a problem in the view of the CCP, it seems likely that the Party will continue to be restrained from seeking to subvert and communise Overseas Chinese in order to subvert and communise Southeast Asia. The direction of Overseas Chinese policy since 1957 indicates, moreover, that the Party not only doubted the effectiveness of the non-communist Overseas Chinese masses as a political weapon, but that it had even stronger reservations about the value of Overseas Chinese communists, and that it was prepared to assist actively in contributing to the ultimate desinification or 'elimination' even of the hard core of patriots and communists, those who are prepared to act in the service of China because they are Chinese, rather than Southeast Asians.

OVERSEAS CHINESE POLICY AND FOREIGN POLICY: PROSPECTS
FOR POST-CULTURAL REVOLUTION ERA

What conclusions can be drawn from the Chinese government's handling of this problem about its approach to foreign policy and its relations with Southeast Asia? That the CCP decided that Overseas Chinese could not be an effective revolutionary vanguard for China does not in itself provide grounds for disproving the theory that the Party is responsible for all revolutionary change in Southeast Asia and harbours ambitions of conquest or hegemony within the region. It does, however, tend to destroy one of the conventional props to this theory. As such, it raises questions about some of the other props, and perhaps reveals something of the CCP's approach to revolution generally in Southeast Asia.

The argument that China seeks either conquest or Chinese-client revolutions in Southeast Asia assumes that China is totally insensitive to the feelings and aspirations of the people of Southeast Asia and is prepared to ride roughshod over them, even to the extent of installing unpopular puppets or clients. If this were the case, Overseas Chinese would have been extremely useful to China, since by this theory China would be prepared in any event to run the Southeast Asian revolution and assume the burden of maintaining its clients in office. That China was not prepared to attempt to use Overseas Chinese in this way suggests a number of things about its foreign policy.

First, and contrary to popular belief, it suggests that in its dealings with Southeast Asia the Chinese government has been extremely well-informed, and sensitive to Southeast Asian attitudes towards China. The Overseas Chinese problem is a complex one, and the CCP could have taken a simplistic and outmoded view like the KMT. In particular, it could have listened only to the voice of Overseas Chinese communists and ardent patriots, who made up a significant percentage of the Overseas Chinese with whom Chinese officials came into contact, but who were not necessarily typical. To understand fully the complexities of the Overseas Chinese problem the Chinese government had to understand how it worked in the milieu of regional politics and the internal politics of a variety of states in the region. Its actions appear to have been based on a more penetrating analysis of the Overseas Chinese situation than any other government could claim.

This was important for China's relations with the region in general, because it also necessitated an intimate understanding of Southeast Asian politics; one of the critical factors influencing the decision to decolonise was precisely the hostility of indigenous Southeast Asian nationalism to Overseas Chinese society and, through this and other associations, to China itself, or what Skinner has called the 'anti-Sinitic tradition'. To be aware of or sensitive to a situation does not necessarily mean that a government will act on its awareness or sensitivity. In this case the CCP did so, which suggests, as some observers have long argued, that China has been far more considerate of the aspirations of the peoples of Southeast Asia, including their nationalist aspirations, than it has been given credit for, or than other outside powers involved in the region.

While it might be argued that objectively the CCP's attempted solution was the only logical one, it can only have been logical to a government that was both well-informed and rational. The Party's Overseas Chinese policies tend to call into question hypotheses about China's past or future foreign policy action which start from the premise that the CCP knows nothing or is badly informed about the outside world. The point is not only that the CCP was well-informed, but that its Overseas Chinese policy is also a striking illustration of the Party's capacity for rational foreign policy action, a capacity which is implicitly denied by the Fifth-Column theory and by the wider assumptions about the Party's goals and intentions on which that theory is based.

It was also a departure from tradition. In relinquishing its claim to the Overseas Chinese the CCP abandoned a traditional view of the extent of the mandate of the rulers of China. The tradition may not have been very old, but some of the territorial claims which are alleged to be accepted by the present Chinese government are not so very much older. The CCP's action demonstrated that the Party is not necessarily bound by the past or by traditional Chinese views, as is sometimes suggested, that it is quite prepared to relinquish traditional claims and frame its policies in accordance with the realities of international politics in the twentieth century. This also would seem to have some significance for China's relations with Southeast Asia. It might be inferring too much to suggest from this alone that the CCP has abandoned all claims to territory outside its present borders, but it should serve as a reminder that the CCP is not moved by some irreversible logic of Chinese history or tradition which impels it towards territorial conquest in Southeast Asia.

The CCP's Overseas Chinese policy was very 'non-ideological' in the sense that this is popularly understood; that is, the mindless pursuit of world communism in disregard for China's security, the balance of world forces or the objective situation in the countries of Southeast Asia. But it was also ideologically justified, not simply in terms of decolonisation, but also because it supports the CCP's own contention that it does not and should not run the revolution in Southeast Asia, that revolution cannot be imported, that peoples striving for revolution, independence and liberation must rely on the strength of their own efforts. Publicly, the Chinese government has never supported the idea of Overseas Chinese making revolution by themselves; and it has supported Overseas Chinese participation in indigenous revolution only rarely, when in the Party's view such revolutions are approaching the point of victory and it is expedient for the Overseas Chinese to declare for the revolutionaries. Cultural Revolution sources, the decolonisation policy, and a number of quite explicit statements by Chou En-lai in the 1950s, indicate that the Chinese leaders actively curbed Overseas Chinese revolutionary activity. The implication is that Overseas Chinese should not participate, not only because they were an alien minority, but specifically because of their association with China. It was because of this association that the CCP saw difficulties in Overseas Chinese participation in Southeast Asian revolution and itself forbore to attempt to use them for this purpose. In other words, while China may provide the model, the propaganda and even the training, the revolution in Southeast Asia belongs to the Southeast Asians.

These observations do not deny the possibility of irrational behaviour on the part of the Chinese government. But it is suggested that in Overseas Chinese policy such irrationality inevitably will be counter-productive and is unlikely to be sustained for long enough to have any more than a marginal effect on relations with the countries of Overseas Chinese residence, particularly as more Overseas Chinese sever their links with the homeland. As suggested earlier, changes in the Overseas Chinese situation cannot be effected simply by a change in Chinese foreign policy, and any Overseas Chinese policy which ignores this fact will have little chance of success.

It is for this reason that there seems every likelihood that the direction of Overseas Chinese policy in the post-Cultural Revolution era will be essentially the same as it was before the Cultural Revolution. At the time of writing, the CCP itself has still not commented in any detail on its present policy, although the information which has appeared indicates that to the extent that the Party is thinking about Overseas Chinese affairs, it is thinking along the same lines as it was before the Cultural Revolution. But it is the nature of the Overseas Chinese problem itself which will probably determine the course of the CCP's policy; the position of the Overseas Chinese in the countries of residence, their traditional relationship with China, and the attitudes of indigenous Southeast Asians. The CCP's policy was incapable of providing quick or easy solutions to the Overseas Chinese problem. But while the Party is both well-informed and acting rationally it will in all probability continue to accept this policy as the only viable approach to the Overseas Chinese, irrespective of the goals of foreign policy.

It may be true, as Chou En-lai said in 1956, that there will always be some who will remain Overseas Chinese. But if the CCP maintains this policy, and the prevailing trend among Overseas Chinese continues, then the number of Nanyang Chinese will continue to grow and the number of Chinese 'sojourners' to diminish. The answer lies partly with the non-Chinese Southeast Asians. If they are willing to acknowledge the distinction between attachment to China and the attachment to Chinese culture, if they will accept the readiness of ethnic Chinese to identify with their countries and the contributions they can make to their societies without attempting to obliterate their Chineseness, then the Overseas Chinese problem, both for Southeast Asia and for China, will be one of steadily diminishing proportions. Recent events in some countries are far from propitious.

Appendix A

Selected estimates of the Overseas Chinese population in Southeast Asia[1]

Area	1960 Purcell[2]	1965 W. E. Willmott[3]	Percentage of total	1965 Chinese Nationalists[4]	1965 Williams[5]	Percentage of total
Brunei	21,745	25,000	26.3	28,000	25,000	26.3
Burma	350,000	400,000	1.6	320,000	400,000	1.6
Cambodia	350,000	425,000	6.8	300,000	435,000	7.0
Indonesia	2,690,000	2,750,000	2.6	2,545,000	2,750,000	2.6
Laos	35,000	45,000	1.8	30,000	45,000	2.1
Malaysia[6]	2,893,291	3,310,000	34.5	3,140,986	3,315,000	35.1
Philippines	181,626	450,000	1.4	300,000	450,000	1.4
Portuguese Timor	5,000	5,000	0.9	5,646	5,000	0.9
Singapore	1,230,700	1,400,000	74.9	1,383,000	1,400,000	74.5
Thailand	2,670,000	2,600,000	8.5	3,790,000	2,600,000	8.5
Vietnam, North	55,000	190,000	1.1 }	1,200,000	190,000	1.1
Vietnam, South	800,000	860,000	5.3 }		860,000	5.3
Total	11,282,362	12,460,000		13,042,632	12,475,000	

Notes:

[1] For comparison, Peking's 1953 census produced a total of 11,743,320. *Jen-min jih-pao*, 1 November 1954. Subsequently the Chinese used a round figure of 'over 12 million'. A recent Russian estimate gives 13 million. N. Simonia, *Izvestia*, 7 September 1967, in *The Current Digest of the Soviet Press*, 27 September 1967, p. 15.

[2] Victor Purcell, *The Chinese in Southeast Asia*, 2nd edn (London: Oxford University Press, 1965), p. 3.

[3] W. E. Willmott, 'The Chinese in Southeast Asia', *Australian Outlook*, vol. 20, no. 3 (December 1966), p. 254.

[4] Collated from *Hua-ch'iao ching-chi nien-chien* (*Overseas Chinese Economy Yearbook*) (Taipei: Overseas Chinese Economy Yearbook Editorial Committee, 1965). The Nationalist estimate at June 1969 was 18,301,126, including Hong Kong and Macao. *China Yearbook 1969–70* (Taipei: China Publishing Company, 1970), p. 394.

[5] Lea E. Williams, *The Future of the Overseas Chinese in Southeast Asia* (New York: McGraw Hill, 1966), p. 11.

[6] Breakdown of figures for Malaysia:

	Purcell	Willmott	(%)	Chinese Nationalists	Williams	(%)
Malaya	2,552,276	2,920,000	35.3	2,877,986	2,920,000	36.1
Sabah	104,542	125,000	24.8	no figure	120,000	23.3
Sarawak	236,473	275,000	33.5	263,000	275,000	32.5

There is a discrepancy between Willmott's total of 3,310,000 for the whole of Malaysia, and the sum of his estimates for Malaya, Sabah, and Sarawak, 3,320,000.

Appendix B

Overseas Chinese Affairs organisations

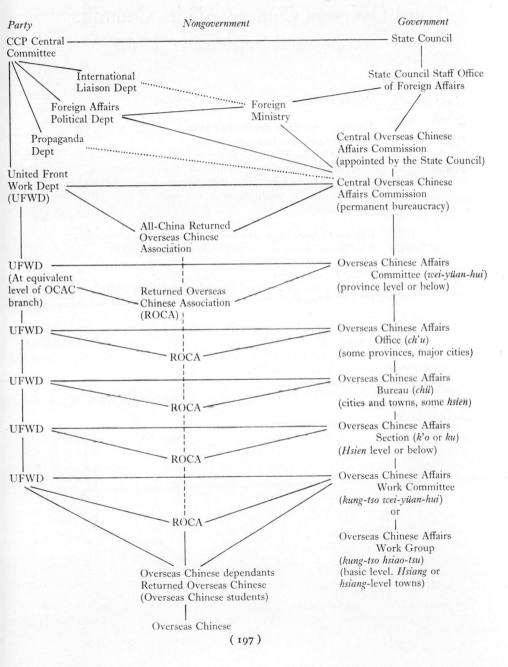

Party   *Nongovernment*   *Government*

CCP Central Committee ——————————————————— State Council

International Liaison Dept

State Council Staff Office of Foreign Affairs

Foreign Affairs Political Dept

Foreign Ministry

Propaganda Dept

Central Overseas Chinese Affairs Commission (appointed by the State Council)

United Front Work Dept (UFWD)

Central Overseas Chinese Affairs Commission (permanent bureaucracy)

All-China Returned Overseas Chinese Association

UFWD (At equivalent level of OCAC branch)

Overseas Chinese Affairs Committee (*wei-yüan-hui*) (province level or below)

Returned Overseas Chinese Association (ROCA)

UFWD

ROCA

Overseas Chinese Affairs Office (*ch'u*) (some provinces, major cities)

UFWD

ROCA

Overseas Chinese Affairs Bureau (*chü*) (cities and towns, some *hsien*)

UFWD

ROCA

Overseas Chinese Affairs Section (*k'o* or *ku*) (*Hsien* level or below)

UFWD

ROCA

Overseas Chinese Affairs Work Committee (*kung-tso wei-yüan-hui*) or

Overseas Chinese Affairs Work Group (*kung-tso hsiao-tsu*) (basic level. *Hsiang* or *hsiang*-level towns)

Overseas Chinese dependants Returned Overseas Chinese (Overseas Chinese students)

Overseas Chinese

Appendix C

Members of the
Third Overseas Chinese Affairs Commission.
Appointed September 1959

Key

Name in italic type	Member of the Chinese Communist Party
*	Appointment since September 1959
(Name)	Died since September 1959
(1, 2)	Member of the First and/or Second Commissions
(Date)	Last identification as member of the Commission. Two dates indicate appointment after the announcement of the Commission, and the first of such dates is the date of first identification or appointment

(CR)	Known to have been attacked in the Cultural Revolution
ACROCA	All-China Returned Overseas Chinese Association
CCP	Chinese Communist Party
CNS	*China News Service*
CPPCC	Chinese People's Political Consultative Conference
DD	Deputy Director
KMT	Kuomintang
NPC	National People's Congress
OC	Overseas Chinese
OCAC	Overseas Chinese Affairs Commission
UFWD	United Front Work Department
VC	Vice-Chairman

Name	Other positions	Other relevant information
Chairman		
廖承志 *Liao Ch'eng-chih* (CR) (1, 2) (9/66) Liao was a Vice-Chairman of the Commission from 1949, and was appointed Chairman in April 1959	Mbr, CCP Central Committee; DD State Council Office of Foreign Affairs; Mbr, Presidium, NPC; NPC deputy (OC); Chmn, Afro-Asian solidarity C'ttee; VC Chinese People's C'ttee for World Peace; VC Sino-Japanese Friendship Assn; VC Sino-Soviet Friendship Assn; President, Overseas Chinese University	Born 1908, Japan
Vice-Chairmen		
庄希泉 Chuang Hsi-ch'uan (CR) (1, 2) (9/66)	Acting Chmn, ACROCA; Mbr, Standing C'ttee and Presidium, 3rd NPC; NPC deputy (OC)	Born 1889. Singapore Overseas Chinese
庄明理 Chuang Ming-li (CR) (1, 2) (10/66) Appointed Vice-Chmn 10/56	VC ACROCA; NPC deputy (OC)	Born 1910. Malayan Overseas Chinese
方方 *Fang Fang* (CR) (1, 2) (9/66) Appointed Vice-Chmn 10/54	DD Central UFWD; D OCAC party c'ttee; VC ACROCA; NPC deputy (OC)	Born 1904. P'u-ning *hsien*, Kwangtung Province
黄長水 Huang Ch'ang-shui (CR) (1, 2) (10/66) Appointed Vice-Chmn 10/56	VC ACROCA; NPC deputy (OC); Dep. Sec.-Gen., China Democratic National Construction Assn; VC All-China Federation of Industry and Commerce; DD International Liaison Dept, All-China Journalists Assn; Deputy Chairman of Directors, Kwangtung Overseas Chinese Investment Corporation	Born 1905. Philippines Overseas Chinese
李任仁 Li Jen-jen (CR) (1, 2) (5/66)	Vice Governor, Kwangsi Province; Mbr Standing C'ttee KMT Revolutionary C'ttee; NPC deputy (Kwangsi)	Born 1883. Linkuei *hsien*, Kwangsi Province

Name	Other positions	Other relevant information
	Vice-Chairmen (cont.)	
林修德 *Lin Hsiu-te*＊ (CR) (4/64 10/66)	Dep. Sec. OCAC Party C'ttee; Mbr, Presidium and Chief Overseas Chinese Section CPPCC	Former Director, Fukien UFWD
林一心 *Lin Yi-hsin*＊ (1/56 9/66)	Secretary, CCP Fukien Provincial C'ttee; NPC deputy (Fukien)	
	Members	
張楚琨 Chang Ch'u-k'un (2) (9/59)	VC and Acting Sec.-Gen. ACROCA; Mbr, 4th National C'ttee CPPCC (OC); Vice-Mayor, Amoy	Former mbr, Fukien OCAC
張帆 *Chang Fan* (CR) (7/64)	Dir., 2nd Dept, OCAC; Mbr, OCAC party c'ttee; Dir., Editor in Chief, and mbr of party c'ttee, *CNS*	
章欣潮 Chang Hsin-ch'ao＊ (10/65 10/65)		
常任俠 Ch'ang Jen-hsia (9/59)	Mbr, Standing C'ttee, ACROCA; Mbr, 3rd Central C'ttee, China Democratic League	Indian Overseas Chinese
張殊明 Chang Shu-ming (1, 2) (9/59)	DD, Production Relief Office, OCAC; Mbr, Standing C'ttee, ACROCA; Mbr, China Democratic League	Singapore Overseas Chinese
張永勵 *Chang Yung-li* (9/63)	Vice Minister of Commerce	Former Chmn, South China Regional C'ttee for Assisting & Guiding Overseas Chinese Investment
趙昱 Chao Yü (2) (9/59)	Mbr, ACROCA; Mbr, 4th National C'ttee, CPPCC (OC); Procurator General, Hunan Province	Born 1885. United States Overseas Chinese. Veteran of 1911 Revolution
陳其尤 Ch'en Ch'i-yu＊ (4/60 4/60)	Chmn, Chih Kung Tang; Mbr, Standing C'ttee, 3rd NPC; NPC deputy (Kwangtung); Mbr, Standing C'ttee, and 4th National C'ttee, CPPCC (Chih Kung Tang)	Born 1893. Returned student from Japan

Name	Other positions	Other relevant information

Members (cont.)

Name	Other positions	Other relevant information
陳其瑗 (Ch'en Ch'i-yüan) (1, 2) (Died 5/68)	Mbr, Standing C'ttee, KMT Revolutionary C'ttee; Vice Minister of Internal Affairs; NPC deputy (OC); Mbr, 4th National C'ttee, CPPCC (Social Relief and Welfare Organisations); VC, ACROCA	Born 1887. Lived in United States from 1929 to 1946
陳曼雲 Ch'en Man-yüan (f) (CR) (2) (10/65)	DD, General Office, OCAC; Dep. Sec.-Gen, and head of Liaison Dept, ACROCA; VC, Peking ROCA; Mbr, Exec. C'ttee, All-China Women's Federation	Indonesian Overseas Chinese
陳伯源 Ch'en Po-yüan* (10/65 10/65)		
鄭鉄如 Cheng T'ieh-ju (2) (9/59)	NPC deputy (Kwangtung)	Hong Kong Chinese
金仲華 Chin Chung-hua (CR) (2) (9/59)	Vice-Mayor, Shanghai; NPC deputy (Shanghai); VC, All-China Journalists Assn; VC, Chinese People's C'ttee for World Peace; VC, Sino-Rumanian Friendship Assn	
秦力真 *Ch'in Li-chen* (9/59)	Director, Consular Affairs Dept, Ministry of Foreign Affairs (until Feb. 1962)	Ambassador to Norway, Apr. 1962– Jan. 1965; Ambassador to Zambia, Feb. 1965
周錚 Chou Cheng (1, 2) (9/59)	NPC Deputy (OC); DD, Hainan Island Administrative District; VC, Kwangtung Province ROCA; VC, Hainan OCAB; Chmn, Hainan ROCA	Thai Overseas Chinese
朱曼平 *Chu Man-p'ing* (4/60)	Director, 3rd Dept, OCAC; Mbr, ACROCA	
朱毅 Chu Yi* (11/66 11/66)	DD, Counsellor's Office of State Council	

Name	Other positions	Other relevant information

Members (cont.)

Name	Other positions	Other relevant information
鐘慶發 Chung Ch'ing-fa (CR) (9/59)	Director, General Office, OCAC; NPC deputy (OC); VC, Sino-Indonesian Friendship Assn	Former Counsellor and Chargé d'Affaires, Chinese Embassy, Djakarta
方君壯 Fang Chün-chuang (1, 2) (9/53 9/59)	Mbr, Kwangtung Province OCAC; VC, Canton OCAB; NPC deputy (OC); Chmn, Canton ROCA; Director, Kwangtung Overseas Chinese Investment Corp	Malayan Overseas Chinese
費振東 Fei Chen-tung (1, 2) (9/59)	Alt. Mbr, 3rd Central C'ttee China Democratic League	Indonesian Overseas Chinese. Former President, Peking O/seas Chinese School; Former Director, Education and Propaganda Dept, OCAC. Labelled rightest in 1957, this label was removed in late 1959
夏斌 Hsia Pin* (10/65 10/65)		
夏衍 *Hsia Yen* (2) (4/64)	Vice Minister of Culture (until April 1965); NPC deputy (Shanghai); VC, All-China Federation of Literary and Art Circles; VC, Chinese People's Assn for Cultural Relations with Foreign Countries	Returned student from Japan. Criticised in 1965
肖林 *Hsiao Lin* (2) (9/59)	DD, Shanghai 2nd Bureau of Commerce	Former Sec, CCP Overseas Work Dept; Former DD, Educ. and Cult. Propaganda Dept, OCAC
肖澤寬 Hsiao Tse-k'uan* (10/65 10/65)		
謝南光 Hsieh Nan-kuang (9/59)	Mbr, NPC Standing C'ttee; NPC deputy (OC); Mbr, Peking ROCA	Born Taiwan Province, under Japanese occupation

Name	Other positions	Other relevant information
Members (cont.)		
黃潔 (Huang Chieh) (2) (Died 11/66)	NPC deputy (OC); Vice Governor, Kwangtung Province; Exec. Mbr, All-China Assn for Industry and Commerce; Mbr, Standing C'ttee, ACROCA; VC, Kwangtung Province ROCA; VC, Canton ROCA; Dep. Chmn of Directors, Kwangtung Overseas Chinese Investment Corp	Born 1910. Indonesian Overseas Chinese
黃欽書 Huang Ch'in-shu* (CR) (1/60 1/60)	Mbr, Standing C'ttee, ACROCA; Chmn, Shanghai ROCA; NPC deputy (OC)	Indonesian Overseas Chinese
洪絲絲 Hung Szu-szu (CR) (1, 2) (11/50 9/59)	Dep. Sec.-Gen., ACROCA; NPC deputy (OC); DD, 2nd Dept, OCAC; Mbr, China Democratic League	Born 1908. Overseas Chinese from Indonesia/Singapore/ Malaya
高明軒 Kao Ming-hsüan (2) (9/59)	VC, ACROCA; Chmn, Fukien ROCA	Philippines Overseas Chinese. Former Chmn, Fukien OCAC
郭瑞人 Kuo Jui-jen (2) (9/59)	VC, Fukien OCAC; VC, Fukien ROCA; General Manager, Fukien Overseas Chinese Investment Corp; NPC deputy (Fukien); Vice Mayor, Amoy	Indonesian Overseas Chinese
雷任民 *Lei Jen-min* (2) (9/59)	Vice Minister of Foreign Trade; VC, China Committee for the Promotion of International Trade	
雷沛鴻 Lei P'ei-hung (2) (9/59)	Chmn, Kwangsi OCAC; Chmn, Kwangsi ROCA; Mbr, Standing C'ttee, ACROCA; Mbr, Standing C'ttee, of 6th Central C'ttee, Chih Kung Tang, and Director of its Overseas Chinese Work Research C'ttee	United States Overseas Chinese
李梅 Li Mei (f) (4/64)	Mbr, ACROCA; Mbr, Peking ROCA; Mbr, 4th National C'ttee, CPPCC (OC)	Indonesian Overseas Chinese

Name	Other positions	Other relevant information
Members (cont.)		
連貫 *Lien Kuan* (1, 2) (5/65)	VC Peking ROCA; Mbr, Standing C'ttee, NPC; NPC deputy (OC); Vice-Pres., Chinese People's Institute for Foreign Affairs; Chmn, Sino-Laotian Friendship Assn	Former (?) Director, 3rd Office, central UFWD
劉型 *Liu Hsing* (CR) (9/63)	Vice Minister of State Farms and Land Reclamation	
劉瑞龍 *Liu Jui-lung* (2) (9/59)	Director, Rural Work Dept, CCP East China Regional Bureau	
羅俊 Lo Chün (CR) (4/64)	Director, State Council Foreign Language Publications and Distribution Bureau	
羅范羣 Lo Fan-ch'ün (CR) (9/59)	Vice Governor, Kwangtung Province	Former Director, Kwangtung Province UFWD
盧心遠 Lu Hsin-yüan (2) (10/65)	DD, 3rd Office, OCAC; Dep. Sec.-Gen., ACROCA; Sec.-Gen. Peking ROCA; Dep. Chief, OC Section, 4th National C'ttee, CPPCC	
毛齊華 *Mao Ch'i-hua* (CR) (2) (9/63)	Vice Minister of Labour (until Feb. 1965)	
牛得清 Niu Te-ch'ing* (10/65 10/65)		
邵力子 (Shao Li-tzu) (1, 2) (Died 12/67)	Mbr, Standing C'ttee, NPC; Mbr, 4th National C'ttee, CPPCC; Mbr, Standing C'ttee, KMT Revolutionary C'ttee	
沈茲九 *Shen Tz'u-chiu* (f) (2) (4/64)	Mbr, Standing C'ttee, ACROCA; NPC deputy (Chekiang); Mbr, Presidium, All-China Federation of Women	Returned student from Japan
蘇惠 *Su Hui* (f) (CR) (2) (10/65)	Director, 2nd Dept, OCAC; NPC deputy (OC)	Wife of Fang Fang

Name	Other positions	Other relevant information
Members (cont.)		
陳 嘉庚 (Tan Kah-kee (Ch'en Chia-k'eng)) (1, 2) (Died 8/61)	Mbr, Presidium and Standing C'ttee, 2nd NPC; NPC deputy (OC); Chmn, ACROCA; Mbr, 3rd National C'ttee, CPPCC	Tan was one of the most eminent of all the returned Overseas Chinese. He made his name, and his fortune, in Singapore, and had associated with the CCP from the Yenan days
蔡 廷鍇 (Ts'ai T'ing-k'ai) (1, 2) (Died 4/68)	VC, National Defence Council; VC, National C'ttee, CPPCC; Mbr, Standing C'ttee, NPC; NPC deputy (Kwangtung); Mbr, Standing C'ttee of Central C'ttee, KMT Revolutionary C'ttee	
曹 菊如 *Ts'ao Chü-ju* (CR) (9/63)	President, People's Bank of China	
董 純才 Tung Ch'un-ts'ai (CR) (9/59)	Vice Minister of Education, until April 1965 Mbr, China Assn for Promoting Democracy	
王 紀元 *Wang Chi-yüan* (1, 2) (10/53 9/59)	DD, Educ. and Cult. Propaganda Office, OCAC; DD, *CNS*; Dep. Sec.-Gen., ACROCA; Mbr, 4th National C'ttee, CPPCC (OC)	Indonesian Overseas Chinese
王 汉杰 *Wang Han-chieh* (CR) (9/59)	Director, Fukien UFWD; Chmn, Fukien OCAC; Chmn, Fukien ROCA; Mbr, 4th National C'ttee, CPPCC (OC)	
王 本珍 Wang Pen-chen (2) (9/59)	Mbr, ACROCA	
王 炎之 Wang Yen-chih (2) (9/59)	Dep. Chief, OC section, 4th National C'ttee, CPPCC	
王 一知 *Wang Yi-chih* (f) (CR) (10/65)	Director, 4th Dept, OCAC; Mbr, ACROCA; Mbr, 4th National C'ttee, CPPCC (OC)	Former Director Yunnan OCAB

Name	Other positions	Other relevant information
Members (cont.)		
王有山 Wang Yu-shan (9/59)		
王雨亭 Wang Yü-t'ing (1, 2) (9/59)	DD, General Office, OCAC; Sec.-Gen., ACROCA; Sec.-Gen., Peking ROCA; Mbr, 4th National C'ttee, CPPCC (OC)	
王源興 Wang Yüan-hsing (2) (9/59)	VC, Kwangtung OCAC; VC, Canton OCAB; VC, ACROCA; NPC deputy (OC); Chmn, Peking ROCA	Indonesian Overseas Chinese
吳濟生 Wu Chi-sheng (CR) (10/65)	Director, 1st Dept, OCAC	
伍治之 Wu Chih-chih (9/59)		Former Chmn, Kwangtung OCAC
吳益修 Wu Yi-hsiu (2) (9/59)	NPC deputy (OC); VC, Peking ROCA; Mbr, Standing C'ttee, ACROCA; Director, Peking T'ien T'an Hospital	Indonesian Overseas Chinese
楊靜桐 Yang Ching-tung (2) (9/59)		
楊春松 (Yang Ch'un-sung) (2) (9/59) (Died 5/62)	Mbr, National C'ttee, CPPCC; Mbr, ACROCA	Japanese Overseas Chinese
顏希純 Yen Hsi-ch'un (9/59)	Mbr, Chih Kung Tang	
顏廼卿 Yen Nai-ch'ing (9/59)		
蟻美厚 Yi Mei-hou (1, 2) (10/59)	VC, Kwangtung OCAC; NPC deputy (OC); VC ACROCA; Chmn, Kwangtung ROCA	Thai Overseas Chinese
尤揚祖 Yu Yang-tsu (2) (9/59)	VC, ACROCA; NPC deputy (OC); Vice Governor, Fukien	Indonesian Overseas Chinese

Appendix D
Overseas Chinese farms

From 1960, Overseas Chinese Farms became the focus of domestic Overseas Chinese policy, and in themselves a basic unit of Overseas Chinese affairs administration. Only eighteen out of the fifty-one farms listed below were established before 1960. The population figures refer only to Overseas Chinese, some 70 per cent of the total. The overall total of 70,000 is taken separately from an item in the Chinese press and does not represent the sum of the totals given. References to *Tsu-kuo* are for the issue no. 5, May 1965.

	Name	Location	Established	Population
		FUKIEN PROVINCE		
		I *State*		
長龍連江縣	Ch'ang-lung	Lien-chiang *hsien*	1963	—
常山云霄縣	Ch'ang-shan	Yün-hsiao *hsien*	Dec. 1952	4,000[1]
赤港莆田縣	Ch'ih-kang	P'u-t'ien *hsien*	1960[2]	400
竹圳同安縣	Chu-pa	T'ung-an *hsien*	1958	300
泉上寧化縣	Ch'üan-shang*[3]	Ning-hua *hsien*	1966	—
崇安寧化縣	Ch'ung-an	Ning-hua *hsien*	1966	—
雪峯南安縣	Hsüeh-feng	Nan-an *hsien*	1959	—
寧德寧德縣	Ning-te	Ning-te *hsien*	1966	—
北郊福州市	Pei-chiao	Foochow Municipality	1961	500
北磴永春縣	Pei-k'ung*	Yung-ch'un *hsien*	1954	3,000
上街閩候縣	Shang-chieh	Min-hou *hsien*	1960	—
双第龍海縣	Shuang-ti	Lung-hai *hsien*	1955	400
双陽晉江縣	Shuang-yang	Chin-chiang *hsien*	1960	2,000
天馬山夏門市	T'ien-ma (-shan)	Amoy Municipality	1960	
東湖塘寧德縣	Tung-hu-t'ang	Ning-te *hsien*	1964	—
東閣福清縣	Tung-ke	Fu-ch'ing *hsien*	1963	1,000
		II *Private*[4]		
黃邦山龍岩縣	Huang-pang-shan	Lung-yen *hsien*		
美里福清縣	Mei-li	Fu-ch'ing *hsien*		
東寶山龍岩縣	Tung-pao-shan	Lung-yen *hsien*		
		KWANGTUNG PROVINCE		
		I *State*		
蕉嶺蕉嶺縣	Chiao-ling*	Chiao-ling *hsien*	1960	4,000
清遠清遠縣	Ch'ing-yüan	Ch'ing-yüan *hsien*	1960	500

	Name	Location	Established	Population
奮勇海康縣	Fen-yung	Hai-k'ang *hsien*	1952	700
海晏台山縣	Hai-yen*	T'ai-shan *hsien*	1964	—
興隆万寧縣	Hsing-lung*	Wan-ning *hsien*	1951	12,000[5]
花縣花縣	Hua *hsien*	Hua *hsien*	1955	1,000
陸丰陸丰縣	Lu-feng*	Lu-feng *hsien*	1952	8,000
梅縣梅縣	Mei *hsien*	Mei *hsien*	1960	—
彬村山琼海縣	Pin-ts'un-shan	Ch'iung-hai *hsien*	1960	1,000
普宁普宁縣	P'u-ning	P'u-ning *hsien*	1954	400
大南山惠來縣	Ta-nan-shan	Hui-lai *hsien*	1960	2,000
台山台山縣	T'ai-shan	T'ai-shan *hsien*	1966	—
潼湖惠陽／東莞縣	T'ung-hu*	Hui-yang/Tung-kuan *hsien*	1969?	—
万頃沙東莞	(Wan-ch'ing-sha)	Tung-kuan *hsien*	1951[6]	—
翁沅翁沅縣	Weng-yuan	Weng-yuan *hsien*		—
陽春陽春縣	Yang-ch'un	Yang-ch'un *hsien*	1964[7]	1,100
英德英德縣	Ying-te	Ying-te *hsien*	1957	2,000

II *Kwangtung Overseas Chinese Investment Corporation*[8]

保亭保亭縣	Pao-t'ing	Pao-t'ing *hsien*	1959	—

KWANGSI PROVINCE

State

桂林桂林市	Kuei-lin*	Kweilin Municipality	1960	1,000
來賓來賓縣	Lai-pin*	Lai-pin *hsien*	1961	600
柳城柳州市	Liu-ch'eng*	Liu-chow Municipality	1958	2,000
宁明宁明縣	Ning-ming*	Ning-ming *hsien*	1953	1,000
百色百色縣	Pai-se*	Pai-se *hsien*	1960	700
武鳴武鳴縣	Wu-ming	Wu-ming *hsien*	1958[9]	*c.* 3,000

KWEICHOW PROVINCE

State

望謨望謨縣	Wang-mu[10]	Wang-mu *hsien*	1960	1,000

YUNNAN PROVINCE

State

稼依	Chia-yi	Unidentified	1964	—
紅河元江縣	Hung-ho	Yüan-chiang *hsien*	1955	2,800
甘庄元江縣	Kan-chuang	Yüan-chiang *hsien*	1958	4,000
陸良陸良縣	Lu-liang	Lu-liang *hsien*	1964	—
賓居賓川縣	Pin-chü	Pin-ch'uan *hsien*	1960	—
太和祥云縣	T'ai-ho	Hsiang-yün *hsien*[11]	1960	—

Name	Location	Established	Population
	LIAONING PROVINCE		
大連旅大市　Dairen Orchard Farm*			—
	Total Overseas Chinese population, 1965[12]		70,000

Notes

* Indicates cited in Chinese sources since 1968.

1 4,000 in *CNS*, 28 November 1966. *Tsu-kuo* gives 8,000.
2 *Jen-min jih-pao*, 15 February 1961. *Tsu-kuo* gives 1959.
3 Referred to in 1971 as the Ning-hua State Overseas Chinese Farm. *Jen-min jih-pao*, 16 February 1971.
4 Identified in *CNS*, 31 March 1960, as having been established for some time.
5 *Jen-min pao*, Rangoon, 30 June 1964. *Tsu-kuo* gives 10,000.
6 One of the original Overseas Chinese farms, in January 1954 it was joined with a state farm to form the Chu-chiang State Machine Farm. *Ta kung pao* (Hong Kong), 24 February 1954. However, Wang Yüan-hsing and Yu Yang-tsu referred to it as an Overseas Chinese Farm in 1959. *Jen-min jih-pao*, 3 May 1959.
7 *Ching-chi tao-pao*, no. 4443, 6 June 1966. *Tsu-kuo* date is 1959. In the Cultural Revolution identified as 'K'ang-mei ('Resist America') Overseas Chinese Farm'. *SCMP*, no. 4122 (20 February 1968), p. 10.
8 *Ta kung pao* (Hong Kong), 14 January 1960. According to *CNS* on 9 December 1959, this was an ordinary State Overseas Chinese farm.
9 *CNS*, 7 April 1958. *Tsu-kuo* gives 1960.
10 This is often referred to as the 'Kweichow Overseas Chinese Farm'. It is possible that it is no longer an Overseas Chinese farm, since the reference to farms in five provinces and regions in 1966 became farms in four provinces, omitting Kweichow, in *CNS*, 4 February 1966.
11 *CNS*, 7 February 1961. *Tsu-kuo* gives Pin-ch'uan *hsien*. Converted in 1960 from a State farm established in 1958. *CNS*, 6 June 1964.
12 *Ch'iao-wu pao*, no. 1, February 1965.

Notes to the text

1 The term 'colonies' as it is generally understood is not an accurate description of the origins of Chinese migration, of the position of Overseas Chinese in the countries of residence, or of their relationship with China. There were, however, 'colonial' elements in the relationship, which are discussed below.

2 Lea E. Williams cites an example of an 'enthusiastic' scholar who arrived in Southeast Asia with a long questionnaire designed to test the attitudes of Overseas Chinese towards the Chinese government, only to discover the futility of such techniques in that situation. *The Future of the Overseas Chinese in Southeast Asia* (New York: McGraw Hill, 1966), p. 22. See also Sheldon Appleton, 'Communism and the Chinese in the Philippines', *Pacific Affairs*, vol. xxxii, no. 4 (December 1959), p. 376.

3 *Jen-min jih-pao* (*People's Daily*), 21 April 1950, gave the proportion of Overseas Chinese in the Nanyang as 95 per cent.

4 The CCP appears to have believed that Chinese in the Americas were capable of making a greater financial contribution to China in proportion to their numbers than were the Chinese in Southeast Asia. This did not, however, affect the Party's political objectives.

5 *China Yearbook 1969–1970* (Taipei: China Publishing Company, 1970), p. 394.

6 Nationality Law of the Republic of China, promulgated February 1929, in Kao Hsin (ed.), *Ch'iao-wu fa-kuei* (*Laws and Regulations on Overseas Chinese Affairs*) (Taipei: Overseas Chinese Affairs Commission, 1964), p. 78.

7 A detailed breakdown of the 1969 KMT figure is not available. See the 1965 figures in Appendix A.

8 Williams, *The Future of the Overseas Chinese in Southeast Asia*, p. 11.

9 *Jen-min jih-pao*, 1 November 1954.

10 See, for example, *Jen-min jih-pao*, 27 October 1949, citing a pre-war KMT estimate of 8,546,000. There is, of course, no reason to suppose that the KMT's own estimates are derived by any means other than 'indirect investigation' where census figures are not available.

11 *Jen-min shou-ts'e* (*People's Handbook*) (Peking: Ta kung pao she, 1965), p. 115.

12 Interview, Peking, 6 February 1968. It is possible that the reluctance to provide even a rough figure for Overseas Chinese population reflected a Cultural Revolution debate on the criteria for determining who was Overseas Chinese.

13 This is not the first occasion on which Peking has claimed not to have registered the Overseas Chinese. In the Indian crisis of 1962–3 the Chinese government stated: 'The Indian government knows clearly that the Chinese government has never carried out a universal registration of the Chinese in India.' *Ch'iao-wu pao* (*Overseas Chinese Affairs Journal*), no. 1 (February 1963), p. 8.

14 *Jen-min jih-pao*, 1 November 1954; *Jen-min shou-ts'e* (1965), p. 115.

15 Lo Li-shih, Vice-Chairman and subsequently Chairman of the Kwangtung Overseas Chinese Affairs Committee (OCAC) and Secretary of its Party Committee, addressing the First Enlarged Conference of the Kwangtung OCAC. *Ta kung pao* (Hong Kong), 13 March 1956.

16 They were specifically excluded, for example, in the 'Regulations governing the administration of Overseas Chinese land during land reform'. *Ch'iao-wu fa-kuei hui-pien* (*Collection of Laws and Regulations on Overseas Chinese Affairs*), vol. 1 (Peking: Lien-ho shu-tien, 1951), p. 7. But they were included in measures for

the protection of remittances introduced in 1955. *Ta kung pao* (Hong Kong), 22 March 1956.

17 According to one published definition, a dependant was one who had immediate relatives who had lived and worked outside China for more than one year. *Fu-chien ch'iao-hsiang pao* (*Fukien Overseas Chinese District News*), 14 September 1956.

18 According to pre-war KMT figures, 95 per cent of the Overseas Chinese originated from the provinces of Fukien and Kwangtung. *Jen-min jih-pao*, 27 October 1949. In 1954, there were said to be 6,400,000 dependants in Kwangtung, and 2,000,000 in Fukien. *Jen-min jih-pao*, 6 October 1954.

19 *Fu-chien jih-pao* (*Fukien Daily*), 30 September 1952.

20 The figures were 65 per cent poor and hired peasants, 25 per cent middle peasants, 8 per cent other labourers, and 2 per cent landlords and rich peasants. *Nan-fang jih-pao* (*Southern Daily*), 2 October 1952.

21 There is unlikely to have been significant increase, since there has been very little emigration since 1949; and with deaths among the Chinese abroad and their dependants in China, the number has probably decreased. In 1957, Lo Li-shih, then Chairman of the Kwangtung OCAC, stated that the ratio of arrivals to departures since 1949 had been two to one. *Nan-fang jih-pao*, 10 August 1957.

22 P. C. Campbell, *Chinese Coolie Emigration to Countries within the British Empire* (London: P. S. King, 1923), p. 68; Harley F. McNair, *The Chinese Abroad; their position and protection* (Shanghai: The Commercial Press, 1925), p. 284.

23 In 1958 the Viceroy of Chihli told an American diplomat who suggested that Chinese consuls should be sent abroad to protect Chinese subjects: 'The Emperor's wealth is beyond computation; why should he care for those of his subjects who have left their home, or for the sands they have scraped together,' W. A. P. Martin, *A Cycle of Cathay*, cited in McNair, *The Chinese Abroad*, p. 11.

24 For a discussion of the activities of Chinese consuls in the Straits Settlements at the end of the nineteenth century, see Eddie Tang, 'British Policy Towards the Chinese in the Straits Settlements: Protection and Control 1877–1900', Unpublished M.A. thesis, Australian National University, 1971. Chinese officials had been involved with Chinese communities in other countries, such as the United States, but their activities in the Straits Settlements exemplify almost the full range of interest and involvement, from politics to finance.

25 For details concerning the Nationality Law, see McNair, *The Chinese Abroad*, ch. 4.

26 There were six Overseas Chinese representatives in the first National Assembly, elected in China by delegates from Overseas Chinese organisations. In 1913 there were 180 in this 'electoral college', and after the restoration of the Assembly in 1917, there were over 700. This practice, or something like it, carried through to the Communist period, where the Central Overseas Chinese Affairs Commission (OCAC) meeting in enlarged session elects representatives to the National People's Congress (NPC). For details of the earlier period, see Feng Tzu-yu, *Hua-ch'iao ke-ming k'ai-kuo shih* (*A History of the Overseas Chinese in the Revolution and the Founding of the Nation*) (Shanghai: Shang-wu yin-shua-kuan, 1947), pp. 121–2.

27 Chinese consuls were appointed concurrently Advisers on Overseas Chinese Education, and each year school inspectors were sent to the countries of residence. *Hua-ch'iao-chih tsung-chih* (*General Gazetteer of the Overseas Chinese*) (Taipei: Hua-ch'iao-chih Editorial Committee, 1956), pp. 261–2. This is a post-1949 official history of the KMT's Overseas Chinese policy.

28 Wang Gungwu, *A Short History of the Nanyang Chinese* (Singapore: Eastern Universities Press, 1959), p. 34.

29 William Skinner, for example, has noted the disillusionment of Thai Chinese with the failure of the Peking governments to protect their rights and interests, and their subsequent enthusiasm for Sun Yat-sen. *Chinese Society in Thailand* (New York: Cornell University Press, 1957), pp. 234–5.

30 *Hua-ch'iao-chih tsung-chih*, pp. 535–9. The OCAC established branches in the provinces and in major ports, as well as a number of agencies for various aspects of Overseas Chinese affairs, such as the Overseas Chinese News Service (*Hua-ch'iao t'ung-hsün she*). In 1944, the KMT approved a recommendation to transform the Commission into a Ministry, but this proposal was subsequently abandoned. Ibid. p. 532.

31 Ibid. pp. 526 *et seq.*

32 The word chauvinism is not intended here to have military connotations, but to indicate extreme nationalism and intense, assertive patriotism. This may be a corruption of the original meaning, but it is widely used in this sense in writings on the Overseas Chinese, and by the Chinese government itself. See the discussion of Chou En-lai's Rangoon speech below.

33 *Hua-ch'iao-chih tsung-chih*, p. 529.

34 Constitution of the Republic of China, effective December 1947, Article 167(2). *China Yearbook 1969–1970*, p. 710.

35 *Hua-ch'iao-chih tsung-chih*, p. 530.

36 This point emerges very clearly in Yoji Akashi's study, *The Nanyang Chinese National Salvation Movement, 1937–1941* ([Lawrence]: Center for East Asian Studies, The University of Kansas, 1970).

37 '*Kung-t'ung kang-ling*' (*The Common Programme*), adopted at the First Plenary Session of the CPPCC, 29 September 1949, Article 58. *Chung-hua jen-min kung-ho-kuo k'ai-kuo wen-hsien* (*Documents on the Founding of the People's Republic of China*) (Hong Kong: Hsin-min-chu ch'u-pan she, 1949), p. 274.

38 G. William Skinner, 'Overseas Chinese in Southeast Asia', *Annals of the American Academy of Political and Social Science*, vol. 321 (January 1959), p. 138.

39 *Ch'iao-wu pao*, 17 October 1956, p. 2.

40 This was stimulated by the first united front with the KMT and again by the anti-Japanese united front of the war period. See, for example, Skinner, *Chinese Society in Thailand*, pp. 234–5; and Victor Purcell, *The Chinese in Southeast Asia*, 2nd edn (London: Oxford University Press, 1965), p. 48.

41 Many Overseas Chinese who were given positions in China after 1949 had been involved in left-wing 'patriotic' activities in Southeast Asia. Fei Chen-tung, for example, who became a member of the OCAC and the first Director of the Peking Returned Overseas Chinese Supplementary Middle School, was twice expelled from Indonesia by the Dutch, the second time at the request of the Nationalist Chinese Consul in Medan. *Chung-kung jen-ming lu* (*Who's Who in Communist China*) (Taipei: Chung-kung jen-ming lu Editorial Committee, 1967), p. 535.

42 It has been claimed that this was when the CCP first became aware of the financial potential of Overseas Chinese. See Lu Yu-sun, *Programs of Communist China for Overseas Chinese* (Hong Kong: The Union Research Institute, 1956), p. 7. It seems highly improbable that the CCP remained in ignorance of Overseas Chinese financial contributions to China until the 1930s.

43 Ibid. p. 8.

44 Chang Hsi-che, *Kung-fei ti ch'iao-wu cheng-ts'e yü ch'iao-wu kung-tso* (*The Overseas Chinese Policies and Overseas Chinese Work of the Communist Bandits*) (Taipei: Overseas Chinese Association, 1962), pp. 5–6.

45 The Party's Draft Programme for Peaceful National Construction presented to the Political Consultative Conference in January 1946, proposed that the Foreign Ministry and diplomatic missions abroad 'should actively protect the interests of the Overseas Chinese, relieve their sufferings, and facilitate the movement of those who return to China; the central and local governments should provide assistance for those who have returned'. Ibid. pp. 6–7.

46 'Protect the interests of the Overseas Chinese, help those who return to China.' 'On Coalition Government', *Mao Tse-tung hsüan-chi* (*Selected Works of Mao Tse-tung*), vol. III (Peking: Jen-min ch'u-pan she, 1961), p. 1065.

47 It is true, of course, that Moscow and the Comintern had been active in Southeast Asia, particularly in Malaysia and Singapore, in the 1920s and 1930s. But that was a rather different problem. It was not aimed solely at Overseas Chinese or at subverting the Kuomintang, nor was it a policy directed by the CCP. The question of CCP involvement with Southeast Asian communism before 1949 has been the subject of some highly speculative writing which does not really prove very much. It is a question which demands a proper investigation.

48 In Lyman Van Slyke's study of the united front, Overseas Chinese are not even mentioned in the pre-1949 period. *Enemies and Friends. The United Front in Chinese Communist History* (Stanford: Stanford University Press, 1967).

49 Constitution of the Republic of China, Article 141. *China Yearbook 1969–1970*, pp. 707–8.

CHAPTER 2: *Administration of Overseas Chinese affairs* (pp. 12–34)

1 *Ch'iao-wu pao*, 17 October 1956, p. 2.

2 For example, 'the range of their organisations, from the central government down to the local communities, gives an idea of the importance attached to this objective (protection of the rights and interests of Overseas Chinese)'. Richard Coughlin, *Double Identity. The Chinese in Modern Thailand* (Hong Kong: Oxford University Press, 1960), p. 183.

3 *Jen-min jih-pao*, 6 October 1954. In Yunnan Province, for example, there were only 50,000 domestic Overseas Chinese in 1956, and one-third of these were concentrated in one *hsien*. *Chung-kuo hsin-wen she* (*China News Service*, hereafter *CNS*), 25 August 1956, and 17 October 1956. In Kwangsi, there were reported to be 100,000 dependants in 1957. *Kuang-hsi jih-pao* (*Kwangsi Daily*), 16 April 1957.

4 This is sometimes referred to as a Committee, since the Chinese term, *wei-yüan-hui*, is identical for both. Although there were administrative reasons for adopting this structure, which the Kuomintang also had found to be the most suitable, it may be that the CCP considered that the adoption of the same title which the KMT had used would assist in legitimising the new government in the eyes of Overseas Chinese.

5 References in the Chinese press to the Commission staff usually refer to them by their rank in the Commission. Otherwise they are called 'responsible persons', 'personnel', etc., but never 'members' of the Commission. Where the Commission is mentioned without other designation, it indicates only the Central OCAC and not the subordinate offices in the provinces.

6 For a description of branch agencies and coordinative committees see Franz Schurmann, *Ideology and Organisation in Communist China* (Berkeley and Los Angeles: University of California Press, 1966), pp. 173–94.

7 In the period of the Hundred Flowers, non-Party members and staff of the OCAC complained of 'having positions but no authority' (*yu-chih wu-ch'üan*). See a report on criticism in the OCAC in *Jen-min jih-pao*, 25 May 1957.

8 For example, it was Ho and not one of the Party members in the Commission who delivered the first major repudiation of the attacks and criticisms of the OCAC of May 1957. '*Teng-ch'ing tui ch'iao-wu-kung-tso ti yi-hsieh hu-t'u ssu-hsiang*' ('Clear up some muddle-headed thinking about Overseas Chinese work'), *Jen-min jih-pao*, 12 July 1957.

9 Liao was born in Tokyo, and spent some time in Hong Kong during the war against Japan. As the son of Liao-Chung-k'ai he also represents a link with Sun Yat-sen, although he was only eighteen when Sun died. He was first appointed an alternate member of the CCP Central Committee in 1946 and was raised to full membership in 1949.

10 Announcement of the appointments and name lists are given in *Jen-min jih-pao*, 20 October 1949, 24 April 1957, and 18 September 1959. A number of appointments have been made in addition to those promulgated on these dates. The announcement of Ho Hsiang-ning's appointment as Chairman was made in *Jen-min jih-pao*, 30 September 1949, and of Liao Ch'eng-chih's succession to this post in ibid. 29 April 1959.

11 They did not, however, coincide with the convening of the National People's Congress or even the Chinese People's Political Consultative Conference (CPPCC). They may have been related to Central Party meetings, but on the evidence available this can only be assumed, not verified. The second Commission came nine months after the announcement of an extensive reorganisation in Overseas Chinese affairs administration. Of its fifty-one members only thirty-seven were reappointed to the Third Commission. Some had come under attack in the Anti-Rightists Campaign of 1957; for example Director of the OCAC General Office, Chang Kan-ch'eng (*Jen-min jih-pao*, 2 June 1957), and Director of the OCAC Culture and Education Propaganda Department, Fei Chen-tung, who was subsequently rehabilitated and reappointed to the Third Commission (*Jen-min jih-pao*, 5 December 1959). Others, such as Chang Ts'an-ming, Director of the Consular Affairs Department of the Foreign Ministry, and Ch'en Tseng-ku, a Vice-Minister of Education, were transferred to areas of work which did not involve Overseas Chinese affairs. Others may have been affected by the decentralisation which began in 1957 or by long periods of *hsia-fang*.

12 For example, since the first major intake of repatriates was to come from Indonesia, one of the new appointees was Chung Ch'ing-fa, former Counsellor and Chargé d'affaires in the Chinese Embassy in Djakarta. In 1960, Chung was appointed concurrently head of a repatriation office in Canton. *CNS*, 5 February 1960.

13 Since 1949, the Commission has been enlarged, although not significantly. Including the Chairman and Vice-Chairmen, the First Commission had a total of fifty members, the Second Commission fifty-eight, and the Third Commission sixty-three when appointed in 1959. The number of Vice-Chairmen increased from four in 1949 to seven in 1966. Estimating from reported deaths and new appointments, the Commission would have had a total of seventy members in December 1966; almost certainly, however, there have been deaths, retirements or dismissals which have not been reported.

14 Lien Kuan, a member of the Second Commission, was identified in the central UFWD in 1949 but has not been identified in this capacity since the early 1950s.

15 Concurrent offices of the members of the First Commission are given in *Jen-min jih-pao*, 20 October 1949. Sixteen names were not promulgated at the time; these positions may not all have been filled, since only four new members were identified between 1949 and 1957.

16 It may be that for routine meetings the full Commission does not convene, but that such meetings are simply a question of gathering together those members who happen to be in Peking, or somewhere in the provinces, at a particular time. One such meeting was reported in July 1957, for Commission members who were in Peking to attend the Fourth Session of the First NPC. *Ta kung pao* (Hong Kong), 18 July 1957.

17 One of the few indications of its size was a report in 1955 that P'eng Tse-min had addressed several hundred (*shu-pai*) Overseas Chinese affairs workers in the OCAC. *CNS*, 22 June 1955. In 1959 140 cadres of the OCAC were reported to have returned from a year's *hsia-fang* in Hainan Island. *CNS*, 20 March 1959. Even assuming that the barest skeleton staff had been left behind in Peking, as was the case in some ministries, that would mean a total of over 200, but the figure is probably much greater.

18 The departments were first designated as *ch'u*, and from 1951 as *szu*. The directors and some of the deputy directors of the departments are usually members of the appointed Commission.

19 *CNS*, 25 January 1958.

20 *Ch'iao-wu pao*, no. 2 (April 1962), p. 39.

21 '*Ch'iao-wu wei-yüan-hui tsu-chih fa*' (Statute of the Overseas Chinese Affairs Commission), revision of 27 September 1942, in Kao, *Ch'iao-wu fa-kuei*, p. 3.

22 The Fourth Enlarged Conference of the First OCAC, for example, held in June 1956, was attended by representatives from the OCAC, Overseas Chinese deputies to the NPC, Overseas Chinese members of the National Committee of the CPPCC, returned Overseas Chinese, dependants, Overseas Chinese workers, and representatives of other central organs. There were 363 attending the conference, of whom only 88 participated in discussion and voting. *Jen-min jih-pao*, 9 June 1956.

23 *Jen-min jih-pao*, 24 November 1953.

24 *Hsin pao* (*New Daily*), Djakarta, 7 September 1954. According to Liao Ch'eng-chih, the candidates were proposed by Overseas Chinese associations or decided by consultation among leading Overseas Chinese figures. In some countries, the Overseas Chinese 'expressed the wish' that they should be represented by returned Overseas Chinese. *Ta kung pao* (Hong Kong), 2 September 1954.

25 The 'figurehead' deputies were returned Overseas Chinese who had been prominent members of the communities in which they had lived. Most of them had other non-governmental positions, in the Returned Overseas Chinese Associations or, for example, in the Overseas Chinese Investment Corporations. Yang T'ang-ch'eng, for example, a New Zealand Chinese, was a member of the All-China Returned Overseas Chinese Association (ACROCA), the Kwangtung Returned Overseas Chinese Association (ROCA), and a director of the Kwangtung Overseas Chinese Investment Corporation. Wu Huan-hsing, a returned Chinese from South Africa, worked in a hospital in Peking, but did not hold any government positions. There have been some deputies actually resident abroad. One of the most prominent was Hsü Ssu-min, who represented the Chinese in Burma at the First NPC. So far as is known, not one of the thirty presently resides outside China.

26 Overseas Chinese are represented also in the CPPCC. The CPPCC has an Overseas Chinese Section, and there are Overseas Chinese representatives on the CPPCC National Committee. The role of the CPPCC, however, has not been significant in Overseas Chinese affairs administration, even in the period before the establishment of the NPC.

27 Work conferences were held in Fukien and Kwangtung rather than in Peking. Conferences on State Overseas Chinese Farms, for example, were held on Hainan Island, where the exemplary Hsing-lung Overseas Chinese Farm was located. Work conferences were held also by the province-level branches of the Commission.

28 At the First Session of the Second Canton People's Congress in December 1956, Overseas Chinese affairs cadres criticised the lack of understanding of Overseas Chinese policy, and called for an 'Overseas Chinese Policy Propaganda Week' in which all cadres of the municipality were to participate. See joint statement by Wang Yüan-hsing, member of the Kwangtung Province OCAC, Hsieh Ch'uang, Chairman, and Yü Hsiu, Vice-Chairman, of the Canton Overseas Chinese Affairs Bureau (OCAB), in *Kuang-chou jih-pao (Canton Daily)*, 2 December 1956.

29 See for example, the criticisms by Wang Yü-t'ing, Deputy Director of the General Office in the OCAC, in *Jen-min jih-pao*, 25 May 1957.

30 The attacks were made in a conference convened by the Party Committee in the Kwangtung OCAC to discuss united front work. *Nan-fang jih-pao*, 2 June 1957.

31 *Shan-t'ou pao (Swatow Daily)*, 22 June 1957.

32 Whereas higher branches are known as 'Overseas Chinese Affairs' (*ch'iao-wu*) branches, the Work Committees are called 'Overseas Chinese Dependants' (*ch'iao-shu*) committees.

33 Schurmann, *Ideology and Organisation*, pp. 188–94.

34 Reported in *Ta kung pao* (Hong Kong), 17 November 1955.

35 In Taishan *hsien* in Kwangtung Province, for example, there were 700,000 domestic Overseas Chinese in 1956. *Ch'iao-wu pao*, 17 October 1956, p. 29.

36 *Fu-chien ch'iao-hsiang pao*, 13 April 1968. Doak Barnett, in his description of the Overseas Chinese Affairs Section in County X, reports that the Section convened a congress in 1959 to solve the problem of the rapid decline in the flow of family remittances. *Cadres, Bureaucracy, and Political Power in Communist China* (New York: Columbia University Press, 1967), pp. 253–4. See also *Fu-chien ch'iao-hsiang pao*, 3 April 1958, for a detailed directive on how Overseas Chinese congresses should be organised and run.

37 In cities, work committees were established at street level, under the jurisdiction of the municipal Overseas Chinese affairs branch. In December 1956, the Canton OCAB organised a course for directors and deputy directors from 145 of these committees from the city of Canton. *Kuang-chou jih-pao*, 23 December 1956.

38 *Ta kung pao* (Hong Kong), 17 November 1955.

39 *Ta kung pao* (Hong Kong), 17 January 1956.

40 *Ch'iao-wu pao*, 20 May 1957, p. 22. No explanation was given for the suggested membership of between nine and seventeen.

41 *Ch'iao-wu pao*, 20 May 1957, p. 23.

42 *Kuan-yü kuo-nei ch'iao-wu kung-tso ti jo-kan cheng-ts'e* (Certain policies concerning domestic Overseas Chinese work), *Kuang-ming jih-pao (Kwangming Daily)*, 10 June 1956.

43 Branches of the Commission were not established simultaneously with the Central Commission in 1949. The Kwangtung and Fukien OCACs were formed early in 1950, the Kwangsi Office not until 1955, the Yunnan Office in mid-1956, and the Chekiang Office at the end of 1956. The Shanghai branch had been upgraded twice. The important Canton Bureau was not formally established until July 1954. Some provinces with a small Overseas Chinese population did not have a separate administrative organ for Overseas Chinese affairs. At lower levels there was widespread inconsistency. On 22 August 1950 the *Jen-min jih-pao*

reported that in Kwangtung Province, apart from the provincial Committee, almost none of the special districts or *hsien* had Overseas Chinese organs. Subsequently branches were established in East Kwangtung and West Kwangtung and then were abolished.

44 *Jen-min jih-pao*, 27 September 1954. According to Hsü Ssu-min, the shortcomings in Overseas Chinese affairs in the period to 1954 had been due to gaps in the administration. Ibid. 29 September 1954.

45 '*Chung-hua ch'üan-kuo kuei-kuo hua-ch'iao lien-ho-hui tang-ch'ien ti chi-pen jen-wu*' (The present basic tasks of the ACROCA). (Hereafter, '*ACROCA tang-ch'ien ti chi-pen jen-wu*'), Report to the inaugural meeting of the ACROCA in October 1956, *Ch'iao-wu pao*, 17 October 1956, p. 15.

46 Although much remains to be learnt about top-level decision-making, some new information came to light during the Cultural Revolution. See, for example, Parris H. Chang, 'Research Notes on the Changing Loci of Decision in the Chinese Communist Party', *China Quarterly*, no. 44, October–December 1970. On the function of Central Work Conferences in the 1960s, Chang points out, however, that there has been little information on the discussion of foreign policy problems.

47 The Staff Office of Foreign Affairs was established in 1958; prior to that time, foreign affairs were handled by the Premier's Secretariat. There is no record of Liao, or Ho Hsiang-ning, having been formally associated with the Premier's Secretariat, but it seems probable that Liao was responsible for external policy before the Office of Foreign Affairs existed. He was appointed to this Office when it was first established.

48 Since the end of 1954, Fang Fang appears to have had responsibility for domestic work. One indication of Liao's sole responsibility in external affairs was that in 1967, the revolutionary rebels in the OCAC attacked Liao, and Liao only in the Commission, for the external Overseas Chinese policy.

49 Liao Ch'eng-chih has made frequent trips abroad to attend peace and friendship or solidarity conferences. Both Liao and Tan Kah-kee went to Bandung in 1955, but as members of the Chinese delegation to the Afro-Asian Conference, and not specificially as members of the OCAC.

50 *Jen-min jih-pao*, 28 December 1949. The letters also asked that copies of all Overseas Chinese publications be sent to the Commission to be held as records. It appears to have been envisaged also that the Commission would have a quasi-consular function. In temporary regulations for returning Overseas Chinese issued in 1950, it was stated that returnees should have either a passport, or documents issued by the OCAC. *Ch'iao-wu fa-kuei hui-pien*, p. 25. It is not known to what extent this system operated, but subsequently it appears to have been left entirely to the Foreign Ministry.

51 See ch. 9.

52 Ch'in Li-chen was Director of the Consular Affairs Department in the Foreign Ministry. Although his work would have concerned Chinese overseas, it had to do with issuing travel documents and arranging for repatriation, which are not strictly matters of external Overseas Chinese policy. Chung Ch'ing-fa had been counsellor and chargé d'affaires in the Chinese Embassy in Djakarta.

53 For surveys of Liao's career, see *Who's Who in Communist China* (Hong Kong: The Union Research Institute, 1966), pp. 373–6; and *Chung-kung jen-ming lu*, pp. 591–3. It should be noted also that in official listings of the central administrative organs under the State Council, the OCAC has always been among the last five, and the most recent listings before the Cultural Revolution placed it last.

54 A full account of KMT policies is beyond the scope of the present study. KMT sources are quite fruitful and in most cases fairly open.

55 The KMT's Third Department is responsible for Overseas Chinese affairs, similar in its relation to the government organ to the CCP's United Front Work Department. The difference is that the Third Department also operates overseas.

56 The first was established in the Canton Branch in November 1949. *Jen-min jih-pao*, 6 May 1950. In her New Year Broadcast to Overseas Chinese in January 1950, Ho Hsiang-ning announced that the banks would assume responsibility for the remittance offices and finance institutions which formerly handled Overseas Chinese remittances.

57 *Ta kung pao* (Hong Kong), 10 April 1950.

58 Report on the operation of the service department in the Shanghai branch of the Bank of China in *Ta Kung pao* (Shanghai), 26 October 1950.

59 Ts'ao Chü-ju, President of the People's Bank of China, was a member of the Third Commission. In 1956, the Fukien branch of the Bank of China organised jointly with the Fukien OCAC training classes for Overseas Chinese affairs cadres. *Fu-chien ch'iao-hsiang pao*, 28 July 1956.

60 In June 1951 they existed in Canton, Chiang-men, Foochow, Amoy, Shanghai, Peking, Mei *hsien*, and Swatow.

61 *Jen-min jih-pao*, 3 April 1957. The full title is Overseas Chinese Travel and Service Agency (*Hua-ch'iao lü-hsing fu-wu she*). The head office was in Peking and there were at that time thirty-five main branches.

62 On occasion, the OCTS has had to publicise the fact that it does not have agencies overseas, in connection with swindles committed by people posing as agents for OCTS. See, for example, one such statement in *Ta kung pao* (Hong Kong), 5 May 1960.

63 There was at one time a State Council Staff Office for United Front Work. Barnett, *Cadres, Bureaucracy, and Political Power*, p. 8. Presumably this office shared in the direction of Overseas Chinese work.

64 *Jen-min jih-pao*, 20 October 1949.

65 Of the Director and nine Deputy Directors of the UFWD in 1965, only one was concerned with Overseas Chinese affairs. Other organs of the CCP have been claimed to direct Overseas Chinese work; the Overseas Work Committee (Purcell, *The Chinese in Southeast Asia*, p. 13), and the Social Affairs Department (Lu Yu-sun, *Programs of Communist China*, p. 13). The work of the Overseas Work Committee is unknown, and the Social Affairs Department, believed to have been concerned with discipline and security, is thought to have ceased to exist. Barnett, *Cadres, Bureaucracy, and Political Power*, p. 5.

66 *Enemies and Friends*, p. 241.

67 UFWD cadres were still identified in leading positions in the Overseas Chinese affairs bureaucracy, and in April 1960 Fang Fang was identified as a Deputy Director of the Department.

68 Since the date at which persons cease to be listed in a position or are officially removed is not necessarily the date on which they cease to occupy that position, it is possible that Liao had not been a member of the UFWD for some time.

69 *P'i Liao chan-pao* (*Criticise Liao Combat Bulletin*), 18 June 1967. *Survey of China Mainland Press* (*SCMP*), no. 4013 (1 September 1967), pp. 5–11.

70 The functions of many of the CCP central departments are by no means clear. It is assumed that the International Liaison Department directed foreign affairs. See Barnett, *Cadres, Bureaucracy, and Political Power*, p. 456.

71 See *Jen-min shou-ts'e*, 1957, p. 313, and 1965, p. 127.

72 Propaganda Department cadres have been identified in some of the lower-level branches. In 1956, following Fang Fang's speech at the June conference of the OCAC, the Propaganda Department in Fukien Province issued a directive for cadres to study Overseas Chinese policy, particularly the broad external implications of the domestic policy. *Fu-chien ch'iao-hsiang pao*, 28 July 1956.

73 The UFWD is discussed further in ch. 8.

74 *Jen-min jih-pao*, 15 January 1966.

75 *Ke-ming ch'iao-pao* (*Revolutionary Overseas Chinese Affairs Bulletin*), 9 April 1967. *SCMP*, no. 3939 (16 May 1967), pp. 5–13. For the July instruction see *Ch'iao-wu pao*, nos. 5–6 (July 1966), p. 45. A former member of the Nationalities Research Institute in Peking said in Hong Kong in 1967 that the OCAC had not reported to the UFWD for some years, and reported instead to the Foreign Affairs Office of the State Council. It is possible, since he was not concerned directly with Overseas Chinese affairs, that he may have remembered the State Council's *wai-shih pan-kung-shih*, Staff Office for Foreign Affairs, for the Central Committee's *wai-shih cheng-chih-pu*, or Foreign Affairs Political Department.

76 According to a report on Overseas Chinese affairs work in Kwangtung Province in 1950, the reason for the establishment of the associations was that Overseas Chinese work was becoming too complex for the OCAC branches to handle alone. *Jen-min jih-pao*, 22 August 1950.

77 Chuang Hsi-ch'üan, '*ACROCA tang-ch'ien ti chi-pen jen-wu*'. Chuang was a Vice-Chairman of the ACROCA, and Acting Chairman after the death of Tan Kah-kee in August 1961.

78 *CNS*, 14 October 1963. The branches in Urumchi and some other unlikely centres appear to have been for returned Overseas Chinese and former Overseas Chinese students assigned to work in these areas. In Liaoning Province, for example, there were reported to be 2,933 returned Overseas Chinese in 1956, mostly from Korea and the Soviet Union. *CNS*, 9 June 1956.

79 A report in the *Kuang-tung ch'iao-pao* (*Kwangtung Overseas Chinese News*), on 21 October 1956, mentions two which apparently were still strong enough to warrant continued consideration by the government, the *Chiu-chiang hua-ch'iao ts'u-chin hui*, and the *P'an-yü hsing-fu hui*.

80 Since 1956, all but two of the Vice-Chairmen (of whom there were twelve at the latest count), one director of a department, and ten members of the standing committee (which totals approximately forty-five) of the ACROCA have been members of the Central OCAC.

81 For example, Wang Yü-t'ing was a Deputy Director of the OCAC secretariat and Secretary-General of the ACROCA; Ch'en Man-yün was in the liaison departments of both organisations; Wang Chi-yüan was a Deputy Director of the Education and Cultural Propaganda Department of the OCAC and Director of the Propaganda Department in the Association. The Acting Chairman and three of the Vice-Chairmen of the Association were all Vice-Chairmen of the OCAC.

82 *Kuang-ming jih-pao*, 27 December 1957.

83 '*Chung-hua ch'üan-kuo kuei-kuo hua-ch'iao lien-ho-hui chang-ch'eng*' (Regulations of the ACROCA), adopted 12 October 1956. *Ch'iao-wu pao*, 20 January 1957, p. 32.

84 *Ch'iao-wu pao*, 20 January 1958, p. 1.

85 The Chairman, Ch'en Ch'i-yu, was appointed to the Commission in 1960.

86 *Jen-min shou-ts'e*, 1957, p. 256.

CHAPTER 3: *Communication with the Chinese abroad* (pp. 35–51)

1 For a discussion of the problems of interpreting the Chinese communications media, see, for example, Schurmann, *Ideology and Organization*, pp. 56–68.

2 For a statement on illiteracy, see 'Success of People's Education', report by Ma Hsü-lun, Minister of Education, in 1952. Stewart Fraser, *Chinese Communist Education* (New York: Science Editions, 1966), p. 131. Over 80 per cent of Overseas Chinese dependants lived in rural areas, where educational facilities were even more sparse than in the cities and towns, and 90 per cent of these were described as 'basic masses'. See report by Su Hui, member of the OCAC, to the Third National Congress of the All-China Federation of Women, in *Ch'iao-wu pao*, 20 September 1957, p. 2. The majority of dependants, therefore, were among that section of the Chinese population which had the least opportunity for education.

3 On 1 February 1950 the Finance and Economic Commission of the Government Administration Council issued a registration form for *shui-k'e*. The information which applicants were required to give included the places in China and abroad where remittances were delivered or collected, the number of trips made each year, the amount of remittances collected from each place in 'normal times', an estimate of the amount to be collected in the future, and whether the remittances were made in the form of cash or goods. A sample form is given in *Ch'iao-wu fa-kuei hui-pien*, p. 11.

4 For a report on *shui-k'e* and currency smuggling, see *Kuang-chou jih-pao*, 2 December 1956. It appears that *shui-k'e* have continued to operate, illegally, from Hong Kong and Macao. The government also continued to permit remittances to be taken into China by Overseas Chinese Exchange Dealers (*ch'iao-p'i-yüan*).

5 See, for example, *Ta kung pao* (Shanghai), 9 June 1951.

6 Publications for domestic Overseas Chinese frequently reminded readers that delivery of letters in the countries of residence was hampered by the fact that addresses were written in Chinese. See, for example, *Ch'iao-wu pao*, 20 December 1957, p. 11.

7 One of the aims of the early literacy classes in the home districts was to enable domestic Overseas Chinese to write to their relatives. *Fu-chien jih-pao*, 30 September 1952.

8 Written statement in *Jen-min jih-pao*, 2 June 1957.

9 *Ch'iao-wu pao*, 20 March 1957, p. 13.

10 *Fu-chien ch'iao-hsiang pao*, 2 September 1956.

11 See, for example, report on the Second Kwangtung Conference on Overseas Chinese Dependants Rural Production, *Kuang-tung ch'iao-pao*, 11 January 1957.

12 The question of remittances was not usually put so delicately, but in a speech by a Vice-Chairman of the OCAC to recently arrived students, it was apparently thought necessary to be a little less blunt. See also a special letter by the Editorial Office of the *Ch'iao-wu pao*, instructing cadres and students that contact with relatives abroad and accepting remittances were approved policies of the state. *Ch'iao-wu pao*, 20 July 1958, p. 7.

13 An article in the *Fu-chien ch'iao-hsiang pao* on 12 January 1957, quoted from a letter by an Overseas Chinese dependant describing deplorable conditions and a state of near-starvation in his district. The article stated that, while it was desirable to seek remittances from abroad, such exaggeration and distortion would have a bad political influence on relatives abroad. From such reports domestic Overseas Chinese could assume that their letters were subject to surveillance.

14 In 1957, it was reported that 500,000 letters a month were sent to Overseas Chinese from Kwangtung Province alone. *Ch'iao-wu pao*, 20 February 1957, p. 12.

15 It is impossible to make a statistical evaluation of these letters, but it seems that apart from the question of remittances, recipients in Southeast Asia rarely receive the requests to act on behalf of China which the dependants are supposed to make.

16 Amoy, Ch'ao-chou, Hakka, and Cantonese. *Jen-min jih-pao*, 7 April 1950. This was the first official announcement of the Overseas Chinese broadcasts, although they had in fact begun in 1949, before the establishment in April 1950 of the Central People's Broadcasting Station and its international service, Radio Peking. A *CNS* report of 6 May 1957, announcing the addition of Taishan broadcasts, reported that Overseas Chinese visiting Radio Peking had also requested broadcasts in Foochow dialect.

17 *Jen-min jih-pao*, 4 March 1950. The Commission was assisted in this task by the Service Departments in the Bank of China. Ibid. 21 April 1950. Local authorities in Kwangtung and Fukien also compiled material for distribution to Chinese abroad by relatives and dependants in China. *Hsing-tao jih-pao* (Hong Kong), 29 July 1950.

18 *Jen-min jih-pao*, 30 September 1952.

19 *Ch'iao-wu pao*, no. 2 (April 1962), p. 40, and a report in a Canadian Overseas Chinese newspaper, the *Ta-han kung-pao*, cited in *Tsu-kuo (China Monthly)* (Hong Kong), May 1966, p. 26. A survey of Radio Peking's broadcasts is given in *Current Scene* (Hong Kong: United States Consulate General), March 1960. According to this survey, the total number of broadcast hours per day for Overseas Chinese in 1959 was 33:40. The number of hours cited by the *Ch'iao-wu pao* in April 1962 was only 17:30, a decrease of almost 50 per cent.

20 The number of hours broadcast by *CNS* has not varied significantly since it began its daily service in 1954. In December 1954, it broadcast three times a day, on six frequencies each time, and for two and three-quarters hours each time, making a total of eight and a quarter hours. *CNS*, 27 December 1954. The number of frequencies was subsequently increased to eight, and the total number of hours to nine. From 1961, the total number of hours fell to seven and a half, and has remained at that level until 1970. *CNS*, 9 October 1970.

21 Early in 1970, the Canton office of *CNS* was moved to Peking. No announcement was made; the address on the cover page was simply changed on 1 March 1970. Publication in Canton was presumably to facilitate delivery to Hong Kong and Southeast Asia. The move to Peking may be related to a post-Cultural Revolution tightening of control over Overseas Chinese affairs.

22 *Hsin-wen chan-hsien (News Front)*, 14 April 1967. In *Ming pao* (Hong Kong), 29 July 1967. One of the examples cited to demonstrate that *CNS* ignored politics is that it is alleged to have cut two-thirds of the communique of the Fourth Plenary Session of the Seventh Central Committee concerning Kao Kang and Jao Shu-shih. The chief of the special features section, Fang T'u, is said to have written historical articles satirising contemporary China and indirectly attacking Mao.

23 A report in 1956, for example, stated that art and literture for Overseas Chinese should avoid too many slogans and 'isms'. *Ch'iao-wu pao*, 17 November 1956.

24 There was, of course, no question that *CNS* was anything but a government organ, and if there was, the Cultural Revolution provided an answer. In one unofficial newspaper, it was asserted that some of the content of *CNS* was more like the advertisements in the Hong Kong capitalist press than the 'official

reports of a government newsagency'. *Chan tao ti* (*Fight to the End*), April 1967, in *Hsing-tao jih-pao*, 1 and 4 May 1967.

25 Apart from the *Hsin Yüeh hua-pao* (*New Vietnam Chinese Daily*) in Hanoi, the three Southeast Asian newspapers which regularly used and attributed *CNS*, the Phnom Penh *Mien-hua jih-pao* (*Khmer Chinese Daily*), the Rangoon *Jen-min pao* (*People's Daily*), and the Djakarta *Hsin pao* (*New Daily*), have all now been suppressed. The other regular uses of *CNS* have been the communist newspapers in Hong Kong and Macao, one paper in the United States and one in Canada. Some of the non-communist press in Hong Kong frequently cites *CNS* reports.

26 The *Ch'iao-wu pao* was published monthly from October 1956 to June 1960, and bi-monthly from then until December 1966 when it suspended publication.

27 Although it carried items on the Chinese abroad, it concentrated on policies and problems in domestic affairs. Many issues were devoted almost entirely to directives, criticisms, and experiences on particular questions like education, Overseas Chinese farms, or the work of Returned Overseas Chinese Associations. It also discussed the role of domestic Overseas Chinese work in national movements. The issue for March 1958, for example, announced that by a joint directive by the OCAC and the ACROCA the next five issues of the journal would publish a series of articles on Overseas Chinese affairs in the Great Leap Forward.

28 Notices and advertisements in the *Ch'iao-wu pao* also indicate that it was aimed mainly at domestic readers. It published advertisements for Overseas Chinese newspapers in the provinces of Fukien, Kwangtung, and Kwangsi, which were not for sale outside China. A readership survey in March 1958 was addressed to a variety of people, but not to Chinese abroad. Subscription notices advised how the journal could be ordered in China only. It was still stated to be for Overseas Chinese readers early in 1960, but the Chinese abroad were dropped from the published list of readers at the end of that year. See subscription notices, 20 February 1960, p. 34, and 20 December 1960, p. 44.

29 The Hong Kong *Chou-mo pao* (*Weekend News*) is aimed at Overseas Chinese readers. It is not, however, officially under the auspices of the Chinese government, and it is not known whether it has any substantial readership outside Hong Kong and Macao.

30 An article by Huang Kuang-t'an in the *Ch'iao-wu pao* in 1957, discussing the importance of this work in communicating with the Chinese abroad, stressed that it was necessary in the replies 'to propagate state policies correctly, to explain the situation patiently, and to point out earnestly where their thinking is incorrect'. *Ch'iao-wu pao*, 20 September 1957.

31 Ibid. The letters were also said to reflect 'the ideas and demands of the Chinese masses overseas concerning work in the home districts', and the 'benefit' may have been largely in domestic affairs. It was reported, for example, that Overseas Chinese had written describing 'excesses' in the home districts, and exposing 'bad elements' who had wormed their way into positions of authority.

32 KMT members were told that they would be allowed to leave China as freely as they had come. It is not known how many, if any, were tempted to take up the offer. On one occasion, T'ao Chu was reported to have said that Chiang Kai-shek was welcome to visit China and return afterwards to Taiwan. *Wen hui pao* (Hong Kong), 8 April 1956. T'ao was attacked on this point during the Cultural Revolution.

33 For example, *Jen-min jih-pao*, 27 September 1959. The thirty or forty countries usually included, however, a large percentage of European, Latin American, and African countries, and Asian countries outside the Southeast Asia region.

34 At the Second Plenary Conference of the Second OCAC in 1959, Fang Fang

stated that 5,451 Overseas Chinese had visited China since 1954. *Ch'iao-wu pao*, 20 April 1959, p. 6. No totals were given for the period before 1954, but the annual figure seems to have been rather less than 1,000. According to Liao Ch'eng-chih, the 2,100 Overseas Chinese in Peking for the National Day celebrations in 1964 represented the largest number since 1949. *CNS*, 4 October 1964. The number has fallen since 1964; in 1967 and 1968 Overseas Chinese were not reported at Peking celebrations; and the numbers attending National Day in 1969 and 1970 were not given.

35 Chinese in Southeast Asia who have attended these receptions have confirmed in private conversation that the official reports were an accurate reflection of what was actually said. This does not mean, of course, that the CCP did not hold private discussions with selected individuals.

36 They were met on arrival at the border, accommodated in special guest houses, and provided with guides and interpreters. If they were visiting relatives, they were offered sightseeing tours before proceeding to their destination, and when they arrived in the home districts they were entertained by the local Returned Overseas Chinese Association, and encouraged to visit development projects. Special arrangements were made for families to receive extra rations while they had relatives from abroad staying with them. *Ta kung pao* (Hong Kong), 22 March 1956. Visitors from Hong Kong and Macao were given a similar reception, although their numbers, particularly during traditional Chinese festivals, were too great to enable the kind of individual attention which is given to Overseas Chinese. At Chinese New Year, for example, their numbers were often in excess of 100,000. Prominent Chinese from Hong Kong and Macao were included in the receptions for Overseas Chinese on May Day and National Day.

37 One important consideration in entertaining Overseas Chinese was the prospect of persuading them to invest in China. One of the first groups of Overseas Chinese to visit China after 1949, from Burma and Indonesia, was reported to have agreed to invest in construction enterprises in China. *Ta kung pao* (Hong Kong), 1 January 1952.

38 The Singapore government requires the Bank of China to be locally staffed, although that need not prevent the staff from representing the policies of Peking. In Tokyo the Chinese government has a trade office, which might serve as a useful point of contact for Chinese from other countries, although it would seem more likely that such contact is made through Hong Kong. The NCNA representatives, and latterly the diplomatic mission, in Canada might attempt to do the same for the Chinese in the Americas, although it must be assumed that they are under the closest surveillance, not only by the Canadian government, but also by the United States authorities.

39 Most known cases occurred in the very early years of the CCP rule, consistent with current Chinese policy. The first Chinese ambassador to Indonesia, Wang Jen-shu, certainly had an Indonesian background, with a close involvement in anti-Japanese activities during the occupation. See Herbert Feith, *The Decline of Constitutional Democracy in Indonesia* (Ithaca, N.Y.: Cornell University Press, 1962), p. 193. The first Chinese Ambassador to Rangoon is reported to have had on his staff a Chinese who had been expelled from Burma. Virginia Thompson and Richard Adloff, *Minority Problems in Southeast Asia* (Stanford, Calif.: Stanford University Press, 1955), p. 17. From incomplete listings of senior diplomatic and consular officials I have been able to find, it does not seem that this practice was continued, although it would not be surprising if Overseas Chinese were used in missions abroad as interpreters and translators.

40 If, as seems likely at the time of writing, China is no longer willing to buy Australian wheat, it is not so much a political decision as one based on other economic considerations with an incidental, if gratifying to the CCP, political payoff.

41 Williams (*The Future of the Overseas Chinese in Southeast Asia*, p. 71) asserts that 'the frequency of reports and rumours...points to extensive use of trade as a political tool'. See also Robert Elegant, *The Dragon's Seed. Peking and the Overseas Chinese* (New York: St Martin's Press, 1959), p. 253, for an example of the way in which such reports and rumours can be misinterpreted.

42 The substance of Chou's talks is discussed in later chapters.

43 Few members of the Overseas Chinese Affairs Commission have visited Southeast Asia in any capacity. Liao Ch'eng-chih was a member of the Chinese delegation to the Afro-Asian conference in Bandung, but since he was also one of the top Chinese representatives in the international peace movement and the Afro-Asian solidarity movement he may have been included for these reasons as much as for his connection with Overseas Chinese affairs.

CHAPTER 4: *Domestic Overseas Chinese Policy: 1949–1966* (pp. 52–73)

1 In addition to the national media and *CNS* and the *Ch'iao-wu pao*, a great deal of attention is devoted to Overseas Chinese affairs in the provincial and local media, particularly in the provinces of Kwangtung and Fukien. There were also special newspapers for Overseas Chinese affairs in these two provinces and in Kwangsi province; the *Kuang-tung ch'iao-pao* (*Kwangtung Overseas Chinese News*), formerly *Kuei-ch'iao yü ch'iao-hsiang* (*Returned Overseas Chinese and Home Districts*), the *Fu-chien ch'iao-hsiang pao* (*Fukien Overseas Chinese District News*), and the *Kuang-hsi ch'iao-pao* (*Kwangsi Overseas Chinese News*). Below province level there were special news sheets in the Overseas Chinese home districts.

2 Ho Hsiang-ning, New Year Broadcast message to Overseas Chinese, 1950. Hereafter cited as New Year Broadcast 1950. *Ch'iao-wu fa-kuei hui-pien*, pp. 1–3.

3 Regulations for South China are given in *Hsin Chung-kuo kung-shang-yeh-chia ti tao-lu* (*The Path for Industrialists and Businessmen in New China*) (Hong Kong: Hua-ch'iao ching-chi ch'u-pan she, 1950), p. 260. Regulations for Fukien Province are given in *Ta kung pao* (Hong Kong), 20 March 1950. For texts of other regulations on remittances and foreign exchange, see *Hsin Chung-kuo kung-shang-yeh-chia ti tao-lu*, pp. 206–84, and *Ch'iao-wu fa-kuei kui-pien*.

4 *Jen-min jih-pao*, 6 May 1950.

5 Ibid. 31 May 1950.

6 The basic investigation in areas of domestic Overseas Chinese concentration was completed towards the end of 1950. Report on Overseas Chinese work in Kwangtung Province, ibid. 22 August 1950.

7 Investigation of returned and student Overseas Chinese was unnecessary since they were registered on arrival in China. On 2 August 1951, the Public Security Bureau promulgated 'Temporary Regulations for Exit and Entry of Overseas Chinese', by which returning Overseas Chinese were required to have either a Chinese passport or a 'Returned Overseas Chinese Certificate', 'to prove their Overseas Chinese status and facilitate the People's Government in according them necessary consideration'. For text see *Nan-fang jih-pao*, 3 August 1951.

8 '*T'u-ti kai-ke chung tui hua-ch'iao t'u-ti ts'ai-ch'an ti ch'u-li pan-fa*'. For text see, *Ch'iao-wu fa-kuei hui-pien*, pp. 7–8. Overseas Chinese land and property was defined as that belonging to 'Chinese people who have resided outside China continuously for one year or more', or their immediate successors.

9 Liao Ch'eng-chih, report to First Enlarged Conference of the OCAC. *Jen-min jih-pao*, 12 July 1951.

10 *Fu-chien jih-pao*, 30 September 1952. At the same time, dependant wives enjoyed the new freedom accorded to all Chinese women. Special measures granting them the right to divorce absent husbands were promulgated in ' *Tui hua-ch'iao hun-yin wen-t'i ti chiu-fen ti ch'u-li pan-fa* ' (Regulations for handling disputes related to the question of Overseas Chinese marriages), *Nan-fang jih-pao*, 30 October 1953.

11 Report on the Second Conference of the Amoy Returned Overseas Chinese Friendship Association. *Ta kung pao* (Hong Kong), 22 January 1952.

12 See, for example, Ho Hsiang-ning's report to the First National People's Congress in September 1954. *Jen-min jih-pao*, 27 September 1954. As early as 1950 there were admissions of excesses in the implementation of land reform for domestic Overseas Chinese. According to one report, for example, basic-level cadres were determining class status on the amount of remittances received. Ibid. 22 August 1950. Some accounts of the experiences of domestic Overseas Chinese during land reform are given in Lu, *Programs of Communist China*, ch. 3.

13 For example, see a speech by one of the best-known returned Overseas Chinese, Ssu-t'u Mei-t'ang. ' *Yü kuo-wai hua-ch'iao t'an ai-kuo ta t'uan-chieh* ' (A talk with Overseas Chinese about great patriotic unity). *Ta kung pao* (Shanghai), 1 January 1952.

14 Justifying the changes which occurred after 1953 and the treatment of domestic Overseas Chinese in the first three years, Lo Li-shih, Chairman of the Kwangtung OCAC, said in 1956 that 'it was natural that in the situation of the Korean War and the attacks on the peasants by southern feudal forces, the first task was to mobilise the masses'. *Ch'iao-wu pao*, 17 November 1956, p. 18.

15 For example, *Hsing-tao jih-pao*, 20 June 1953; *Chung-nan jih-pao* (*Central South Daily*), 23 June 1953; *Kung-shang jih-pao* (*Kung Shang Daily*), 1 July 1953.

16 Report by Feng Pai-chü, Vice-Chairman of the Kwangtung People's Government, in *Nan-fang jih-pao*, 30 October 1953.

17 *Ta kung pao* (Hong Kong), 1 January 1954.

18 *Nan-fang jih-pao*, 30 October 1953.

19 Kao Ming-hsüan, Chairman of the Fukien OCAC, address to the first class of the Overseas Chinese Affairs Cadre Training School. *Fu-chien ch'iao-hsiang pao*, 28 July 1956.

20 Two enlarged conferences of the OCAC were held in this period: in November 1953 and June 1954. Published reports on these conferences stated only that they had discussed the question of elections to the NPC. At the Fourth Enlarged Conference in June 1956, however, Chuang Ming-li, a Vice-Chairman of the OCAC, revealed that three important proposals had been made at the 1954 conference (all related to Overseas Chinese foreign exchange), all of which had been accepted and implemented since 1954. They concerned remittances, donations to public works, and the use of state-owned wastelands by Overseas Chinese. *Ta kung pao* (Hong Kong), 14 June 1956.

21 *Jen-min jih-pao*, 27 September 1954.

22 In a speech on 25 September, Huang Ch'ang-shui, a Vice-Chairman of the OCAC, had announced that reform of returned Overseas Chinese businessmen was particularly necessary because of their intimate relationship with Chinese abroad. But Huang also emphasised the need for patience in this work. *Jen-min jih-pao*, 26 September 1954.

23 'Some New Decisions Adopted by the Government Administration Council', in *The Agrarian Reform Law of the People's Republic of China and Other Relevant Documents*, 4th edn (Peking: Foreign Languages Press, 1953), p. 50.

24 The exact date of the decision has not been identified. According to Jao Chang-feng, Chairman of the Kwangtung OCAC (*Ta kung pao* (Hong Kong), 1 January 1955), and Yi Mei-hou, a Vice-Chairman of the Kwangtung OCAC (*Nan-fang jih-pao*, 14 August 1956), the South China Bureau of the CCP made such a decision at the end of 1954. This must have been preceded by a decision at the Party centre. Gordon Bennett has pointed out that the actual experience of Overseas Chinese was that while status might be changed, background did not, leaving the whole question open for reclassification. 'Political Labels and Popular Tension', *Current Scene*, vol. VII, no. 4 (26 February 1969), p. 5.
25 *Ta kung pao* (Hong Kong), 9 February 1955; and *Wen hui pao* (Hong Kong), 11 February 1955.
26 Proclamation by Kwangtung Provincial Government, cited in *Jen-min jih-pao* editorial, 3 March 1955.
27 Fang Fang, Report to the Third Session of the Second National Committee of the CPPCC. *Ta kung pao* (Hong Kong), 17 March 1957.
28 In Fang's report to the CPPCC (ibid.), it was stated that the 95 per cent of reclassified households represented 38,000 households in the two provinces of Kwangtung and Fukien. In March 1956, it had been reported that 30,000 house-holds had changed in Kwangtung. *Wen hui pao* (Hong Kong), 10 March 1956. Whereas, in October 1956, only 4,200 households had changed in Fukien. *Fu-chien ch'iao-hsiang pao*, 7 October 1956.
29 *Jen-min jih-pao*, 21 April 1950.
30 Elegant, *The Dragon's Seed*, p. 27.
31 '*Chung-hua jen-min kung-ho-kuo kuo-wu-yüan kuan-yü kuan-ch'e pao-hu ch'iao-hui cheng-ts'e ti ming-ling*' (State Council of the People's Republic of China order concerning the implementation of the policy for protection of Overseas Chinese remittances), promulgated 23 February 1955, and published in *Jen-min jih-pao*, 3 March 1955.
32 See, for example, Ho Hsiang-ning's written statement on shortcomings and mistakes in Overseas Chinese affairs work published in *Jen-min jih-pao*, 2 June 1967; and Tu P'ei-lin, Director of the Chekiang Overseas Chinese Affairs Office, who spoke of 'forced donations, savings, loans, purchase of bonds, and investment in credit cooperatives, and infringements of the right to use remittances'. *Ch'iao-wu pao*, 20 January 1957, p. 4.
33 *Jen-min jih-pao* editorial, 2 March 1955; and *Nan-fang jih-pao* editorial, 30 March 1955.
34 For example, see a report by Kao Ming-hsüan, a Vice-Chairman of the Fukien OCAC, to the First Fukien Conference of Returned and Dependant Overseas Chinese. *Fu-chien jih-pao*, 16 April 1955.
35 *Wen hui pao* (Hong Kong), 14 April 1955.
36 Report to the Second Session of the First NPC. *Jen-min jih-pao*, 23 July 1955.
37 These conferences were not confined to Fukien and Kwangtung. In Yunnan Province, for example, which had never figured prominently in Overseas Chinese affairs, the Overseas Chinese Affairs Office held its First Enlarged Conference in August. *Yün-nan jih-pao* (*Yunnan Daily*), 17 August 1956.
38 *Ta kung pao* (Hong Kong), 27 March 1956. In June 1955, for example, the ration of rice for domestic Overseas Chinese in Chang-chou municipality averaged ten per cent more than for the ordinary Chinese. Ibid. 16 July 1955.
39 *Fu-chien ch'iao-hsiang pao*, 14 September 1956.
40 The Overseas Chinese store in Taishan *hsien*, for example, offered over forty special items for Overseas Chinese. *Wen hui pao* (Hong Kong), 12 May 1957.

41 For example, see *Wen hui pao* (Hong Kong), 12 May 1957, and *Hsin pao* (Djakarta), 15 June 1957.

42 *Jen-min jih-pao*, 3 March 1955. In September 1955, the Kwangtung People's Government issued a directive on the protection of Overseas Chinese ancestral graves. *Kuang-tung ch'iao-pao*, 21 October 1956. This is interesting also as an example of direct response to external criticisms, since stories about desecration of Overseas Chinese graves had appeared frequently in the Overseas Chinese press since 1949.

43 See, for example, a joint directive on Overseas Chinese work issued by the Party and government committees in Fukien Province. *Fu-chien jih-pao*, 3 August 1956. And a report by Lo Li-shih, Chairman of the Kwangtung OCAC, to the Fourth Session of the First Kwangtung People's Congress. *Nan-fang jih-pao*, 11 August 1956. According to the *Fu-chien ch'iao-hsiang pao* on 21 July 1946, domestic Overseas Chinese who had income from abroad could refuse to take part in labour and still remain members of cooperatives. But there were still reports that they were being forced to participate in labour. See, for example, a report on Mei *hsien* in Kwangtung Province, in *Nan-fang jih-pao*, 8 September 1956.

44 See Ho Hsiang-ning's report to the Second Session of the First NPC. *Jen-min jih-pao*, 23 July 1955.

45 See for example, Fang Fang, report to the Third Session of the CPPCC National Committee. *Kuang-ming jih-pao*, 17 March 1957. The percentage appears to have been lower in Fukien Province, where it was reported that over 60 per cent had joined the cooperatives. *Fu-chien ch'iao-hsiang pao* editorial, 2 January 1957. As pressures on domestic Overseas Chinese to conform began to increase in 1957, 'increasing income' became a euphemism for making them take part in labour. See, for example, two editorials 'On assisting Overseas Chinese dependant cooperative members to increase their income', in *Fu-chien ch'iao-hsiang pao*, 22 January 1957, and 7 February 1957.

46 See report by Huang Chieh to the Fourth Session of the First Kwangtung People's Congress. *Nan-fang jih-pao*, 11 August 1956.

47 *CNS*, 25 June 1956.

48 *Fu-chien ch'iao-hsiang pao* editorial, 2 January 1957. Also *Ch'iao-wu pao*, 20 February 1957, p. 1.

49 See statement by Lo Li-shih in *Nan-fang jih-pao*, 11 May 1957. Resentment against domestic Overseas Chinese was exemplified in the popular reaction to anti-smuggling exhibitions held in Fukien and Kwangtung in 1956 and 1957, when the authorities had to caution that the illegal activities of a few did not mean that all domestic Overseas Chinese were bad, and should not be taken as a pretext for indiscriminate denunciations. See *Shan-t'ou pao*, 22 June 1967.

50 *Ch'iao-wu pao*, 20 May 1957, p. 16.

51 *Ch'iao-wu pao*, 20 October 1957, p. 32. See also Ch'en Pi-sheng: 'Consideration is given in order to reform; it should be integrated with reform.' *Kuang-ming jih-pao*, 17 December 1956.

52 Report by Ho Hsiang-ning, *Ta kung pao* (Hong Kong), 22 November 1957; and *Ch'iao-wu pao*, 20 November 1957, pp. 2–4.

53 *Chung-kuo chin-jung (China's Currency)*, no. 139, 7 July 1957, reported a fall of 9.87 per cent in the first quarter of 1957 in Fukien Province alone. See also ch. 7 and 8.

54 See Report on the Anti-Smuggling Exhibition at Shumchun, on the Hong Kong border. *Kwang-chou jih-pao*, 1 May 1957.

55 At the same time as it began to exert a new pressure on the domestic Overseas Chinese, the government introduced a number of measures designed to attract direct Overseas Chinese investment.

56 *Fu-chien jih-pao*, 26 November 1957; *Ta kung pao* (Hong Kong), 15 December 1957. The period of validity of remittance certificates was extended subsequently to twelve months.

57 In February 1957, it was reported that one-third of dependants relied primarily on remittances for their livelihood, and another third relied partly on remittances. *Ch'iao-wu pao*, 20 February 1957, p. 10.

58 '*Kuei-ch'iao, ch'iao-chüan ju-ho ken ch'üan-kuo jen-min yi-ch'i ku-chi-kan-ching, li-cheng-shang-yu*' ('How should the returned Overseas Chinese and Overseas Chinese dependants go all out and aim high together with the people of the whole country'), *Ch'iao-wu pao*, 20 March 1958, pp. 2–4.

59 '*Teng ch'ing tui ch'iao-wu kung-tso ti yi hsieh hu-t'u ssu-hsiang.*'

60 Report to the First Enlarged Conference of the Second OCAC. *Ch'iao-wu pao*, 20 June 1958, p. 5.

61 In 1956, Overseas Chinese work had been listed as the central task in Kwangtung and Fukien. According to Kao Ming-hsüan, Chairman of the Fukien OCAC, 'where the Overseas Chinese are numerous, Overseas Chinese work should come first; where they are less numerous, it should come second or third'. *Fu-chien ch'iao-hsiang pao*, 28 July 1956. Subsequently, this order of priorities was attributed to a directive by Vice-Chairman Teng Tzu-hui. *Kuang-ming jih-pao*, 17 December 1956. For a discussion of 'central tasks', see James Macdonald, 'The Use of Slogans and "Uninterrupted Revolution" in China in the early part of 1964', Ch'en and Tarling (eds.), *Studies in the Social History of China and South-East Asia* (Cambridge: Cambridge University Press, 1970).

62 Ho Hsiang-ning, National Day broadcast. *Ch'iao-wu pao*, 20 October 1958, p. 4.

63 Conference report, *Ch'iao-wu pao*, 20 December 1958, p. 2.

64 *Ch'iao-wu pao* Editorial Office, 20 January 1959, pp. 7–8.

65 *Ta kung pao* (Hong Kong), 11 August 1959. Wang had recently become Chairman of the Fukien OCAC.

66 *Ch'iao-wu pao*, 20 November 1959, p. 3.

67 *Ch'iao-wu pao*, 20 October 1959, p. 4.

68 Measures for supplying commodities were revised in October 1959, July 1962, and again in September 1962, when supplies became more plentiful. See *Fu-chien ch'iao-hsiang pao*, 30 June 1962, 3 September 1962, and 5 November 1962; and *Ch'iao-wu pao*, no. 6 (December 1962), p. 33. For a summary of these measures, see *Chin-jih ta-lu* (*Mainland Today*), no. 184 (25 May 1963), pp. 3–6.

69 For accounts of the traffic in food parcels from Hong Kong, see *Far Eastern Economic Review*, 14 September 1961, pp. 496–8, and 23 August 1962, p. 334; and *South China Morning Post* (Hong Kong), 13 March 1962. Another scheme introduced in 1961 was the fertiliser bond system, whereby relatives could remit foreign exchange equivalent to the cost of a given amount of fertiliser, and the dependants would receive extra ration coupons or cash. See *Far Eastern Economic Review*, 7 December 1961, p. 446; *Ming pao* (Hong Kong), 17 July 1962; and Wu Chun-hsi, *Dollars, Dependants, and Dogma. Overseas Chinese Remittances to Communist China* (Stanford: The Hoover Institution, 1967), p. 73.

70 The sentiments of Chinese expatriates in Hong Kong and elsewhere who did not enjoy these privileges reflect the bitter animosity towards Overseas Chinese which existed in China. This also surfaces in the Chinese press quite regularly.

71 *Ch'iao-wu pao*, no. 2 (April 1962), pp. 2–3.

72 *Ch'iao-wu pao*, no. 1 (February 1965), pp. 4–6.
73 Chinese sources claimed 300,000 to the end of 1959 (*CNS*, 1 January 1960), 94,000 repatriated from Indonesia in 1960 (*Ta kung pao* (Hong Kong), 8 February 1961), another 10,000 from Indonesia to the end of October 1961 (*CNS*, 10 December 1961), and 2,300 from India in 1963 (*Ch'iao-wu pao*, no. 6 (December 1963), p. 1). On 28 February 1961, the *Jen-min jih-pao* reported that the number of returnees in 1960 equalled the total for the first ten years, i.e. 300,000. This appears to have been an error, since there was no mass exodus of Overseas Chinese from other parts of Asia, and subsequent published totals only give 'over 400,000'. *Ch'iao-wu pao*, no. 5 (October 1963), p. 3.
74 One example of the status and consideration to which returned Overseas Chinese felt they were entitled were complaints, in 1954, that there were no special provisions guaranteeing them a privileged status in the new constitution. See statement by Tan Kah-kee, attacking these complaints, in *Jen-min jih-pao*, 16 June 1954. According to one of the Cultural Revolution attacks the reason why so many returned Overseas Chinese and students wanted to leave China was that they had been misled by reports of a life of luxury and ease in China carried in the despatches of the *China News Service*. *Chan tao ti* (*Fight to the End*).
75 The least enthusiasm for Overseas Chinese to return to China has been shown during and after the Cultural Revolution.
76 Commenting on the repatriation programme for 1960, for example, Foreign Minister Ch'en Yi asserted that 'this could never have been done in old China by the Northern Warlords or the Kuomintang government'. *Ch'iao-wu pao*, no. 1 (February 1962), p. 3. The KMT has made one attempt at large-scale repatriation, following the South Vietnamese government's implementation of a decree forcing local-born Chinese to take Vietnamese citizenship in 1957. For obvious reasons, this was minute by comparison with the CCP's repatriation programme of 1960.
77 See, for example, Lu Hsin-yüan, report to the inaugural session of the ACROCA, in *Ch'iao-wu pao*, 17 November 1956, p. 13. Lu pointed out that appropriate use had not always been made of skilled persons. He cited several examples, including one of a veterinary surgeon who was assigned to work in a contagious diseases hospital.
78 An example of 'representative' Overseas Chinese was the famous Cantonese opera singer, Hung Hsien-nü, who owned a house in the Canton village.
79 In 1962, twenty-four Overseas Chinese villages had been identified, mostly in Kwangtung and Fukien, and between fifteen and twenty apartment buildings, including one in Peking and one in Shanghai.
80 The Canton village, established in 1955, became a showpiece for both Overseas Chinese and foreign visitors.
81 It was not possible to visit the Canton village in February 1968.
82 For example, 60,000 of the 133,000 who returned from 1949 to 1954 required government assistance because they had 'genuine difficulties'. *Jen-min jih-pao*, 6 October 1954.
83 *Jen-min jih-pao*, 3 March 1959; and *Wen hui pao* (Hong Kong), 5 October 1960.
84 *Ch'iao-wu pao*, no. 1 (February 1965), p. 12. The total population of the farms at the end of 1963 was 103,000, of which only 70,000 were returned Overseas Chinese. Most of the farms were in Kwangtung and Fukien. There were six in Kwangsi, seven in Yunnan, one in Kweichow, and one in Dairen. See Appendix D. For a documentary survey of ordinary state farms, see Robert Carin, *State Farms in Communist China* (Hong Hong: The Union Research Institute, 1962).

85 Most returned Overseas Chinese were given at least a month's free accommodation and food, clothing, cigarettes, and spending money if they required it.
86 Of the total of 300,000 who returned in the period from 1949 to 1959, some two-thirds had already returned by 1954. *Jen-min jih-pao*, 6 October 1954; *CNS*, 1 January 1960.
87 *Ch'iao-wu pao*, 20 February 1960, p. 6.
88 *Ch'iao-wu pao*, no. 1 (February 1962), pp. 4–8.
89 Fang Fang, ibid. no. 1 (February 1965), pp. 4–5.
90 Ibid. p. 5.

CHAPTER 5: *The 'colonial' legacy; identification of problems.*
Overseas Chinese policy, 1949–1954 (pp. 74–101)

1 *Ta kung pao* (Hong Kong), 26 July 1950.
2 There are of course many analyses of Overseas Chinese society, from as many points of view, but on the question of identifiable categories of attitudes, particularly as they affect Overseas Chinese views of their position in relation to China and to the countries of residence, the most illuminating analysis in recent writing is that developed in two papers by Wang Gungwu: 'Chinese Politics in Malaya', *China Quarterly* no. 43, July–September 1970; and 'Political Chinese. An aspect of their contribution to modern Southeast Asian history' (Hamburg: Institut für Asienkunde, 1971).
3 The Ch'ing government also had attempted to take a similar position in the last years of its rule. For example, see Tang, 'British Policy Towards the Chinese in the Straits Settlements'.
4 Details of this case may be found in the *Far Eastern Economic Review*, vol. LXIX, no. 29 (16 July 1970), and no. 34 (20 August 1970).
5 Editorial in the inaugural issue of the *Ch'iao-wu pao*, 17 October 1956, p. 2.
6 Other indications that the Party made a conscious effort to present itself to the Overseas Chinese as the legitimate successor to the Kuomintang were the adoption of the KMT title 'Overseas Chinese Affairs Commission', the appointment of Ho Hsiang-ning as Commission Chairman, and the regular use of prominent returned Overseas Chinese and members of the KMT Revolutionary Committee to make public statements to Overseas Chinese.
7 Naosaku Uchida, *The Overseas Chinese: A Bibliographical Essay Based on the Resources of the Hoover Institution* (Stanford: Hoover Institution on War, Revolution, and Peace, 1960), p. 13.
8 '*Kung-t'ung kang-ling*', Article 17.
9 Article (iii). *Ch'iao-wu fa-kuei hui-pien*, p. 7.
10 *Chou-mo pao* (Hong Kong), 10 August 1953.
11 '*K'ung-t'ung kang-ling*', Preamble and Article 13.
12 The exact figure was 11,743,320, but since this included Chinese students abroad, the figure for Overseas Chinese would have been slightly lower.
13 *Jen-min jih-pao*, 11 August 1954. Hu was former Editor in Chief of the Singapore *Nan-ch'iao jih-pao*, and was deported by the British in 1952.
14 A similar ambiguity occurs with the term *ch'iao-min*, used frequently to refer to Overseas Chinese. In a legal sense it is translated as 'national', but it may also mean 'emigrant', or 'compatriot living abroad'.
15 In August 1950, for example, a conference convened by the Kwangtung OCAC called for the speedy appointment of Chinese ambassadors, since there were 'serious problems awaiting solution, such as the problem of Overseas Chinese nationality'. *Nan-fang jih-pao*, 14 August 1950.

16 '*Kung-t'ung kang-ling*', Article 58.
17 *Ch'iao-wu fa-kuei hui-pien*, p. 3.
18 For a good example of this kind of statement as late as 1954, see the following passage which appeared in the Hong Kong *Ta kung pao* on 6 October 1954: 'Our 12 million Overseas Chinese compatriots can now go anywhere in the world without being afraid that they have black hair and yellow skin; they can face any man without having to lower their heads and feel ashamed. Why is this? It is because China is independent, China is strong.'
19 Ssu-t'u Mei-t'ang, '*Yü kuo-wai hua-ch'iao t'an ai-kuo ta t'uan-chieh*'.
20 For example, see Lien Kuan, '*Hsien-fa t'sao-an yü hua-ch'iao*' ('The Overseas Chinese and the Draft Constitution'). *Jen-min jih-pao*, 3 August 1954.
21 *Ch'iao-wu fa-kuei hui-pien*, p. 6. The situation was still 'daily worsening' at the end of 1953. See Ho Hsiang-ning's 1953 National Day broadcast. *Ta kung pao* (Hong Kong), 1 October 1953.
22 Ho Hsiang-ning, National Day broadcast, October 1951. *Jen-min jih-pao*, 5 October 1951.
23 Chou En-lai, for example, in his political report to the National Committee of the CPPCC in October 1951, referred to the 'predicament' of the Chinese abroad, but said nothing at all about alleviating their plight. *Hsüeh-hsi* (*Study*), vol. 5, no. 2 (16 November 1951), p. 7. This statement, which promised only the 'attention' and 'concern' of the Chinese people, remained the authoritative pronouncement on Overseas Chinese policy until September 1954. It was still quoted, for example, by Lien Kuan in '*Hsien-fa ts'ao-an yü hua-ch'iao*'.
24 See, for example, a telegram sent by the First Enlarged Conference of the OCAC to all Overseas Chinese, supporting their 'protection of their own proper rights and interests', in *Jen-min jih-pao*, 12 July 1951.
25 The CCP's attitude to the Malayan emergency is discussed more fully below.
26 *Ta kung pao* (Hong Kong), 26 July 1950.
27 One example which the KMT has carefully documented, was the response to President Diem's decree forcing the Chinese in South Vietnam to take Vietnamese citizenship in 1956. See *Yüeh-nan hua-ch'iao kuo-chi wen-t'i yen-chiu* (*A Study of the Overseas Chinese Nationality Question in Vietnam*) (Taipei: Hai-wai ch'u-pan she, 1957).
28 See, for example, an editorial in *Ta kung pao* (Hong Kong), 28 October 1952.
29 See, for example, Fang Fang's report to the Second Plenary Conference of the Second OCAC. *Ch'iao-wu pao*, 20 April 1959, p. 7.
30 *Jen-min jih-pao* short commentary, 18 November 1949.
31 *Constitution of the People's Republic of China*, Article 58 (Peking: Foreign Languages Press, 1954), p. 53.
32 See, for example, Ho Hsiang-ning's New Year broadcast in January 1950: 'This broad democratic united front should include all classes, societies and people from all walks of life. Any patriotic elements may participate so long as they love peace and democracy. Even those compatriots who in the past blindly followed the KMT reactionaries to a greater or lesser extent...should be welcomed equally.'
33 Li Wei-han, Director of the United Front Work Department, spoke of the Overseas Chinese 'patriotic united front' in this sense at the Eighth Party Congress in 1956. *Ch'iao-wu pao*, 17 October 1954, p. 1. The qualifications appended to his remark together with similar statements by other Chinese leaders at this time indicate clearly that the term was little more than a slogan or posture statement.

34 A similar phenomenon occurred for a short time during the Cultural Revolution, when the Party was again isolated and withdrawn from the world.
35 Report to the First Enlarged Conference of the OCAC. *Jen-min jih-pao*, 12 July 1951.
36 Ho Hsiang-ning, New Year broadcast January 1951.
37 National Day broadcast. *Jen-min jih-pao*, 5 October 1951.
38 National Day broadcast. *Ta kung pao* (Hong Kong), 1 October 1953.
39 *Jen-min jih-pao*, 24 November 1953.
40 Ibid. 24 April 1954.
41 Ibid. 3 August 1954.
42 A. Doak Barnett, *Communist China and Asia, Challenge to American Policy* (New York: Harper, 1960), p. 186. Barnett's argument is used also by Alain-Gérard Marsot in 'La Chine Populaire et les Communautés Chinoises du Sud-est Asiatique', *Revue Juridique et Politique*, no. 2 (April–June 1965), p. 187.
43 The 'patriotic Overseas Chinese' (*ai-kuo hua-ch'iao*, or *ai-kuo ch'iao-pao*) have been a distinct category in the CCP's Overseas Chinese terminology. They are not necessarily communist, but may be pro-China. At times, the Party has claimed that the majority of Overseas Chinese is 'patriotic', but such statements appear to be no more significant than the term patriotic unity itself, since they have been clearly contradicted by the CCP's own actions.
44 *Ch'iao-wu fa-kuei hui-pien*, p. 1.
45 *Jen-min jih-pao*, 12 July 1951.
46 According to Mary F. Somers, in 1951 there was open fighting between pro-KMT and pro-CCP Chinese in Palembang. *Peranakan Chinese Politics in Indonesia* (New York: Cornell University Modern Indonesia Project, 1964), p. 20. This was not, however, a common phenomenon.
47 *Nan-fang jih-pao*, 14 August 1950; *Jen-min jih-pao*, 12 July 1951, and 3 October 1951.
48 See Ho Hsiang-ning's protest in October 1950 at the closure of two minor pro-Peking Chinese newspapers in Singapore and the fact that a KMT paper the *Chung Hsing Daily* continued to operate, allegedly with British encouragement. *Nan-fang jih-pao*, 5 October 1960.
49 For example, see Lien Kuan, '*Hsien-fa ts'ao-an yü hua-ch'iao*'.
50 For a long exposition of the CCP's arguments on patriotism and the Kuomintang, see Ssu-t'u Mei-t'ang, ' *Yü kuo-wai hua-ch'iao t'an ai-kuo ta t'uan-chieh*'.
51 Ho Hsiang-ning, Spring Festival broadcast, *Ta kung pao* (Hong Kong), 7 February 1954.
52 The Party introduced one scheme, for example, whereby Overseas Chinese could provide the cash for purchase of aircraft which would be known as 'Overseas Chinese' (*hua-ch'iao hao*) aircraft. *Jen-min jih-pao*, 6 June 1951, 12 June 1951, and 21 June 1951. In the late 1930s Chinese in the Philippines had considerable success in raising money through a China Association for the Construction of Airplanes. Akashi, *The Nanyang Chinese National Salvation Movement*, p. 50.
53 *Jen-min jih-pao*, 12, 19, 22, 23, 25 February 1951.
54 Lu Yu-sun, for example, asserts that Ho Hsiang-ning in her first New Year broadcast called on Overseas Chinese 'to create friction and opposition between races, and to act as the vanguard of international communism'. *Programs of Communist China*, p. 15. In fact, there is nothing in this speech either stated or implied, to justify any such assertion.
55 See, for example, Ssu-t'u Mei-t'ang, ' *Yü kuo-wai hua-ch'iao t'an ai-kuo ta t'uan-chieh*'. The Party claimed that only five per cent of the Overseas Chinese

were petty bourgeois, industrialists, and commercialists. For a discussion of the background and class composition of Overseas Chinese, see *Chung-kuo ch'ing-nien pao* (*China Youth Daily*), 14 September 1956.

56 *Jen-min jih-pao*, 9 October 1949, and Ho Hsiang-ning's 1951 National Day broadcast in ibid. 5 October 1951.

57 See Tan Kah-kee, statement on the eve of Anti-Colonialism Day, in *Fu-chien jih-pao*, 28 February 1952.

58 Ho Hsiang-ning in *Nan-fang jih-pao*, 5 October 1950.

59 Ibid.

60 This practice has not been confined to Malaya or the period of the emergency. It has been widely used in writings about the Overseas Chinese, in some cases carelessly, and in others deliberately, where to distinguish would be to undermine an argument that the CCP controls an Overseas Chinese fifth column. For an example of the blurring of this distinction, see Justus M. van der Kroef, 'Peking and South-East Asia's Dominoes', *Quadrant*, September–October 1968, pp. 33–42. A related problem, which also is sometimes attributable to careless writing, is the argument that the CCP maintains branches of its own among the Chinese in Southeast Asia. Coughlin, for example, says without supporting evidence that 'branches of both the Kuomintang Party and the Chinese Communist Party have been formed in Thailand'. *Double Identity*, p. 182. Evidence that the CCP has formed branches of its own in Southeast Asia is extremely difficult to come by. There are Overseas Chinese communist parties and cells, which may or may not be controlled from Peking. There are possibly CCP couriers and 'contact men' who could be said to form a kind of underground network. There may conceivably be CCP cadres whose purpose is to direct the activities of communist parties among Overseas Chinese. But there is good reason to doubt, since it would be contrary to the CCP's theory, its dogma, and its experience with Moscow, that the CCP actually maintains branches of its own party outside China to direct local revolutions.

61 For a description of the early history of the communist movement in Malaya, see J. H. Brimmell, *Communism in South East Asia* (London: Oxford University Press, 1959); and Gene Z. Hanrahan, *The Communist Struggle in Malaya* (New York: Institute of Pacific Relations, 1954).

62 The closest the CCP has come to its own International has been since the rupture with the Soviet Union. The nature of the splits in communist parties around the world, however, suggests that most pro-Peking splinters chose to follow the Peking line of their own volition (E. F. Hill's pro-Peking, or 'Marxist-Leninist' party in Australia is one good example), and that the alliance is more ideological than organisational. There are, of course, some self-styled Maoist groups which have no connection whatever with the Chinese Communist Party.

63 See Ruth T. McVey, *The Calcutta Conference and the Southeast Asian Uprisings* (New York: Cornell University Modern Indonesia Project, 1958).

64 According to Brimmell (*Communism in South East Asia*, p. 210), at the end of 1947 the Secretary-General of the MCP and some of the Central Committee paid a visit to China, but they apparently obtained no help from the Chinese Party.

65 Ibid. p. 313.

66 Despite many claims that the MCP was the creature of Peking, an examination of these claims fails to reveal any substantiating evidence. Gene Hanrahan, for example, who is quoted by a number of other writers on this particular point, cites as evidence of the CCP's 'hegemony' over the MCP an unidentified but 'usually reliable source' to the effect that 'the real command of the Malayan

struggle is now (1954) based in Nanning, South China, functioning under a so-called "United Operations Department" of the Chinese Communist Party'. *The Communist Struggle in Malaya*, p. 80. In Hinton (*Communist China and World Politics*, p. 403), this becomes: 'There can be no serious doubt that the MCP has always been and is still under Communist Chinese (not Soviet) influence, if not outright control.' Victor Purcell, on the other hand, pointed out in his revision of *The Chinese in Southeast Asia* (p. 329) that even in 1963 the question of external direction and control had still not been established. Richard Harris asserts that the British government does not regard Overseas Chinese communists in Malaya and Singapore as 'potential arms of Peking'; 'they are not directly related to China, and they are not viewed as part of a generalised Chinese threat in the area'. 'Britain and China', A. M. Halpern (ed.), *Policies Towards China: Views from Six Continents* (New York: McGraw Hill, 1965), p. 39.

67 *The Chinese in Southeast Asia*, p. 344.
68 In 1950, some sources in Hong Kong reported that the CCP prepared printed matter for domestic Overseas Chinese to send to relatives in Malaya urging them to join the Malayan communists. For example, *Hsing-tao jih-pao*, 29 July 1950.
69 *Nan-fang jih-pao*, 5 October 1950.
70 Some observers believe that this was partly the cause of Overseas Chinese failure to support the MCP, that they were waiting to see which way the Chinese government would go.
71 *Hsin-hua yüeh-pao* (*New China Monthly*), vol. 3, no. 2 (December 1950), p. 311.
72 Statement by Foreign Ministry spokesman. *Jen-min jih-pao*, 30 December 1950.
73 Ibid. 18 November 1949.
74 Ibid. 7 December 1950.
75 Ibid.
76 Ibid. 9 March 1951.
77 Ibid. 25 April 1951.
78 Ibid. 4 December 1951.
79 Chou En-lai's Political Report to the National Committee of the CPPCC in October 1951, for example, pointedly avoided all mention of the Malayan question or support for Overseas struggle against imperialist oppression and persecution.
80 For details of the MCP directive, see Brimmell, *Communism in South East Asia*, p. 327.
81 According to Victor Purcell, it was argued in 'higher political circles in Malaya' that the reason why the CCP did not support the Malayan communists was that it would be 'embarrassing to many thousands of influential Chinese in Southeast Asia who were called upon by the new regime to build up trade and provide foreign exchange'. *The Position of the Overseas Chinese in Southeast Asia* (New York: Institute of Pacific Relations, 1950), p. 61.
82 Hinton, *Communist China in World Politics*, p. 404.
83 For example: 'expression of concern for the affairs of Chinese residing abroad still takes second place to the maintenance of good relations with the host nations concerned. Where relations are not particularly good, Overseas Chinese problems receive more attention, and actions against their interests may attract more vehement protests.' Mary F. Somers Heidhues, 'Peking and the Overseas Chinese; the Malaysian Dispute', *Asian Survey*, vol. VI, no. 5 (May 1966), pp. 285–6. 'Only the Chinese in countries hostile to the People's Republic, however, are called upon to be disobedient to their governments. Elsewhere, Chinese are encouraged to be inconspicuous, decent settlers.' Lea E. Williams, *The Future of the Overseas Chinese*, p. 69. 'Peking's protests over anti-Chinese measures are

made with great vehemence against governments aligned with the West...they are non-existent or *sotto voce* against neutral regimes.' W. E. Willmott, 'The Chinese in Southeast Asia', *Australian Outlook*, vol. 20, no. 3 (December 1966), pp. 260–1.

84 The Chinese government recognised, for example, that there were special problems for United States Chinese in remitting money, or for Philippines Chinese in visiting China, or that the position of Chinese in Japan was quite different from that of the Chinese in Indonesia. But nowhere is there evidence of a separate policy for the Chinese in separate countries. Even in the case of Malaya, the Chinese government had not gone any further in its public statements than it had for the Chinese in other parts of Southeast Asia. In Burma and Indonesia, the approach to the governments may have been different, but the policy towards the Chinese was the same.

85 Where the CCP did make distinctions, these were usually between the Chinese in Southeast Asia and those in all other parts of the world. For example, on the question of investment, in 1958 the Party stated that its policy of encouraging Overseas Chinese to invest locally was intended for the Chinese in Southeast Asia, out of consideration for their long-term interests in the region; while its appeals for Overseas Chinese to invest in China were intended mainly for those in Europe and the Americas. *Ch'iao-wu pao*, 20 October 1958, p. 38.

CHAPTER 6: *Self-determination, nationality, and peaceful coexistence: 1954–1956* (pp. 102–15)

1 *Cheng-fu kung-tso pao-kao* (*Government Work Report*) (Peking: Jen-min ch'u-pan she, 1954), pp. 30–1.

2 '*ACROCA tang-ch'ien ti chi-pen jen-wu.*'

3 Chou's announcement appears to have been preceded by a review of Overseas Chinese policy, between September 1953 and September 1954. In November 1953, the OCAC convened its Second Enlarged Conference, and although the official reports mentioned only that the conference had discussed the problem of selecting nominees for election to the NPC, it was probably at this conference that discussions on the future of Overseas Chinese policy were initiated. *Jen-min jih-pao*, 24 November 1953. The Third Enlarged Conference followed only eight months after the second, in July 1954. This conference also was concerned with the NPC elections, but it was not mentioned in the Chinese press until September, and although it had approved reports by Ho Hsiang-ning and at least three of the Commission Vice-Chairmen, neither texts nor summaries of these reports were released. *Ta kung pao* (Hong Kong), 2 September 1954. In the whole period from October 1953 to September 1954 there was no detailed public statement on external Overseas Chinese policy. Ho Hsiang-ning's broadcasts, for example, were devoted to the state of the Chinese economy and to the potential of the Overseas Chinese for assisting China's economic development. *Ta kung pao* (Hong Kong), 1 January 1954, 7 February 1954. The *Jen-min jih-pao* carried a series of articles by returned Overseas Chinese on the subject of the draft constitution, but these gave no indication of current thinking on external policy. It was only after Chou's announcement at the NPC that Overseas Chinese affairs officials broke their silence on the future of China's relations with the Chinese abroad.

4 For a discussion of Overseas Chinese and Asian nationalism, see Skinner, 'Overseas Chinese in Southeast Asia', pp. 136–47.

5 The meeting was reported in *Jen-min jih-pao* on 27 June 1954, but details of discussions were not given.

6 *Jawaharlal Nehru's Speeches*, vol. 3, March 1953–August 1957 (New Delhi: Government of India Ministry of Information and Broadcasting, 1958), pp. 271–2.

7 The question of Overseas Chinese nationality had been discussed when the Indonesian Prime Minister, Ali Sastroamidjojo, visited New Delhi in September 1954. Donald E. Willmott, *The National Status of the Chinese in Indonesia 1900–1958* (New York: Cornell University Modern Indonesia Project, 1961), p. 45. According to Krishna Menon, the Indians 'were the conciliators' between China and Indonesia. Michael Brecher, *India and World Politics. Krishna Menon's View of the World* (London: Oxford University Press, 1968), p. 55.

8 Purcell, *The Chinese in Southeast Asia*, p. 482.

9 The details did not emerge until the treaty with Indonesia 1955. In 1954 it was only known that the Party considered dual nationality as the first and most important problem in Overseas Chinese affairs, but not what solutions it had in mind. See Ho Hsiang-ning's report to the NPC, *Jen-min jih-pao*, 27 September 1954.

10 Barnett, *Communist China and Asia*, p. 187. This point has been made also in a recent Soviet attack on past and present Overseas Chinese policies of the CCP. See N. Simonia 'Maoists use Blackmail', *Izvestia*, 7 September 1967, in *The Current Digest of the Soviet Press*, 27 September 1967, pp. 15–17.

11 See reports to the NPC by Ho Hsiang-ning and Yeh Yi-tung in *Jen-min jih-pao*, 27 September 1954. Yeh was an Overseas Chinese deputy representing Indonesia. At the end of the decade, it was sometimes claimed that it had been the consistent policy of the Chinese government since 1949 to instruct Overseas Chinese to respect local laws and customs. For example, Liao Ch'eng-chih in *CNS*, 1 January 1960. On the basis of public statements there is no evidence to support this claim for the period before 1954.

12 '*Chung-hua jen-min kung-ho-kuo pao-hu kuo-wai hua-ch'iao ti cheng-tang ch'üan-li ho li-yi. Ch'iao-wu kung-tso ti hui-ku*' ('The People's Republic of China protects the rights and interests of the Chinese resident abroad. A review of Overseas Chinese work'), by the Propaganda Team of the OCAC. *Jen-min jih-pao*, 6 October 1954.

13 The Chinese government itself did not use the term 'instrument' about the Overseas Chinese.

14 In her first New Year broadcast, Ho had pointed out that many Overseas Chinese had already come to regard the countries of residence as a 'second home'. See also William Skinner's observation on this point: 'The very definition of a Chinese becomes intricate in the overseas context, for neither ancestry nor legal citizenship is a realistic criterion of Chineseness in Southeast Asia. Millions of Chinese in this region neither claim nor exercise any prerogative of Chinese citizenship and, because of widespread miscegenation and assimilation, untold thousands of persons descended from Chinese immigrants are identified completely as Southeast Asians.' 'Overseas Chinese in Southeast Asia', p. 137. See also Maurice Freedman, *The Chinese in South-East Asia: A Longer View* (London: The China Society, 1965), for a discussion of these trends in Malaysia/Singapore, Indonesia and Thailand.

15 Fang Fang, in a speech to domestic Overseas Chinese. *Ta kung pao* (Hong Kong), 23 December 1960.

16 In South Vietnam, for example, all locally born Chinese had been required to

take Vietnamese citizenship by a decree of August 1956. According to one report there were only 2,000 Chinese nationals (of the Republic of China) in South Vietnam by 1961. *Far Eastern Economic Review*, 20 July 1961, p. 147. In Thailand, the nationality law had been amended three times between 1952 and 1956, ending up with a law based on the principle of the *jus soli*. Coughlin, *Double Identity*, pp. 170–3. Malaya had become independent, and if the Chinese government had counted Chinese residents in Malaya as Chinese nationals before independence, which is by no means certain, then following independence there would have been a very large increase in the total number of dual nationals in the CCP's assessment.

17 The Indonesian Ambassador in Peking had attempted to open negotiations on the nationality question in late 1953. Harold C. Hinton, 'The Overseas Chinese and Peking', *Far Eastern Economic Review*, vol. XIX, no. 14 (6 October 1955), p. 422. Peking's refusal to begin negotiations until the end of 1954, may have been due to the fact that all aspects of Overseas Chinese policy were at that time being subjected to reexamination.

18 Joint Communique, *Jen-min jih-pao*, 13 December 1954.

19 William C. Johnstone, *Burma's Foreign Policy* (Cambridge, Mass.: Harvard University Press, 1963), p. 171.

20 For a detailed examination of the Sino-Indonesian Treaty and the extraordinary complications involved in the nationality of Chinese in Indonesia, see Willmott, *The National Status of the Chinese in Indonesia*.

21 Briefly, the treaty provided for a two-year period in which adult dual nationals would opt for either nationality; those who failed to opt at the end of two years would retain the nationality of their parents. Dual nationals under eighteen would opt when they turned eighteen, and children born of Chinese nationals were themselves to remain Chinese. For text of the treaty and related documents, see *Ch'iao-wu cheng-ts'e wen-chi* (*Collected Documents on Overseas Chinese Policy*) (Peking: Jen-min ch'u-pan she, 1957), pp. 220–38. The supplementary agreement is given in *Jen-min jih-pao*, 24 December 1960.

22 *The National Status of the Chinese in Indonesia*, p. 44.

23 Ibid. In the negotiations for the supplementary agreement in 1960, the Chinese again pressed for the widest possible interpretation of who should be regarded as Indonesian nationals. Somers, *Peranakan Chinese Politics in Indonesia*, p. 30.

24 Barnett, *Communist China and Asia*, p. 195. The provision is contained in Article 7.

25 Early in 1958, two years before the problem arose in Indonesia, it was stated publicly that China might have to anticipate large-scale resettlement of Overseas Chinese. See the discussion of resettlement below.

26 '*Ho-p'ing hsieh-shang kuo-chi wen-t'i ti yu yi fan-li*' ('Another example of solving international problems through peaceful consultation'), *Jen-min jih-pao* editorial, 23 April 1955.

27 The Chinese government hailed the treaty as a victory for its policy of peace and friendship, and an important contribution to the promotion of Afro-Asian and world peace. It demonstrated that independent Asian countries could solve even the most difficult problems inherited from former colonial or feudal rulers. *Jen-min jih-pao* editorial, 23 April 1955: and statement by Ho Hsiang-ning, '*Kuan-yü shuang-ch'ung kuo-chi wen-t'i ti t'iao-yüeh ti t'an-hua*' ('A talk on the dual Nationality Treaty'), in ibid. 28 April 1955.

28 Ho Hsiang-ning, '*Kuan-yü shuang-ch'ung kuo-chi wen-t'i ti tiao-yüeh ti t'an-hua*'.

29 Ibid. Chou also directed his offer at specific countries. For example, he answered

a query by the Thai Foreign Minister with the response that China was willing to conclude such a treaty with Thailand. See David Wilson, 'China, Thailand, and the Spirit of Bandung', Part II, *China Quarterly*, no. 31 (July–September 1967), p. 98.

30 At the Sino-US ambassadorial talks which began in August 1955, the Chinese appear to have hoped to use the question of Chinese nationals in the United States both as a starting point for more substantive proposals and as a means of manoeuvring the US into recognition. The US government, however, was not interested in Chinese nationals, but in US nationals in China, which deprived the Chinese of their bargaining position. See Kenneth T. Young, *Negotiating with the Chinese Communists: the United States Experience, 1953–1967* (New York: McGraw-Hill, 1968), ch. 3.

31 Ho Hsiang-ning, '*Kuan-yü shuang-ch'ung kuo-chi wen-t'i ti t'iao-yüeh ti t'an-hua*'.

32 '*Ho-p'ing hsieh-shang kuo-chi wen-t'i ti yu yi fan-li.*'

33 In the Sino-Indonesian Treaty, the Chinese side had inserted a clause in which the two sides agreed to urge their nationals to respect local laws and social customs. The wording of the relevant phrase was identical with the one Chou En-lai had used in his NPC announcement, and Chinese statements drew attention to the fact that this represented the practical implementation of Chinese policy. See Ho Hsiang-ning's '*Kuan-yü shuang-ch'ung kuo-chi wen-t'i ti t'iao-yüeh ti t'an-hua*'. The clause was contained in Article 11.

34 '*Hsin Chung-kuo ti ho-p'ing wai-chiao cheng-ts'e hohua-ch'iao shuang-ch'ung kuo-chi wen-t'i*' ('New China's peaceful foreign policy and the question of Overseas Chinese dual nationality'), *Jen-min jih-pao*, 10 May 1955.

35 Ibid. 4 June 1955. It would appear to be this appeal which Robert Elegant refers to as an example of 'Communist pressure (which) daily becomes more intense, regardless of its effect on the lives of the *hua-ch'iao* themselves'. *The Dragon's Seed*, p. 19.

36 Cheng Yen-fen, Chairman of the Nationalists' Overseas Chinese Affairs Commission, in *Hsing-tao jih-pao*, 27 June 1955.

37 Ibid.

38 '*Kuan-yü shuang-ch'ung kuo-chi wen-t'i ti t'iao-yüeh ti t'an-hua.*'

39 New Year speech for Overseas Chinese, *Ta kung pao* (Hong Kong), 4 January 1955.

40 Willmott, *The National Status of the Chinese in Indonesia*, p. 46; Skinner, 'Overseas Chinese in Southeast Asia', p. 146. According to Williams (*The Future of the Overseas Chinese*, p. 52), 'it is reported that policy towards the Chinese abroad has figured in factional differences within the political hierarchy in Taipei'.

41 In October 1955, for example, Chou En-lai repeated this formula in response to questions put by two Filipino correspondents about China's attitude to Chinese nationals in the Philippines. *Jen-min jih-pao*, 30 October 1955.

42 '*Hsin Chung-kuo ti ho-p'ing wai-chiao cheng-ts'e ho hua-ch'iao shuang-ch'ung kuo-chi wen-t'i.*'

43 *Jen-min jih-pao*, 26 September 1956.

44 *Ch'iao-wu cheng-ts'e wen-chi*, pp. 45–6.

45 Ibid. p. 44. Earlier in the week, Chou had made a public statement on similar lines about nationality in both Singapore and Malaya. See *Nan-yang shang-pao* (Singapore), 5 October 1956.

46 *Ch'iao-wu cheng-ts'e wen-chi*, pp. 1–10.

47 Fang Fang, report to the National Committee of the CPPCC in March 1957. *Ch'iao-wu pao*, 20 March 1957, p. 2.

48 Ibid. 20 February 1957, p. 8.

49 See also, report on Chou's visit to Hanoi in ibid. 20 January 1957, p. 23.

50 See, for example, Chou's report to the CPPCC in March 1957. *Jen-min jih-pao*, 6 March 1957. And his report to the same body in April 1959. Ibid. 19 April 1959.

51 In his Rangoon speech, for example, Chou referred to the fact that some Chinese in Burma had displayed pictures of Chiang Kai-shek during celebrations of the anniversary of the 1911 Revolution, and that many members of the Overseas Chinese community had disapproved; 'but displaying a picture of Chiang Kai-shek won't make him live for another hundred years or return to the mainland. That is impossible. (Enthusiastic applause.) This does not depend on a photograph. So there is no need to regard this affair as anything of importance.' *Ch'iao-wu cheng-ts'e wen-chi*, p. 8. This attitude possibly stemmed from a general devaluation of the importance of the KMT. The former Hungarian diplomat János Rádvanyi, for example, reported that in 1959 Mao told the Hungarian Prime Minister that 'in his opinion, Chiang Kai-shek was not powerful enough to influence any mass movement in China'. 'The Hungarian Revolution and the Hundred Flowers Campaign', *China Quarterly*, no. 43 (July–September 1970), p. 128.

52 A comprehensive account of this affair is given in *Yüeh-nan hua-ch'iao kuo-chi wen-t'i yen-chiu*. See also Bernard Fall, 'Viet-Nam's Chinese Problem', *Far Eastern Survey*, vol. XXVII, no. 6 (May 1958), pp. 65–72.

53 *Jen-min jih-pao*, 7 September 1956.

54 Ibid. 21 May 1957.

55 Ibid.

56 Ibid. 28 May 1957.

57 Ibid. 5 June 1957. In June 1957, the *Ch'iao-wu pao* (pp. 31–2) carried an account of the affair, together with a short statement by Overseas Chinese students at the Tientsin Teachers' College.

58 This position may be compared with the CCP's position on territorial questions. In seeking to negotiate border agreements, the Party has not necessarily sought to lay claim to disputed territories, but to solve existing problems on the basis of recognition of the CCP's right to claim or dispose of territories formerly claimed as Chinese.

CHAPTER 7: *Policy reassessment, 1956. Foreign exchange and education* (pp. 116–34)

1 '*Kuan-yü kuo-nei ch'iao-wu kung-tso ti jo-kan cheng-ts'e.*'

2 *Jen-min jih-pao*, 19 June 1956.

3 See, for example, Chou En-lai's speech in Rangoon in December 1956. *Ch'iao-wu cheng-ts'e wen-chi*, pp. 4–5. It has been pointed out by some writers that Overseas Chinese businessmen, while responsive, perhaps, to the call of patriotism, have tended to be the least responsive to the appeals of communism. See, for example, C. P. FitzGerald, *The Third China* (Melbourne: F. W. Cheshire, 1965), p. 60, and Willmott, 'The Chinese in Southeast Asia', p. 261.

4 Wang Gungwu, for example, has pointed out that there is an almost total response from Overseas Chinese businessmen to opportunities for trade with China, irrespective of the degree to which they might identify with China or the countries in which they live. 'The Overseas Chinese Response to Peking's Overseas Chinese Policy', Unpublished seminar paper, Australian National University, 14 November 1968. See also Sheldon Appleton (op. cit. p. 383), who quotes the editor of

a Chinese newspaper in the Philippines to the effect that 'at least half of the Chinese businessmen in the Philippines would be willing to do business with Peking, if the opportunity arose'.

5 The clearest illustration of this argument is China's trade with Hong Kong and, in recent years, Singapore. To have disregarded the advantages of Hong Kong, Chinese territory 'stolen' by the British, would have been severely damaging to China's international balance of payments. Even at the height of the Cultural Revolution frenzy the people in control in Peking seemed reluctant to support the activities of the Maoists in Hong Kong, and from the end of 1967 the Hong Kong communists abandoned their terrorist campaign, and the communist stores mounted an operation to lure customers back to their counters with bargains, discounts, and free gifts. In Singapore, China has accepted the conditions that the Bank of China should be locally staffed and that the department stores should not sell or display communist propaganda; and Singapore officials have stated privately that there has been no apparent attempt to use this trade as a 'political weapon'. The result has been a massive increase in China's trade with Singapore.

6 *CNS*, 6 November 1958. Dulles' statement is given in Department of State *Bulletin*, vol. XXXIX, no. 1017 (22 December 1958), p. 991.

7 *Jen-min jih-pao*, 21 April 1950.

8 *Hsin Chung-kuo kung-shang-yeh-chia ti tao-lu*, p. 89.

9 There is some question about the exact amount of Soviet aid to China. For a discussion, see Alexander Eckstein, *Communist China's Economic Growth and Foreign Trade* (New York: McGraw Hill, 1966), pp. 154–9.

10 *Jen-min jih-pao*, 27 October 1949.

11 For a survey of the CCP's policies for remittances and investment, see Chun-hsi Wu, op. cit., ch. 3. Wu's study is also one of the only detailed examinations to have been published on any aspect of Overseas Chinese policy. See also *Tsu-kuo*, no. 3, no. 14 and no. 38, and *Hua-ch'iao t'ou-tzu shou-ts'e* (*Overseas Chinese Investment Handbook*) (Canton: Kwangtung Overseas Chinese Investment Corporation, 1959).

12 For example, *Kuang-chou jih-pao*, 6 May 1957; *Ch'iao-wu pao*, 20 November 1957, pp. 13–14; and *Chou-mo pao*, 15 February 1958. In 1957 and 1958, anti-smuggling exhibitions were held in Fukien and Kwangtung.

13 In 1957 it was reported that 2 per cent of family remittances was invested, 3 per cent was deposited in savings accounts, and 90 per cent was used for family support. *Ch'iao-wu pao*, 20 February 1957, p. 10. An interesting insight into the process by which investment capital was raised was given in an editorial in the *Fu-chien ch'iao-hsiang pao* on 13 April 1958. The stages of 'implementation' were as follows: 'Where will (this money) come from? Which people have funds to invest? Are they willing to do so? Are there any difficulties which might be encountered in mobilising them to invest? How will such difficulties be handled? *When they are willing to invest, how can their relatives be persuaded to agree?*' (Italics added.) In other words, the Corporations decided in advance how much they required, and it was then up to each *hsien* to raise the money from abroad through the domestic Overseas Chinese.

14 In 1955, joint state–private Overseas Chinese investment companies, which had been established in Kwangtung and Fukien since 1951, were placed under full state control, and similar corporations were established subsequently in other areas of China. In 1964, there were fourteen such Corporations, in Chekiang, Fukien, Heilungkiang, Kwangsi, Kwangtung, Liaoning, and Shantung, and in Nanking, Shanghai, Tientsin, Wenchow, Wuhan, and Wuhsi. *Tsu-kuo*, no. 5

(May 1955), p. 3. The corporations in Kwangtung and Fukien also had branches in the main Overseas Chinese home districts; in 1966, for example, there were thirty branches and twenty agencies of the Kwangtung corporation. Ibid. no. 38, May 1967.

15 From 1952, when the Hsing-lung Overseas Chinese farm was established on Hainan Island, the basic policy for resettlement of Overseas Chinese who had no relatives, or technical or professional skills, was to attempt to exploit their experience in tropical agriculture in South China. See the discussion of Overseas Chinese farms in Chapter 4. To supplement the practical experience of returned Overseas Chinese the government established a Faculty of Agriculture in the Overseas Chinese University, and a special school for tropical agriculture on the Hsing-ling farm. *CNS*, 16 May 1964.

16 The overseas students were those who had left China to study abroad before 1949, and were not strictly Overseas Chinese. The great majority was in North America and Europe. The most notable of the 'returned students' was the rocket specialist, Ch'ien Hsüeh-sen, who returned in 1955 after being prevented from doing so by the United States government in 1950.

17 See, for example, *Ta kung pao* (Hong Kong), 4 September 1956; and *Nan-fang jih-pao*, 21 July 1956.

18 A set of figures was issued by the Bank of China in Hong Kong for the amount it had handled for the period 1950 to 1960. See Wu, *Dollars, Dependants, and Dogma*, p. 18.

19 *Communist China's Economic Growth and Foreign Trade*, p. 197.

20 In *Dollars, Dependants, and Dogma*.

21

Year	Chun-hsi Wu (US $ million)	United States Government Central Intelligence Agency (US $ million)
1950	60.10	133
1951	56.81	145
1952	41.05	148
1953	45.34	108
1954	41.22	100
1955	46.49	92
1956	45.85	76
1957	45.42	54
1958	41.69	52
1959	36.05	36
1960	41.69	52
1961	38.89	62
1962	39.77	62
1963	42.42	62
1964	44.92	62

Sources: Wu, *Dollars, Dependants and Dogma*, p. 142; and 'Communist China's Balance of Payments', *An Economic Profile of Mainland China* (Washington: United States Congress Joint Economic Committee, February 1967), p. 654.

22 Wu, op. cit. pp. 18–19.
23 Ibid. p. 162.
24 'Communist China's Balance of Payments', p. 627.

25 Estimates have ranged as low as US $12 million for some years. Wu, op. cit. p. 18. A recent Russian estimate claimed that £50 million was remitted through Hong Kong in 1966. *Izvestia*, 18 June 1967, *The Current Digest of the Soviet Press*, vol. XIX, no. 24 (5 July 1967), p. 19.

26 *Jen-min jih-pao*, 24 December 1949.

27 *Ch'iao-wu pao*, no. 1 (February 1965), pp. 4–6.

28 See Bank of China advertisement in *Chou-mo pao*, no. 47 (18 November 1967), p. 21. I was told by an official of the China Travel Service in Peking in February 1968 that dividends would continue to be paid, but at a lower rate, and that only 25 per cent could be repatriated. The last dividends announced for the Fukien, Kwangtung, and Yunnan Corporations were in January 1966. See *CNS*, 4, 14, and 18 January 1966.

29 The other concerned the CCP's attempts at decolonisation, discussed in the following chapter.

30 *Jen-min jih-pao*, 27 September 1954.

31 Ibid. 24 December 1954.

32 *Wen hui pao* (Hong Kong), 5 April 1955.

33 *Jen-min jih-pao*, 23 July 1955.

34 *Kuang-ming jih-pao*, 17 December 1956.

35 *Communist China and Asia*, p. 186.

36 '*Chung-hua jen-min kung-ho-kuo hua-ch'iao shih-wu wei-yüan-hui fu-tse-jen fa-piao t'an-hua huan-ying ch'iao-pao t'ou-tzu ho pan-hsüeh*' ('Statement issued by responsible person of the Overseas Chinese Affairs Commission of the People's Republic of China welcoming investment and establishment of schools by overseas compatriots': hereafter cited as 'Statement on investment and schools'). *Ch'iao-wu cheng-ts'e wen-chi*, pp. 105–7.

37 *Ta kung pao* (Hong Kong), 7 December 1957.

38 *Chou-mo pao*, 15 December 1958.

39 See *Chung-kuo chin-jung*, no. 139, 7 July 1957; Ho Hsiang-ning, report to the NPC, *Jen-min jih-pao*, 12 July 1957; and Huang Chieh, in *Nan-fang jih-pao*, 8 August 1957.

40 See Wu, *Dollars, Dependants, and Dogma*, p. 163.

41 Skinner, 'Overseas Chinese in Southeast Asia', p. 146.

42 See Wu, *Dollars, Dependants, and Dogma*, p. 166 for a summary of these restrictions.

43 This was not necessarily the case with Hong Kong and Macao.

44 In the period 1950 to 1956, only 113,105 Chinese were reported to have left China from Kwangtung Province. *Ta kung pao* (Hong Kong), 19 August 1957.

45 See, for example, percentages of China-born and local-born Chinese in Thailand, Malaya, and Indonesia, in Wu, *Dollars, Dependants and Dogma*, p. 144.

46 *Jen-min jih-pao*, 24 April 1950.

47 *Dollars, Dependants and Dogma*, p. 160.

48 Remittances from Hong Kong account for 27.8 per cent of Wu's total for 1950–64. Ibid. p. 160.

49 For a survey of Chinese education in Southeast Asia and the restrictions imposed by Southeast Asian governments, see Douglas P. Murray, 'Chinese Education in Southeast Asia', *China Quarterly*, no. 20, October–December 1964.

50 It is alleged by the Kuomintang that the CCP has despatched large numbers of teachers to infiltrate Chinese schools in Southeast Asia. This may be true, although there is almost no evidence to support the allegation.

51 The most recent examples of the disastrous effects of undisciplined political

activity by Overseas Chinese schools were the activities in 1967 of Overseas Chinese 'Red Guards' in Burma, and to a lesser extent in Cambodia.

52 For the same reasons which prompted it to attempt to solve the nationality problem, the Chinese government could not have been anxious to publicise a programme for controlling or communising Overseas Chinese schools. It is surprising, nevertheless, how little reference there is in the domestic Chinese press to positive support for Chinese education abroad, or, for example, to achievements of Overseas Chinese schools in 'great patriotic unity' or contributions to relations between China and the countries of residence. One possible reason is the decline in the number of children attending Chinese schools. According to Murray (op. cit. p. 70), in 1962 the number of ethnic Chinese students in Southeast Asian schools in which Chinese was either the main medium of instruction or taught to all students as the second language, was about 1,050,000. The point is that only in Sabah and Sarawak were the majority of school-age Chinese children enrolled in Chinese schools (ibid. p. 71).

53 A figure of 40,000 for the first seven years was given in *Chung-kuo ch'ing-nien pao*, 8 April 1957.

54 The official aggregate figure of 60,000 Overseas Chinese students is given in *Jen-min jih-pao*, 15 April 1960.

55 Statements on education for Overseas Chinese addressed to the Chinese abroad invariably stressed the difference between the CCP's policy and that of the KMT. See, for example, Fei Chen-tung, Director of the Peking Overseas Chinese Supplementary Middle School, in *Ta kung pao* (Hong Kong), 1 January 1955.

56 *Jen-min jih-pao*, 6 October 1954.

57 Fei Chen-tung, statement at the inaugural meeting of the All-China Returned Overseas Chinese Association, in *Ch'iao-wu pao*, 17 October 1956, p. 18.

58 *Fu-chien ch'iao-hsiang pao*, 7 September 1956; and Liao Ch'eng-chih in a talk with Overseas Chinese students reported in *Ch'iao-wu pao*, 20 March 1957, p. 13.

59 *Nan-fang jih-pao*, 14 August 1956.

60 *Jen-min jih-pao*, 6 October 1954.

61 Statement by the Correspondence Office of the OCAC, in *Ch'iao-wu pao*, 20 June 1957, p. 12. See also T'ao Chu in *Jen-min jih-pao*, 9 May 1957.

62 Rangoon *Jen-min pao* (*People's Daily*), 30 September 1955. Lo was a Vice-Chairman and subsequently became Chairman of the Kwangtung OCAC.

63 There were originally two committees, in Peking and Canton. In 1954, the two were merged in a single committee in Canton. *Jen-min jih-pao*, 2 July 1954.

64 The Chinese authorities were plagued by demands from Overseas Chinese students to transfer to other schools or institutions, and former students now in Hong Kong report numerous examples of assignments quite contrary to their own requests; for example, students wishing to study journalism being sent to engineering institutes.

65 There were seven main supplementary schools, located in Peking, Canton, Amoy, Swatow, and from 1960, in Nanning, Kunming, and Wuhan. In other centres and in the rural areas, there were supplementary schools or classes on a smaller scale. In 1964, there was a rationalisation of the seven main schools, the first three taking senior middle schools graduates only, and the other four, middle schools students, 'to train qualified people for higher education'. *CNS*, 16 May 1964. It is not known how many supplementary schools there were beside the seven main ones. They appear to have been fairly widespread in the provinces of Fukien and Kwangtung. For example, there were six such schools for girls alone in Chin-chiang Special District in Fukien in 1955. *CNS*, 13 June 1955.

66 *Jen-min jih-pao*, 6 October 1954.
67 Fang Fang to visiting Overseas Chinese, Peking, 2 October 1960. *CNS*, 4 October 1960.
68 In 1969, the policy for Overseas Chinese supplementary schools was attacked for advocating that the schools 'should be a bridge for entering university', and that 'after graduation, Overseas Chinese should be sent to the big cities rather than small cities, to the south rather than the north, and to factories rather than the countryside'. *CNS*, 25 January 1969.
69 In 1956, 20 per cent of Overseas Chinese students were reported to be in institutes of higher education. *Ch'iao-wu pao*, 17 October 1956, p. 18. The Amoy University, established by the Singapore millionaire Tan Kah Kee in 1921, had a long association with Overseas Chinese, and in 1954 the CCP recognised this fact in a decision stipulating that the university should direct its attention to the Chinese in Southeast Asia. *Jen-min jih-pao*, 8 October 1956.
70 *Kuang-tung ch'iao-pao*, 1 March 1958; *Fu-chien ch'iao-hsiang pao*, 6 May 1958; and *Jen-min jih-pao*, 8 April 1960. For a brief account of the genesis of this institution see Lea E. Williams, *Overseas Chinese Nationalism* (Glencoe, Ill.: The Free Press, 1960), pp. 92–4.
71 *New China News Agency Daily Release*, 1 August 1961. In 1963 a Fine Arts Faculty of the Overseas Chinese University was formed in Peking from a former department of the Peking Overseas Chinese Supplementary Middle School. *CNS*, 13 February 1963. According to a Hong Kong report, the 3,000 students in the Overseas Chinese University in 1966, mostly from Indonesia, had no formal education and were enrolled for political education and training in the cultivation of tropical crops. *Tsu-kuo*, no. 38 (May 1967), p. 12.
72 *CNS*, 15 June 1965.
73 The most famous Overseas Chinese school was the Chimei School in Amoy, established by Tan Kah Kee in 1913.
74 *Nan-fang jih-pao*, 7 August 1962.
75 For example, *Kuang-chou jih-pao*, 5 October 1956.
76 According to one report, 'the majority of returned Overseas Chinese are young students'. *Ch'iao-wu pao*, 20 January 1957, p. 12.
77 See, for example, Kenneth Priestley, 'Waning Enthusiasm of Overseas Chinese for Mainland Education', *Current Scene* (Hong Kong: US Consulate General), 19 January 1961. Priestley gives figures issued by the Immigration Department in Singapore of 893 students in 1957, declining to 152 in 1959.
78 *Ta kung pao* (Hong Kong), 27 April 1955.
79 See, for example, answers to questions by the OCAC, published in *Kuang-ming jih-pao*, 27 August 1956. See also *Ch'iao-wu cheng-ts'e wen-ta* (*Overseas Chinese Policy: Questions and Answers*) (Foochow: Fu-chien jen-min ch'u-pan she, November 1956), pp. 38–45; and *Ch'iao-wu pao*, 17 December 1956, pp. 5–6.
80 *Ch'iao-wu pao*, 20 January 1957, p. 12.
81 *Shan-t'ou pao*, 22 January 1957.
82 *Ch'iao-wu pao*, 20 January 1957, p. 12.
83 *Kuang-chou jih-pao*, 6 December 1956. Students now in Hong Kong report that gang fighting occurred in other parts of China not only between Overseas Chinese, but between them and national minority students who enjoyed a similarly privileged position.
84 From April to September 1957, almost half of each issue of the *Ch'iao-wu pao* was devoted to the problems of Overseas Chinese students. See also the issue for November 1957, pp. 19–21.

85 Statement by Yang Ching-t'ung, member of the OCAC, in *Ta kung pao* (Hong Kong), 23 November 1947.

CHAPTER 8: *An experiment in decolonisation* (pp. 135–61)

1 '*Chung-hua ch'üan-kuo kuei-kuo hua-ch'iao lien-ho-hui chang-ch'eng*' (Regulations of the ACROCA). *Ch'iao-wu pao*, 20 January 1957, p. 32.
2 *Ch'iao-wu pao*, 20 April 1958, pp. 9–10.
3 Li Wei-han, report to the Eighth Congress of the CCP, *Jen-min jih-pao*, 26 September 1956; and Liu Shao-ch'i, report to the same Congress, *Ch'iao-wu pao*, 17 October 1956, p. 1.
4 *Jen-min jih-pao*, 26 September 1956.
5 *Kuang-ming jih-pao*, 17 December 1956. The article was by Ch'en Pi-sheng, a member of the Nanyang Research Institute of Amoy University.
6 '*Teng-ch'ing tui ch'iao-wu kung-tso ti yi-hsieh hu-t'u ssu-hsiang.*'
7 Fang Fang, in *CNS*, 4 October 1960.
8 Werner Klatt, review of Chun-hsi Wu's *Dollars, Dependants, and Dogma*, in *China Quarterly*, no. 35 (July–September 1968), p. 170.
9 Wang Gungwu, for example, has stated that remittances from Overseas Chinese are purely personal, and 'may not be related in any way to their own views'. 'The Overseas Chinese Response to Peking's Overseas Chinese Policy.'
10 '*Hua-ch'iao t'ou-tzu yü kuo-ying hua-ch'iao t'ou-tzu kung-szu ti yu-tai pan fa*' ('Preferential measures for Overseas Chinese investment in State-owned Overseas Chinese Investment Corporations'), State Council Order, promulgated on 2 August 1957; and '*Hua-ch'iao chüan-tzu hsing-pan hsüeh-hsiao pan-fa*' ('Measures governing financing of schools by Overseas Chinese'), State Council Order, promulgated 2 August 1957. *Jen-min jih-pao*, 3 August 1957.
11 'Statement on investment and schools.'
12 *Ch'iao-wu pao*, 20 January 1957, p. 2.
13 *CNS*, 20 May 1957. See also, statement by Fei Chen-tung, Director of the Peking Overseas Chinese Supplementary School, in *Ta kung pao* (Hong Kong), 18 July 1957.
14 Statement by Fei Chen-tung, ibid.
15 See Fang Fang, '*Kuei-ch'iao, ch'iao-chüan ju-ho ken ch'üan-kuo jen-min yi-ch'i ku-ch'i-kan-ching, li-cheng-shang-yu*'.
16 'Statement on investment and schools.'
17 Students from Indonesia in 1960 were expected to conform in the same way. See statement by Liao Ch'eng-chih, in *Ch'iao-wu pao*, 20 January 1960, p. 4.
18 For example, see the case of 1,300 students who in 1964 were assigned directly from the Swatow Overseas Chinese Supplementary School to work on an Overseas Chinese farm in Tai-shan *hsien*. *CNS*, 27 November 1969.
19 See, for example, *CNS*, 3 January 1959, and 5 August 1962; and *Fu-chien ch'iao-hsiang pao*, 1 April 1963.
20 Ho Hsiang-ning, '*Teng-ch'ing tui ch'iao-wu kung-tso ti yi-hsieh hu-t'u ssu-hsiang*'.
21 'In this way, they will be able to...study the culture and the economy of the countries of residence so that they may live for a long time in friendly coexistence with the local people.' Ibid.
22 Ibid. See also, statements by Ho Hsiang-ning in *Ta kung pao*, 22 November 1957, *Ch'iao-wu pao*, 20 January 1958, pp. 3–4, *Jen-min jih-pao*, 7 February 1958; the *Jen-min jih-pao* editorial of 13 August 1957; and the report of the

decisions of the First Plenary Conference of the Second OCAC in *Jen-min jih-pao*, 22 November 1957.

23 *Jen-min jih-pao* editorial, 13 August 1957.

24 Ibid. See also an article by the Editorial Office of the *Ch'iao-wu pao* in the issue for December 1957, p. 20.

25 Ibid.

26 *Ta kung pao* (Hong Kong), 22 November 1957. See also the decisions adopted by the conference, in *Jen-min jih-pao*, 12 December 1957.

27 '*Tsai hsin-ti hsing-shih hsia sheng-li ch'ien-chin*' ('Advance victoriously in the new situation'), *Ch'iao-wu pao*, 20 January 1958, pp. 3–4.

28 *Kuang-tung ch'iao-pao*, 1 March 1958. See also Ho Hsiang-ning's statement at the same session of the NPC, '*Ch'iao-chüan kuei-ch'iao t'ung-yang yao ku-ch'i-kan-ching li-cheng-shang-yu*' ('Overseas Chinese dependants and returned Overseas Chinese must also go all-out and aim high'), *Jen-min jih-pao*, 7 February 1958; and Fang Fang's speech to returned and student Overseas Chinese, '*Kuei-ch'iao, ch'iao-chüan ju-ho ken ch'üan-kuo jen-min yi-ch'i ku-ch'i-kan-ching, li-cheng-shang-yu*'.

29 *Jen-min jih-pao*, 12 December 1957; *Ch'iao-wu pao*, 20 January 1958, pp. 3–4.

30 See, for example, the references to *hua-jen*, rather than *hua-ch'iao*, in reports on Malaysia in 1969. *CNS*, 21 May 1969.

31 For example, Mary F. Somers Heidhues, 'Peking and the Overseas Chinese; the Malaysian dispute', pp. 285–6. The CCP made every effort to communicate this policy to the Chinese abroad; it attempted also to ensure that the governments of Southeast Asia would be aware that it had taken this clear, unequivocal position. See, for example, Chou En-lai's talk with Prince Sihanouk in Peking in August 1958. *Ch'iao-wu pao*, 20 September 1958, p. 4.

32 In this statement, as with Chou's use of the term *jen-min* (see ch. 6), there was the suggestion that the CCP's proposals envisaged more than the solution of the legal problem of nationality. The statement that 'if they are still Overseas Chinese, that means they are still Chinese nationals', implies that if they were not Chinese nationals they were no longer 'overseas' Chinese.

33 Ho Hsiang-ning in *Jen-min jih-pao*, 7 February 1958.

34 '*1958 nien ch'iao-lien ti kung-tso fang-chen ho jen-wu*' (Work, policies, and tasks for the ACROCA in 1958). *Ch'iao-wu pao*, 20 January 1958, p. 7.

35 See the two-part article by 'Ai Hua' in *Ch'iao-wu pao*, 20 July 1959, pp. 12–15, and 20 August 1959, pp. 27–30.

36 Ho Hsiang-ning, '*Ch'iao-chüan kuei-ch'iao t'ung-yang yao ku-ch'i-kan-ching li-cheng-shang-yu*'.

37 The joint statement by the sixteen Overseas Chinese deputies, for example, pointed out that among those who might be compelled to return, 'there will be some who have no home to go to, and no relatives to look after them, and even some who do not know where their native place is'. *Kuang-tung ch'iao-pao*, 1 March 1958.

38 Ibid.

39 *Ch'iao-wu pao*, 20 April 1958, pp. 4–6.

40 Ibid. pp. 9–10.

41 On 14 May 1959, the Indonesian Ministry of Trade announced that from 1 January 1960 alien retail traders would be banned in rural Indonesia.

42 *Far Eastern Economic Review*, 10 September 1959, p. 389.

43 According to Mary F. Somers (*Peranakan Chinese Politics*, p. 24) the decree meant that Overseas Chinese could do business only in 85 cities and towns in Java and about 120 outside Java.

44 There had been continuing pressures on Chinese schools and newspapers since 1957 (See Skinner, 'Overseas Chinese in Southeast Asia', pp. 141–3). The Chinese government made no public comment on this development until the end of 1959. In 1960, it claimed that the number of Overseas Chinese operated schools in Indonesia had fallen from 1,800 to 500, and the number of enrolled students from 400,000 to 150,000. *Ch'iao-wu pao*, 20 March 1960, p. 32.

45 *Jen-min jih-pao* editorial, 12 December 1959.

46 '*Tang-ch'ien hsing-shih yü ch'iao-wu kung-tso*' ('The present situation and Overseas Chinese work'), *Ch'iao-wu pao*, 20 December 1959, p. 13.

47 See Liao Ch'eng-chih (*CNS*, 1 January 1960), Ho Hsiang-ning (*CNS*, 30 January 1960), Wang Han-chieh, Chairman of the Fukien OCAC (*CNS*, 9 February 1960), and the *Ching-chi tao-pao* (*Economic Reporter*) (Hong Kong), no. 657, 22 February 1960.

48 For example, a statement by Liao Ch'eng-chih at a May Day reception for Overseas Chinese in Peking in 1960: 'Our plan of repatriating (*chieh-yün*) Overseas Chinese will remain the same both now and in the future.' *Jen-min jih-pao*, 4 May 1960. The phrasing of statements on resettlement also indicates that the government expected Overseas Chinese to comply with its wishes, regardless of their own thoughts on the matter. See for example, Wang Han-chieh, Chairman of the Fukien OCAC: 'our government has decided that they should be resettled in China' (*CNS*, 9 February 1960); and Liao Ch'eng-chih: 'if the Indonesian authorities do not want them, we intend to bring them back to China' (*Ch'iao-wu pao*, 20 March 1960, p. 7).

49 *Ta kung pao* (Hong Kong), 23 December 1960.

50 '*Kuo-wu-yüan kuan-yü chieh-tai ho an-chih kuei-kuo hua-ch'iao ti chih-shih*' ('State Council Directive concerning the reception and resettlement of returned Overseas Chinese'), promulgated 2 February 1960. *Ch'iao-wu pao*, 20 February 1960, p. 3. This directive appears to have come from a Party decision taken at the end of 1959, since Chinese statements at that time referred to a 'decision', a 'proclamation', and a 'directive', and since the State Council directive itself embodied most of the proposals which had already been outlined in December 1959.

51 Established by order of the State Council, 2 February 1960.

52 Ibid. See also, *CNS*, 5 February 1960, 6 July 1960.

53 In Fukien, for example, they were already established in three special districts and nine cities or *hsien* by February 1960. *CNS*, 9 February 1960.

54 *CNS*, 5 February 1960.

55 *Ch'iao-wu pao*, 20 February 1960, p. 4.

56 Ibid. p. 9.

57 Ibid. p. 5.

58 *Fu-chien ch'iao-hsiang pao*, 3 September 1962.

59 This was calculated on the basis of 300 yüan (US $118) per person on arrival.

60 Fang Fang, '*Tang-ch'ien hsing-shih yü ch'iao-wu kung-tso*'.

61 Customs duties were waived, Overseas Chinese were guaranteed that personal belongings would remain their own property, that they could return to their home villages if they wished, and that if they had had no socialist education they would not be compelled to undergo 'study'. Liao Ch'eng-chih, New Year broadcast, *CNS*, 1 January 1960. See also the State Council directive of February 1960. For details of preparations in Kwangtung Province, see *Ch'iao-wu pao*, 20 February 1960, pp. 15–16, and in Hainan, see ibid. p. 17.

62 See Liao's speech to Indonesian returned Overseas Chinese, in ibid. 20 March

1960, pp. 6–10. This reorientation is reflected clearly in the content of the *Ch'iao-wu pao*. The final issue for 1960, for example, was concerned entirely with Overseas Chinese farms, labour, and production; and although the journal tended throughout the 1960s to devote less and less space to Overseas Chinese affairs, the declining portion concerned with specifically Overseas Chinese matters was overwhelmingly concerned with problems associated with resettlement.

63 *Jen-min jih-pao* editorial, 12 December 1959; and Fang Fang, '*Tang-ch'ien hsing-shih yü ch'iao-wu kung-tso*'.

64 *P'i-Liao chan-pao*.

65 For the Chinese announcement and Ch'en Yi's accompanying statement, see *Ch'iao-wu pao*, 20 February 1960, p. 2.

66 The exchange of notes following the signing of the treaty in 1955 had provided for the establishment of a joint committee on implementation. This was established on 25 January 1960 (ibid.). The text of the supplementary agreement negotiated by this committee is given in *Jen-min jih-pao*, 24 December 1960. For regulations on implementation promulgated by the Public Security Bureau in China, see *Fu-chien ch'iao-hsiang pao*, 6 May 1961.

67 *Jen-min jih-pao*, 28 February 1961.

68 *CNS*, 10 December 1961. Another 2,300 were repatriated from India in 1963, and some 4,000 from Indonesia in 1966–7.

69 *Jen-min jih-pao*, 12 December 1959.

70 On the basis of 300 yüan per person, announced in Fang Fang's speech in December 1959, the initial resettlement would have cost the government some US$12 million to the end of 1961. This, however, was only the first problem. Most of the returnees were settled in rural areas, particularly on the Overseas Chinese farms, most of which were in areas of barren wasteland. There was difficulty enough in making them productive, let alone self-sufficient. By the end of 1960, self-sufficiency had already become the main slogan for Overseas Chinese farms. *Ch'iao-wu pao* editorial, 20 December 1960, pp. 2–4.

71 The 'small freedoms' were the right to more rations and better clothing than the masses, and the right to retain special living habits, so long as these did not conflict with 'social order'. See Fang Fang in *Ch'iao-wu pao*, 20 February 1960, p. 5.

72 Ibid. no. 1 (February 1962), p. 5.

73 Letter to Subandrio, *Jen-min jih-pao*, 12 December 1959.

74 In his speech of March 1958, for example, Fang Fang actually claimed that there had been no change whatsoever in domestic Overseas Chinese policy; it was just that unreasonable demands and excessive consideration were no longer condoned. *Ch'iao-wu pao*, 20 March 1958, pp. 2–4. A *Jen-min jih-pao* editorial began one sentence with the positive declaration that 'the greater part' of the Overseas Chinese have the homeland constantly in their hearts, and ended with an assertion that the Overseas Chinese were becoming lost in identity with the people of the countries of residence. 13 August 1957.

75 Chou En-lai's Rangoon speech, pp. 7–8. The legal concept of nationality does not describe satisfactorily the distinction which Chou appeared to be making. Several times, Chou referred to categories of 'patriotic', 'conservative', and 'chauvinist' Overseas Chinese.

76 Ibid. pp. 1–3. Chou referred with approval to the fact that 'many' Overseas Chinese had married local people, not only in Burma, but in Korea, Vietnam, Laos, Cambodia, Nepal, and India.

77 See, for example, Ho Hsiang-ning's 1957 New Year broadcast, calling on Overseas

Chinese to consolidate and expand kinship relations with the local people. *Ch'iao-wu pao*, 20 January 1957, p. 1. In 1967, a group of returned students from Indonesia accused the Indonesian government of attempting to force 'complete assimilation' (*ch'üan-mien t'ung-hua*) of Overseas Chinese. *CNS*, 10 February 1967. The measures which the Indonesian government is said to have taken to achieve this end were identical to those which in June the revolutionary rebels of the OCAC accused Liao of urging on the Overseas Chinese for 'permanent survival'. See below, ch. 9.

78 Chou said that when he was told in Hanoi that Overseas Chinese schools only taught two lessons of Vietnamese a week, he instructed them that they should have a minimum of one hour a day (ibid. p. 6).

79 Chou referred, discreetly, to the resentment of Overseas Chinese domination of Southeast Asian commerce, by saying that on his visit to 'southern Asia', he had heard it said that Overseas Chinese were 'good businessmen', and he warned that they should not engage in profiteering, black-marketeering, or exploitation of the people (ibid. p. 4).

80 Two years later, an article in the *Ch'iao-wu pao* confirmed the political motive of this proposal. See the issue for 20 October 1958, p. 38.

81 Chou had, in fact, already outlined the policy in Cambodia in November 1956, but his remarks were not reported in detail. See Roger M. Smith, *Cambodia's Foreign Policy* (Ithaca, New York: Cornell University Press, 1965), pp. 105–6.

82 Decision of the First Plenary Conference of the Second OCAC, November 1957. *Jen-min jih-pao*, 12 December 1957.

83 Fang Fang, talk with visiting Overseas Chinese, *CNS*, 4 October 1960.

84 *Jen-min jih-pao* editorial, 13 August 1957.

85 '*Tsai hsin ti hsing-shih hsia sheng-li ch'ien-chin*', New Year Broadcast.

86 '*Ch'iao-chüan kuei-ch'iao t'ung-yang yao ku-ch'i-kan-ching li-cheng-shang-yu*',Report to the Fifth Session of the First NPC.

87 Joint Statement of sixteen Overseas Chinese deputies at the Fifth Session of the First NPC.

88 *Jen-min jih-pao* editorial, 18 March 1960.

89 *CNS*, 4 October 1960.

90 Ch'en-Yi/Subandrio Joint Communique, *Jen-min jih-pao*, 12 October 1959.

91 *Jen-min jih-pao*, 12 December 1959. According to Subandrio, the CCP had undertaken to repatriate the displaced Chinese during the talks in Peking in October. *Far Eastern Economic Review*, 29 October 1959, p. 688. In the event, it was the Chinese side which assumed responsibility for repatriation.

92 Ch'en Yi, letter to Subandrio, *Jen-min jih-pao*, 12 December 1959.

93 *Jen-min jih-pao* editorial, 24 December 1960. See also Fang Fang in *Ch'iao-wu pao*, 20 April 1960, pp. 5–7.

94 *Far Eastern Economic Review*, 10 September 1959, p. 390.

95 *Ch'iao-wu pao*, 20 July 1959, pp. 12–15, and 20 August 1959, pp. 27–30.

96 Directive attributed to Liao Ch'eng-chih, in *P'i Liao chan-pao*.

97 *Ta kung pao* (Hong Kong), 5 October 1956. T'ao was at that time First Secretary of the Party Committee in Kwangtung Province.

98 For example, an editorial in the *Ch'iao-wu pao* (no. 6, December 1963, p. 1) stated that 'the overwhelming majority of Overseas Chinese support the three red banners, and the general line of China's foreign policy'.

99 *Ch'iao-wu pao*, no. 6 (December 1963), p. 22; no. 2 (April 1964), p. 36; no. 5 (October 1964), p. 2. It will be recalled that Chou En-lai's Rangoon speech implied that 'Overseas Chinese' was synonymous with 'Chinese national'.

100 Liao Ch'eng-chih in *Ch'iao-wu pao*, no. 1 (February 1965), p. 3; and Fang Fang in *CNS*, 3 October 1963, and 4 May 1965.
101 Fang Fang, *CNS*, 4 May 1965.
102 May F. Somers Heidhues, 'Peking and the Overseas Chinese; the Malaysian Dispute', p. 287.
103 Liao Ch'eng-chih, *Ch'iao-wu pao*, no. 5 (October 1964), p. 2.
104 See Fang Fang, talk with visiting Overseas Chinese, *CNS*, 4 May 1965. The ambiguity of the Chinese government's position is demonstrated in this statement by Fang Fang. Having referred to the contributions and sacrifices made by Overseas Chinese in the anti-imperialist struggle in various parts of the world in the past, Fang said: 'At present, Overseas Chinese in the *liberated areas* of Vietnam and Laos are taking part in the anti-imperialist struggle together with the local people. Wherever there is anti-imperialist or anti-colonialist struggle, there must the Overseas Chinese stand together with the local people, and this glorious tradition must be continued and developed' (italics added).
105 *P'i Liao Chan-pao.*
106 Overseas Chinese 'should coexist in friendship with the local people, contribute to the economic and cultural development of the local countries, and not take part in local political quarrels'. Fang Fang, report to the CPPCC, December 1961. *Ch'iao-wu pao*, no. 6 (December 1961), p. 2. See also Liao Ch'eng-chih's Spring Festival broadcast, in ibid. no. 1 (February 1962), p. 2.
107 *CNS*, 3 October 1962.
108 *Wen hui pao* (Hong Kong), 7 October 1964. See also, a note from the Chinese Embassy in Djakarta on 4 November 1965 to the Indonesian Foreign Ministry, in *Ch'iao-wu pao*, no. 6 (December 1965), p. 23, and Liao Ch'eng-chih's New Year broadcast, January 1966, *CNS*, 2 January 1966.
109 Justus M. van der Kroef, for example, is one of the persistent exponents of the theory of 'Peking's...strategy of exporting revolution throughout Southeast Asia through its *hua ch'iao*'. 'Nanyang University and the Dilemmas of Overseas Chinese Education', *China Quarterly*, no. 20 (October–December 1964), p. 126. See also Frank Trager: 'Peking's use of the Overseas Chinese as a "fifth column" is a standard ploy.' 'Sino-Burmese Relations', *Orbis*, vol. XI, no. 4 (Winter 1968), p. 1053. And T. B. Millar: 'There is considerable evidence that the government of the Chinese People's Republic uses the "Overseas Chinese"...to provide from among their number a built-in fifth column, a source of agents for intelligence and subversion, a valuable instrument of foreign policy.' *Australia's Defence* (Melbourne: Melbourne University Press, 1965), p. 54. It is on the basis of such generalised statements and totally unsupported claims about 'considerable evidence' that the fifth column theory persists.

CHAPTER 9: *The Cultural Revolution. Overseas Chinese policy under attack* (pp. 162–84)

1 This chapter is based on information available up to February 1971.
2 *Jen-min jih-pao*, 4 July 1967.
3 Liao's name was retained in the Liao–Takasaki Office of Sino-Japanese trade, until renegotiation of the trade agreement in March 1968. *CNS*, 8 March 1968.
4 *CNS*, 26 February 1968. The OCAC was mentioned only on five other occasions after 1 July 1967.
5 Ch'en Ch'i-yu, member OCAC, last identified as such April 1960; Chuang Hsi-ch'üan, Vice-Chairman OCAC, last identified as such September 1966; Ho

Hsiang-ning, Chairman OCAC until April 1959 and subsequently associated with Overseas Chinese affairs; and Hsieh Nan-Kuang, member OCAC, last identified as such September 1959. Hsieh Nan-kuang died in July 1969, and Ch'en Ch'i-yu died in December 1970; and the deaths of three other members of the Commission have been reported since July 1967: Shao Li-tzu, Ts'ai T'ing-kai and Ch'en Ch'i-yüan. In no case did the death notices mention their association with Overseas Chinese affairs. Ch'in Li-chen, ambassador to Zambia, probably ceased to be a member of the OCAC when first appointed to Zambia in 1965.

6 *Chan tao ti.* In the course of the struggle one of the Deputy Directors of the Shanghai Overseas Chinese Affairs Bureau, Liu Hsiang-wen, attempted to commit suicide.

7 *CNS*, 15, 17, 18 February 1967; 14 April 1967.

8 The following account is based on a number of articles in the *Ke-ming ch'iao-pao* (*Revolutionary Overseas Chinese Affairs Bulletin*).

9 Fang Fang, Vice-Chairman of the OCAC and head of its Party Committee; Su Hui, wife of Fang Fang, member of the OCAC, director of one of its departments, and member of its Party Committee; Wu Chi-sheng, member, head of a department, and member of the Party Committee of the OCAC; Wang P'ing, Deputy Director of the CCP Foreign Affairs Political Department, and Deputy Director of the Hopei Province OCAC; Chang Fan, member and head of a department in the OCAC, Director, and member of the Party Committee of *CNS*.

10 It was probably in this connection that an Overseas Chinese Affairs Political Work Conference was held in Peking in April 1966. *Jen-min jih-pao*, 5 June 1966. The Foreign Affairs Political Department is discussed in Chapter 2.

11 This latter organisation was identified also in the official press in what appeared to be a leading capacity in Overseas Chinese Affairs. *CNS*, 27 and 29 April 1967.

12 Lin was dragged back by rebels from Fukien, indicating that his ‘crimes’ may not have concerned his work in the Central Commission.

13 *Hsiang-kang shih-pao* (*Hong Kong Times*), 28 February 1968. Ch'en was a member of the OCAC and Deputy Secretary-General of the ACROCA. She is alleged to have sold secrets to US intelligence organisations for seventeen years.

14 Interview, 6 February 1968.

15 *Wen-ke feng-lei* (*Cultural Revolution Storm*), Canton, no. 3, March 1968. Translated in *SCMP*, no. 4177 (14 May 1968), p. 5.

16 *Hsiang-kang shih-pao*, 28 February 1968.

17 *CNS*, 10 February 1968. In the same item it was reported that revolutionary committees existed in the Peking Returned Overseas Chinese Supplementary Middle School, and the Fine Arts Faculty of the Overseas Chinese University. The Revolutionary Committee of the Middle School was first identified in *CNS*, 21 November 1967.

18 See ‘Yang Ch'eng-wu's Eight Major Crimes’, in *SCMP*, no. 4186 (27 May 1968), p. 2.

19 *Kwang-chou kung-jen* (*Canton Worker*), Canton, 10 July 1968. Reprinted in *Tsu-kuo*, no. 53 (August 1968), p. 407.

20 *CNS*, 15 February 1968.

21 *CNS*, 2 February 1967.

22 *CNS*, 14 May 1967.

23 See *Jen-min jih-pao*, 11, 12 October 1966, 30 November 1966, 6 February 1967; and *CNS*, 14 May 1967. Liao made a special visit (*chuan-ch'eng*) to Chan-chiang to meet the first group. *Ch'iao-wu pao*, nos. 8–9 (November 1966), p. 41.

24 See Liao Ch'eng-chih's New Year and Spring Festival speeches in *CNS*, 1 and 20 January 1966.

25 *CNS*, 1 October 1969. In the intervening years, there were visitors from Hong Kong and Macao and Overseas Chinese visitors not reported in the official media. See, for example, a group of Cambodian Chinese who hurriedly left China in September 1967, fearing a break in Sino-Cambodian relations which might leave them stranded in China. *South China Morning Post* (Hong Kong), 26 September 1967. Informants in Singapore told me that in 1968 Overseas Chinese were told that they were not welcome in China unless they were engaged in trade.

26 A western government official who spent six weeks in Canton for the Autumn Fair in 1967 spoke with several Overseas Chinese businessmen who remarked on this treatment. The official himself observed that Overseas Chinese appeared to be treated equally with other businessmen.

27 *CNS*, 21 November 1968; 28 July 1968.

28 *CNS*, 16 September 1968.

29 *Jen-min jih-pao*, 5 June 1966. The details of the report indicate that the decisions of the conference must have been condemned soon afterwards as representing the Liu Shao-ch'i line, not so much on specifically Overseas Chinese issues, but for the adoption of more general 'Liuist' slogans.

30 *Wen hui pao* (Hong Kong), 8 November 1966; and 20 December 1966; and *Ta kung pao* (Hong Kong), 1 November 1966.

31 Statement by a responsible person of the Bank of China in Hong Kong. *Wen hui pao* (Hong Kong), 5 January 1967. There is some uncertainty about the date of the cancellation, but an official of China Travel Service claimed in Peking in February 1968 that it was mid-September 1966. The same official claimed that interest on investments in the Overseas Chinese Investment Corporations would continue to be paid, but according to one Hong Kong report, the Fukien Corporation was no longer paying interest in March 1968. *Hsiang-kang shih-pao*, 3 March 1968.

32 *Chen pao* (*Truth Daily*) (Hong Kong), 24 April 1967.

33 One of these notices was sighted in Hong Kong in 1967.

34 Fang Fang, in a report to the NPC in 1960, stated that many of the repatriates from Indonesia had, before repatriation, made 'written decisions expressing the need to conform with state requirements and agreeing (to abide by decisions of) the government on work allocation' on arriving in China. *Wen hui pao* (Hong Kong), 12 April 1960. In the interview in Peking in 1968, I was told that there was prior investigation of the repatriates from Indonesia in 1966–7.

35 Reports in the Chinese press indicate that returned Overseas Chinese and students had great difficulty in joining the Party or the Communist Youth League because of their backgrounds. See, for example, Yang Ching-t'ung, a member of the OCAC, in *Ch'iao-wu pao*, 20 April 1957, pp. 30–2.

36 *Hsin-sheng wan-pao* (*New Life Evening News*) (Hong Kong), 15 and 25 July 1968.

37 Established 28 October 1957, with Ch'en Yü as Chairman. *CNS*, 30 October 1967.

38 Trager, 'Sino-Burmese Relations', p. 1040.

39 Following the discrediting of the extremist groups in the Foreign Ministry it was revealed that 'Without permission, they despatched telegrams to foreign countries, sent notes to the country of xx, "appointed" diplomats to foreign countries, searched and closed the Party Committee of the Foreign Ministry, and detained the Vice Foreign Ministers, thus seriously damaging the diplomatic activities.' *Yeh chan pao* (Canton), combined issue of nos. 12 and 13, March 1968.

SCMP, no. 4158, 16 April 1968. Elsewhere in this and other bulletins, it is reported that the 'extremists' constantly resisted and opposed specific directives from Chou En-lai and the Central Committee concerning activities in the Foreign Ministry. Trager ('Sino-Burmese Relations', p. 1053) attempts to interpret the incidents of 1967 as part of a declared policy 'to strike out'. He dismisses irrationality as the explanation, at a time when irrationality and chaos ruled in Peking, particularly in the foreign affairs sector. Subsequent developments in 1968 would seem to cast serious doubt on his theory, and Mao's interview with Edgar Snow in 1970 confirms the interpretation of events suggested above. See Edgar Snow, 'A Conversation with Mao Tse-tung', *Life*, vol. 70, no. 16 (30 April 1971), pp. 46–8.

40 See, for example, *Far Eastern Economic Review*, 28 September 1967, p. 631.

41 Stanley Karnow in *International Herald Tribune*, 4–5 November 1967.

42 *CNS*, 30 June 1968.

43 There are a number of accounts of the position of the Chinese in post-coup Indonesia. For example, see Harold Munthe Kaas in *Far Eastern Economic Review*, vol. LVIII, no. 6 (9 November 1967), p. 281; Justus M. van der Kroef, 'The Sino-Indonesian Rupture', *China Quarterly*, no. 33 (January–March 1968), pp. 17–46. van der Kroef suggests that the repatriation programme came to an end because the Indonesian government obstructed it, 'For reasons of "face"'... national security, or economic self-interest' (ibid. p. 32). See also *Tsu-kuo*, no. 38 (May 1967), pp. 13–14.

44 Articles of the 'XX Love Chairman Mao' type in *CNS* in 1967 show that in the majority of cases it is possible to substitute for 'Overseas Chinese', terms like 'world's people', 'people of five continents', 'world's seamen', 'Russian masses', etc., without substantially altering the meaning.

45 For example, a cable from the OCAC to the Chinese in Burma stated: 'patriotic Burmese Overseas Chinese will arm themselves even better with the thought of Mao Tse-tung, unite more closely with the revolutionary Burmese, dare to fight, fight well, and fight to the end against the common enemy'. *CNS*, 26 August 1967.

46 Most of the newspapers concerned with Overseas Chinese affairs in the Cultural Revolution which have become available were published between April and June 1967.

47 Translated in *SCMP*, no. 4013, 1 September 1967.

48 I am indebted to Daniel Tretiak for bringing this article to my attention.

49 The article was published when the Cultural Revolution struggle in the Overseas Chinese Affairs Commission was reaching its height, and some of its expressions were echoed in the official media. For example, it accuses Liao Ch'eng-chih of assisting in 'strangling and ruining' Chinese education, a phrase which occurred in official protests over the Chinese in Burma. See, for example, note of 1 November 1967, from the Chinese Foreign Ministry to the Burmese Embassy in Peking. *CNS*, 2 September 1967. The article also attacks the integration policy for Overseas Chinese, and a similar attack was directed at the Indonesian government in the official media in February 1967. *CNS*, 10 February 1967.

50 Capitulation to imperialism, modern revisionism and all reactionaries, and annihilation of world revolution.

51 The original Chinese text has not been sighted, but assuming 'Overseas Chinese affairs' to be a translation of *ch'iao-wu*, then it almost certainly refers to internal affairs only. Although the term *ch'iao-wu* embraces both external and internal affairs, directives of this kind in past political movements and campaigns have not concerned the Chinese abroad. For example, it was pointed out at the

OCAC Conference in November 1957 that 'the Overseas Chinese live outside China and their situation is completely different from that of the domestic Chinese. The domestic anti-rightist struggle and the rectification campaign, therefore, are unnecessary outside China and should on no account be copied.' *Jen-min jih-pao*, 12 December 1957. In the early stages of the Cultural Revolution, in April 1966, an Overseas Chinese Affairs Work Conference directed *domestic* Overseas Chinese to engage in class struggle. Ibid. 5 June 1966.

52 This does not exclude, of course, giving allegiance to a revolutionary government, or to a revolutionary movement on the point of success.

53 This was stated as early as November 1967, in a note from the Chinese Embassy in Rangoon to the Burmese government. *CNS*, 25 November 1967. See also Chinese statements in *CNS*, 14 December 1967; 26 February 1968; 30 March 1968; and 4 April 1968.

54 *Kuang-ming jih-pao*, 5 October 1970.

55 *Communist Chinese Affairs, Facts and Features*, vol. 1, no. 3 (29 November 1967), p. 11. Taiwan sources on China during the Cultural Revolution established a credibility which they had not had before.

56 The last official protest about Overseas Chinese was issued by the Foreign Ministry in December 1968. *CNS*, 18 December 1968. From November 1968 to March 1969 *CNS* carried only four items on Overseas Chinese affairs, and none at all from 25 January to 1 April 1969.

57 The T'ung-hu farm, on the boundary of Hui-yang *hsien* and Tung-kuan *hsien*. *CNS*, 22 November 1969.

58 *CNS*, 17 September 1969; 26 September 1969; 22 November 1969; 15 October 1970.

59 *CNS*, 28 July 1968.

60 The Nanning Supplementary School was producing graduates in 1969. *CNS*, 7 August 1970.

61 *CNS*, 21 November 1967; 28 July 1968; 24 September 1970.

62 The Taishan No. 1 Middle School, for example, was referred to as having been established 'originally' with Overseas Chinese funds, but in the same report there was no further reference to present connection between the school and Overseas Chinese. *CNS*, 22 June 1970. 'Patriotic Overseas Chinese', however, have been among those enrolled at higher institutions in Kwangtung. Canton Radio, 2 December 1970. Amoy University reopened in late 1970.

63 *Jen-min jih-pao*, 16 February 1971. Also *Kuang-ming jih-pao*, 22 February 1971. It is not known what happened to the decision reported by Anna Louise Strong (*Letter from China*, nos. 58–9, 10 May 1968) that ten seats on the Kwangtung Province Revolutionary Committee were to be reserved for 'other concerned circles such as intellectuals and patriotic Overseas Chinese'.

64 Canton Radio, 29 September 1970.

65 Foreign Ministry protest to the Burmese government, *CNS*, 18 December 1968.

66 *CNS*, 5 October 1969.

67 Ibid.

68 Ch. II, Sec. 1, Art. 16, in various unauthenticated drafts.

69 *Jen-min jih-pao*, 5 October 1970.

70 Moscow Radio, 28 June, 18 July 1970. Moscow's motives on this question are quite transparent. It began launching such attacks in the context of its own initiatives in the Southeast Asian area in mid-1967.

71 See statement by OCAC spokesman on the imprisonment of Chinese in Burma. *CNS*, 26 February 1968.

72 For example, *CNS*, 18 December 1968.
73 *CNS*, 15 November 1968.
74 The Treaty was repudiated in Law Number 4 of 1969, passed by Parliament on 7 March and signed by the President on 16 April. *Kompas (Djakarta Daily)*, 8 March and 17 April 1969.
75 *Jen-min jih-pao*, 20 May 1969.
76 *CNS*, 3 April 1970.
77 *CNS*, 7 September 1969.
78 *CNS*, 18 May 1970.

CHAPTER 10: *Overseas Chinese policy, Overseas Chinese communism, and foreign policy* (pp. 185–95)

1 See, for example, Brimmell, who comments that 'Peking replaced Moscow as the major source of inspiration and advice to the Communist movement in South East Asia'. *Communism in South East Asia*, p. 313.
2 An example of this latter technique is given in Justus M. van der Kroef's *Communism in Malaysia and Singapore* (The Hague: Martinus Nijhoff, 1967, p. 32), in which, in the context of detailed discussions of purely local developments in Overseas Chinese communism without mention of the role of the CCP, there are suddenly appended statements such as 'and all the while Peking's shadow loomed larger and darker over Malaysia and the rest of Southeast Asia, continuing to draw much of the restless *hua-ch'iao* into its cultural and political orbit, and reinvigorating the Communist movement in an arc from Perlis to Sabah'.
3 See, for example, Doak Barnett, 'the Chinese Communist Party itself maintains an underground apparatus among Overseas Chinese' (*Communist China and Asia*, p. 141); and Harold Hinton, 'the CPC undoubtedly maintains its own organization among the Overseas Chinese' (*Communist China in World Politics*, p. 414).
4 Appleton, 'Communism and the Chinese in the Philippines', pp. 378, 389–90.
5 Hinton, *Communist China in World Politics*, p. 400.
6 Williams (*The Future of the Overseas Chinese in Southeast Asia*, pp. 109–10) regards the 'Chineseness' of the Overseas Chinese parties as an important factor, and suggests that the Overseas Chinese communists are 'driven by chauvinism, not ideology'. C. P. FitzGerald (*The Third China*, p. 62) sees Overseas Chinese communism as arising partly from exclusion of the young educated class from Asian nationalism, and partly from identification with the politics of China. See also, Lucien W. Pye, *Guerilla Communism in Malaya* (Princeton: Princeton University Press, 1956), for a discussion of the motivations of Chinese who joined the communists in the Malayan insurgency.

Bibliography

I CHINESE COMMUNIST PARTY SOURCES

A *Newspapers and periodicals*

Ao-men jih-pao (*Macao Daily*), Macao
Che-chiang jih-pao (*Chekiang Daily*), Hangchow
Ch'iao-wu pao (*Overseas Chinese Affairs Journal*), Peking
Ching-chi tao-pao (*Economic Reporter*), Hong Kong
Chou-mo pao (*Hong Kong Weekend*), Hong Kong
Chung-kuo chin-jung (*China's Currency*), Peking
Chung-kuo ch'ing-nien pao (*China Youth Daily*), Peking
Chung-kuo hsin-wen she (*China News Service*), Canton, Peking
Fu-chien ch'iao-hsiang pao (*Fukien Overseas Chinese District News*), Foochow
Fu-chien jih-pao (*Fukien Daily*), Foochow
Fu-chou jih-pao (*Foochow Daily*), Foochow
Hsia-men jih-pao (*Amoy Daily*), Amoy
Hsin-hua yüeh-pao (*New China Monthly*), Peking
Hsin wan-pao (*New Evening News*), Hong Kong
Hsüeh-hsi (*Study*), Peking
Jen-min jih-pao (*People's Daily*), Peking
Kuang-chou jih-pao (*Canton Daily*), Canton
Kuang-hsi ch'iao-pao (*Kwangsi Overseas Chinese News*), Nanning
Kuang-hsi jih-pao (*Kwangsi Daily*), Nanning
Kuang-ming jih-pao (*Kwangming Daily*), Peking
Kuang-tung ch'iao-pao (*Kwangtung Overseas Chinese News*), Canton
Nan-fang jih-pao (*Southern Daily*), Canton
Shan-t'ou pao (*Swatow Daily*), Swatow
Shih-chieh chih-shih (*World Culture*), Peking
Ta kung pao (*Ta Kung Daily*), Shanghai, Tientsin, and Peking
Ta kung pao (*Ta Kung Daily*), Hong Kong
Wen hui pao (*Wen Hui Daily*), Hong Kong
Yang-ch'eng wan-pao (*Yangcheng Evening News*), Canton
Yün-nan jih-pao (*Yunnan Daily*), Kunming

B *Books, documents and speeches*

(Documents and speeches listed are only those of major importance
cited frequently in the text)

The Agrarian Reform Law of the People's Republic of China and Other Relevant Documents, 4th edn. Peking: Foreign Languages Press, 1953.
Chan tao ti (*Fight to the End*). n.p.: United Rebel Committee of Shanghai Revolutionary Returned Overseas Chinese, April 1967. Reprinted in *Hsing-tao jih-pao* (Hong Kong), 1 and 4 May 1967.
Chang Hsi-jo. '*Hsin chung-kuo ti ho-p'ing wai-chiao cheng-ts'e ho hua-ch'iao shuang-ch'ung kuo-chi wen-t'i*' (New China's peaceful foreign policy and the question of Overseas Chinese dual nationality). *Jen-min jih-pao*, 10 May 1955.
Ch'iao-wu cheng-ts'e wen-chi (*Collected Documents on Overseas Chinese Policy*). Peking: Jen-min ch'u-pan she, 1957.

258 Bibliography

Ch'iao-wu cheng-ts'e wen-ta (*Overseas Chinese Policy: Questions and Answers*). Foochow: Fu-chien jen-min ch'u-pan she, 1956.

Ch'iao-wu fa-kuei hui-pien (*Collected Laws and Regulations on Overseas Chinese Affairs*), vol. 1. Peking: Lien-ho shu-tien, 1951.

Chou En-lai. *Cheng-fu kung-tso pao-kao* (*Government Work Report*), 1954. Peking: Jen-min ch'u-pan she, 1954.

'*Chou En-lai tsung-li tui Mien-tien hua-ch'iao ti chiang-hua*' (Premier Chou En-lai's speech to Overseas Chinese in Burma), printed in *Ch'iao-wu cheng-ts'e wen-chi.*

Chuang Hsi-ch'üan. '*Chung-hua ch'üan-kuo kuei-kuo hua-ch'iao lien-ho-hui tang-ch'ien ti chi-pen jen-wu*' (The present basic tasks of the All-China Returned Overseas Chinese Association). Report to the inaugural meeting of the ACROCA. *Ch'iao-wu pao*, 17 October 1956.

'*Chung-hua ch'üan-kuo kuei-kuo hua-ch'iao lien-ho-hui chang-ch'eng*' (Regulations of the All-China Returned Overseas Chinese Association). Adopted 12 October 1956. *Ch'iao-wu pao*, 20 January 1957.

'*Chung-hua jen-min kung-ho-kuo ho Yin-tu-ni-hsi-ya kung-ho-kuo kuan-yü shuang-ch'ung kuo-chi wen-t'i ti t'iao-yüeh*' (Treaty on the question of dual nationality between the People's Republic of China and the Republic of Indonesia). Signed 22 April 1955. *Jen-min jih-pao*, 26 April 1955.

'*Chung-hua jen-min kung-ho kuo hsien-fa*' (Constitution of the People's Republic of China). *Hsüeh-hsi*, no. 10, 2 October 1954.

'*Chung-hua jen-min kung-ho-kuo hua-ch'iao shih-wu wei-yüan-hui fu-tse-jen fa-piao t'an-hua huan-ying ch'iao-pao t'ou-tzu pan-hsüeh*' (Statement by responsible person of the Overseas Chinese Affairs Commission of the People's Republic of China welcoming investment and establishment of schools by overseas compatriots). Issued 12 August 1957. *Jen-min jih-pao*, 13 August 1957.

Chung-hua jen-min kung-ho-kuo k'ai-kuo wen-hsien (*Documents on the Founding of the People's Republic of China*). Hong Kong: Hsin-min-chu ch'u-pan she, 1949.

'*Chung-hua jen-min kung-ho-kuo kuo-wu-yüan kuan-yü kuan-ch'e pao-hu ch'iao-hui cheng-ts'e ti ming-ling*' (State Council of the People's Republic of China order concerning the implementation of the policy for protection of Overseas Chinese remittances). Promulgated 23 February 1955. *Jen-min jih-pao*, 3 March 1955.

'*Chung-hua jen-min kung-ho-kuo pao-hu kuo-wai hua-ch'iao ti cheng-tang ch'üan-li ho li-yi*' (The People's Republic of China protects the proper rights and interests of the Chinese resident abroad), by the Propaganda Team of the Central Overseas Chinese Affairs Commission. *Jen-min jih-pao*, 6 October 1954.

Fang Fang. '*Kuan-yü kuo-nei ch'iao-wu kung-tso ti jo-kan cheng-ts'e'* (Certain policies concerning domestic Overseas Chinese work). Report to the Fourth Enlarged Conference of the First Overseas Chinese Affairs Commission. *Kuang-ming jih-pao*, 10 June 1956.

'*Kuei-ch'iao, ch'iao-chüan ju-ho ken ch'üan-kuo jen-min yi-ch'i ku-ch'i-kan-ching, li-cheng-shang-yu*' (How returned Overseas Chinese and Overseas Chinese dependants can go all-out and aim high together with the people of the whole country). *Ch'iao-wu pao*, 20 March 1958.

'*Tang-ch'ien hsing-shih yü ch'iao-wu kung-tso*' (The present situation and Overseas Chinese work). *Ch'iao-wu pao*, 20 December 1959.

Ho Hsiang-ning. '*Kuan-yü shuang-ch'ung kuo-chi wen-t'i ti t'iao-yüeh ti t'an-hua*' (A talk on the dual nationality treaty). *Jen-min jih-pao*, 28 April 1955.

'*Teng-ch'ing tui ch'iao-wu kung-tso ti yi-hsieh hu-t'u ssu-hsiang*' (Clear up some muddle-headed thinking about Overseas Chinese work). Report to the Fourth Session of the First NPC. *Jen-min jih-pao*, 12 July 1957.

'*Tsai hsin-ti hsing-shih hsia sheng-li ch'ien-chin*' (Advance victoriously in the new situation). *Ch'iao-wu pao*, 20 January 1958.

'*Ch'iao-chüan kuei-ch'iao t'ung-yang yao ku-ch'i kan-ching li-cheng-shang-yu*' (Overseas Chinese dependants and returned Overseas Chinese must also go all-out and aim high). Report to the Fifth Session of the First NPC. *Jen-min jih-pao*, 7 February 1958.

'*Ho-p'ing hsieh-shang kuo-chi wen-t'i ti yu yi fan-li*' (Another example of solving international problems through peaceful consultation). *Jen-min jih-pao* editorial on the Sino-Indonesian Dual Nationality Treaty, 23 April 1955.

Hsin Chung-kuo kung-shang-yeh-chia ti tao-lu (*The Path for Industrialists and Businessmen in New China*). Hong Kong: Hua-ch'iao ching-chi ch'u-pan she, 1950.

Hsin-wen chan-hsien (*News Front*). n.p.: Lu Hsün Detachment of China News Service, 14 April 1967. Reprinted in *Ming pao* (Hong Kong), 29 July 1967.

'*Hua-ch'iao chüan-tzu hsing-pan hsüeh-hsiao pan-fa*' (Measures governing financing of schools by Overseas Chinese). State Council Order, promulgated 2 August 1957. *Jen-min jih-pao*, 3 August 1957.

Hua-ch'iao t'ou-tzu shou-ts'e (*Overseas Chinese Investment Handbook*). Canton: Kwangtung Overseas Chinese Investment Corporation, 1959.

'*Hua-ch'iao t'ou-tzu yü kuo-ying hua-ch'iao t'ou-tzu kung-szu ti yu-tai pan-fa*' (Preferential measures for Overseas Chinese investment in State-owned Overseas Chinese Investment Corporations). State Council Order, promulgated 2 August 1957. *Jen-min jih-pao*, 3 August 1957.

Jen-min shou-ts'e (*People's Handbook*) (1957 and 1965). Peking: Ta kung pao she.

Ke-ming ch'iao-pao (*Revolutionary Overseas Chinese Affairs Bulletin*). n.p.: 7 April 1967. Translated in *SCMP*, no. 3939 (16 May 1967), pp. 5–13.

'*Kuan-yü kuei-kuo hua-ch'iao hsüeh-sheng sheng-hsüeh ho chiu-yeh wen-t'i*' (On the question of schooling and employment for returned Overseas Chinese students), by the Correspondence Office of the Central Overseas Chinese Affairs Commission. *Ch'iao-wu pao*, 20 June 1957.

'*Kung-t'ung kang-ling*' (The Common Programme). *Chung-hua jen-min kung-ho-kuo k'ai-kuo wen-hsien*.

'*Kuo-chia tui hua-ch'iao shih-wu to yu yi chung-yao ts'o-shih*' (Another important measure of the state in Overseas Chinese affairs). *Jen-min jih-pao* editorial, 13 August 1957.

Kuo-nei ch'iao-wu cheng-ts'e wen-chien hui-pien (*Collected Documents on Domestic Overseas Chinese Policy*). n.p.: All-China Returned Overseas Chinese Association, 1956.

'*Kuo-wu-yüan kuan-yü chieh-tai ho an-chih kuei-kuo hua-ch'iao ti chih-shih*' (State Council directive concerning the reception and resettlement of returned Overseas Chinese). Promulgated 2 February 1960. *Ch'iao-wu pao*, 20 February 1960.

Lien Kuan. '*Hsien-fa ts'ao-an yü hua-ch'iao*' (The Overseas Chinese and the draft constitution). *Jen-min jih-pao*, 3 August 1954.

Mao Tse-tung hsüan-chi (*Selected Works of Mao Tse-tung*). Peking: Jen-min ch'u-pan she, 1961.

P'i Liao chan pao (*Criticise Liao Combat Bulletin*). n.p.: Preparatory Group for Liaison Post of Criticism and Repudiation of Liao Ch'eng-chih and Fang Fang, 18 June 1967. Translated in *SCMP*, no. 4013 (1 September 1967), pp. 5–11.

Ssu-t'u Mei-t'ang. '*Yü kuo-wai hua-ch'iao t'an ai-kuo ta t'uan-chieh*' (A talk with Overseas Chinese about great patriotic unity). *Ta kung pao* (Shanghai), 1 January 1952.

Tsu-kuo yü hua-ch'iao (*The Homeland and the Overseas Chinese*), 2 vols. Hong Kong: Wen hui pao, 1956.

'*T'u-ti kai-ke chung tui hua-ch'iao t'u-ti ts'ai-ch'an ti ch'u-li pan-fa*' (Regulations governing the administration of Overseas Chinese land and property during land reform). Enacted 6 November 1950. *Ch'iao-wu fa-kuei hui-pien.*

II   OTHER SOURCES
A   *Newspapers and periodicals*

Chen pao (Truth Daily), Hong Kong
Chin-jih ta-lu (Mainland Today), Taipei
Chung-nan jih-pao (Central South Daily), Hong Kong
Communist Chinese Affairs: Facts and Features, Institute of International Relations, Taipei
Current Scene, United States Consulate-General, Hong Kong
Far Eastern Economic Review, Hong Kong
Hsiang-kang shih-pao (Hong Kong Times), Hong Kong
Hsin pao (New Daily), Djakarta
Hsin-sheng wan-pao (New Life Evening News), Hong Kong
Hsin Yüeh hua-pao (New Vietnam Chinese Daily), Hanoi
Hsing-chou jih-pao (Hsingchow Daily), Singapore
Hsing-hsien jih-pao (Hsingsien Daily), Bangkok
Hsing-tao jih-pao (Hsingtao Daily), Hong Kong
Jen-min pao (People's Daily), Rangoon
Kung-shang jih-pao (Kungshang Daily), Hong Kong
Mien-hua jih-pao (Khmer Chinese Daily), Phnom Penh
Ming pao (Ming Daily), Hong Kong
Nan-yang shang-pao (South Seas Commercial Daily), Singapore
South China Morning Post, Hong Kong
Tsu-kuo (China Monthly), The Union Research Institute, Hong Kong

B   *Articles and books*

Akashi, Yoji. *The Nanyang Chinese National Salvation Movement, 1937–1941.* [Lawrence]: Center for East Asian Studies, The University of Kansas, 1970.

Appleton, Sheldon. 'Communism and the Chinese in the Philippines'. *Pacific Affairs*, vol. XXXII, no. 4, December 1959.

Barnett, A. Doak, *Communist China and Asia. Challenge to American Policy.* New York: Harper, 1960.
  Cadres, Bureaucracy, and Political Power in Communist China. New York: Columbia University Press, 1967.

Bennett, Gordon A. 'Political Labels and Popular Tension'. *Current Scene*, vol. VII, no. 4, 26 February 1969.

Brecher, Michael. *India and World Politics. Krishna Menon's View of the World.* London: Oxford University Press, 1968.

Brimmel, J. H. *Communism in South East Asia.* London: Oxford University Press, 1959.

Campbell, P. C. *Chinese Coolie Emigration to Countries within the British Empire.* London: P. S. King, 1923.

Carin, Robert. *State Farms in Communist China.* Hong Kong: The Union Research Institute, 1962.

Chang Hsi-che. *Kung-fei ti ch'iao-wu cheng-ts'e yü ch'iao-wu kung-tso. (The Overseas Chinese Policies and Overseas Chinese Work of the Communist Bandits).* Taipei: Overseas Chinese Association, 1962.

Chang, Parris H. 'Research Notes on the Changing Loci of Decision in the Chinese Communist Party'. *China Quarterly*, no. 44, October–December 1970.

China Yearbook, 1969–1970. Taipei: China Publishing Company, 1970.

Chung-kung jen-ming lu (Who's Who in Communist China). Taipei: Chung-kung jen-ming lu Editorial Committee, 1967.

The Conditions of Overseas Chinese Labourers in the South Seas. Nanking: Overseas Chinese Affairs Commission, 1947.

Coughlin, Richard J. *Double Identity. The Chinese in Modern Thailand*. Hong Kong: Oxford University Press, 1960.

Eckstein, Alexander. *Communist China's Economic Growth and Foreign Trade*. New York: McGraw Hill, 1966.

Elegant, Robert. *The Dragon's Seed. Peking and the Overseas Chinese*. New York: St Martin's Press, 1959.

Fall, Bernard, 'Vietnam's Chinese Problem'. *Far Eastern Survey*, vol. XXVII, no. 6, May 1958.

Feith, Herbert. *The Decline of Constitutional Democracy in Indonesia*. Ithaca, N.Y.: Cornell University Press, 1962.

Feng Tzu-yu, *Hua-ch'iao ke-ming k'ai-kuo shih (A History of the Overseas Chinese in the Revolution and the Founding of the Nation)*. Shanghai: Shang-wu yin-shua-kuan, 1947.

FitzGerald, C. P. *The Third China. The Chinese Communities in South-east Asia*. Melbourne: F. W. Cheshire, 1965.

Fraser, Stewart. *Chinese Communist Education*. New York: Science Editions, 1966.

Freedman, Maurice. *The Chinese in South-East Asia: A Longer View*. London: The China Society, 1965.

Fried, Morton H. (ed.). *Colloquium on the Overseas Chinese*. New York: Institute of Pacific Relations, 1958.

Hanrahan, Gene Z. *The Communist Struggle in Malaya*. New York: Institute of Pacific Relations, 1954.

Harris, Richard. 'Britain and China', A. M. Halpern (ed.). *Policies Towards China. Views from Six Continents*. New York: McGraw Hill, 1965.

Hertslet, Godfrey E. P. *Hertslet's China Treaties*. London: H.M. Stationery Office, 1908.

Hinton, Harold C. 'The Overseas Chinese and Peking'. *Far Eastern Economic Review*, vol. XIX, no. 14, 6 October 1955.

Communist China in World Politics. London: Macmillan, 1966.

Hsu, Immanuel. *China's Entrance into the Family of Nations: the Diplomatic Phase. 1858–1880*. Cambridge, Mass.: Harvard University Press, 1960.

Hua-ch'iao ching-chi nien-chien (Overseas Chinese Economy Yearbook). Taipei: Overseas Chinese Economy Yearbook Editorial Committee, 1965, 1968, 1969.

Hua-ch'iao-chih tsung-chih (General Gazetteer of the Overseas Chinese). Taipei: Hua-ch'iao-chih Editorial Committee, 1956.

Huang Tsen-ming. *The Legal Status of the Chinese Abroad*. First published 1934, republished without revision (Taipei: China Cultural Service), 1954.

Jawaharlal Nehru's Speeches, vol. 3, March 1953–August 1957. New Delhi: Government of India Ministry of Information and Broadcasting, 1958.

Johnstone, William C. *Burma's Foreign Policy*. Cambridge, Mass.: Harvard University Press, 1963.

Kao Hsin (ed.). *Ch'iao-wu fa-kuei (Laws and Regulations on Overseas Chinese Affairs)*. Taipei: Overseas Chinese Affairs Commission, 1964.

Lu Yu-sun. *Programs of Communist China for Overseas Chinese*. Hong Kong: The Union Research Institute, 1956.

Macdonald, James. 'The Use of Slogans and "Uninterrupted Revolution" in China in the early part of 1964'. Jerome Ch'en and Nicholas Tarling (eds.). *Studies in the Social History of China and South-East Asia* (Cambridge: Cambridge University Press, 1970).

Marsot, Alain-Gérard. 'La Chine Populaire et les Communautés Chinoises du Sud-Est Asiatique'. *Revue Juridique et Politique*, no. 2, April–June 1965.

McNair, Harley F. *The Chinese Abroad: their position and protection*. Shanghai: The Commercial Press, 1925.

McVey, Ruth T. *The Calcutta Conference and the Southeast Asian Uprisings*. New York: Cornell University Modern Indonesia Project, 1958.

Mitchison, Lois. *The Overseas Chinese*. London: Bodley Head, 1961.

Murray, Douglas P. 'Chinese Education in South-East Asia'. *China Quarterly*, no. 20, October–December 1954.

Priestley, Kenneth. 'Waning enthusiasm of Overseas Chinese for Mainland Education'. *Current Scene*, 19 January 1961.

Purcell, Victor. *The Position of the Overseas Chinese in Southeast Asia*. New York: Institute of Pacific Relations, 1950.

The Chinese in Southeast Asia, 2nd edn. London: Oxford University Press, 1965.

Pye, Lucien W. *Guerilla Communism in Malaya*. Princeton: Princeton University Press, 1956.

Rádvanyi, János. 'The Hungarian Revolution and the Hundred Flowers Campaign'. *China Quarterly*, no. 43, July–September 1970.

Schurmann, Franz. *Ideology and Organization in Communist China*. Berkeley and Los Angeles: University of California Press, 1966.

Simonia, N. *Overseas Chinese in Southeast Asia – A Russian Study*. Translated by US Joint Publications Research Service. New York: Cornell University, Department of Far Eastern Studies, 1961.

'Maoists use Blackmail'. *Izvestia*, 7 September 1967. *The Current Digest of the Soviet Press*, 27 September 1967.

Skinner, G. William. *Chinese Society in Thailand*. New York: Cornell University Press, 1957.

'Overseas Chinese in Southeast Asia', *Annals of the American Academy of Political and Social Science*, vol. 321, January 1959.

Smith, Roger M. *Cambodia's Foreign Policy*. Ithaca, New York: Cornell University Press, 1965.

Somers Heidhues, Mary F. 'Peking and the Overseas Chinese; the Malaysian Dispute'. *Asian Survey*, vol. VI, no. 5, May 1966.

Somers, Mary F. *Peranakan Chinese Politics in Indonesia*. New York: Cornell University Modern Indonesia Project, 1964.

Staunton, Sir George Thomas. *Ta Tsing Leu Lee. Being the Fundamental Laws and a Selection of the Supplementary Statutes of the Penal Code of China*. London: T. Cadell and W. David, 1810.

Tang, Eddie. 'British Policy Towards the Chinese in the Straits Settlements: Protection and Control 1877–1900'. Unpublished M.A. thesis, Australian National University, 1971.

Thompson, Virginia, and Adloff, Richard. *Minority Problems in Southeast Asia*. Stanford: Stanford University Press, 1955.

Ting Wang (ed.). *Chung-kung wen-hua ta ke-ming hui-pien (Collection of Materials on Communist China's Great Cultural Revolution)*. Hong Kong: Ming pao yüeh-k'an she, 1967.

Trager, Frank. 'Sino-Burmese Relations'. *Orbis*, vol. XI, no. 4, Winter 1968.

Uchida, Naosaku. *The Overseas Chinese. A Bibliographical Essay Based on the Resources of the Hoover Institution.* Stanford: Hoover Institution on War, Revolution, and Peace, 1960.

United States Government, Central Intelligence Agency. 'Communist China's Balance of Payments', *An Economic Profile of Mainland China.* Washington: US Congress Joint Economic Committee, 1967.

van der Kroef, Justus M. 'Communism and Communalism in Sarawak'. *China Quarterly*, no. 20, October–December 1964.

'Nanyang University and the Dilemmas of Overseas Chinese Education'. *China Quarterly*, no. 20, October–December 1964.

'Philippines Communism and the Chinese'. *China Quarterly*, no. 30, April–June 1967.

Communism in Malaysia and Singapore. The Hague: Martinus Nijhoff, 1967.

'The Sino-Indonesian Rupture'. *China Quarterly*, no. 33, January–March 1968.

'Peking and Southeast Asia's Dominoes'. *Quadrant*, September–October 1968.

Van Slyke, Lyman P. *Enemies and Friends. The United Front in Chinese Communist History.* Stanford: Stanford University Press, 1967.

Wang Gungwu, *A Short History of the Nanyang Chinese.* Singapore: Eastern Universities Press, 1959.

'The Overseas Chinese Response to Peking's Overseas Chinese Policy'. Unpublished seminar paper, Australian National University, Canberra, November 1968.

'Chinese Politics in Malaya'. *China Quarterly*, no. 43, July–September, 1970.

'Political Chinese. An aspect of their contribution to modern Southeast Asian history'. Hamburg: Institut für Asienkunde, 1971.

Who's Who in Communist China. Hong Kong: The Union Research Institute, 1966.

Williams, Lea E. *Overseas Chinese Nationalism. The Genesis of the Pan-Chinese Movement in Indonesia, 1900–1916.* Glencoe, Ill.: The Free Press, 1960.

The Future of the Overseas Chinese in Southeast Asia. New York: McGraw Hill, 1966.

Willmott, Donald E. *The National Status of the Chinese in Indonesia 1900–1958.* New York: Cornell University Modern Indonesia Project, 1961.

Willmott, W. E. 'The Chinese in Southeast Asia'. *Australian Outlook*, vol. 20, no. 3, December 1966.

The Chinese in Cambodia. Vancouver: University of British Columbia, 1967.

Wilson, David. 'China, Thailand and the Spirit of Bandung'. *China Quarterly*, no. 30, April–June 1967, and no. 31, July–September 1967.

Wu, Chun-hsi. *Dollars, Dependants, and Dogma. Overseas Chinese Remittances to Communist China.* Stanford: The Hoover Institution, 1967.

Young, Kenneth T. *Negotiating with the Chinese Communists: the United States Experience, 1953–1967.* New York: McGraw Hill, 1968.

Yüeh-nan hua-ch'iao kuo-chi wen-t'i yen-chiu (A Study of the Overseas Chinese Nationality Question in Vietnam). Taipei: Hai-wai ch'u pan she, 1957.

C   *Serial translations*

American Consulate General, Hong Kong. *Current Background.*

Survey of China Mainland Press.

Index

Administration, 12–34, 126, 197; All-China Returned Overseas Chinese Association, 23, 30–2; banking system, 27–8; cadre training, 21, 24; consolidation of (1956), 23–4; function of, 13–14; impact of the Cultural Revolution on, 162–6; non-governmental organisations, 30–3; Overseas Chinese Affairs Commission, 16–27; Party control of, 28–30; and policy implementation, *see* Communication; and policy-making, 24–7, 33–4; reorganisation of (1959–60), 146–7; service departments, 14, 27–8

Africa, 19, 183

All-China Returned Overseas Chinese Association, 23, 24, 25, 27, 29, 30–2, 34, 46, 58, 70, 114, 136, 145; impact of the Cultural Revolution on, 163, 166

Americas, 4n, 19, 60, 100n, 183

Amoy University, 131

Assimilation, 148, 150–1

Australia, 48, 70

Bandung Conference, 108, 109

Bank of China, 27–8, 39, 47, 48, 124

Burma, 19, 25, 37, 49, 88, 90, 100, 101, 104, 107, 112, 113, 162, 169, 170, 171, 180

Burmese Communist Party, 171

Cadres, 20, 21, 22, 23, 24, 39, 40, 55, 57, 59, 63, 93, 122, 128, 164, 165, 167

Calcutta Youth Conference, 93

Cambodia, 47, 49, 113, 169, 171, 183–4

Census (1953), 3, 79

Central Administrative Office for Distribution, 147

Central Cultural Revolution Group, 170

Central tasks, 61, 66, 67, 73, 124

Ceylon, 183

Chang Fan, 163

Chang Hsi-jo, 109

Chang T'ieh-t'ao, 165

Chang Wen-tien, 176

Chauvinism, 7n, 143, 151, 160

Chekiang Province, 4, 21

Ch'en Ch'i-yu, 180

Ch'en Man-yün, 164

Ch'en Yi, 46, 148, 149, 152, 155, 163, 164

Chiang Ch'ing, 165

Chiang Kai-shek, 45n, 113n, 172

Ch'iao-wu pao, 44, 166, *passim*

Chih Kung Tang, 21, 31, 32–3

China News Service, see *Chung-kuo hsin-wen she*

Chinan University, 8, 31

Chinese Communist Party, *passim*; comprehension of Southeast Asian politics, 192–3; control of Overseas Chinese affairs, 28–30; and Kuomintang, 45, 49–50, 69, 77, 80, 84, 86–8, 105, 109, 113–14, 124, 128, 129, 135, 150, 173, 183; pre-1949 policy towards Overseas Chinese, x, 10–11; priority of Overseas Chinese affairs, 11, 15, 26, 29, 44, 66, 91, 157; problems with Overseas Chinese, 2, 5, 9–10, 20–1, 37, 51, 73, 83, 99–101, 103, 119–20, 133–4, 155, 175, 184, 186–7; and relations with Southeast Asia, 1–2, 6, 9, 12, 33–4, 36, 58, 74–6, 77, 97, 98, 102–3, 104, 113, 116, 127, 134, 141–9, 154, 157, 161, 183, 185, 186, 187, 192–5; undifferentiated Overseas Chinese policy, 37–8, 83, 98–101, 113, 154, 158; views on political behaviour of Overseas Chinese, 102, 105–6, 109, 110–11, 112–13, 136, 140–1, 142–3, 149–55, 157–61, 174; views on relationship with Overseas Chinese, 25, 30, 67, 71–2, 74, 76, 77, 78, 80, 82, 84–9, 98–101, 106, 121, 129, 130, 137, 140–1, 147, 157–9, 182

Chinese language, 140–1, 151, 177

Chinese Nationalists, *see* Kuomintang

Chinese People's Political Consultative Conference, 20n, 32, 46, 79

Ch'ing Government, 5–6, 11, 103; Nationality Law of, 6

Chou En-lai, 46, 50, 59, 80, 102, 103, 104, 105, 107, 108, 112, 113, 142, 150, 164, 171, 174, 175, 194, 195

Chuang Hsi-ch'üan, 24, 102

Chung Ch'ing-fa, 11n, 147

Chung-kuo hsin-wen she, 41–4, 163, *passim*

Chungshan University, 131

Clan and welfare associations, 25

'Colonial' legacy, 1, 9, 74–6, 77, 102–3, 104, 106, 119, 121, 176, 186; *see also* Decolonisation

Commerce, Ministry of, 17, 146, 147

Committee for Reception and Resettlement, 146–7

Common Programme, 9n, 77, 79, 81, 83

Communalism, 93, 97, 98, 153, 154, 159, 183, 190

(264)

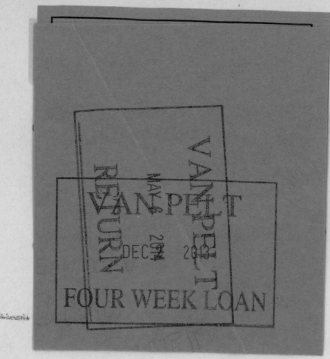